Reform in America

A revolution must come on the due instalments plan.
James Joyce

We are all a little wild here with numberless projects of social reform. . . . I am gently mad myself and am resolved to live cleanly.
Ralph Waldo Emerson

Social justice is . . . something we must continue looking for, even though we all know it can never be found.
Kenneth Boulding

ROBERT H. WALKER

Reform in America
The Continuing Frontier

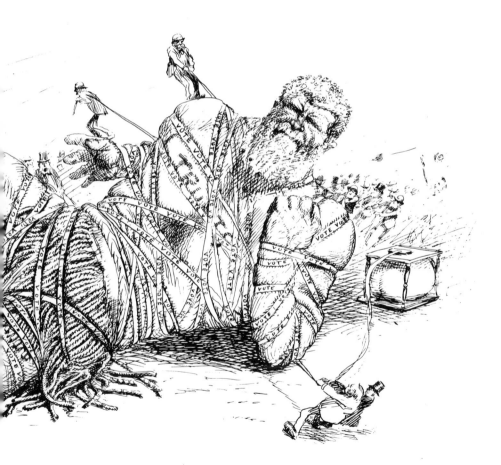

THE UNIVERSITY PRESS OF KENTUCKY

For those who taught me to look for the large patterns, the unexpected connections:

in memory of Ray Billington, Wally Davies, Roy Nichols; and for Tom Cochran, Ralph Gabriel, Anthony Garvan, and Robert Spiller.

Scholarly publisher for the Commonwealth,
serving Bellarmine College, Berea College,
Centre College of Kentucky, Eastern Kentucky University,
The Filson Club, Georgetown College, Kentucky Historical Society,
Kentucky State University, Morehead State University,
Murray State University, Northern Kentucky University,
Transylvania University, University of Kentucky,
University of Louisville, and Western Kentucky University.

Editorial and Sales Offices: Lexington, Kentucky 40506-0024

Library of Congress Cataloging-in-Publication Data

Walker, Robert Harris, 1924-
  Reform in America.

  Bibliography: p.
  Includes index.
  1. United States—Social conditions. 2. Social change—Case studies. 3. Social reformers—United States—History. 4. Social action—United States—History. I. Title.
HN57.W26   1985   303.4′84′0973   85-15711
ISBN 0-8131-1549-3

The title page drawing is by Homer Davenport, ca. 1900.
Prints and Photographs Division, Library of Congress.

CONTENTS

PREFACE

Perhaps the study of reform can be taken as a metaphor that applies to the national and scholarly temper as well. We have passed through a period devoted to examining the distinctive traits of certain groups and experiences. In the field of reform we have been rewarded with a number of impressive monographs depicting a leader, a movement, a time, or a place. In the larger world we have been learning to appreciate the special situation of disadvantaged groups, the contributions of regional and ethnic minorities, and the idiosyncrasies of folk and vernacular subcultures.

Lately, however, there are signs that the charm of diversity has a rival. The 1984 Olympic Games saw members of American minorities conspicuously singing the national anthem on platforms where, not long ago, there were raised fists and silence. That same summer the political conventions vied with one another for the number of flags and the voltage of patriotic testimonials. Beyond the symbols and the rhetoric, moreover, is a mounting call for balancing the centrifugal with a concern for those factors that have made this country recognizable as a single nation. Academic as well as political conventions have witnessed the call for parity between diversity and synthesis.

The present work is attuned to this rising spirit. Although many pages are devoted to distinguishing between and among the plurality of reforms, the underlying purpose is to promote the perception of directed social change as a single phenomenon. Literally this work concerns itself with the underside of diversity: inequity and the attacks thereon. Metaphorically, at least, it is also about what unites Americans.

This work contains its own challenge. In it are described episodes as varied as a California constitutional convention and a New York City kangaroo court. Even the major cases in point—from the money question to the search for utopia—do not immediately suggest a contiguous subject matter. The challenge is to give these elements a consistent structural and chronological dimension.

The result, even if the challenge has been met, is an argument with many examples missing. This product may also be viewed as an incipient map of a relatively neglected frontier. Key features remain to be charted. The cartographical principles themselves will need adjustment. There does appear, nevertheless, a set of coordinates that may eventually transform some familiar but isolated landmarks into a grand *terra cognita*.

A number of distinctive traits and biases show themselves in the pages that follow. None has marked the work more strongly than its beginnings as a search for reform patterns so strong that the mere arrangement of the documents would make evident its validity. The first result of this search, *The Reform Spirit in*

America: A Documentation of the Pattern of Reform in the American Republic (1976; reprint R.E. Krieger, 1985) implicitly proposed the revision of reform's main categories, the identification of certain constant and variable elements, and the functional redefinition of the historical study of social change. Although the present work goes beyond the document collection in many ways, it still bears the stamp of the original quest for pattern and structure. The most fortunate consequence of this order of procedure is in the existence of two books, parallel in organization, one describing a thesis and the other furnishing documentary evidence.

Direct contact with the record of reform soon taught mistrust of prevailing generalizations. My notes are filled with disputations. Eventually I developed a bias against revisionism for its own sake. Given a choice between iconoclasm and constructive synthesis, I chose the latter. Instead of refuting concepts that proved unworkable I have attempted to replace them. Finding the division of reform vague and the vocabulary inconsistent, I have proposed three major categories, fully exemplified, and a taxonomy of common terms. Finding the reformer dismissed with caricature, I have projected a differentiated set of social actors, individual and collective. Finding the larger meanings of reform buried under the assumption that it is a series of isolated struggles for fixed objectives, I have substituted the concept of an interrelated continuum. Finding American values resting heavily on competitive individualism, I have located a compensatory stress on morality, reason, practicality, altruism, and process.

The bias against lateral controversy has created some special bibliographical problems within a subject already choked with contradictory indications. Many useful studies lose their credibility when they shift from close analysis to general improvement. One recent study of antebellum reform, for example, served up the following gratuitous and unsubstantiated statements: that the period of this study was the most intense and active; that reform eras are killed by war and followed by apathy; that social action before Sumter left no postwar legacy; that progressivism had no influence on reforms of the 1930s; and that discontinuity is the rule of reform.

There are not many cases of a leap off the deep end so heedless of evidence; yet many otherwise reliable works are marred by the urge to make one corner of reform appear unique. Rather than argue with assertions such as these, I have chosen to avoid using certain monographs at the risk of appearing unaware of them, following the principle that too much disputation discourages synthesis. On the other hand, I am disproportionately grateful for those lucid and ambitious works that have made successful connections beyond a single reform topic. I have cited them with a gratitude matched only by the feelings of the uncertain navigator sighting a familiar beacon on the darkened shore. Inevitably, in a subject of this scope, I have missed some beacons and for these omissions I take full blame.

As my work progressed, I became increasingly convinced that a central error lay in seeing reform as a series of neat specimens bottled in time. With this conviction came an unconscious bias against period histories of reform which, too often, develop misleading particular traits (among the genuine) and thus stand in the way of locating the common elements. On the other hand, I became increasingly prejudiced in favor of the importance of the creative imagination in the process of social change. Sometimes only inspired art, literature, and music—at all cultural levels—appear able to generate the emotional intensity essential for overcoming the burden of inertia. This conviction may well have led me to overuse the products of the muse.

The bias that may be most thoroughly hidden is the aversion to unnecessary risk. Although it is hard to imagine a high wire more precarious than the attempt to organize this enormous and varied subject, it will become clear, I hope, that I have also strung the safety net. Given my choice I would suggest nothing "by assertion" but would assemble layers of evidence. My plan for the document collection called for thrice the 664 pages that eventually appeared. The present book was hewn from a much larger manuscript. Restrained by the economics of publishing, I have used the notes to summon additional evidence, friendly interpretations, and supportive bibliography. For my most controversial argument (about periodization) I have compiled a detailed chronology. I have taken heroic measures to avoid the misstep of loose terminology. To guard against the dizziness of trivia and inconsequence I have illustrated each major section with the largest cases in point.

In spite of these precautions I am neither hoping nor expecting that my proposals will escape controversy. The main position will be reflexively resisted by those who are convinced that comprehension of this subject is limited to disconnected insights in a context of chaos. Having shared this point of view for so long, I have considerable sympathy with it. And I have not devised a perfect model: who could? My fondest hope is that some scholars will be encouraged to make more cumulative sense of reform history and that, in so doing, they will use, revise, and improve upon this structure. Toward this end I have eschewed the smoke of mystical perceptions and have laid out a plan in plain detail.

My most transparent prejudice is a direct product of the research that produced this work. I approached reform full of the accepted skeptical stereotypes and relinquished them with a gradual reluctance. At some point, however, I became convinced that directed social change constitutes a vital and undervalued part of this nation's meaning. I have made no real effort to conceal this point of view.

ACKNOWLEDGMENTS

My heaviest debt is to that long-time student of reform, Daniel Aaron, who reviewed my first draft, point by point, asking the hard questions that led to greater clarity. Other constructive critics of the work-at-large were Astere E. Claeyssens, J. Merton England, Ralph H. Gabriel, and Clifford S. Griffin. Both in conversation and through his own continuing work Thomas C. Cochran, my former professor, proved an apt guide to rationale and method. Guy E. Noyes, once director of research at the Federal Reserve, along with Walter T.K. Nugent and Robert P. Sharkey, amended my account of the money question. Phyllis Palmer reviewed the section on the woman question; John Hancock and Robert Kenny, aspects of the ideal community. My colleague Sar Levitan, a mentor on many counts, criticized the final section. My friend and neighbor, Carl Bode, talked me over some hurdles and, with his wife Charlotte Smith, furnished knowledgeable encouragement.

A fellowship at the Huntington Library gave me the particular joy and profit of working again under the sympathetic eye of the late Ray Billington who, as my undergraduate instructor in 1944, provided an intellectual shove that eventually proved decisive to me. The acumen of the Huntington's legendary staff would be hard to exaggerate. Parts of this work were also done while enjoying the hospitality of the Hoover Institution on War, Revolution and Peace; the Rockefeller Center at Bellagio; and the Woodrow Wilson International Center for Scholars. In all these settings I both learned from my fellows and profited from the benign logistics. My own University Research Committee has furnished financial support. The Library of Congress, my intellectual home for many years now, I am in danger of taking for granted. Not only are its resources unmatched, but its staff includes people like Edward MacConomy, John Sartain, and Bruce Martin who literally go out of their way to help the scholar. For the really hard work, my thanks to the tireless Carole Tuchrello.

Jack London Meets London

At the end of the Boer War the American Press Association wired Jack London in California, asking if this exciting writer of rising reputation would go to South Africa and do a series of articles on postwar conditions.[1] Putting aside his final corrections for *Children of the Frost*, London started eastward by Pullman on the Overland Limited. The soft sheen of the veneered sleeping compartment, the attentive ministrations of dining-car waiters, the worldly conversation of the club car—all brought back to his sensitive conscience the memories of an earlier trip along the same route but in a decidedly different class of passenger accommodation. How many of his club-car confreres, he wondered, would even know the meaning of "side-door Pullman," let alone appreciate the trickery necessary to outwit the railroad police for the sake of a freight-car berth. The memory of his own impoverished past, contrasted with his new opulence, brought a journalistic scheme to mind. His route to Africa would take him through England, where a coronation was about to take place. Why not transfer his own recently recalled perceptions of class difference to the English soil? Why not descend into the slums of London for a view from the bottom of that quintessential monarchical pageant?

In New York he talked with his Macmillan editor, George Brett. Two days in London's East End would do it. The author spoke to the editor about the human beasts he had observed on New York's Lower East Side. The London slumdwellers would be no different. Their comments on royalty would be trenchant, salty, perhaps irreverent, maybe even revolutionary. It sounded good to Macmillan.

As it cannot help doing, the crossing on a passenger steamer intensified the author's sense of social stratifications. London's guilt at being higher than steerage was expunged, anticipatorily, by his plans to descend into the steerage of the world's greatest city. Once ashore he completed his arrangements with dispatch. A handsome cab took him over the terrain; a secondhand clothing store furnished his disguise; a visit to Thomas Cook's and the American consulate brought him some tactical advice and informed them of his whereabouts in case he should fail to surface. Engaging a modest working room as headquarters, the former sailor put on a worn stoker's shirt, battered shoes, a filthy hat, and trousers to match. Secreting a little folding money in his sleeve, he put a knife and an odd coin in his pocket, bid himself a nervous farewell in his astounded mirror, and began his descent.[2]

Two days had become seven weeks. It was an amazed, aged, and—even for him—wrackingly exhausted London who wrote to his close friend, Anna Strunsky Walling:

East London
Sept. 28/02

Dear You:

The book is finished. I typed the last word of the last chapter ten minutes ago—63,000 words. Now I shall have to move out of this room I have occupied seven weeks. Shall I give you the last paragraph?

"When the people who try to help, cease their playing and dabbling with day nurseries and Japanese art exhibits, and go back and learn their West End and the sociology of Christ, they will be in better shape to buckle down to the work they ought to be doing in the world. And if they do buckle down to the work, they will follow Dr. Barnardo's [sic] lead, only on a scale as large as the nation is large. They won't cram yearnings for the Beautiful & True & Good down the throat of the woman making violets for three farthings a gross, but they will make somebody get off her back and quit cramming himself till, like the Romans, he must go to a bath and sweat it out. And to their consternation, they will find that they will have to get off that woman's back themselves, as well as the backs of a few other women and children they did not dream they were riding upon."

I am afraid that I have hit out too strongly right along to get serial publication. But, try as I would, I could not curb my wrath enough to make it sufficiently innocuous for a bourgeois publication. . . .[3]

Jack London had indeed "hit out too strongly" for the publishers. The affluent magazines refused *People of the Abyss;* it was eventually serialized in *Wilshire's*, a radical monthly whose pay was as modest as its circulation. Even Macmillan found parts of it too forceful, and for the sake of the contract, London removed references to King Edward himself and softened some other passages. Still it was and is an angry book. The East Enders he found bore little resemblance to even the "beasts" of the New York slums. Assuming the role of a seaman without a ship, Jack London fell in with two former seagoing laborers, scavenging the streets for castoff rinds and crusts, their eyes never leaving the pavement. At night they hoped for a workhouse where a day's labor would produce a place to lie down and two thin meals. Otherwise they would have to loiter outside the public parks until daybreak when the police would no longer prevent their entering and stretching out on grass or benches. His heart wrenched by this set of circumstances beyond any spectacle he had thereto witnessed, the supposedly detached reporter did not get through the first level of his descent before tearing the hidden currency from his sleeve, buying his mates a decent meal and leaving them with the change.

The descent continued. Before his eyes caricatured forms that only faintly resembled human beings fought over gutter refuse while the young took what rottenness was left. The detached observer felt his distance shrinking. He apologized to his own body for the filth he put in it and the outrages of environment to which he exposed it. In the end he had written what he sometimes referred to as his favorite book. No experience had cost him more of his youth nor tried his optimism more severely. *People of the Abyss*, fortified with photographs and statistics, achieves that mixture of passion and objectivity which defines muckraking at its most effective.

Implicitly, *People of the Abyss* is an emotional revelation about degradation so thorough and institutionalized that—Jack London assumed—the only relief would come through an explosion. The rich were riding the backs of the poor, as he wrote to Anna Strunsky. The social mechanisms for dealing with this problem are ineffectual. The exploited, therefore, had revolution as their only recourse. Yet Jack London also thought otherwise. Taking his personal philosophy from a group of thinkers themselves contradictory, London did not always penetrate their ideas completely. He blurred them further by filtering them through a personality that combined a vast talent for friendship and a true love for the freemasonry of the living with a recurrent belief in elitism and the innate inferiority of certain groups. Fortunately, *People of the Abyss*, sustained by a pure outrage, used no special philosophy to color its meaning or to soften its impact. In his original closing he even implies that social philosophies would only stand in the way of dealing with this problem.

Although London's publishers shied away from some of the new anger in his depiction, the American public was ready for the turning of the searchlight of public attention onto the evils of the modern city. Jacob Riis with his pictures; Stephen Crane with his realistic fiction; Lincoln Steffens with his profiles of urban political corruption—all were assaulting the public mind with a message climaxed in many ways by Jack London's descent. It mattered not that London's subject was London, England, and not Boston or San Francisco or Cincinnati. The problem, as American readers were beginning to see, was as prevalent as the modern city. It was not restricted to the greatest city in the British Empire at a time when economc conditions were relatively good. It would not disappear, in good times or bad, without drastic remedial work: hard, unflinching work that would take some privileged minds and pampered bodies into situations that would outrage them mentally and physically. Jack London's voyage inspired many others. It began, as is often the case, innocently enough: a traveler resting his forehead against the window of a moving train, watching and musing. It required coincidence: the cancellation of the African trip and the birth of a publishable idea. Before this voyage was over it took at least one sailor into waters so deep and dark that he feared his ability to surface.

Introduction

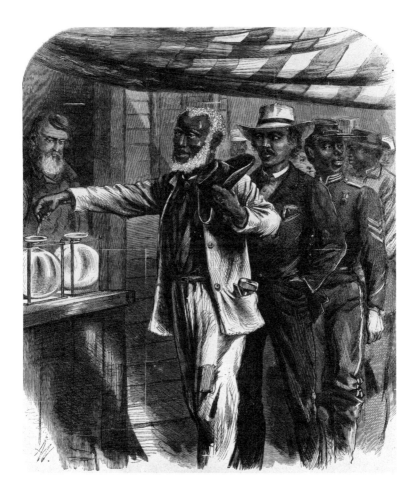

Soldiers oversee the exercise of the newly won franchise by former slaves as the government becomes a principal actor in reform. A.R. Waud, *Harper's Weekly*, November 16, 1867.

The immediate purpose of this work is to propose a way of organizing what we know about reform. This is not a simple proposition. It is complicated by our knowing both too much and too little. Our bookshelves are full of biographies of Frances Willard and Horace Greeley, analyses of the silver question and populism, samplings of protest and voting behavior, histories of abolition and chronicles of the woman's rights movement. Yet there are but a handful of large views of reform. Added to the problem of scope is the fact that insights come from so many directions: not only from sociology and social history but from politics and economics, religion and literature, journalism and art. It is small wonder that our perceptions have been limited to a figure, a problem, a movement, or an era. What we might learn about American society, could we but view the grand sweep of social change, remains something of a mystery.

Ralph Waldo Emerson opened his central discussion of this mystery by inventing a "lost fragment" of classical mythology in which Uranus (the reformer) chides Saturn (the conservative) for spending a thousand years making only the race of oysters. To illustrate the companion essay Emerson might have used an actual myth: the story of Proteus, son of Neptune, who would tell the truth only after appearing in a number of astonishing forms. "Man the Reformer," he wrote, must be sunshine in winter, shade in summer. He will take many shapes but "should not be a subject of irregular and interrupted impulses of virtue, but a continent, persisting, immovable."[1]

The student of society cannot learn the truth about reform unless he recognizes it in a number of shapes and guises. Only then will he find reform to be "persisting"—an inevitable half of the eternal debate which may have begun with Saturn's stubborn mollusk monomania. This debate, as Emerson argues, centers on the very nature of society. In discussing slavery and woman's rights, social security and the graduated income tax, the reformers have defined and redefined America. Because of the amount and nature of attention it has attracted, the reform record is a prime source for the discovery of cultural priorities. Because the general contours of the subject have been relatively neglected (compared with, say, the frontiers of unsettled land and technology) the analysis of this record can be expected to alter the accepted picture of the American character. The ultimate purpose of this work is to present this altered picture.

Method

The first thing one notices in approaching the subject of reform is that nearly everyone defines the term differently. The second obvious trait is the looseness

7

and inconsistency with which the subject has been divided. "Social reform," the most common descriptive term, usually means nothing more nor less than "economic reform." "Economic reform" may mean labor reform; it is frequently a euphemism for a Marxist interpretation. "Humanitarian reform," which ought to be as broad as social reform, is frequently used only to denote movements on behalf of handicapped groups and often connotes private charity. "Moral reform," which ought to describe rationale, is often used as though it pertained only to certain subjects.[2]

Even this degree of confusion may be natural in a subject which, Emerson insists, is as wide as society and as long as history. Therefore, instead of pursuing still another definition of reform I have sought a way of arranging the reform experience so that its collective patterns can be seen. When, after assuming a score of astonishing Protean shapes, this principle finally appeared, it resembled more a scientific than a historical method. It calls for the dissection of the subject, the examination of its vital parts, and its eventual reconstruction.

The trick is in finding where to cut. All parts belong to the same corpus; none will be mutually exclusive or totally unconnected. The main parts, however, will bear not only the unmistakeable features of the whole but a set of distinctive traits as well. These parts turned out to be politico-economic reform, reform for special groups, and the presentation of model societies. They were discovered by a method that had little to do with logic, a lot to do with trial-and-error, and almost nothing to do with prior procedures.

This technique does not promise a description of all of reform. Its usefulness does depend on the importance of the three parts, and this condition raises a question that may need no proof or may be beyond proof. One argument in favor of the three divisions is that they do represent the general direction of social change. American society has moved toward increased political democracy in the cause of economic equity, toward full social participation by groups perceived as outside the mainstream, and toward the continuous presentation of ideal forms and emblems.[3] These topics carry the burden of this study. Their separate examination and collective assessment become an argument for what is important about reform and reformers, about the way society changes and about the goals it tries to achieve. If this argument succeeds it will not end the task of describing reform but it will offer a structure, a vocabulary, and an open-ended method for generalizing about reform.

Thus far we have been talking about a method for discovery which merits no label beyond the heuristic. The method of presentation arises directly from the way the problem of discovery was solved. It opens with analysis and ends with narrative. Once the parts of reform are identified they are treated historically. This technique should not, in my opinion, be confused with social science. If a name for it is needed, perhaps "analytical social history" will serve.

The three segments of reform (which will be called modes) are the subject of the three parts of this book. The particular method in each part varies with the problem confronted. Part One uses a single case study in order to say something specific about the way reform works in an enormous arena. Part Two comprises an area not so large but probably more complex. No single case study could ever represent this mode. Since the area can neither be covered nor represented, the method relies on an examination of the three most important movements within this mode: reform on behalf of women and blacks; the defense of civil liberties. In Part Three the problem is connecting a number of well-recognized activities and showing that they form a continuum of substantial importance from the viewpoint of reform. The method here involves the subjective selection of those examples that best make the case.

There is also the question of a larger method verging on a philosophy of history. The study of reform confirmed an attitude toward understanding the past that had already seemed attractive. The process of coming to understand social change was, in large part, a process of breaking down barriers. Many of these barriers had been erected around movements, epochal events, violent conflicts, supposedly unique figures, or even recurring cycles. The barriers were replaced by a sense of the cumulative impact of certain ideas and social movements. Singular occurrences and patterned recurrences exist, but their importance is significantly less than the ability to see the uninterrupted incremental power of connected events. It may be that no one theory of history serves all needs, yet the study of American reform is remarkably well served by the "nondialectical" or cumulative approach.[4]

The investigative method, to recapitulate, could be called problem solving; the method of presentation, analytical social history with variations of the case-study technique; the philosophy, cumulative or incremental history. There is one important disclaimer that should accompany this statement of method. Although this work is clearly aimed at raising the esteem in which reform is held, it is not dedicated to the proposition that reform causes social change. Other forces are also important: environmental, demographic, attitudinal, technological. Reform is a process of adjusting social attitudes and institutions to meet an evolving set of basic conditions. Reform does other things as well: it plays a part in curing social ills and setting goals—but it is not a separable element in the chain of cause and effect.

Among the thorny bushes in the garden of reform none is more prickly than the definition of the reformer himself and the related question of motivation. As this work unfolds, a certain position on these subjects will become clear; a few words at the outset will also be helpful.

Who are the reformers? I am tempted to say, with Emerson, that they are all of us—at certain times, under certain conditions. Yet this study does not really follow Emerson's assertions all the way. The reformer, in this study, is a person, an association, or an agency that seeks to direct social change. From what can be learned about individual "directors of social change," they are not part of a profession, as it is often assumed. Most social actors work at some familiar occupation. Reform may be a by-product or an avocation. There are paid reformers, it is true, but the very large majority of social actors cannot be shown to have profited from their reform activities.

One of the major concerns of this study is to show how social actors try to move their fellow citizens: their arguments as well as their techniques. This study is *not* concerned, beyond the circumstantial level, with how social actors are moved to assume their roles. It seems both clear and important that Lizzie Boynton would not have become an active feminist had she not been denied study at a male college; that Edward Kellogg would not have turned to economic theory without having gone bankrupt in 1837; or even that Jack London might not have written *People of the Abyss* without the coincidence of a coronation and a Pullman trip. (See Encounters 1 and 4, and Chapter 1). To recognize the force of events on individuals, however, is quite different from searching for a standard theory of what causes reformers to behave as they do. The evidence already rules out economic self-interest. Is there a psychological pattern? Are reformers compensating for social or sexual frustrations? Some are. Are they products of broken homes? Are they the consequence of radical educations? Yes, some are. But is there a standard psychological profile that explains the internal motivations of social actors? No.

Taxonomy

To describe reform in an organized manner requires no new or invented terms but a set of accepted terms used consistently within their standard meanings. In order to avoid historical ambiguities there has been some tampering with the conventional vocabulary of reform but as little as possible. What follows is not a jargon but a consistent and slightly narrowed use of words as defined in common dictionaries. It is this taxonomy that gives structure to the subject of reform and allows for ordered comparison and contrast.[5]

The least-familiar term, "mode," has been used to designate the largest divisions of reform. Since the identification of these divisions constitutes the major "discovery" on which the work is based, it needed a designation free from shopwear. A standard definition of mode is "a manner of arranging some underlying substance." Here the substance is reform; each mode becomes the manner in which a major aspect of reform is arranged. They are:

Mode I: the improvement of politico-economic democracy
Mode II: the improved treatment of specific individuals and groups.
Mode III: the alteration of society by reference to a substantially different model.

The use of "mode," a term unfamiliar in the context of reform, not only suggests a fresh approach to the subject but also offers a mercifully compact substitute for some unavoidably distended descriptive phrases. In common the modes share a discontent with the status quo and a belief in process of social meliorism. They are not mutually exclusive in that many movements (even some individual documents) can be explained only by reference to more than a single mode. They use the same arguments to persuade the public. Their greatest points of distinction are in their goals and their dynamic patterns. Together the three modes define the limits of this study.

Each large aspect of reform may be analyzed under logical subheadings. The vocabulary has been provided by students of society. It is only necessary to recognize these headings and to use the terms predictably; otherwise, the ability to compare and contrast evaporates. The essential subheadings are: actors, forms, dynamics, arguments and assumptions.

The term used to describe an entity that attempts to affect society is "social actor"; four types are commonly cited: independent individuals, unorganized groups, voluntary associations, and institutions including all levels and branches of government. The first of these terms is self-explanatory. A group is distinguished from an association by its lack of structure and/or permanence. Group actions (riots, demonstrations) are spontaneous. Associations are characterized by charters, officers, publications, and all the organizational trappings. Many voluntary associations are purely recreational and have nothing directly to do with reform. Some, like the American Anti-Slavery Society, have only to do with reform; others, like labor unions and political parties, mix self-interest with altruism. A reform association, by definition, operates for the benefit of a group other than or larger than its own membership. Many well-structured, long-standing associations fall within the definition of an "institution," yet the main purpose of this category is to call attention to governments—at all levels and in all branches—as important social actors.

Social actors in all modes use a wide variety of "forms" ranging from private fasting to mass demonstrations, from platforms and conventions to contemplative verse, from the painstaking documentation of suffering to the rapier slash of the daily cartoon. Theoretically all varieties of social expression are available to all causes. In fact each movement develops an affinity for certain characteristic forms and, in so doing, helps define itself. Furthermore, attention to the extreme range of expression helps correct the unfortunate tendency to associate reform with only a few narrow stereotypes.

No aspect of reform would seem, at first glance, to be so obvious and predictable as the stages through which an issue evolves. Surely, one would think, all causes begin with spontaneous response to a problem (random negative). Next, the interested individuals would organize to spread awareness of the problem (structured negative). Although many movements would get no further than this stage, others would turn from a complaint to a solution. At first there might be many proposed solutions (random positive), followed by a selection of a single aim or a set of priorities (structured positive). Finally, if the measure does not fail, it will be institutionalized by a legislative act, a court decision, or an executive agency. Thus the "dynamics" of reform may be summarized as a five-step sequence: random negative (unorganized protest), structured negative (organized protest), random positive (various remedies), structured positive (organized movement with constructive aim), watchdog (surveillance of institutionalized reform).

This sequence is, indeed, as common as any in describing social change, particularly within Mode I. The other modes tend to define themselves, in part, by their distinctive variations from this pattern: Mode II by a double transit of the cycle, Mode III by opening the sequence in the fourth (structured positive) or fifth (institutional) stage. Listing the natural sequence not only leads to modal distinctions but helps clarify the problems encountered in certain movements which did not pass through a normal set of stages: the greenbacks and prohibition, for example. The list should not suggest that reform dynamics expire with institutionalization. Instead, the issue begins a second life in the "watchdog" phase: for example, the money question under the Federal Reserve.

Beyond the general commitment to meliorism, nothing unifies reform as profoundly as the "arguments" for social change, which are based on explicit appeals to: a higher law, reason, and a sense of the practical.

Contrary to the expectations aroused by either the history of ideas or the enormous subcultural variety in value structures, the rationales used by social actors to persuade their fellow citizens seems almost eerily constant. Differences in time and place, issue and audience, produce variations in rhetoric and stress. As the record of reform is brought into view, however, it will become clear that one of its most important, unvarying characteristics is its basic reliance on the interrelated threefold justification of morality, rationality, and feasibility.

Some of the underlying assumptions are equally universal. All reformers seem to agree that the general welfare is the ultimate goal or test for any proposition even though the means for approaching it may vary. All reformers start with a dissatisfaction with conditions as they find them. As a rule, reformers find challenge in defeat and success alike. To fail is to try again; to reach one milestone is to start toward the next. In fact the entire reform experience, it will be argued, is incomprehensible without the implicit assumption of an underlying and continuous social process which serves as both a means and an end.

Only one assumption is not totally shared and that is the efficacy of gradual change. All reformers assume the unacceptability of the status quo. Modes I and II generally call for a moderate process of melioration; Mode III, in presenting notably different alternative, commends the abandonment of the present society and the adoption of the alternative model—as soon as possible. Reform arguments and assumptions are closely related to cultural values and will be reviewed in this light—including a discussion of negative and implicit as well as positive and explicit values—in Chapter 8.

A clear and standard vocabulary for reform is not an end in itself. It is essential, however, to the removal of certain barriers that have impeded the understanding of both particular and general traits. In the largest sense, the act of dividing and finding the skeletal structure is the act of defining.

To concentrate on the components of reform is to expand its scope. To consider the variety of social actors that have moved against the status quo is to appreciate that reform cannot be imprisoned in its historical stereotype. Reform is a poem by Whittier; it is a citizen's angry letter to the press. Protest means something when it is a spontaneous sidewalk demonstration, not just when it enters a presidential campaign or congressional debate. It also helps to be reminded that social change does not end with elections and enactments but extends to the vigilant surveillance of officials and agencies.

Only close attention to the elements of reform makes possible the differentiation between the multitude of causes. Some causes attract a crown of charismatic leaders while others labor through the proceedings of anonymous associations and committees. Some crusades are ever threatening to explode into song; others are the stuff of films and fiction. Social solutions sometimes appear full grown; sometimes they must survive cycles of protest and proposals. In some cases—communes, visionary plans—the form taken by a proposal is nearly synonymous with the mode itself.

The most important reason for treating the components of reform with consistent attention is to discover what unifies the whole enterprise. We know reformers are discontented with the status quo; we know they have a vision of a better society. We respect the diversity of crusades and techniques but we have a right to expect some unifying goals and assumptions beyond the obvious. The approach that insists on a logic of distinctions must—and does—ultimately produce a logic of consanguinity. Toward this end, each major section of this work climaxes in both a narrative and an analytical summary. In the end (chapter 7) they are assembled in a way that identifies what unites as well as what distinguishes.

Organization

The presentation that follows, with one exception, is perfectly straightforward. It is in three main parts. Each part equates with a mode. The organization wthin each part follows the same general pattern. At first the mode is defined in terms of scope, objectives, and historical and philosophic origins. This definition is followed by a narrative sketch which sets the background for the cases in point. Following the discussion of the exemplary materials is a two-part summary: one, analytical, uses taxonomic categories to tighten the definition of the mode; the second, chronological, continues the introductory sketch by tracing the modal history up to the present.

The interior method in each part differs and is described in introductions to these principal sections, including the Conclusion. Chapter 7 expands on the pattern established in the separate parts by summarizing the collective materials both narratively and anlytically. Only in Chapter 8 has an effort been made to go outside the subject and assess its impact on the perception of the national character.

The deliberate exception to the logical presentation of the reform argument is the six "encounters," which punctuate the major sections. The very range and variety of these vignettes are intended as a caution against overly pat theories of reform. They explore the unlikely circumstances which motivate individual reform actions. Several of them defy probability in a way that intentionally inhibits overly simple theories of cause and effect.

Any series that moves, without transition, from a Yale commencement speech through a California constitutional convention to a midnight trial in Manhattan is clearly intended to retain some aura of the random. Yet each case, in one way or another, is a case in point and is used as such in the text. Each illustrates some classic reform situation. They all focus on some of the more important and characteristic forms utilized within the social process. In their order of presentation the encounters illustrate the two major modes in the same succession followed by the text, moving from politico-economic reform to issues involving blacks, women, and civil liberties. Furthermore, they represent, collectively, the normal stages in the dynamics of reform: from an exposé through varieties of negative and then positive movements and climaxing in a subject long in its institutional stage.

ENCOUNTER 2

Connecticut Meets Abraham Bishop

In the early years of Yale a banner occasion was the annual Phi Beta Kappa address presented on the eve of the college commencement. The most exciting of these ceremonial occasions took place in the year 1800. The excitement was caused not by the Phi Betta Kappa lecture but by the man who did *not* deliver it.

Abraham Bishop was born in 1763 to Samuel Bishop, a respected pillar of Connecticut political life who served fifty years as assemblyman, town clerk, deacon, and mayor.[1] The precocious son qualified for college just before his twelfth birthday and entered the notable Yale Class of 1778, which included Joel Barlow and Noah Webster among its illustrious members. In a few years he appeared successfully for the bar examination, but much more important was his decision to spend nearly two years in the politically fermenting Europe of 1787 and 1788. He returned, according to an oft-cited diary entry of Yale's President Stiles, "full of Improvement and Vanity."[2]

In fact he returned full of he same kind of political ideas that had motivated Jefferson and his followers: a sense of the natural rights of political man and of the need to press, combatively when appropriate, against historic controls and toward a more open society with an enlarged scale of popular participation. He returned, moreover, to one of the new nation's most conservative states, where a rather small number of favored families combined behind an orthodoxy in religion and politics to extend an unchallenged control over education, commerce, and industry. Property qualifications for voting still existed, and the percentage of adult white males who could meet suffrage conditions was actually shrinking in many parts of the state.[3]

The elders may have noted Bishop's increased vanity; they also apparently saw a much more serious and sober young man than the one who had left. Rumors reached them that he had been displaying a certain knack for oratory and that he had some interesting ideas on education. Hoping that at last Deacon Samuel's son had matured toward orthodoxy, they saw a chance to fill the ceremonial lectern with a prodigal native. Custom dictated a Phi Beta Kappa address on a question in moral philosophy or an aspect of natural science. To deal with contemporary politics was unheard of, even during an election year as high-spirited as 1800. The fact that Connecticut enjoyed a distinct conservative majority did not eliminate partisanship but rather intensified it in some quarters.

Against this setting Abraham Bishop prepared his best known of many pamphlets. He called it "An Oration on the Extent and Power of Political Delusion," and he submitted it to the governing committee of the Phi Beta Kappa Society but twenty-four hours prior to the meeting.[4] The committee read this forthright campaign speech with amazement, quickly located a substitute speaker and inserted a last-minute announcement in the morning paper. Bishop was hardly taken by surprise. In that same paper was a somewhat longer notice that Bishop would present his speech in another hall already engaged for this purpose. Bishop's speech was scheduled at the same time as the society's. The challenge had been delivered.

Those who chose the hall of the White Haven Society, which Bishop had engaged, instead of the hallowed Centre Church, where the substitute speaker held forth (his name and subject of indifferent interest to history), were in for a treat. Bishop opened with a brief parody of the typical learned discourse which measured the "diameter of the antediluvians" or explained "why an elm tree does not bear apricots." Instead of a fat feast, Bishop promised a "plain dish." He then plunged into a series of sharp, hyperbolic remarks aimed at shocking the audience with the degree to which Connecticut, once a leader in a revolution, had become a closed corporation, operating virtually without a state constitution and leaving little room for anyone not born to the establishment.

Bishop's prose pudding was hardly a "plain dish," but it was bubbling over with inflamatory rhetoric and ready for consumption. As the audience left the hall they were offered copies of the pamphlet whose flavor was accurately anticipated in the author's preface. Here the crowning metaphor was that of a palace inhabited by those who manipulated the state's pursestrings so as to choke off any symptoms of economic democracy.

> These pages present the corner-stone of an AMERICAN PALACE, and the dark vault where are to be entombed, in eternal sleep, the liberties and hopes of this, and future generations The foundation of a MONARCHY is already laid in 6 per cent. 3 per cent. and deferred stock, in millions of civil list and indirect taxation. The aristocracies already formed, are to be the pillars of this magnificent building. The glory of this latter house is to transcend that of the edifice of freedom, which, erected on the ruins of palaces, lately presented a massy colonnade of human bones. What infant, in his nurse's arms, is to be the progenitor of an illustrious race of AMER-ICAN MONARCHS, is yet unknown.[5]

Bishop outdrew his rival speaker both in attendance and furor. A number of replies were evoked, one of the most vicious attributed to Bishop's erstwhile classmate Noah Webster, who titled his riposte "A Rod for the Fool's Back."[6] The appearance of these vituperative rejoinders showed that the speaker had hit his mark. As a Jeffersonian, he had very little to lose. His fellow Republicans may have been spirited but they were abysmally in the minority. Bishop's only hope for making Connecticut a two-party state was to play on partisanship itself; and this he surely did. He did it in a way that was not original but was nonetheless effective. The Revolution was a recent enough memory so that any crowd could still be dependably aroused by the assertion that the courage and wisdom of the

Revolutionary leaders had been in vain. According to Bishop, the mass of Connecticut's citizens might as well have stayed subject to the English throne. Instead of a House of Lords and a monarch, there was now an aristocratic governor and legislature. Instead of a Church of England, there was a religious orthodoxy every bit as compelling. Instead of the tyranny of British mercantilism, there was a tight oligopoly of wealth, including a self-serving, rising class of middlemen called lawyers. The answer? A broadened suffrage to remove privilege and to assert the rights of man.

Bishop's oratory did not sway the majority, but it made the campaign more interesting. There were enough Connecticut Republicans to rejoice in Jefferson's election and to invite Bishop to repeat his oratorical triumph at Hartford. Recognized as a party leader, he earned for his father a political appointment from Jefferson's hand. Abraham Bishop continued to lead a life that should fascinate a biographer: an early, stormy marriage to the daughter of the controversial Timothy Dexter ended in divorce and was followed by two others. A bright beginning, turned dissolute and then radical, turned again toward wealth and respectability, losing interest at every milestone to the student of social change.

Yale, New Haven, Phi Beta Kappa, and Connecticut all survived the year 1800 without notably altering their conservative courses. Yet Bishop's moment in the spotlight serves as a prototype for much of the debate that has ensued. *Connecticut Republicanism* typified the sense of economic grievance (a monarchy built on deferred stock) that underlay the call to political action. Bishop, one of the first in a long sequence of politico-economic reformers, showed his successors how to open with a broad cannonade, narrow quickly to a vulnerable target (bankers will always serve), then charge forth with a remedy (broadening suffrage), an association (the Republican party), and a leader (Jefferson). Bishop's Phi Beta Kappa maneuver is as vivid as any early example of mainstream reform.

Politico-economic Reform

Cartoonist Homer Davenport portrayed the "trusts" as an extravagantly muscled giant, ca. 1900. Prints and Photographs Division, Library of Congress.

The largest element within American reform is the effort to improve political democracy and, in so doing, to eliminate special privilege and undue poverty. For reformers participatory democracy was not to be tested just by its ability to reflect the popular will but also by its ability to move the society toward improved distribution of wealth. This aspect of reform includes suffrage movements, labor reform, and taxation for social purpose. Among these and other options, the politics of money was selected as the most revealing example of how reform works within this mode. The money question, as a case in point, is examined in considerable detail for that period (1832–1913) when the United States, technically, had no national banking system.

Part One opens with a definition of Mode I, its origins and scope. The case study of the politics of money occupies the end of Chapter 1 (narrative) and the opening of Chapter 2 (analysis). Both discussions are buttressed by the chronology that appears in the Appendix. This unusual amount of evidence supports some crucial and revisionary assertions: that reform has a characteristic dynamic pattern; that the perception of this pattern depends on the complete fusion of political with economic events and the recognition of social change in many forms and stages; that the assessment of the full dimensions of reform reveals some gross errors in the conventional periodization of reform. Part One concludes with a historical synopsis of Mode I followed by the identification of those actors, forms, and dynamic patterns peculiar to this mode.

CHAPTER 1

The Mainstream and the
Politics of Money

Because it was, among other things, a politico-economic reform movement, the American Revolution makes a good starting place for a consideration of the main currents in reform. The Revolution, however, did not open without a prologue—a prologue stretching back to the earliest records of Western civilization. While it is not essential here to make these connections in detail, it is important to note that the impulse which guided the Revolution and pointed the new nation toward a continuing process of social change did not spring miraculously into being with the signing of the Declaration of Independence or the tolling of the famous bell.

Origins of Mode I

Of the many aspects of the European Renaissance a few were especially germane to the political environment that produced the new nation. There was a return to the legacy of the classical civilizations and with it a rediscovery of the ideas of humanism, democracy, civil liberties, and human rights. The concept of natural rights led to a set of social theories alien to oppressive monarchies and hierarchical churches. The French political philosophers kindled passionate verbal fires against tyranny. In England there arose the concept of the "independent whig"—made popular in the colonies through *Cato's Letters*—who learned through bitter experience to mistrust all power and authority.[1]

It is possible to see the rising discontent of the colonists as an inevitable outgrowth of a restless *saeculum politicum*. It is necessary to see the Revolution as a kind of funnel through which the broad experience of Western civilization was narrowed into the framework for a particular style of social change. From this viewpoint the Revolution becomes a stage in a prototypical reform movement with extremely broad consequences.

Although most colonists clearly thought of themselves as loyal British citizens throughout the prerevolutionary years, there appeared a rising tide of resentment that typifies the early stages of social change. There were, to begin, economic hardships: difficulties with credit, rising indebtedness among the planters, and unfair restrictions on the incipient commerce of New England. In this first stage the complaints are diverse, the protest unorganized.

In the second stage the problems are still more evident than the solutions, but the protest is becoming organized: by informal groups, colonial legislatures, and committees of correspondence. As the complaints become structured, remedies begin to appear (stage three): full citizenship rights for the settlers; more self-government; an expanded role in the mercantilist formula. The frustrations felt by these loyal-but-long-suffering Englishmen may be fairly gauged by John Adams's whimsical proposal that Parliament follow the shifting British population and meet in America every third year.

The movement to improve the politico-economic status of the American colonies did not reach the fourth stage, organized positive action, until the convening of the Continental Congress, the drafting of the Articles of Confederation, and the signing of the Declaration of Independence. Although the issues between the Crown and the people were many, the idea of political redress for economic grievance remained at the center. Taxation without representation is tyranny.

The climax of this reform movement was not "the shot heard round the world," the surrender at Yorktown, nor even the Treaty of Paris. It was the ratification of state and federal constitutions that would assure citizens a political voice in their economic fate. The victory was only incidentally a military victory. It was, as Benjamin Rush calmly stated, the chance to bring European forms of government "to perfection" by diffusing what James Wilson called the "vital principle" of representation throughout the system."[2]

To the student of social change there are some surprises in the way this first great reform movement was institutionalized and applied. Considering the many restrictions imposed on the erstwhile colonists, why did they leave their Bill of Rights as a constitutional afterthought? In light of the categorical mistrust of power inherent in so much revolutionary literature, why would some framers of the Constitution find the enumeration of civil liberties a redundancy? With so many of the Founding Fathers outspokenly in favor of passive government and states' rights, why was the federal government so promptly invoked by the new nation to curb monopoly, protect workers, and inhibit the spread of slavery?

The answer seems to rest squarely on Wilson's "vital principle": representation. Considering the narrow and sometimes shrinking enfranchisement (see Encounter 2) of the new American citizen, it may be puzzling to see so much faith in the probity of those elected bodies which would comprise the main forum for social debate. In search of a reason for this trust one might look at the New York convention of 1821 and a speech by David Buel, Jr., that struck a note of optimistic compromise. Voting, declared Buel, is the bedrock on which rests the chance for achievement. It cannot, therefore, be limited to the wealthy. Although property must be protected it cannot form the "basis of representation. Our community is an association of persons—of human beings" and not of property.[3] The social actors of this era made Buel's arguments the basis for unprecedented trust in government. With the removal of property qualifications and the steady expansion of the suffrage, what had the "independent whig" to fear from his own government?

With the ratification of the federal Constitution and the redrawing of the state charters the stage was set for the central and continuing drama of reform. Its plots have concerned suffrage and representation but also tax and tariff, currency and credit, the regulation of commerce and manufactures, the protection of workers' rights. The actors on this stage have been the largest organizations— political parties, labor unions, a multitude of special interest groups—with the governments themselves playing increasingly prominent roles in all their branches and at all levels. The central plot has not changed: it is the search for improved economic equity through the perfection of the democratic process. Dramatic tension is guaranteed by the basic juxtaposition of values underlying any capitalistic democracy: civil rights versus property rights. Exceptionally well covered by the media and reflected in virtually all social forms, this show has played in factories and slums, in guerrilla theater and in the most elegant supper clubs. Even the matinees have sold out.

The Money Question

The charting of the mainstream will be resumed, in the next chapter, with a summary discussion of its boundaries, its salient traits, and its narrative flow. In order to understand the workings of this mode—and some of its characteristics are seriously misunderstood—it is necessary to take a close look at one of its major aspects. Many issues would serve admirably as cases in point—suffrage, taxation, and labor among them. In the end the money question nominated itself, not because of any suspected glamour but because it was unavoidable.

The literature of reform is filled with the concern of workers over the real value of their pay, farmers over the terms of credit. Partisan oratory and political platforms have concentrated on money issues above all else save praising the Founding Fathers. The major parties have splintered over gold, silver, and greenbacks. The state of the nation, in good times and bad, always seems to rest on the couch of money.

In spite of the prominence of the money question, textbooks in general history seem anxious to avoid more than a quick brush with booms and panics. If a student wants to learn whether Andrew Jackson was justified in attacking the Second Bank of the United States, or whether Herbert Hoover was right in anticipating that a departure from the gold standard would increase the concentration of wealth, then he will have to consult an economic history or a special study. For the student of reform, however, there is no avoiding this question. Since colonial times the questions related to money have not only attracted basic adversarial positions but also have represented a form of social conflict that may be distinctive.[4]

Having accepted the primacy of the money question, one takes the next step with an ease that is unfortunate because of the amount of labor involved. There is only one natural division in the chronology of this subject: from 1832 when the national bank was effectively terminated to 1913 when a national banking system was again established. With the 1830s, banking became national and political instead of local and legal. Between 1832 and 1913 there arose a series of reform movements based on financial convictions which we have learned to understand separately and which we need to view as part of a vital continuum. During this period—from the administration of Andrew Jackson to the administration of Woodrow Wilson—the issues relating to currency, interest, and banking constituted a major political preoccupation. After 1913 the money question surely did not disappear, but its setting shifted from the social to the institutional.

A "case study" that lasts eighty years and includes many separable political movements is a virtual contradiction in terms. The difficulties, however, are precisely appropriate to the problem. What is missing in the understanding of this subject is not the appreciation of any limited period or issue but the recognition of connections and continuity. No specimen study that was limited to a single generation, region, or group could effectively supply the missing perceptions. To make this necessarily extensive case in point manageable, while giving it the substance to support revisionary observations about the entire subject of reform, a three-part exposition has been prepared. Immediately following is a narrative account of the politics of money, identifying its chief figures and issues. Chapter 2 opens with an analysis of these same topics. The Appendix supports both these presentations with a detailed chronology that brings together the key financial, political, and social events.

The personality that hovers influentially over the questions of money and banking in the early Republic is that of Alexander Hamilton. It was he who argued, in his famous essay on the loose construction of the Constitution, that the chartering of a national bank was within the power of the federal government. It was he who convinced a sufficient number of his colleagues that the commercial future of the young nation lay with paying its debts and establishing, thereby, credentials for issuing currency and loans. Famous for his prophetic view of America as a rising nation of commerce and industry while it was still predominantly an agricultural nation in population, economics, and metaphor, Hamilton also saw the necessity of an institution that could collect income, safeguard funds, issue money, meet payrolls, and extend credit to those entrepreneurs who would fulfill Hamilton's vision of America.

Hamilton's task was not easy. The colonies had encountered currency problems as diverse as their geography. In the process most of them had learned to despise the Bank of England, which had hardly extended itself on behalf of these remote British outposts. The historic antipathy to the Bank of England surfaced whenever the idea of an American national bank was proposed. Even in the exigencies of wartime, when the Continental Congress found that a bank of some kind was essential to the business of revolution, James Madison and others questioned its legitimacy. During George Washington's first term the subject arose again. A committee composed of Madison, Thomas Jefferson, and Edmund Randolph met at the president's request and advised—predictably— that there was no constitutional basis for a national bank. Meanwhile, congressional debates on the subject had produced little enthusiasm. One congressman was quoted as saying that he would as soon be seen entering a house of ill fame as a bank.[5] His hyperbole, if such, was not unique. As the first Bank of the United States (BUS) was receiving its charter in 1791, Philip Freneau was about to turn the journalistic guns of the *Gazette of the United States* on the alleged insidious alliance between Federalist politics and the interests of certain bankers and businessmen. Another enemy of federalism, Abraham Bishop, in satirizing the role of the bankers in what he viewed as an aristocratic conspiracy, wrote, "The foundation of a MONARCHY is already laid in 6 per cent. 3 per cent. and deferred stock."[6]

With the second bank these sentiments grew. Part of the opposition was rhetorical. The Anti-Federalists were developing their appeal to the voters by equating the new establishment with the one overthrown in the Revolution. They characterized the Federalists as a group of wealthy, propertied, Episcopalian gentlemen, accoutered in tie wigs and lace. They were the officer class of wartime who were not reluctant to draw the sword of martial memory when the situation demanded. This upper-class "royalty," as depicted by the Republicans, had its attendant institutions. At the top of this list came a transplanted Church of England and reborn Bank of England, now called by a different name but run by a blueblood named Nicholas Biddle.

Some of the Republican rhetoric made it seem that a country had best have no bank at all. Serious discussions, however, began to produce a pattern of issues. One concern was for foreign domination. At one time the first BUS had 18,000 of its 25,000 shares in foreign hands; the threat of manipulation from abroad continued into the Biddle era. Local interests—led by Martin Van Buren— noted the rising financial prominence of New York and argued that the bank was misplaced. Other regional interests resented an apparent tendency of the BUS to draw on branch depositories in a way that tightened money in the South and West at times when credit was acutely needed.

Not all of these criticisms were fair. Both Banks of the United States had been more ready to extend credit to businessmen than to farmers, but before the recharter was vetoed, Biddle had used bank bills to expand currency and credit in the West and South. None of these measures would change the minds of those spokesmen for the common man, who, in increasing numbers, saw a threat in all monopolies, the most virulent of which they identified as a federally chartered national bank.

Moreover, as the BUS began opening branches in the several states, the sensitive issue of federal versus state powers came into play. Banks had been chartered by the states in order to retain local authority. When the federal branch banks entered the picture, chaos resulted. Two kinds of governmental monies competed with a variety of issues already in circulation. The U.S. Mint, newly established, was of little help. In fact it had such a limited supply of precious metals that foreign coins were passed on as legal tender. The wage earner had to look more than once into his pay envelope before he could determine the purchasing power of his earnings. Thus the bank became a focal point of contention between debtor and creditor, worker and employer, buyer and seller. It also pitted region against region and placed in destructive competition the various levels of government: local, state, and national.

General feelings about money and class were kept alive and often exacerbated by the series of constitutional conventions which marked the early years of the Republic. Banks and bankers were not always prominent in these arguments, but they were never far removed. In all states some feelings were expressed against an overly broad attribution of power to the central government. One of the prime examples of excessive central power was the national bank. The bank issue, thus, appeared on two of the favorite debating grounds: federal versus states' rights and democracy versus privilege.

In this atmosphere of continuously charged feelings—with the constitutionality of the BUS questioned by some of the Revolution's leading figures, with the states already wounded and sensitized on the subject of national charter, and with a popular president already publicly declared against a national bank—Henry Clay advised Nicholas Biddle to make recharter an election issue for 1832!

When Biddle took Clay's dubious advice, and when Jackson, predictably, met him head on, a memorable politico-economic war was declared. The conflict, echoing with the salvos of congressional debate, crackling with the sniping of the press, and marshaled within the frontal assault of a presidential campaign, remains one of the most dramatic and well studied of events. Coupled with the movement for an independent treasury, the war on the bank has a special meaning for the student of reform. It brought financial issues into unavoidable prominence and invested the contending sides with partisanship based on class and occupation, region and party. It showed many reformers that public interest lay in concrete issues like money and banking as opposed to panaceas like universal education or religious experiments in the wilderness. Once the public was convinced of how vitally its personal and collective well-being was bound up in monetary and financial issues, it was never to let the candidates forget.

Andrew Jackson no more *discovered* how to make a play to the populace by tweaking the bankers than Franklin Roosevelt *invented* "social justice." Both these presidents knew good political rhetoric when they saw it, however, and both were quick to borrow, adapt, and polish. Thus Jackson's veto message is a classic not because of its originality but because of its knowing use of what was already there.[7] Throughout the speech he inveighs against wealth and privilege, condemning the bank as a source of improper rewards to a small group of native and foreign elite. In a paragraph that might be taken as the literary climax, Jackson admits that nature guarantees no equality and charges government to protect whatever "fruits of superior industry" the individual can fairly attain. However, he continues,

> when the laws undertake to add to these natural and just advantages artificial distinctions, to grant titles, gratuities, and exclusive privileges, to make the rich richer and the potent more powerful, the humble members of society—the farmers, mechanics, and laborers—who have neither the time nor the means of securing like favors to themselves, have a right to complain of the injustice of their Government.

A just government must, "as Heaven does its rains, shower its favors alike on the high and the low."[8]

This message is but the best-remembered part of two intense and powerfully adumbrative battles—one for the presidency and one to override the incumbent's veto—that defined the issues and set the rhetorical tone for a century of politico-economic reform.

Two proposals emerged as alternatives to the BUS. One was the free-banking movement. Since the granting of charters was to be removed from federal supervision, this program represented an extension of the states' rights sentiment which helped defeat the BUS. But the free-banking movement went further. It attacked the scandals rampant in the granting of state charters by making banking virtually available to all. Only minimum requirements faced anyone who wished to open a bank. Bank notes were backed by bonds, and specie reserves were required, but at a very low ratio. Supported by some farm and labor elements, free banking was enacted in Michigan and New York, where it enjoyed some success in diluting the favoritism inherent in limited charters. But free banking was inflationary and lacked sufficient regulation. It did not attack the problem of private control over fiscal matters of public interest. Support by labor faltered. Court decisions against free banking's constitutionality eventually terminated this experiment.[9]

The second alternative was one that sought increased participation by the federal government. As a carefully studied proposal it is traceable to William M. Gouge. Born in Philadelphia in 1796, Gouge first earned public notice as part owner and editor of the *Philadelphia Gazette* and as a reporter of the Delaware state constitutional convention. Gouge was a methodical man with a taste for detailed knowledge of how things worked, especially banks. From the first he had a particular interest in state banks and continued this preoccupation throughout his life, publishing accounts of state banking in Texas and Arkansas, as well as using details from state banking systems to illustrate his more general arguments. Appointed a clerk in the U.S. Treasury by Levi Woodberry, he produced, sometimes without pausing to ask permission of his superiors, the most thorough and useful work to emanate from that department. His two most influential books were *A Short History of Paper-Money and Banking in the*

United States . . . (1833) and *An Inquiry into the Expedience of Dispensing with Bank Agency and Bank Paper . . .* (1837).

Today the importance of Gouge seems to be taken lightly, if at all.[10] At the height of his career, however, he was influential both at home and abroad. He contributed regularly to financial journals in terms which meant something to the financial community. His exhaustive knowledge of banking, and his capacity for absorbing details, enabled him to support his postulations with impressive evidence. His experience as a journalist gave him a knack for saying things with a terminal directness rare in politics. At a time when reformers were beginning to argue the virtues of a flexible currency, Gouge declared that fluctuations serve not the community but "the profits and safety of banks." Echoing Jacksonian rhetoric, he identified paper-money banking as a source of "*artificial* inequality" which "adds nothing to the substantial happiness of the rich, and detracts much from the happiness of the rest of the community."[11]

In spite of this antiestablishment tone, Gouge was surprised and offended when he was accused—by bankers and their friends—of being a conscienceless rabble-rouser. In response Gouge had no trouble compiling lists of his respectable supporters. He was taken seriously in all circles, but his ideas were most in tune with the demands of the workers and their advocates. In the first place, he furnished ammunition to those who historically and emotionally opposed banks. He attacked all banks on all counts. He was appalled that banks were allowed to charge the community for services that made them money. Rather, he wrote, payment should flow from the banks to the community. He saw the banks wielding unjustifiable power, often endorsed by state charters and confirmed by government deposits. The instability that profited the bankers was particularly burdensome to the producing class, which depended on a predictable amount of purchasing power at the end of a day's work or a season's harvest and which also needed credit on dependable terms.

Gouge's remedy for this problem was not a simple one, but in the popular mind it boiled down to two essential points. The first was that all "artificial" money should be gradually removed from circulation so that, eventually, coins and currency would be based only on precious metals (Gouge favored silver). The second, and the more consequential in the long run, was that the government should cease giving artificial advantage to some banks by chartering them or by depositing money in them or by paying them interest. This meant that the government would have to store its money in the United States Treasury or in branches thereof. Thus Gouge became one of the principal sources of support for what became known as the subtreasury or independent treasury plan.[12]

It is instructive to observe the way these issues permeated a group as diverse and bright as those workingman's friends who gathered in New York City around that benign and tolerant enthusiast George Henry Evans. At one time or another this group included true radicals like Mike Walsh and Thomas Skidmore, who wanted all real property divided by lot to every family in equal measure; Robert Dale Owen, who believed in the universal remedy of education;

and Evans himself, whose primary loyalty went to land reform. In spite of the variety of personalities and vast amounts of ideological energies represented in this group, they probably agreed more fully on the importance of financial issues than on any other common ground. The first issue of Evans's paper, for example, predictably gave first place to the question of land ownership. Second only to that, the problems created by banking institutions were labeled a deserving target of "the artillery of your suffrage."[13]

The importance and the appeal of financial issues to reformers can be illustrated by the career of Frances Wright, who began as an unlikely advocate for an issue as limited and mundane as the treasury. Like many early American reformers she was born abroad. Her father, a radical thinker of means, promoted Thomas Paine's *Rights of Man* in the area surrounding Dundee, Scotland, where his daughter was born in 1795. Frances's parents died before she was three and she was moved to London, where she was reared by more conventional relatives. On completing her formal education she was offered the customary grand tour of Europe, which she declined, stating that she would prefer to see free America instead of oppressed Europe. The book she published as a result of this visit attracted the favorable notice of the Marquis de Lafayette. Hence she was invited to accompany him on his famous triumphal tour of America in 1824 and came to speak directly with Thomas Jefferson and James Madison. She used these occasions to test her ideas for the emancipation of American slaves, which she later put into practice at Nashoba.[14]

Particularly in her early days, Wright did have a leaning toward sweeping, simplified remedies for all social ills. She interested herself in New Harmony, the Fourieristic experiment of another famous Scottish immigrant, Robert Owen. She joined forces with his son in the promotion of free and compulsory public education as the essential basis for social melioration. In its communitarian aspect Nashoba itself was something of a universal solvent not only for the ills of slavery but also for social repressions. But the career of this woman does not end with panaceas.

Although she never lost her sense of the philosophical underpinnings of social behavior, Fanny Wright became a star performer on the stage of the early labor movement by vigorously, explicitly, and emotionally addressing concrete issues. She came down hard on the side of an independent treasury and endowed it with values similar to those argued by Jackson and Gouge, sometimes stated even more forcefully. Perhaps twisting the English lion's tail came naturally to this Scotswoman, but she did it in a way that appealed strongly to both native pride and xenophobia. She called the BUS "the American Branch Bank of England," explaining how the state and national banks had been manipulated by the Bank of England in order to rob the South of cotton, the North of labor, and the whole country of its wealth. Insisting on the term "independent," Wright hailed this measure as the chance to end "odious enthralment" to the "overwhelming tyranny of the money power," and to reverse a history of foreign exploitation. The Independent Treasury she called the "day-star of constitutional liberty," "the first practical, efficient, decisive realization of the Declaration of '76."[15]

With the verbal guns of Frances Wright and Evans's circle now aimed directly at this issue, support began to increase. In 1837 Martin Van Buren, backed by his cabinet and key members of the Congress, called a special session to propose the basic outline of a subtreasury plan. The subsequent bill, calling for the deposit of federal funds in branches of the treasury without recourse to private or state banks, passed the Senate but was tabled in the House. With the seating of the Twenty-sixth Congress the bill was reintroduced, passed, and signed. Meanwhile the National Republican party (Whigs), whose members had opposed the bill in 1837, was meeting in Washington, D.C., to compose what some consider the first true party platform. Its eighth plank resolved that "the separation of the moneys of the government from banking institutions, is indispensable for the safety of the funds of the government, and the rights of the people."[16]

In spite of this seeming bipartisan support, a Whig victory in 1840 was followed by a repeal of the Independent Treasury Act of 1840 and the dissolution of the subtreasuries that had been established in Boston, Charleston, New Orleans, New York, Philadelphia, St. Louis, and Washington. The return to power of the Democrats in 1844 led to the third submission of an independent treasury bill. This time it passed (1846), was signed into law, and remained in effect until after the passage of the Federal Reserve Act. (The subtreasuries established under the act of 1846 were not actually abolished until 1921.)

As Gouge had intended, the impact was twofold. The act directed that debts to the government were acceptable only in specie. Thus the flow of specie was increased, and bank notes which could not be redeemed at par with "hard money" were eventually forced from circulation. The early days of the Independent Treasury, however, saw a continuation of paper-money chaos which might or might not have been worse without the new legislation.[17] The second effect was to remove government monies from private banks, thus making the federal government its own banker and, it was assumed, ending the privileged status of certain banks and the improper influence of private banks on public policy.

The Independent Treasury did not solve all the money and credit problems of the United States. The act did not even create a truly independent treasury. The ink was hardly dry on the new enactment before the secretary of the treasury found himself forced to act more like the head of a national bank than like the director of an "independent" repository which simply collected what was due the government and met the payroll.[18] The Civil War shattered whatever remained of the Treasury Department's resolve to adhere to the original limitations. There was simply no way to meet an emergency on this scale within the provisions of the Independent Treasury. Too, the "money market," centered more and more in New York City, had a growing power far beyond what the antibank backers of the legislation would have liked. (In the 1980s, as the nation continues a war against inflation, the same complaint can be heard from still other secretaries of the treasury.)

Although the act did not solve the money problem, it did climax one of the first—and in many ways representative—politico-economic movements. Its negative stages lay in a long seige of sporadic muckraking, which coalesced into a sustained attack on the national bank. From among many proposed solutions the subtreasury idea came to define the positive goal. Although individual actors began the agitation, structure was eventually provided by labor groups and political parties. The forms were typical of Mode I (the cartoon, the tract, the platform) as was the rhetoric (inveigh against special privilege, invoke the Declaration). In its institutional form the measure added to the responsibilities of the federal government. In this, as in all respects, the independent treasury movement offered a reasonable prototype for the five-stage cycle of social change.[19]

The link between the subtreasury and the next episode in the politics of money is the panic of 1837, which led to the bankruptcy of a New York merchant, Edward Kellogg, who, shocked by the part that money and credit had played in his commercial decline, turned from business to theory. Kellogg was born on a farm outside Norwalk, Connecticut, the American family seat of the Kelloggs. His father, James, a prosperous farmer, had eight children by his first wife (of whom Edward was the sixth) and six by a second wife. When the family was still young, James moved across the line into Dutchess County, New York, and eventually back to Northfield, Connecticut. Edward was not lost, even among a brood of fourteen; his clear visage, penetrating eyes, and notable initiative set him apart. One of his early discoveries was that selling things to farmers was more profitable than farming. He became a drygoods retailer, then a wholesaler with an office on Pearl Street, in Manhattan, whence he conducted a thriving business until he became unable to collect his debts during the panic. This shrewd merchant, praised by employers as having the keenest judgment of human character, had also acquired a judgment for land values. While conducting his business he had been buying land on Long Island. In 1838 he moved to Brooklyn, with his wife and five children, and spent the rest of his business life managing his own estate.[20]

Kellogg's starting point was not an uncompromising hatred of banks but rather a bewilderment that the supply of money was so poorly managed and that the resulting fluctuation in interest rates could be so harmful. The remedy he offered in 1841 was a national bank with a branch in every state.[21] This plan resembled the independent treasury in that it would distribute government deposits throughout the land; but there the similarity ended. The backers of the subtreasury wanted a stable money based solely on specie and dependably inflexible. Kellogg's branch banks, on the other hand, were to accumulate a "safety fund" to be available when scarcity of currency would otherwise cause depressions.

In a further departure from the hard-money friends of labor, Kellogg argued that money could not be satisfactorily defined in terms of a fixed relationship to gold or silver but drew its value from the national product and measured itself against the rate of interest charged for loans. A dollar that could command 6 percent interest, he pointed out, was worth twice the dollar which drew 3 percent. If the value of money was functional, then the government had the right and duty to control those conditions which affect this value. From the first, Kellogg saw that the government must set standards for money as it did for weights and measures. The hard part of the equation, according to Kellogg's daughter, was the determination of what the government might offer as security for currency once a metallic basis had been abandoned. For years he belabored this problem. At last, in one of those moments of insight which are remembered forever, the inventor cried "Eureka! Why not exchange the dollar for a bond?"

Kellogg elaborates his proposal by describing two kinds of paper the government should print. One was the circulating medium and the other was a low-interest bond, based on the credit of the government itself, and interchangeable with currency on demand. Through these twin issues the government could—and should—control the supply of money and its value as measured in its capacity to earn interest. With such a system—and only with such a system—will money accurately reward a day's work and protect the honest merchant: "The laboring classes of all civilized nations have been, and are, as a body, poor. Nearly all wealth is the product of labor; therefore, laborers would have possessed it had not something intervened to prevent this natural result." What had intervened? Special interests in the money marketplace. What was needed? Public acceptance of responsibility for controlling currency and credit.[22]

Having made his central discovery, Kellogg then tried to spread the gospel. He sent copies of his work, *Labor and Other Capital,* abroad, where he thought it might be received with sympathy. He mailed a copy to Henry Clay and then paid him a visit for the sake of further persuasion. Horace Greeley—that master propagator of new ideas—was tempted to the Kellogg home where Kellogg's daughter Mary dutifully read the manuscript to the famous editor. Greeley was immediately impressed, carried the manuscript home with him, arranged for its printing in newspaper format with cheap and wide distribution in mind, and then published a flattering notice in the *Tribune.* Yet Kellogg's contemporaries, even when they applauded the direction of his thinking, could not imagine it as an immediate possibility. He died in 1858, still mentally revising his prose, searching for that dramatic presentation which would galvanize his audience to action.

The next major step in the political history of the money question was the issuance by the wartime government of the North of fiat currency in 1861 and the subsequent passage of the Legal Tender Act making those greenbacks the authorized currency and underwriting additional issue. The question of Kellogg's influence on this decision is, in my opinion, both open and complex.[23] There is no question, however, that Kellogg's ideas took a new vitality after his recommendations had, under the argument of wartime necessity, been put into effect. Paper money was indeed in circulation. It was based on no fixed deposit of gold or silver. It was convertible with an interest-bearing bond. *Labor and Other Capital* now provided a guide to the potential political meaning of this monetary fact:

> Of all the drastic doctrines and revolutionary movements thrown up by the sixties and seventies the most puzzling and American was greenbackism. What the socialism of Lassalle and Marx was to Germany, the cooperative anarchism of Proudhon to France, the revolutionary anarchism of Bakunin to Spain, Italy, and Russia, what Feenianism was to Ireland, and land nationalization to England, so was greenbackism to America. The originator of greenbackism was Edward Kellogg.[24]

The man who saw the immediate political application of Kellogg's theories was Alexander Campbell who, in the early 1860s, had put himself into the money picture. He wrote the government advocating fiat currency; he read Kellogg; he published *True American System of Finance; the Rights of Labor and Capital, and the Common Sense Way of Doing Justice to the Soldiers and Their Families. No Banks; Greenbacks the Exclusive Currency.*[25] In this book Campbell advised his readers to make a virtue of a wartime necessity. He argued the Kellogg line in recognizing two crucial elements in the financial equation: the amount of money in circulation and the interest rate. He saw a relationship between the two elements, and seizing on Kellogg's device of grounding the currency on its redemption in interest-bearing bonds, he stressed the notion that this interconvertible feature would automatically regulate both the currency supply and the interest rate. The level at which the government pegged the interest rate would offer either a floor or a ceiling for the money market, depending on the direction of movement. Steadily available money at fixed interest would eliminate usury as it removed the private moneylenders from their position of central control. Furthermore, the relationship between bonds and currency would tend to modulate the currency supply, heading off extreme inflationary and deflationary trends.

Campbell's life, like his ideas, had several points of similarity with Edward Kellogg's. Like Kellogg he had experience as a clerk, then manager of a business: in Campbell's case the business was the manufacture of iron products, which took him steadily westward from his native Pennsylvania. Like Kellogg he became heavily involved in land speculation and eventually moved to occupy and manage his property. Campbell's land investments took him to Illinois where he settled in La Salle and was twice elected mayor on the Whig ticket (also Kellogg's choice) before joining the incipient Republicans.[26]

Campbell's entry into politics signaled the important differences between the two men, differences which provide a clue to the role each served in the propagation of greenbackism. If it is fair to call Kellogg the "father of the greenbacks," it is just as fair to call Campbell the "father of the Greenback

Song covers, especially in the nineteenth century, were an index of popular concerns; this one reveals the ubiquity of the money question. A. McLean, 1863. Music Division, Library of Congress.

party."[27] Campbell followed his service as mayor with election to the state constitutional convention and eventual entry into the Congress of the United States in 1875 as a member of the Independent (Greenback) party. Campbell had made one change in Kellogg's recommendation which, although it might at first appear to be but a minor financial variation, made all the political difference in the world.

In place of Kellogg's recommended national bank, Campbell called for a currency and bond system directed by the government. This change enabled him to tap the historic prejudice against banks in general and against the two Banks of the United States in particular. By making one modification in Kellogg's mechanics, he immediately allied himself with Jefferson, Freneau, and Bishop; with Benton, Jackson, and Gouge; and with Evans, Skidmore and Wright. In short, he placed the greenback issue squarely in the mainstream of politico-economic protest. In so doing, he was stockpiling some important emotional capital. He would need every bit of it, for he and his colleagues were attempting to create one of the great reversals in the history of labor protest: the conversion of the working man from the side of hard money to the side of a flexible paper currency.

In addition to antibank sentiment, the Greenbackers were also able to draw on patriotism. Greenbacks were issued on "faith in the Nation," as the legal-tender proponents somewhat unfairly argued during the 1862 debates. Once adopted, the greenbacks became the currency that freed the slaves, won the war, and saved the Union. In short, their appeal almost exactly paralleled the notorious "bloody shirt" rhetoric of the postwar GOP, which commanded the electorate to "vote the way you shot" and elect the party that saved the nation. Obviously, this was a regional appeal. Before the farmers of the South could be drawn to a soft-money cause, other arguments would be needed.

Immediately following the Civil War most farmers enjoyed a short period of prosperity. It was industrial labor, favored by improved conditions during the war, which began to suffer most quickly. It is hardly surprising, then, that men like William Sylvis and T. V. Powderly were among the first to see the virtues of a change in the economic system. The primacy of the greenback idea may be taken from the National Labor Reform party platform of 1872, which opened:

> *Resolved.* 1. That it is the duty of the Government to establish a just standard of distribution of capital and labor by providing a purely national circulating medium, based on the faith and resources of the nation, issued directly to the people without the intervention of any system of banking corporations, which money shall be legal tender in the payment of all debts.[28]

The election following this declaration was decidedly anticlimactic for the friends of labor (the national slate resigned after the Liberal Republican convention); however, the platform accurately indicated the road labor politics were to follow during the rest of the century.

T. V. Powderly was present at the organization of the National Labor Union in 1866; he was prominent in the formation and expansion of the Knights of Labor, the largest labor organization up to the American Federation of Labor. In his reminiscences he quotes a plank worded almost identically with the one cited above from the 1872 platform and says: "No other section of the preamble has attracted less attention than that, and none other is of more importance to the people."[29] Powderly's views on the money question were as shrewdly political as Andrew Jackson's. He used similar rhetoric of mistrust for money changers and usurers. He insisted that the government accept the issuance of money as a sacred obligation and suffer no intrusion between this function and the public interest. The threat of inflation and the cyclical problems of currency supply worried Powderly less than they had his antebellum colleagues. Rather he invited the support of farm and business interests by recommending an expanding supply of currency keyed to modest interest rates. Only such a fiscal policy would promote national growth and lead to full employment. Although the agenda for the rapidly organizing industrial labor force lengthened notably during these years, the priorities of the leadership kept the politics of money in the forefront of the movement.

Rural interests, although they were often represented at labor's political assemblies, came somewhat tardily into the Kellogg-Campbell camp. As the lot of the Western and Southern farmers grew steadily worse their growing sense of grievance was expressed in a number of issues and in the general rise of associations which gradually formed themselves into statewide, then regional, then national organizations with increasing commitments to direct political action.

One man was particularly important both in organizing rural opinion and in attracting agrarian interest to the money question. He was Dr. Charles W. Macune, son of a Wisconsin blacksmith-preacher, who inherited some of his father's evangelic fervor. Orphaned at age ten, he received little formal education but read for professional examinations and practiced both law and medicine. After some years of living in frontier communities, he appeared in Texas in the 1870s, a propitious time for displaying his talents as an organizer. Like Kellogg a failed businessman, he had also acquired a thorough sympathy with the plight of the Southwestern farmer. A witty and dynamic speaker, he played a vital role in organizing farmers' groups in Texas and elsewhere, moving his constituency steadily toward a point of view which was broad enough to allow for regional, then national support. He held offices in a number of these organizations. He was also effective as a writer, eventually becoming editor of the *National Economist* in 1889 and using this journal of the National Farmers' Alliance and Industrial Union as an outlet for his ideas on currency, credit, and related issues.[30]

C. W. Macune was important for consolidating rural organizations and sensitizing them to political issues of national scope. He was also important for understanding the importance of currency and credit to rural well-being. Macune realized that rural needs and opportunities varied from year to year, from region to region. He called attention to a recurring problem: the seasonal shortage of money and credit at precisely the times when they were most acutely needed—planting and harvest. With currency supplies contracted, and with credit either unavailable or restricted by usurious interest rates, the farmer was forced to buy seed at the seller's price and to sell crops at the buyer's price. To relieve this problem Macune described a new subtreasury plan designed to free the farmer from the tyranny of seasons and the profiteering of the speculators. Branches of the treasury were to be provided with facilities for storing grain and cotton. At harvest time the producer could either sell the product or store it with the government as security for currency: that is, accept a paper-money advance against the eventual sale of the crop. Such a practice would tend to remove from commodity prices those extreme variations brought about by seasonal alternations between abundance and scarcity. As price fluctuations moderated, so would the importance of the trader in futures. The consumer would benefit by lower prices. The economy would be improved by a process that automatically expanded and contracted the currency supply at appropriate times.[31]

Since history thrives on connections, it is interesting to speculate on Macune's resurrection of the term "subtreasury" two generations after its advocacy by Gouge. The coincidence tends to irritate economists, since one was offered in the service of stability and deflation while the other was frankly inflationary. The two plans, however, did have some features in common. They both stressed the need for regional differentiations, for assuring low-interest loans, and for increased governmental participation in financial questions. The most important link between the two subtreasury ideas, however, is the rhetorical link provided by their mutual reliance on that great protest reservoir of antibank sentiments. Ideas for change have a better chance of success if they concentrate on eliminating an unpopular public enemy. Both Gouge and Macune were able to arouse widespread sympathy by attacking the Eastern banker, the speculator, and the usurer.

The particular appeal of Macune's plan was to the farmer who yearned to escape the vicious cycle of low crop prices at harvest and high interest rates at planting. The general appeal was to the producer who resented the intrusion of any real or imagined middleman, profiteer, or parasite. In ways that were as emotional as they were logical, both subtreasury plans attacked unmerited privilege while they promoted economic democracy. Macune, in the manner of Gouge and Campbell, drew skillfully on these emotions.

It is less important to find originality in Macune than to see him as emerging from a well-defined protest tradition. Following Gouge and Campbell he opposed both national banks and undue influence of private banks. Like Gouge in particular he saw a great need for distributing the funds and functions of the U.S. Treasury over the entire country. Like Kellogg and Campbell he saw the necessity of a fiat currency founded on the national product, secured by "faith in

A cartoon cliché imported from Europe used familiar symbols to show the mixture of pride and resentment that fueled agrarian protest. Chicago Lithograph Co., for the Prairie Farmer, 1869.

the nation" and managed in such a way that credit would be broadly available at modest rates. Kellogg had advocated land loans. Macune went a crucial step further and advocated crop loans. In a way this proposal was a basic redefinition of currency.[32]

The greenback movement reached a climax in the election of 1878 when it claimed victories in fifteen congressional contests. In the narrow sense, the movement ended on January 1, 1879, when the resumption of specie payments commenced, although this event was as much a victory as a defeat for the partisans of an expanded currency. (The currency supply was not actually contracted; greenbacks were made redeemable in specie and, under these terms, remained in circulation.) The Greenback party declined not simply because of resumption but also because the philosophy of greenbackism was pervading other parties. In the negative sense this meant calling for the prevention of manipulation of money and credit by the private money market, the land and crop speculators, and the local moneylenders. In the positive sense it meant a commitment to control interest rates and to a currency which would expand and contract in response to need and opportunity. The recommended amount of circulating money was to be pegged not to a fixed dollar sum but to a per-capita figure, thus calling for a currency that would grow along with the population.

One of the parties which took over this philosophy was the People's party which, at its 1892 convention, endorsed the ideas of Kellogg, Campbell, and Macune and demanded the free and unlimited coinage of silver at the ratio of 16:1. Free silver reflected special, regional interests and was, compared with greenbackism, a simplistic response to the currency problem.[33] Nevertheless, it shared with other expansionary views the insistence that money need not be limited by the treasury's holdings of a single precious metal. Gouge, the workingman's economist, had long ago advocated silver as the ideal basis for currency. Adversaries of monometalism referred to gold as the metal of the money changers. William Jennings Bryan brought this imagery to a climax with his famous imprecation, "You shall not crucify mankind upon a cross of gold."

In that famous speech, the candidate showed a good sense of the history of the money question: "What we need is an Andrew Jackson to stand, as Jackson stood, against the encroachments of organized wealth." Like Jackson, Bryan attempted to pit farm and labor against the financial community. In Jackson's day, however, the voice of the common man had called for a reliable currency and paid little heed to the amount of it in circulation. Since that time Kellogg and greenbackism had educated the voter to the crucial and related questions of money supply and interest rates. Anyone who owed money or hoped to borrow money learned to stand for greenbacks or for bimetalism or for any expansionistic plan which would enable him to borrow at reasonable rates and pay back his loan with dollars deflated in value because of the inflation in their number. The creditors, the inhabitants of more settled areas, the vested interests—all wanted the stability of a fixed currency supply as well as the profits to be made by loans if the value of the dollar rose or stayed constant. Though Bryan lost, and lost again and again, his financial platform triumphed. The graduated income tax he defended in that same speech was eventually reenacted and declared constitutional. Silver increased its importance as a basis for securing currency. Finally another great orator, Franklin D. Roosevelt, took the nation off the domestic gold standard. An expanding or at least a flexible currency showed itself to be an idea that would triumph, sooner or later, in a nation that hoped to grow both materially and in the degree to which wealth is shared.

The climactic event for the political heirs of Jefferson and Jackson, Gouge and Wright, was not the silver debate but the passage in 1913 of the Federal Reserve Act. With the establishment of the Federal Reserve System, and particularly after the depression-spurred legislation and policy shifts, many crucial financial functions were permanently removed from the private sector and placed in public hands. Federal Reserve notes, issued by the government directly into the hands of citizens without the intervention of private banks, finally met the criteria of T. V. Powderly. Gouge, although he would have opposed the issue of any paper money unsecured by precious metal, would at least have applauded the federal assurance of stability. Jefferson and the Anti-Federalists would have been pleased by the fact that this national network was composed of regional boards, each empowered to make decisions in tune with local needs. This system had the capacity to influence not only the supply of currency but also discount rates and interest levels. Its board members were appointed so as to represent a balance of special and general interests. In its design, at least, the system incorporated a potential for that responsive flexibility so important to Kellogg and Macune.

The passage of the Federal Reserve Act in 1913 reflected an important change in the political mood of the country. The campaigns of William McKinley were the last in which the interests of Eastern ownership and management were flatly pitted against the interests of farm, labor, and the growing West. As the twentieth century ended its first decade, the issues long supported by the friends of farm and labor began to capture the political center. Progressivism was, among other things, a response to mounting insistence that the government, on all levels, increase its active protection of the citizens' economic well-being. In this sense the Federal Reserve Act was precisely in tune with the progressive spirit. To judge from the political rhetoric of their 1912 campaigns, Eugene Debs, William Howard Taft, and Theodore Roosevelt would all have signed the Federal Reserve Bill.[34]

But the passage of the bill was also a personal triumph for the successful candidate, Woodrow Wilson, who had spoken with particular force against the sinister monopoly of financial decisions by the speculators and private bankers of the Eastern cities. With superb timing the House of Representatives Committee on Banking and Currency, led by Arsène Pujo, had delivered a report early in 1913 documenting much of Wilson's rhetoric. In leading the arguments for the bill from the floor of the U.S. Senate, Claude A. Swanson, a Democrat from Wilson's native state of Virginia, mixed illustrations from the Pujo report with emotive language that would have done credit to Frances Wright or the silver-tongued orator from Nebraska. He praised Wilson's determined leadership against the banking interests as the friends of labor had praised Jackson's veto message:

> In this conflict he has without hesitation and without fear stood by the masses of the people, and determined, as far as he was able, to give the country a banking and currency system promotive of all the interests of all the people and with a view to save the country from the paralyzing influence of monopoly of money and bank credits.

The measure would, promised Swanson, free the nation from "selfish and sinister domination" while speeding the Republic toward "progress, prosperity, and equal opportunity."[35]

The Federal Reserve System (the Fed) has not provided a final answer to the problems of money and banking, speculation and credit. Inflation ran wild after World War I and has been a major issue in every election since World War II. Speculators led the country's investors on a roller-coaster ride through the 1920s with an unpleasant surprise ending in 1929. The Securities and Exchange Commission was voted into existence as a reaction to some of these problems, although there is still much concern about improving the regulation of trading in stocks, bonds, and commodity futures. In theory, the Federal Reserve System should have been able at least to mitigate the extreme crises of the 1930s, which led not only to an abandonment of the gold standard but also to the closing of banks and the resultant loss of savings to many who could ill afford it. Private banks, in concert, can still heavily influence interest rates and credit allocation. Money and credit are huge public issues still. Political leaders today, as in the 1830s, struggle to identify the public interest, and their appointees struggle to turn policy into effective reality.

But if the establishment of the Federal Reserve did not put an end to the money question,[36] it did change the setting. No one could guarantee that the decisions of the Federal Reserve Board would be better than those of J. P. Morgan; however, to paraphrase a Wilsonian phrase from another context, these decisions were now public decisions publicly arrived at. The governors of the Fed were chosen so as to represent a balance of the major sectors of popular concern. The executive branch can influence these decisions through appointments, and the Congress, through confirmation and appropriations as well as further legislation. The public can respond through the ballot box.

In the eighty years between the closing of one national bank and the opening of a national banking system there appeared a number of colorful individuals and distinctive movements in what may resemble a patchwork of social change. The particulars are indeed shaped by time and place. But there is also continuity. Between the message of Andrew Jackson and the speech of Claude Swanson there are connecting threads. The veto and the Fed are parts of the same large pattern.

CHAPTER 2

The Mainstream Analyzed

To superimpose the narrative sketch of a movement (Chapter 2) on a detailed recording of its essential events (Appendix) is to stress one point above all: perspective makes a crucial difference. Although the greater distance provides the final appreciation of the composition, the near view shows the preparation of the canvas and the technique. Each prospect helps in its own way to understand the process of change.

Even to skim lightly over a recapitulation of events, year by year, is to become unavoidably aware of the intertwining of political and economic events. A tract or a platform takes on its true meaning only when seen against the current interest rates, money supplies, or rulings of the treasurer, and vice versa. To insist on this relationship is to iterate what should be obvious; yet the understanding of social change is still seriously inhibited by arbitrary barriers within the politico-economic territory. [1]

The near view calls attention to the often-remarkable lag between the repeated observance of a problem and the formulation of an appropriate response. How long must a nation grow in population and productivity before its leaders recognize the need for proportionately increasing something as basic as currency? How often must a nation register conflicting attitudes from its many corners until the politics of money is seen to depend on occupation and region? How many springs must thaw the earth before the farmer's need for seed and fertilizer, labor and equipment, is appreciated as seasonal? How frequently must a secretary of the treasury put fidelity to fiscal policy before informed realism until the voting public begins to suspect that no single viewpoint serves all conditions? To review these questions season by season, panic by panic, budget by budget, election by election, is to realize that for every situation that produces a response there are dozens which fail to do so. The process of change, seen close at hand, is slow, stubborn, and gradual at best.

The close perspective also provides the most difficult test for any theory of cause and effect. There were nearly a dozen depressions, of varying degrees of seriousness, between 1832 and 1913. Most of them had no immediate impact on reform; all of them, in one way or another, contributed to a cumulative sense that financial affairs should be better managed. Some of them had a quite specific impact: the panic of 1837 led directly to Edward Kellogg's work; the panic of 1893 led indirectly but visibly to the Federal Reserve Act. Hard times sometimes produce social action, as witness the prompt establishment of labor organizations after the Civil War. Western and Southern farmers, on the other hand, suffered through years of annual currency and credit shortages as well as a prolonged slump in farm prices before they produced an effective remedial movement. Good times, as in the earlier twentieth century, sometimes see more effective reform achievement than times of deprivation and protest. The opposite case is made most obviously by the New Deal. Clearly there is no single chain of causation.

Reform Eras Reconsidered

If there is no evidence for cause and effect, at least there is a reasonably consistent sequence. Reform movements usually reveal themselves through random complaints concerning a single problem. In the first episode treated in Chapter 1, the problem was unreliable currency and unavailable credit, both of which came to be associated with the Bank of the United States. The random complaints led to an organized attack on Nicholas Biddle; a positive phase emerged in the independent treasury plan. When this idea was adopted first by voluntary associations and then by political parties, it received its essential structure and was eventually institutionalized.

The period covered by the chronology can be arranged into the four distinctive movements described in the preceding chapter, all but one of which reflect the sequence indicated above. The first movement was in progress as the chronology opens and culminates with the 1846 passage of the Independent Treasury Act. The second had already technically begun with the publication of Edward Kellogg's ideas in 1841. The problem under attack was inflexible currency and high interest. It became a matter of large concern only after the Civil War and ended in 1879 with the resumption of specie.

The third movement—in some ways an extension of the ideas of Kellogg and Alexander Campbell—began in the mid-1880s with the politicization of farm protest. Its positive side was distinguished by the addition of C. W. Macune's subtreasury plan, although the fiscal aspect of this movement was preempted by the silver question, which ended with defeat at the polls in 1896 and 1900. The fourth movement, which pulled together threads from all that preceded, was triggered by the 1893 depression. It eventually developed a broad base of support and culminated in the Federal Reserve Act.

All of these movements began with a problem. Even though they overlapped and built on one another, each had a special target; each was structured in a distinctive way; each developed its own positive response. For the most part, each progressed through the dynamics of social change in the normal manner, beginning with the random-negative phase and moving rather quickly to group sponsorship. Since each of these movements was built around a proposed solution, it tended to pass over the random-positive phase and to adopt a single remedy matched to the problem and usually sponsored by the same group or groups that had provided structure for the negative phase. None of these movements was a total success, but three of the four received a measure of institutionalization within their limited time span.

The interesting exception is the greenback movement which began, as a publc cause, with the fifth stage: institutionalization. Edward Kellogg had foreseen that a state of war would likely demand the kind of fiat money he advocated and, within a few years after his death, his prediction came true. Greenbackers, therefore, had the atypical task of defending the status quo instead of agitating for change. The wartime currency was nearly everything Kellogg had advocated. It was not based on specie, it was expansive, it was redeemable in bonds. Yet even when Kellogg's ideas were intelligently politicized by Alexander Camp-bell, they still failed to muster enough support to maintain their original shape beyond 1879.

All long-suffering agitators should study the greenback movement. They would learn that there may be something worse than a deaf ear: namely, the institutionalization of a program that has not been tested by the fire of a protest movement. The congressmen who had argued for the fiat currency on grounds of expediency did not feel they could escape the tar from the brush of Kellogg-Campbell "radicalism." Almost to a man the wartime defenders of greenbacks denounced them in peacetime. Had these same ideas emerged in response to the hardships created by hard money in short supply, they might well have made some gains in the 1870s and 1880s instead of being disavowed and put on the shelf, in effect, until 1913. The solution, unfortunately, had preceded the politicization of the problem.

It is important to see the money question in terms of the four sequential episodes depicted in Chapter 1: to contrast the rhetoric of Frances Wright with that of William Jennings Bryan, to sympathize with both the worker's fear of unreliable currency and the farmer's dread of insufficient credit. The tendency to focus on a single generation, however, has been largely responsible for the chronological patterns placed on the past: patterns that have acquired sufficient force to prevent scholars from accepting the logical conclusions of their own work. Irwin Unger, after demonstrating that an era previously characterized as devoid of reform was active indeed, still offered the view that the money question was of but periodic concern.[2] Thomas Greer, who documents an extensive period of social action, similarly declared (on no evidential base) that reform could be tolerated only once a generation as a response to "unbearable" conditions.[3] Unger, Greer, and many other chroniclers of social actors and movements have accumulated evidence that seriously questions the prevailing periodization of reform.

With the help of a detailed chronology it is possible to pinpoint three kinds of discrepencies between the accepted periodization and the evidence offered by the money question: (1) an alleged era of great reform activity when the politics of money was relatively quiescent; (2) an era when reform was supposedly dead while, in fact, the politics of money was enjoying great attention; and (3) a more complex case where there is apparent incongruity but actual concurrence.

The first instance lasts from the passage of the Independent Treasury Act in 1846 until the outbreak of the Civil War. Although this was an era of considerable reform activity in labor, education, communitarianism, and—above all—in the antislavery campaign, it appears to have been a genuinely quiet time in the politics of money. The Democrats were stuck with their independent treasury, whether they liked it or not, and their opposition could not muster the votes to reestablish the national bank for which they halfheartedly cried. The problem of unstable money had not been solved, but the party leaders either thought that further measures were unnecessary or failed to conceive of them. Gouge had had his day. Kellogg was publishing his works but had not achieved a wide audience. Here is the one genuinely quiet period in the history of the politics of money. It comes at one of the most active times in the history of other reforms.

Another kind of incongruence occurs between 1860 and 1880. Social historians have maintained that war postwar years are apathetic toward social melioration. This stigma had been widely applied to the 1860s and 1870s in spite of the obvious reform implications of Reconstruction, the numerous signs of labor unrest, the highly visible assumption of new roles by women, and the emergence of "pre-muckraking."[4] In fact these very years comprise the "greenback era" and were, as the chronology exemplifies, among the most active in the history of politico-economic reform.

The first decade of the twentieth century reveals a third kind of incongruence which, in this case, is more apparent than real. With the fading of the silver question after Bryan's second unsuccessful campaign, the politics of money showed a tranquil surface. The Populists, who also went down with silver, lost their platform for promoting the ideas of Macune. Those forces that had kept the politics of money alive from Gouge's subtreasury through Macune's subtreasury had lavished their momentum on silver. When it went down, so did they.

There were also some constructive reasons for the surface calm. Outside the historic combat zone, something was being done about conditions that for so long had provoked active protest. The panic of 1893, apparently, served as a final straw in demonstrating how a sequence of relatively small problems could cripple the camel of financial order. To this largely financial depression the banking community itself reacted promptly with its Baltimore plan of 1893. That same year, Congress appointed a Joint Committee on Executive Departments which, over the next two years, published a number of reports leading to the centralization and tightening of treasury procedures. In 1897 the Indianapolis Board of Trade convened a meeting that established a monetary commission to study the banking systems of other nations. This commission's report, when submitted, combined with the Baltimore plan to produce positive momentum toward a new federal system.

In 1907 and 1908 there was a spate of visible activity. A crisis in the banking community caused the panic of 1907. The Aldrich-Vreeland Act, of 1908, created a special fund to prevent a recurrence of the run on private banks that had occurred the previous year. This act also established the National Monetary Commission, whose multivolumned report eventually laid the detailed research foundation on which the Federal Reserve System was constructed.

This great early twentieth-century effort to create a new national banking system escaped the headlines as it escaped a chronology of public events. The appearance of inactivity was due in part to the lack of controversy and in part to a shift in the source of pressure for change. Instead of third parties and farm-labor groups, the social actors had become bankers and congressional commissions. With this kind of sponsorship, one could argue, the issue had already passed beyond the structured-positive stage and become institutionalized in all but name. In any case, the nature of the advocacy by no means diminishes the importance of the action. The absence of headlines only shows that vital reforms are not always superficially apparent. The climax of the money question, in fact, exemplified progressivism both in timing and in spirit.

These three examples of apparent conflict in understanding eras of reform have different messages. In the antebellum instance, the message is one of caution. If a bellwether issue like money is inactive, then sweeping characterizations of this era as possessed with a universal zeal for reform need to be tempered. Not all the reform fiddles are tuned at once. The message of the disjunction in perceptions of the Civil War and Reconstruction is simply that social historians should have looked more closely at the spectrum of social change before they declared an era of apathy. They were wrong: and not just about money. In the final case, the message is that reform achievements do not always depend on public turmoil. The dynamic character of one era may be imparted by events that are as unobtrusive as they are, at another time, stridently public.

Basic conflicts between the chronology of the money question and the standard periodization of reform may depend less for their resolution on a revised timetable than on the ability to view social change from more than a single perspective. To contemplate this entire case study over its eighty-year span is to invite some corrective insights.

With eighty years on the horizon the particular traits of each generation dissolve into a continuum. The constant problem becomes the mismanagement of currency and credit. At this range it matters less whether the problem is inflation or deflation, whether the offending banks are private or public. Similarly, the remedies appear more as related than as distinctive. One sees the similarities, as well as the differences, between the two subtreasury plans. The hyphens connecting Gouge-Kellogg-Campbell-Macune explain the adaptation of a small number of fiscal theories to meet similar problems in a variety of settings. They are all part of the same idea.

Stepping back far enough to see all eighty years is to notice strong lines that carry across the whole canvas. One such line was applied by the social actors who steadily sought to involve the federal government in the money question.

Their particular needs were different: reliability, sufficiency, availability, flexibility. The general object was to increase government responsibility for the regulation of money, banks, and credit. Thus, from this perspective, the Federal Reserve Act comes as no surprise but as the tracing of a single stroke from Jackson and Gouge through Kellogg and Macune. Little wonder that Senator Swanson's speech sounded familiar.

The long view carries implications well beyond the arbitrary limits of 1832 and 1913. It shows clearly that the general problem is permanent. There will never be an extended period when money, interest, and credit are managed well enough to suit the major economic groups. Protest, therefore, becomes continuous. Complaints often (not always) mature into remedies; remedies often (not always) mature into institutional solutions. The enactment of solutions, however, must not be seen as definitive but, rather, as landmarks along a path of social change.

The standard perception is of three islands of reform activity—1820-60, 1885-1915, the 1930s—set in a sea of apathy.[5] The study of almost any individual issue will show—as has the politics of money—a very poor correlation with this perception; yet it somehow persists. In order to correct some truly damaging as well as puzzling misconceptions it is necessary only to add up the evidence already presented in countless reliable studies and to recognize social change in its many stages, forms, and guises. It will then become clear that each issue has its own timetable and dynamic pattern; that apparent differences in quantity of activity are in reality but differences in the quality of activity; and that, although some eras are more broadly or superficially active than others, no era is without important protest and social movement. In the end it will not be a matter of shifting the periodization of reform so much as appreciating that protest and melioration are major social continuities.

Particularities must be seen as what they are: important to the understanding of time and place but only modifiers of more prevailing problems and solutions. Only the remote perspective reveals the profound continuities: the inevitability of protest, the recurring transformation of goals into starting points, and the steadily increasing involvement of the major social institutions.

Characteristics of Politico-economic Reform

The case study of the money question makes possible some observations about the main categories of social change: actors, forms, dynamics, and arguments. Because of the central position of the case study within Mode I, it is also possible to extend these observations toward a general portrait of politico-economic reform and thus to prepare for the comparison offered in Chapter 7.

The money question shows how the individual social actor tends to give way to the collective one. Jackson's war on the bank is remembered as though he were a lonely hero fighting the wealth establishment for the interest of the common man. In fact, Jackson was bolstered by a decade of rising antibank sentiments and by some party backing; yet his individual act had an undeniable impact. So did the books of Gouge and Kellogg. As the century matured, however, individual acts, per se, mattered less. Campbell needed support from labor and a political party, Macune needed to ride the shoulders of the Farmers' Alliance to the public's attention. It is possible to pick out an individual whom we can call the "father of the greenbacks," but who is the father of the Federal Reserve? The ideas that produced this institution were, by the early twentieth century, so thoroughly cloaked in the platforms of various parties, in committee reports and studies from the private banking community, that fatherhood would be as difficult to establish as if the Fed had been the offspring of a woman of the night.

Like many issues in the mainstream, the money question was not guided through its history by a single voluntary association. Rather, since the issue was seen as nationally important, it appeared in the charters of farm and labor organizations and as a recurring plank in the platforms of political parties, major and minor. The workingmen's parties endorsed the independent treasury plan in the Jacksonian years, while the greenbacks, the interconvertible bond, the new subtreasury plan, free silver, and an expanding currency were successively endorsed by the National Labor Reform party, the Greenback party, the Populists, and the Progressives.

Seen from afar, the politics of money confirms what students of political protest have often described: namely, that a concept will start with an individual, receive the endorsement of a voluntary association, move into the priorities of a minor party, then—sometimes—achieve major party endorsement and, with that prominence, a chance for national testing. But the validity of this general pattern is no more important than the complications inherent in this process. The politics of money reveal these complexities. They also show how difficult it is to assess the role of political parties as social actors because of their inconstancy, their liability to internal strife and even their propensity to splinter. Witness the fate of the idea of an elastic currency from the time greenbacks became a public issue until the passage of the Federal Reserve Act.

The concepts of Edward Kellogg, extended and modified by those of Alexander Campbell, first came together in public view in 1866 when the *Chicago Workingman's Advocate* disseminated Campbell's proposal. The new National Labor Union (NLU) promptly endorsed this plan (1867); its existence surely helped the advocates of the Ohio idea (a compromise between contraction and expansion) defeat the hard-money proponents that same year. In 1868 labor leaders were present at the Democratic convention, trying to persuade the platform committee to endorse the Kellogg-Campbell plan. They failed but did get backing for the Ohio idea.

Progress in the diffusion of these ideas was rapid. In 1869-70 the *Chicago Workingman's Advocate* serialized Kellogg's *Labor and Other Capital*. In 1872 the National Labor Reform party backed Kellogg-Campbell and in 1873 the

NLU offered a second, more formal endorsement. Prospects looked rosy when rural journals joined the cause during the next two years and when Campbell was elected to Congress in 1874. When neither major party picked up the plan in 1876, the Independent (Greenback) party was formed to carry forward the fight, capturing only 80,000 votes but showing considerable strength in the Midwest. By 1878, reflecting rising recognition of the need for flexible money tied to low-interest bonds, the Greenbackers won fifteen congressional seats. Clearly, this financial position had become a political force to be reckoned with. The major parties would compete with each other for soft-money planks and Greenback ideas in 1880.

Oh yeah? In 1880 the Democrats called for "honest" money on a strictly metallic base while the Republicans smugly congratulated themselves on their rapid repayment of the national debt. What had intervened was the passage of the resumption of specie act and the resultant political estimate that the questions raised by the Greenbackers had been answered, definitively and negatively. The estimate was correct only in the most narrow sense. The great silver debate would rouse similar currency and credit issues, while public events, especially the panic of 1893, would dramatize the escalation of banking problems on a national scale.

With the fall of the Greenback party, labor's position on money became divided. Rural organizations stayed behind Kellogg-Campbell and added the ideas of C. W. Macune and his new subtreasury plan. The 1892 platform of the Populists was faithful to this line, but silver was forcing a new focal point and, by 1896, the political atmosphere was characterized by compromises and splinter groups. The Populists stayed true to expanding currency, but the Democrats, who had taken their candidate, inserted a plank against paper money not redeemable in coin. Backing Bryan was as close as the Democrats ever came to supporting the inflationary monetary ideas of the farm-labor groups. Subsequently the Democrats were recaptured by their hard-money wing. The ideas of Kellogg and Campbell received true major party endorsement for the first time in the *Republican* platform of 1908!

The Democrats, of the major parties, were the most continuously and complexly involved in the money question. It was the party of Jackson which declared war on the national bank and afterward supported the independent treasury. The Whigs made a few gestures toward the working class but tended to stand for a national bank. Henry Clay and his fellow Whigs were responsible for killing the first independent treasury bill. At first glance it might therefore appear surprising that Edward Kellogg badgered the Whigs and not the Democrats with his ideas. At second glance it is not illogical at all. Kellogg favored a national bank; so did the Whigs. The Democrats and the spokesmen for labor, supported by Gouge, were for a stable, reliable currency either in specie or convertible directly thereunto. Flexible currency, wrote Gouge, benefited only the bankers and surely not the common people. Hence Kellogg, arguing for a flexible currency redeemable in bonds and not precious metals, would be

With its wheels matching the 16-to-1 ratio of silver to gold, this bicycle makes the money question the driving force in reform. George Y. Coffin, ca. 1890. Prints and Photographs Division, Library of Congress.

anathema to the "hard money" Democrats who dominated the party before the Civil War and at many times thereafter.

As the Democrats reentered political life after the Civil War they did so as a drastically divided party. One wing thought that the future lay with sympathy toward farm and labor. It was this group which listened to the likes of Sylvis, Powderly, Campbell, and Macune, and which brought about the temporary merger with the Populists in the 1890s. This wing also endorsed free silver, although it was often forced to separate the silver issue from the idea of a flexible currency.[6] When William Jennings Bryan lost, the "silver Democrats," many of whom had also been sympathetic to the ideas of Kellogg-Campbell-Macune, were tarred with defeat in the national election and surrendered control of the party to those who wanted a monetary policy based rigidly on specie. The defeat of Alton Parker in 1904, running without a silver plank, did nothing to change this situation.

The Republicans, born as a single-issue party, spent the postwar years struggling to find their political place on the economic spectrum. As Robert Sharkey has shown, many of their leaders were sympathetic to the Kellogg-Campbell ideas.[7] It was Republicans who produced the Ohio idea and who gave this compromise with greenbackism its short-lived success. It was the intransigence of Ulysses Grant, however, which so publicly placed the Republicans on the side of resumption and specie. In state and local elections, however, the Republicans had often sided with farm and labor groups even though their national platform was consistently in favor of a currency based on specie and a prompt retirement of the Civil War debt.

It is therefore at least mildly ironic that it was the GOP which captured the consensus view of banking reform as it took shape after the panic of 1893. Republican leadership, together with the banking community, began to sponsor investigations that led eventually to the Federal Reserve System. The 1908 platform, as has been said, included the first unqualified major-party endorsement of the principles of flexible currency and controlled interest that had been building since Kellogg's day. The GOP platform of 1912 went beyond greenbackism to specify the need for farm loans and seasonal increments in currency supply for rural areas. The Democrats, in that year, only mildly favored banking reform and suggested that private banks bid for public business. It was as though the Democrats had temporarily stolen free enterprise from the party of William McKinley. Then, in an immediate twist of double irony, the Wilsonian Democrats confounded their own platform by introducing federal reserve legislation, shepherding it through both houses under party leadership and crowing to the nation of this Democratic achievement in progressive legislation for the many.

Superficially, the Democrats would seem to have gained the most from the politics of money. Jackson won reelection partly on the bank issue; eighty years later Wilson was there to make political capital out of the installation of the national banking system that was the peacetime successor to the one that

Jackson destroyed. Earlier they had embraced the Populists and the advocacy of free silver.

Yet this is a highly misleading picture of the Democrats. It was the Republican leadership that was most sympathetic after the Civil War to the farm-labor view of money. It was a minority of Republicans who fought most effectively against shrinking the currency through resumption. When the Democrats threw in with Bryan, they took silver only as a supplement to gold, specifically rejecting the notion that silver would provide the basis for a rapidly expanding currency. Well before Woodrow Wilson appeared on the national scene, it was the Republicans who nurtured the idea of a new federal system based on regional differentiation and controlled flexibility.

The relationship between party politics and the money question—for all its bewildering complexity—makes a simple and important point. It is not possible to trace any substantial issue by assuming it to be the property of a single association. All large organizations—political parties, labor unions, associations of manufacturers—are subject to internal strife, the urge for consensus, and the wish to present a moderate and popular position. The result is temporization and vacillation. Thus the student of social change must don his deerstalker and prepare to follow a broken and difficult trail: in and out of associational shadows, on and off the thoroughfare of public attention.

The money question strongly exemplifies the rise of the government as a social actor, a development of importance in all aspects of reform. It also shows something about the balance between branches and levels of government. As with most issues, court decisions furnish some essential cornerstones (those affecting the money questions have been recorded in the Appendix). Yet the judiciary is of considerably less continuing importance than the executive. As soon as the BUS went out of business it was the Treasury Department that became the instrumental arm of monetary policy for the nation, sometimes abetting the banking community and sometimes competing with it. Few secretaries of the treasury kept within the limits of their office as set in the Independent Treasury Act, even as amended. The more they used their office to carry out their own fiscal theories, the more they entered the reform scene both by creating conditions and reacting to problems.[8] In times of emergency the government cheerfully suspended the restrictive aspects of the Independent Treasury.

Without overlooking the importance of the other two branches it is hard to deny the preeminince of the legislative branch in the process of social change. It is the most directly representative branch. It is the scene of those discussions which institutionalize the public interest for better or for worse. Legislatures annually act on large and complex budgets, set tax policy, establish and abolish regulatory agencies. Congress authorized the greenbacks and the Fed. Legislatures regularly attack the problems of privilege and poverty in full view of the electorate. The timing of their actions has much to do not only with economic cycles but also with reform cycles—as most notably in the issue and stabilization of currency.

The tension between federal and other governments is a factor in all reform modes and, to a degree at least, the money question represents what has happened across the board. In the young Republic there seemed to be a clear choice between the confusion of individual state banking systems and the relative stability of firm federal leadership. With the abandonment of a national bank, the balance shifted to the state governments, whose banking methods produced a small number of model arrangements and a large album of chaos and corruption. Even had all states governed impeccably, however, it would have grown steadily apparent that states are not functional economic units and that there are clear national responsibilities that must outweigh local sovereignty.

One consequence of the emergence of federal authority is the chance to deal with problems by region. Since economic problems rarely adhere to political boundaries this is an important consequence. The political campaigns for currency and credit reform identified the agricultural regions (not states) as needing special considerations. The organization of the Federal Reserve System reflects this approach. Federal sponsorship has also made possible a regional approach to homesteading, the Tennessee Valley, Appalachia, and even the inner cities. As the money question shows, there remains a balance between all branches and levels of the government, shifting steadily toward Washington, D.C., while the total force of government as a social actor waxes daily.

Mode I, being the mainstream, utilizes all forms of social action. More than the other modes it features the large-scale events and entities: national campaigns and elections, crowded conventions and monstrous demonstrations, widespread strikes and boycotts. Partly because of these grand settings, Mode I has shown a particular affinity for certain forms: oratory, tracts, platforms and resolutions, cartoons and visual symbols, literature and the press.

Political oratory is not confined to the money question but is strongly marked by financial issues, from the exhortations of Frances Wright to the chats of FDR.[9] What is considered by many to have been the greatest speech in all of American politics featured William Jennings Bryan's views of currency and banking. If one extends the category to the written speech, or message, then one can include another long list of premier political documents authored by Alexander Hamilton, Andrew Jackson, and a legion of successors. Since budgetary items are always primary parts of campaign speeches and presidential messages, it is clear that oratory, although perhaps an art form less valued now than formerly, is still strongly associated with the politics of money.

Another kind of "written speech," the tract or book-length essay, has played an essential role in this mode. The money question would have scarcely progressed without the pamphlets of Gouge, Kellogg, Henry and Mathew Carey, and their modern equivalents. It might be fair to consider a special category of tracts called platforms, declarations of principles, and associational constitutions. As the chronology has exemplified, the money question could have been borne along for generations solely on the wings of these pronouncements.

The nation's presses not only produced tracts and platforms but a variety of newspapers and periodicals which reflect the politics of money both intimately and extensively. The partisan presses that wrangled over the Revolution and gave birth to the two-party system continued their heavy involvement. Horace Greeley assumed that the way to popularize Kellogg's ideas was to praise them in the *Tribune* and then to publish them in the format of a low-priced newspaper. Not only did the press continually take positions on financial questions, but the politics of money was marked by special-interest periodicals springing up all over the country. Leading reformers edited and wrote for them. Thus, journalism not only exposed problems but articulated remedies and philosophies.

The press has also become the primary medium for circulating the cartoon, the distinctive and perhaps most effective of all political forms of attack. The earliest cartoons were political, some of them directly concerned with banks.[10] Thomas Nast helped personify "Dollar Mark" Hanna, and the skillful pens hired by Hearst and Pulitzer made war on the trusts by equating them with omnivorous, outsized giants or with tentacled beasts from the deep. Partisan imaginations drew symbolic value from silver (allegedly favored by the Founding Fathers and called therefore the "dollar of the Daddies") while they invoked Bryan's infamous image of a golden crucifixion. Cartoons, in combination with oratory and campaign rhetoric, have produced that kind of symbolism, special to political battles everywhere, that adds a vivid, often vicious dimension to social debate.[11] A remarkably complete history of protest can be harvested from cartoons, posters, badges, and other mottoes and symbols beginning with the attack on the royal ermine and sceptre, the aristocratic tiewig and smallclothes, passing through the vilification of "King Andrew" Jackson and the eminently caricaturable Abe Lincoln, rising to a height in the Thomas Nast era with his bloated bosses and spoilsmen, and coming uninterrupted to the sinister jowls of one president and the oversized teeth of another.

The political cartoons of Germany, England, Mexico, and Japan are sufficiently celebrated to make the visualization of protest an easily recognized global phenomenon. A case has been made, however, for the unusually high level of social involvement on the part of the American writer. The case opens with that thick sheaf of Puritan sermons that were as often political as they were theological. It includes the colonial counterparts of *Cato's Letters* as well as *The Federalist Papers,* contributed by the more celebrated essayists. Protest literature is inevitably a mixture of the ephemeral with the exalted. Philip Freneau's political verse, for example, was little better than doggerel, although not nearly so unpoetic as this effort—reflected in hundreds of similarly unfortunate literary sallies—to solve the silver question in rhyme:

> Silver's day is bound to come,
> And cause the idle mills to hum . . . [and it]

Will help the farmer pay his debt. . . .
Will lift the mortage off his farm . . .
Will give employment to the masses;
Restrict the greed of money classes;
A bloodless revolution cause,
Restore to Code once-honored laws.[12]

At the other extreme are the labor ballads of John G. Whittier, the flow of Walt Whitman's political philosophy, the moving exhortations of Edwin Markham, William Vaughn Moody, and Carl Sandburg, or the caustic probings of an E. E. Cummings, Ezra Pound, or Lawrence Ferlinghetti. Verse set to music—campaign and labor songs—have been omnipresent as Mode I has run its course, although more memorable music has emanated from the antislavery and civil rights crusades. Song covers often made popular airs politically pertinent even when the words and music were not sharply focused. The money question, for example, contributed any number of "greenback polkas" and "free silver gavottes."

Protest theater began with caricatures of perfidious Albion and the innocent Brother Jonathan. Thence it proceeded to attract public attention to numerous politico-economic issues, including the plight of labor and the problems of political corruption. The favored melodramatic villain, that mustachioed holder of the farm mortgage, was calling attention to the same problem addressed by J. W. Macune and Henry George.

In more recent times the Federal Theater Project took advantage of public sponsorship to explore a number of politico-economic problems, as have such memorable playrights as Elmer Rice, William Inge, and Arthur Miller. The cinema and television studios have also been involved. From Charlie Chaplin through Frank Capra to a recent prize-winning account of the unionizing of southern mills (*Norma Rae*) films have treated labor and industry with a mixture of sentimentality, comedy, and outrage. There are enough movies about machine politics to make a genre of its own.

Of all the literary genres, fiction has made the most important contribution to politico-economic reform. Richard Henry Dana's *Two Years before the Mast* exposed the maltreatment of merchant seaman; *The Littlepage Chronicles* of James Fenimore Cooper centered on the problems of tenant farmers. While Ignatius Donnelly and others were writing parables about currency, Hamlin Garland was dramatizing the theories of Henry George ("Under the Lion's Paw"), and Frank Norris was exposing the evils of monopoly and speculation (*The Pit, The Octopus*). Jack London and Stephen Crane are both famous for protesting ghetto life, but they also depicted the harsh exploitation of labor (*Martin Eden* and *Maggie*, respectively). William Dean Howells (*Rise of Silas Lapham*) and Theodore Dreiser (*The Titan, The Financier*) exposed unethical business practice. Upton Sinclair muckraked a whole industry (meatpacking, in *The Jungle*). John Steinbeck fictionalized the tragedy of the dust bowl and of migrant labor (*Grapes of Wrath, In Dubious Battle*). The inventory is a lengthy one. Fiction, to be sure, deals with all manner of subjects, but it is evident that the United States has made a special place for the social novel and that politico-economic topics have been favored.

The dynamic pattern identified with the politics of money is representative of Mode I. It is the standard five-stage sequence, moving through spontaneous then organized protest, through random then structured solutions, and ending— if the issue survives—in institutionalization. Although these logical steps would seem inevitably to characterize the process of social change at large, they are accurately descriptive only of what usually happens in politico-economic reform. The mainstream, thus, establishes a standard from which the other modes will be shown to offer interesting variations.

Just as the dynamic patterns help distinguish reform modes, so the consistency of arguments attests to the unity of social change. Money, interest, and banking involve highly technical questions. Much of the literature on money consists of closely reasoned theories supported by case studies. Gouge was famous for his detailed knowledge of banking systems; the studies that led to the Federal Reserve System included close analyses of many foreign banking systems and comprised many volumes. In the manner of the Enlightenment both Jackson and Gouge (as has been shown) argued from natural law. The appeal throughout this literature is to reason and experience.

Appeals to a higher law are also present in an abundance that would astonish anyone who thought money to be a purely secular subject. Long before William Jennings Bryan made gold and crucifixion synonymous, demagogues had seen that the money question was a sacred topic to most of the population and that greed and usury and wanton speculation were indeed held as sinful. Edward Kellogg, as important as anyone in the politics of money, grew up preoccupied with moral and scriptural questions. He kept this orientation all his life, salting his work with liberal quotations from the Bible. His daughter wrote:

> The moral effect of his system was always uppermost with him. While he foresaw, as perhaps few others can, the physical benefits to follow on its [his system's] establishment, the prospect of peace and good-will among men was the one which most delighted him. "The millennium can never come," he would say, "until this system goes into operation; but then it can come!"[13]

Kellogg's attitude was more typical than exceptional.[14]

Perhaps it is natural rather than surprising to see a narrow issue, bristling with implications of self-interest, cloaked in the broadest of terms. For whatever reason, that is what happened. For Jackson the issue was privilege versus equality; for Frances Wright it was independence versus foreign control; for Edward Kellogg it was purgatory versus salvation; for Claude A. Swanson it was "selfish and sinister domination" versus "progress, prosperity, and equal opportunity." For the student of reform the money question was not only pragmatic and empirical but consistently related to the ideals of political democracy and the moral imperatives of a higher law.

Continuity and the Mainstream

The revised state constitutions and the ratified federal Constitution were by no means a total triumph for reformers. They were left with one strong fear and one strong hope. Since privilege and property had not been consumed in the fires of egalitarianism, there was constant fear that the injustices that had caused the Revolution would be recreated in the United States.[15] Since the new constitutions provided a clear opportunity to push political representation beyond any European model, reformers were determined to use this chance to promote economic equity.

As Jackson and Biddle commenced their shootout there was already an impressive agenda before the reformers who sought to avoid the sins of Europe and use the ballot effectively. Suffrage itself remained an issue with property qualifications still in force in some constituencies. The connotation of aristocracy made upper houses suspect and unicameralism a popular subject. Banks were only one form of monopoly under attack; other targets included utilities and protected forms of transportation. Regulation of auctions was proposed. Taxation was still a minor issue and arose mainly in a libertarian context: whether church property could properly be exempt; whether government should be allowed to tax beyond its need for revenue. Tariff, a giant among nineteenth-century issues, was looming ever larger to farmer, manufacturer, consumer, and laborer. Labor's concerns, beyond tariff, wages, and hours, were with imprisonment for debt and the lien laws. Panaceas that promised to solve economic among other problems included land reform, universal education, and many varieties of socialism.[16]

As mid-century approached, the slavery issue came to dominate reform. Although this topic is central to Mode II, it is by no means irrelevant to the present context. At odds were two economic systems with two contrasting political bases. The war may or may not have stimulated the growth of commerce and industry; it surely gave labor a better bargaining position. Wartime measures pertaining to Mode I included the issue of greenbacks as well as mildly graduated income and inheritance taxes.

As for the political side of the equation, the sectional controversy tested and proved the power of the federal government, a condition of increasing importance. Slavery was, from one point of view, a question of suffrage and representation. Not only did the Civil War lead to the statutory resolution of this question but the Reconstruction governments, as the revisionist historians have allowed us to see, offered some excellent examples of effective democracy. The Fourteenth Amendment, a direct consequence of the war, not only transformed Mode II but had a large impact on politico-economic affairs in its application to corporate individuals.

For reasons that are difficult to fathom it is common for social historians to depict reform as falling dormant with the firing on Fort Sumter and awakening only to the clarion charge of Theodore Roosevelt and the progressives. While it is true that some of the attributes of social change were shifting, the amount of activity was anything but negligible. The nation's workers swung into action before the echoes of the battlefield were still. The National Labor Union was founded in 1866, the Knights of Labor was born in 1869 (although not under that name), while the forerunner of farmers' political organizations, the National Grange of the Patrons of Husbandry, was established in 1867. Although the politicization of rural America has been chronicled in regard to the money question, it must be remembered that the farmers were after more than soft money and easy credit; they wanted a favorable tariff, railroad regulation, and adjustments in the mechanics of government that would become part of the progressive package. Industrial labor, too, tensed its passive posture by developing national organizations, staging strikes and demonstrations, and flirting with radicalism. The one million members of the American Federation of Labor, as of 1900, were not products of an instant mix.

During this same era the genteel reformers, concerned over the rise of professional politics, were battling bossism and pressing for the enactment, enforcement, and expansion of the civil service. West of the Mississippi the new states admitted in the 1870s and 1880s vied with one another in the refinement of a representative democracy. These diverse voices—coming from a nation infinitely larger and more complex than it was a mere century ago—called for the modification of old political institutions in order to deal with new problems, many of them economic. The new conditions arose from the rising force of technology, professionalization, centralization, and urbanization. It was the reformers, in general, who understood these changes and urged the institutional adjustments: men like William Sylvis, T.V. Powderly, Eugene Debs, Henry George, Carl Schurz, Edward Bellamy, Lincoln Steffens, and John Hay.

The resistance came from those who believed in laissez-faire economics, private charity, the primacy of individual economic freedom, the stewardship of wealth, and social Darwinism. Reformers saw that special interest groups were becoming so large and powerful that the public interest would have to be protected by a commensurately large force. Progressivism, as it emerged at the end of the nineteenth century, was no sudden star shower of ideas but the culmination of growing concerns. The most revolutionary of these concerns was in the attitude toward government. Historically, the enemy of the commonweal was the government. Now the government seemed the only agency available to speak in the name of the public interest. If more powerful governments were needed (city, state, national) they would have to be carefully structured so as not to miscarry the will of the people. Political democracy would have to be further purified through such devices as the simplified and secret ballot, direct election of senators and judges, initiative, referendum, and recall.[17]

Progressivism, this curious combination of political science and public morality, can be seen as the setting in which much of the reform agenda reached maturity. Before the Civil War most action was in the negative stage (anti-Federalist, antimonopoly, antislavery), while the postbellum decades showed these protests reaching a positive stage. From the achievement of civil service reform in the 1880s onward, protest began to elicit remedial response and to gain some measure of institutionalization. To see reform as rising at the end of the century from two generations of sleep is to ignore many aspects of the subject.

From a reform point of view it is logical to see the response to the Great Depression as an extension of progressivism. It is not appropriate to see the administrations of Wilson and Franklin Roosevelt separated by a great chasm called the 1920s. For all its outward signs of reaction and social irresponsibility, this decade also manifested many of the same impulses that characterized progressivism and the New Deal. The 1920s saw the application of such progressive measures as professional management and proportional representation at the state and local levels. Cincinnati, New York, Wisconsin, and Louisiana all sponsored progressive innovations in the 1920s. Even at the national level there was no immediate stoppage of the progressive impulse with the ending of World War I. Heavy taxes continued. A railroad regulation battle was won and the Transportation Act passed in 1920. Water power and conservation legislation was enacted. So was a new child labor act. The woman suffrage amendment was ratified as was Prohibition. Even immigration restriction (1924), which many historians correctly see as a sign of reaction, was progressive in the sense that it established government controls over a situation that had previously been almost unregulated. Herbert Hoover, who is characterized as progressive by most recent biographers, was a contributor to the Progressive party of Teddy Roosevelt and Robert M. La Follette and was supported by many Progressives throughout his career.[18]

The period between the end of World War I and the inauguration of Franklin D. Roosevelt saw, in sum, a doubling of the electorate, the advancement of participatory democracy and of progressive principles in several states and cities, and the general continuation of federal participation in the economy and in the institutionalization of activities formerly confined to the private sector. Perhaps the most conclusive example of this continuing tendency is in an act not signed until 1933 but developed painstakingly through the latter part of this period: the Tennessee Valley Authority, whereby the government entered directly into conservation, flood control, power generation, and regional planning.[19]

The New Deal was part political opportunism and part remedial response to a great crisis. But it was also a climax for many of the trends that had been operating in Mode I since the middle of the nineteenth century. Measures were institutionalized (some temporary, some not) to help farmers, industrial workers, home owners, consumers, the poor, and the jobless. Economic democracy was abetted through graduated income taxes, corporate taxes, and surtaxes.

Enough first aid was applied to banks and small businesses that the New Deal could be called—especially in contrast with many radical responses to the depression—the savior of the free enterprise system. The voters supported Franklin Roosevelt more emphatically than any political leader of the century, and he used that mandate to mitigate the extremes of wealth and poverty, thus acting out the definition of Mode I and incorporating these acts in a rhetoric of "social justice." The New Deal, in fact, began an attack on inequality of wealth so effective that it convinced many observers that the United States had at last found the key to economic democracy.

Also important is the way the New Deal, definitively and irreversibly, placed the center of economic responsibility in Washington, D.C. Roosevelt's first budget represented a quantum leap not just over Hoover's but over any peacetime budget in history. Each year it grew. As the pump of economic recovery was primed with the fluids of deficit financing, the nation mortgaged its future to this central responsibility. No amount of war or prosperity or campaign attacks on the federal bureaucracy has ever been able to dislodge it. Politico-economic reform had always rested on the idea that improved political democracy would increase economic equity. The 1930s made conclusive the argument that the federal government must be the primary agent in the process.

Very little has happened since the New Deal to reverse the trends in politico-economic reform which were underlined in that era; the familiar politico-economic issues are still in evidence. They still center on the economic responsibilities of government and on the improvement of government through extending democracy. Farmers still worry about credit and the Fed. Attacks on BUS and Standard Oil give way to attacks on agribusiness and multinational corporations. Now that senators are elected directly there are movements to abolish the electoral college. Women have the vote; now the question is home rule for the District of Columbia. Strikes for the forty-hour week give way to negotiations for flextime, portal-to-portal pay, and job satisfaction. Aid in kind is provided the needy, and poverty is steadily redefined toward middle-class income. The government is urged—sometimes abruptly—to extend its protection of the consumer from dangerous products falsely advertised and from nuclear accidents and industrial waste.

David S. Broder, a respected and not always optimistic syndicated political columnist, visited Iowa during the 1980 primary caucuses and pronounced that the system was capable of invigorating, grass-roots decision making. The net result of this activity, he found, was "the infusion of thousands of new people into the ranks of party activists."[20] *The more participation the better.*

Arthur S. Miller, a retired professor of constitutional law who does not always view the democratic process with good cheer, joined with Jeffrey H. Bowman, an employee of the Federal Elections Commission, to argue publicly for avoiding the indirect democracy of the party convention and allowing candidates of all shades of opinion to appear on the public ballot.[21] *The more direct the democracy the better.*

At the 1980 Democratic convention, Senator Edward Kennedy, having withdrawn from candidacy for the nomination, takes the floor to influence the platform by invoking the sense of the party's historic mission. Having cited Jefferson and Jackson as the voices of the common man, Kennedy asks his party, as its first priority, to eschew unemployment and high interest rates ("human misery") as weapons against inflation and to guarantee full employment and job security for all workers. This emphasis only underlined the headline on the page that followed the printing of his speech: *"The Essence of Politics: Allotting Shares of the Nation's Wealth"* (italics mine).[22]

ENCOUNTER 3

Garrison Meets Walker

Sometimes the reform experience defines itself in the meeting of two great forces. In the antislavery crusade there were not two men more greatly feared and reviled than William Lloyd Garrison and David Walker. South of the Mason-Dixon line each had a price on his head that escalated as the verbal war against slavery progressed. Garrison spoke out longer, more directly and uncompromisingly than any other white agitator. Walker's famous *Appeal*, found in the hands of a slave, was taken as circumstantial evidence that the slave planned revolt or escape. Garrison and Walker met, in print, on January 8, 1831.

David Walker was born in Wilmington, North Carolina, in 1785, son of a black free mother and an enslaved father who died before the infant was born. Sickened by the treatment of his father's fellow bondsmen, he left the South, entered the clothing business in Boston, and used his means for his own education and in generous support of fleeing slaves and poor Negroes. He was a lifelong Methodist. His book, according to Henry H. Garnet, "produced more commotion among slaveholders than any volume of its size that was ever issued from an American press." It is easy to see why Walker's work so shocked his readers.

At one point Walker quotes at length from an account in the Portsmouth (Ohio) *Columbian Centinel* for August 22, 1829. It descibes the escape of a group of sixty captives being transported by a black driver and his two assistants from Maryland to Mississippi. The insurgents filed through their chains, freed the other captives, and fled the scene leaving the driver for dead. Only wounded, however, the driver was helped into the saddle by one of the female slaves and made his escape. How did Walker regard this Samaritan act?

Brethren what do you think of this? Was it the natural fine feelings of this woman, to save such a wretch alive? . . . I cannot think it was any thing but servile deceit, combined with the most gross ignorance: for we must remember that humanity, kindness and the fear of the Lord, does not consist in protecting devils. Here is a set of wretches, who had SIXTY of them in a gang, driving them around the country like brutes, to dig up gold and silver for them. (Which they will get enough of yet.) Should the lives of such creatures be spared? Is God and Mammon in league? What has the Lord to do with a gang of desperate wretches, who go sneaking about the country like robbers—light upon his people wherever they can get a chance, binding them with chains and hand-cuffs, beat and murder them as they would rattle-snakes? Are they not the Lord's enemies? Ought they not to be destroyed? Any person who will save such wretches from destruction, is fighting against the Lord, and will receive his just recompense.

Walker goes on to revile the "blockheads" who bungled the murder and, forgetting for the moment that the driver was also black, slides into an exhortation of racial superiority that climaxes with the assertion that "twelve black men . . . well armed for battle . . . will kill and put to flight fifty whites."[1]

This is strong medicine for any time or place; but as an incendiary message to the Southern slave from a free black of Boston in 1829! Walker was, of course, not ignorant of the stir he was causing. One group of Southern planters vowed to fast until the author of this "seditious" book was destroyed. His own family urged him to flee and hide; he refused. A rumor persists that his early death (at age forty-five) was due to poison.

Walker has a moderate side. Although he disparaged those demagogues who wanted eventual credit for "giving" slaves a freedom that was not theirs to give, he did urge admiration for the selfless antislavery evangelist. He appealed to God as much as to force. Divine destiny controlled all events; all men were God's agents; Christian piety was the only appropriate attitude. But like the Puritan who worked ferociously in spite of his belief in foreordination, Walker urged human beings to act out God's mandate in ways that were far from passive.[2]

The story of David Walker, long overlooked, is now an accessible part of history. Garrison has remained prominent as a prototype of the unswerving single-cause reformer. When colonization was still popular among his neighbors he began to insist on universal emancipation, immediately arrived at. His *Liberator*, in its bold masthead, declared itself the obdurate foe of compromise as well as thralldom. Although the pages of Garrison's paper reported other reform activity, the focus of the publisher was clear. True to his narrow purpose he printed just one edition following the Emancipation Proclamation, congratulated the nation and himself, and put the paper permanently to bed.

The first issue of the *Liberator* had contained a promise to review *Walker's Appeal*. As good as his word, Garrison took up the chore in the very next issue, thus providing a rare moment for Garrison's critics. For once they could see an agitator they regarded as extreme confronting a work which took the word "extreme" toward a new contemporary definition. Those who knew Garrison knew that he was uncompromising not only toward slavery but also toward violence. Although his own self-righteous rigidity provoked his adversaries to violence, Garrison's personal conduct exemplified the constraints of nonviolence even under extreme conditions.

In Walker, Garrison recognized a man of equal courage who sought the same ultimate goal. Both were religious, albeit Walker had more faith than Garrison in the social efficacy of the church. But their differences were extreme and important. Students of social change dispute the relative effectiveness of violence and passive resistance while slavery and civil rights have offered a continuous setting for this debate. In spite of the nonviolent model of men like Garrison, the first round went to Walker, John Brown, and the armies that fought four years of bloody battles. More recent is the haunting question whether the advance of civil rights in the 1960s owed more to the passive resistance of Martin Luther King, Jr., or to the explosive riots that followed his assassination.

To the foes of emancipation the confrontation between the passive and the incendiary must have been a disappointment. Garrison refused to turn his differences with Walker into an issue that might divide the cause. Although he could not condone the measures advocated by Walker, he denied the South the right to challenge them. After all, wrote the editor, Walker was only turning the weapons of bondage on itself. Garrison ended on a note of common grievance. Like many antislavery agitators, Walker had cited the Declaration of Independence and its guarantee of equality as evidence of a national hypocrisy. "Every Fourth of July celebration," agreed Garrison, "must embitter and inflame the minds of the slaves."[3]

PART TWO / MODE II

Social Justice for All

This most striking icon of reform was widely used by the American Anti-Slavery Society, sometimes chained to the pillars of John C. Calhoun's "Greek democracy." Engraving ca. 1830, Rare Books Division, Library of Congress.

Second only to politico-economic reform are those movements on behalf of groups which have, in some way, been separated from the mainstream and denied a measure of participation in social, political, and economic life. Although these movements (comprising Mode II) might at first seem an extension of Mode I (a further improvement of economic democracy through political means) they have in fact their own types of social actors, characteristic forms of protest, and a distinctive dynamic sequence. Part Two serves to identify these traits.

Reform is characterized as much by constants as by variables. Chapter 3 is the one place where the recurring features of social change are stressed. By using movements for Afro-Americans to exemplify both constant (Chapter 3) and dynamic (Chapter 4) features, it is possible to show how a single cause reveals both familiar patterns and an evolving agenda—sometimes simultaneously. In Chapter 4 civil liberties and woman's rights are used alongside the cause of black Americans to illustrate Mode II.

CHAPTER 3

Outside the Mainstream
Reform Constants

One facet of the national personality shows the mainstream as a strong current which must be navigated upstream. Floating toward the delta induces a softness and Sybaritism alien to the vigorous New World. To be insinuated into the headwaters without vanquishing the rapids. as by inherited wealth or unmerited privilege, is to have been excommunicated from life's central religion: self-help, achievement, success. Therefore, since no serious individual would wish more than the chance to rise as far as merit and diligence would take him, extra difficulties come as a kind of blessing. To be born poor (but of honest parents) is all anyone should expect or desire. To face additional handicaps is only to enhance potential achievement. To overcome orphanhood, physical disability, or social exile is to win the prize. To reach the headwaters having begun outside the mainstream altogether—set apart by race, sex, religion, or other criteria—is to add a golden shimmer to the laurel wreath. Americans generally profess belief in equality of opportunity; yet many Americans have heaped extra measures of admiration on successful individuals who have triumphed over exceptional obstacles.

Contrary to the myth of success runs a set of assumptions which define the second mode of reform. Although the hardworking reformer would be the last to applaud a life spent drifting downstream, he would also abhor the existence of barriers, making achievement more difficult for one citizen than another. Next to politico-economic programs, efforts on behalf of groups seen as outside the mainstream have attracted the great reform energies of the nation. Some of this activity serves large groups—women, for example—and has occupied the nation throughout most of its history. Such movements involve the major parties or voluntary associations with sizable assemblies and serious publications. At the other extreme is the effort to protect the rights of a single individual. Such a movement may begin and end with a brief hearing in a nearly deserted courtroom.

The common concern of this mode is the denial of full access to the politico-economic mainstream of American life. Some individuals have been disadvantaged by mental or physical disabilities. Some have been victimized by institutions: slavery, the prison system. Some have been enslaved by alcohol or drugs.

Temporary conditions—such as extreme youth or age—handicap others. Some have been set apart by a difficult environment (the ghetto, Appalachia) or by occupation (miners, prostitutes). Many groups are not inherently disadvantaged at all: it is just that a large segment of the population has regarded them as different and in some way not fully acceptable. Their only handicap is the attitude of society. This would apply to victims of discrimination by race, sex, and religion. If it seems both rude and illogical to deal with miners and prostitutes, native Americans, and unsighted people in the same category, it must be pointed out that it is society that has created these categories through its similar patterns of reaction.

Movements on behalf of special groups began with the Republic; in fact, some causes—better treatment of Indians, slaves, women—had received sporadic attention in colonial times. The Revolution brought with it a crusading zeal to set a shining example in all aspects of social activity. The Revolution also reflected a commitment to Enlightenment philosophy, a point of view which added rationalistic social arguments to the existing moral ones. Because of the assumption that man is innately good, the Age of Reason developed particular arguments for removing the handicaps or institutional errors that had led many astray. Whereas Calvinists believed that the approach to perfection belonged to the World Beyond, many social philosophers of the eighteenth century felt that perfection was an earthly possibility and that it began with the removal of those obstacles that stood between mankind and its natural, innate goodness. Therefore the patterns of thought that came in with the Revolution were eventually used with special force against the conditions that kept certain groups from realizing their full human capabilities.

As the Republic matured, an increasing number of groups were recognized as being, in one way or another, outside the mainstream of political participation, economic equity, and social equality. With this recognition came the organization of movements first to provide special treatment for these groups and then to provide for their full assimilation. Reform in Mode II came to define itself as movements

> on behalf of the deaf, dumb, blind, insane, or otherwise physically or mentally handicapped
>
> to provide full participation for native Americans, Afro-Americans, religious and ethnic minorities
>
> to assist those who have been victimized by excessive use of alcohol, tobacco, and other drugs/narcotics and to move toward temperance/ Prohibition
>
> to protect and sustain the young (child labor laws, education) and the aged
>
> to provide a more full and fair participation in society for women
>
> to improve police practices, courtroom procedures, prison life

to moderate excessive punishments and to offer more effective
  rehabilitative programs
to assist groups that can be defined by place (e.g., ghetto dwellers,
  residents of Appalachia) or by occupation (e.g., miners, prostitutes)[1]

Most of these movements had at least begun before the Civil War and have been moving through their peculiar cycle ever since. The dynamics of reform on behalf of special groups will be illustrated in the next chapter with the examples of movements for blacks, women, and the special case of civil liberties. The remaining business of the present chapter is to make use of one very special movement from Mode II in order to identify some of the most important constant elements in the reform equation.

In a subject called social *change* there is a self-evident need to establish characteristic progressions and cycles. It may be that reform is preeminently a matter of evolution and fluctuation, but its appreciation also depends on an understanding of the features that prevail and recur. The records of what is surely the premier American reform serve well to demonstrate these constant elements. Movements against slavery and for civil rights have produced a high percentage of great literature: oratory, essays, drama, fiction, verse, and autobiography. Giant historical figures—from Mather and Jefferson through Thoreau and Lincoln to the Kennedys and King—have been prominently involved. Events central to both shaping and understanding the nation have pivoted on slavery and the rights of blacks.

Movements for Afro-Americans were chosen not only because they have been singularly prominent but also because they form part of that aspect of reform which alternates most obviously between frenzy and full stops. To attempt to identify reform constants in this most variable mode is to accept the hardest case. The challenge is heightened by using materials separated by more than a century. If constants in actors, forms, and arguments can be established in this subject, over so considerable an interval, then perhaps they can be found throughout reform.

Actors

Within the category of social actors there has been considerable change from antebellum days to the mid-twentieth century. The most obvious shift has been in the increased participation of government: from the days when Congress was throttled by a conspiracy of silence on the slave question to a day when the Supreme Court—often portrayed as the most reluctant of social actors—would set the legal pace for social change. It may be that the bullhorn and the portable TV camera have given public demonstrations an impact beyond the power of those mobs that confronted the abolitionists. It may be that the individual social actor has lost his potential force in proportion to the rise of collective behavior.

One thing is certain, however, and that is the continuing preeminence of the association among social actors. This fact is hardly surprising. Students of American society—both natives and visitors—have given citizens high marks for joining. It is hard to think of any serious reform issue which has not precipitated the formation of at least one large and sustained voluntary association. In the case of slavery and civil rights, the organizations have been numerous and vital; yet one from each era has overshadowed the others: the American Anti-Slavery Society (AA-SS) and the National Association for the Advancement of Colored People (NAACP). These two organizations are usefully comparable.

Both were formed in response to a point of view which had an aura of beneficence but became philosophically repugnant. In the case of the AA-SS, the American Colonization Society provided the negative stimulus. Colonizers opposed slavery but addressed this problem only by proposing to "repatriate" free Negroes to Liberia. The AA-SS insisted, however, "that slaveholding is a heinous crime in the sight of God, and that duty, safety, and the best interests of all concerned require its immediate abandonment, *without expatriation*" (italics mine). The purpose of the society did not stop with emancipation. Rather,

> This Society shall aim to elevate the character and condition of the people of color, by encouraging their intellectual, moral, and religious improvement, and by removing public prejudice,—that thus they may, according to their intellectual and moral worth, share an equality with the whites of civil and religious privileges.[2]

There is a direct parallel to the AA-SS view in the declaration of W.E.B. Du Bois that the NAACP must insist on "full manhood rights, exposure of the evils of lynching and disenfranchisement, and the widest encouragement of trained ability." As the AA-SS position replaced colonization, so the NAACP replaced the policy associated with Booker T. Washington which Du Bois summarized as stressing "the duty of Negroes to be thrifty and hardworking . . . to insist as little as possible on political, civil and social rights, and above all, not to complain."[3]

However grand the purpose of any reform group, the problem of survival inevitably leads to the humbling question of money. Both of these organizations had some prominent and generous benefactors. Both had to stretch pennies, to exercise their collective imaginations, and to beg. James G. Birney complained that the panic of 1837 and the ensuing hard times had cut off the usual sources and forced the AA-SS to accept support from those who could ill afford it, including a retired revolutionary soldier, a little boy near Boston "not four years old," and "a colored woman who makes her subsistence by selling apples in the streets."[4] Depression or no, things were never easy. Birney estimated that, counting local societies, the antislavery cause probably attracted more contributions than any comparable group. Still they had to sell handkerchiefs and wholesale publications. The *Emancipator* (October 1, 1840) printed a "beautiful contribution box" covered with scriptural reminders, featuring the AA-SS's ubiquitous symbol of the kneeling slave chained to classic pillars. This time, instead of his pathetic question, "Am I not a man and brother?" he exhorts the youthful reader: "Remember your weekly pledge."[5] In spite of ingenious and sometimes desperate measures, Birney conceded that the society was always in debt.

Having a wider canvas than its predecessor, the new abolition society, as the NAACP sometimes called itself, was faced with augmented problems of self-support. As a perusal of any issue of *Crisis* will make clear, the full gamut of fund-raising ploys was constantly in use. Benefit shows and picnics were succeeded by benefit balls and dinners. Organized help came in the form of "church nights," a source that would havve been dubious indeed for the abolitionists of the 1830s. A complex dues structure was invented; yet most paid only a pittance for membership and a subscription to *Crisis*. One plan called for selling life memberships for $500; yet in its first ten years this idea had attracted only sixty subscribers, paid in full or in part. With its growing scope in a growing nation the NAACP, too, was always in debt.[6]

Both for raising money and for carrying out programs, local chapters were important to both organizations. In the emancipation movement, regional, state, and local organizations sometimes antedated the national society and always had complete autonomy.[7] With the NAACP the momentum was otherwise. Yet neither association could have carried out a truly national program without coordinated activity at the local level. It is here that the volunteer is recruited and put to work in ways that responded to the extreme variety of local conditions. Both in *Crisis* and in its annual reports the NAACP recognized the need to single out local problems, take local actions, and recognize local heroes. The longest and most prominent section of the 1959 summary, for example, dealt specifically with local problems in housing, employment, and legislation, supplying a full log of names, dates, and places. Without the local chapters, as the leadership has freely and frequently admitted, the NAACP would have been a much lesser force.[8]

Both organizations chose New York City for their national headquarters. Both also kept their eyes on Washington, D.C., where most of the events that made their program truly national took place. The AA-SS put the legislation of emancipation high on their list of priorities as they furnished the documents for Congressman John Quincy Adams's petition campaign against the South's effort to gag all discussion of matters relating to slavery on the floor of the House. The society's work in Washington was abetted by the patient, painstaking efforts of the unbiquitous Theodore Dwight Weld.[9]

The NAACP, too, kept what it sometimes called its "watch on the Potomac." Confrontations inevitably began at the local level, but they often culminated with federal action. Legislation, particularly the Civil Rights Acts of 1957, 1960, 1964, and 1968, and the Voting Rights Act of 1965, made the Congress of the United States a cynosure equal to the Supreme Court. The NAACP was hardly alone in Washington by this time, but it was largely responsible for a series of court cases which attacked segregation in higher education in a reasoned sequence that led to *Brown v. Board of Education*.[10]

Both groups also knew that, without the media, they were nothing. Out of its relatively small wherewithal (its annual budget never exceeded $40,000 before 1840), the AA-SS not only funded its own publications (*Emancipator, Human Rights, Anti-Slavery Magazine*) but also assisted many others (*National Enquirer, Philanthropist, Colored American*, and of course the *Liberator*). AA-SS leadership was explicitly aware of circulation and readership throughout the nation. They assumed that the printed word was of primary importance and they planned their use of this potent force to the last penny.[11]

The NAACP has been no less sensitive to the power of the media. One of its first acts was to launch the *Crisis*, which quickly became, and has remained, the most important sustained twentieth-century voice on behalf of the interests of black Americans. The association also learned to depend on the informal network of newspapers published by and for blacks, both to discover what was concerning the constituency in various parts of the country as well as to spread the message of Du Bois and his colleagues. Experience promptly taught the NAACP the value of knowing its friends and adversaries in the large daily papers. It compiled and updated lists of newspapers which would print their news releases without disfavor. It often bought advertising space in publications known to be unfriendly. "Public relations" and the NAACP "image" were recurrent topics in the annual report.

Interest also extended to the newer media. A case in point stemmed from an hour-long NBC televised documentary on school desegregation problems in Atlanta, February 1, 1959. Commentator Chet Huntley, at the end of the program, expressed his opinion that things might go better were the NAACP less active. This organization, he said, "may have outlived itself." Prompt and persistent response gave the association a chance for rebuttal, which was effectively performed by Roy Wilkins on February 8. Wilkins got only ten minutes (the association had asked for an hour) and his appearance was "balanced" by the remarks of a pro-segregationist.[12] Even so, this and similar events reveal a pattern of alertness in utilizing the media to turn a gratuitous slap in the face into a chance to change some minds.

The association is an important constant among social actors and many of its characteristics are predictable. The American Anti-Slavery Society was determined, resourceful, innovative, and perpetually in debt. It was a national association headquartered in New York with a lobby in Washington. It badgered Congress daily. It was built on a network of autonomous regional gorups. It used every known method of fund-raising and invented some new ones. It used its funds mainly to keep the issue in front of the public. Although speeches and tracts and meetings and demonstrations were all employed, the greatest stress was on the press. The society not only supported a number of its own journals but also learned the periodical scene intimately and used it judiciously. These traits, taken together, comprise a portrait of socially active voluntarism. The effectiveness of the AA-SS is demonstrated by the fact that the NAACP followed in its footsteps virtually every step of the way.

Forms

Of the many forms used to promote social change none is so controversial as violence and the incitement to violence. We would, most of us, like to minimize it. We would like to think that John Brown only lit the fuse for an explosion that was already past prevention. We would like to think that the impact of the Reverend King came more through his life's work than through the manner of his death. We would like to think that as Garrison confronted *Walker's Appeal* he was prevented from taking violent exception to Walker's incitement only by the repugnance of the evil under attack.[13] We would like to think that those actors who use or encourage violence only interrupt an essentially peaceful process. In general, we may be correct.

Sometimes individual acts and even large-sale violence affect the decision-making process indirectly if at all. Yet those who witnessed the turmoil and response to the shooting of King will know that this is not always true: sometimes a sustained series of brutal and destructive events will attract the public's notice as nothing else. A constructive response must be ready to hand if the arousal is to mean anything in terms of permanent advance; but there is sometimes no way to overlook the effectiveness of the hammer blow.

The incitement to violence is a reform staple. David Walker announced that "one good black man can put to death six white men" and twelve, well armed, "will kill and put to flight fifty whites."[14] One hundred thirty years later one reads:

> The killing of one of my followers [Black Muslims] means the death for ten to ten times ten of the infidels besides the great loss of their property. Believe it or not, but calculate on your ever increasing loss of lives and property on the land, air and sea.[15]

Closely related to the strain of violence is the dependent tactic of nonviolence. Just as the Greek tragedians used the transparently mild deus ex machina to create a shock more profound than the anticipated bloodletting, so certain actors have been able to use the expectation of violence to create a superior impact through passive resistance. This was a favorite trick of William Lloyd Garrison, that master, as Wendell Phillips said, of evoking malignity and, as J.J. Chapman said, of evoking disgust.[16] He did this in the pages of his famous newspaper. He could also do this oratorically with an incendiary quality heightened by his personal magnetism. Crowds were more consistently aroused by Garrison than by other speakers. He was said to be the most assaulted man in America. At the same time, he was able to turn these threatened confrontations from ordinary mob scenes into personal, nonviolent triumphs in social suasion.[17] Martin

Luther King, Jr., was no less a master of this technique, albeit in a different style. The Garrisons and Kings make it possible to say that, although violence is a consistent part of the reform scene, passive resistance is also recurrent and, although less common, may be a superior long-term agent for constructive change.

Not all violence is as decisive as the martyrdom of John Brown or the rioting following the King assassination. Not all appeals to violence are as shrill as those of David Walker or Elisha Muhammad. Not all resistance to violence is as dramatic as that of King and Garrison. On a lesser scale, and much more common, are the acts of token resistance to authority, the gatherings without a permit, the flaunting of minor ordinances, the commission of nuisance property damage and the miscellaneous provocations intended to create public theater, to lead to mass arrests, and to make the jailhouse into a platform for protest. The potential for violence of all kinds may be increased by the presence of racial issues, but the record does not necessarily support this supposition. The history of the labor movement includes a full repertoire of damage and assault. The Woman's party introduced to American protest some of the more boisterous forms of attention getting. Carrie Nation was renowned for liberating spirits with her deadly hatchet. The violence associated with slavery and civil rights may have been more celebrated, but it was not an isolated case.

Whether they entail violence or nonviolence, whether they are dramatized by individuals or launched by organized groups, most reform movements begin with an exposé. The forms taken by these protests recur so strikingly as to indicate some of reform's most important constants. The earliest muckraking blockbuster in the antislavery campaign appeared anonymously in 1839 under the title *American Slavery As It Is: Testimony of a Thousand Witnesses.*[18] It was, as the title suggests, a compilation of firsthand views of the peculiar institution, some from travel accounts, most from newspapers. Here is a sample:

> "In 1811, I was returning from mill, in Shenandoah county, when I heard the cry of murder, in the field of a man named Painter. I rode to the place to see what was going on. Two men, by the names of John Morgan and Michael Siglar, had heard the cry and came running to the place. I saw Painter beating a negro with a tremendous club, or small handspike, swearing he would kill him; but he was rescued by Morgan and Siglar. I learned that Painter had commenced flogging the slave for not getting to work soon enough. He had escaped, and taken refuge under a pile of rails that were on some timbers up a little from the ground. The master had put fire to one end, and stood at the other with his club, to kill him as he came out. The pile was still burning. Painter said he was a turbulent fellow and he *would* kill him. The apprehension of P. was TALKED ABOUT, but, as a compromise, the negro was sold to another man."[19]

Like most successful muckraking works, this one stressed authenticity and detail. If more than one person witnessed an episode this corroboration was cited. The idea was to avoid commentary and let the grim facts speak for themselves. In this, *American Slavery As It Is* succeeded. Southerners and Northerners alike, many for the first time, were moved by this book to respond to the horrors of slavery. It was, according to some sources, America's best-selling book in its first year of publication. Its sales continued to provide the principal support for the AA-SS. Gilbert Barnes and Dwight Dumond called it "the greatest tract of all."[20] Its compiler was Theodore Dwight Weld.

Among the admirers of *American Slavery As It Is* was a conscientious, imaginative young woman named Harriet Beecher Stowe. Offering Weld the sincerest form of flattery, she began imitating him in the collection of a parallel set of episodes. Before this task had been completed Mrs. Stowe was inspired to approach the subject in the form of fiction. Still, when her famous novel came under attack from slavery sympathizers—and this attack was as vicious as it was massive—she was ready with the evidence she had compiled in imitation of Weld. She published it as a defense of *Uncle Tom's Cabin*, claiming that it not only substantiated her treatment of slavery but showed that the novel's major episodes were based on actual events. She called it *A Key to Uncle Tom's Cabin.*[21]

The 1960s produced no tract comparable to Weld's. The famous report compiled by Daniel P. Moynihan for the Department of Labor is similar in spirit and in purpose, dwelling on the modern consequences of slavery which Moynihan sought to remedy as sincerely as Weld sought to end servitude.[22] A closer parallel can be developed between Stowe's *Key* and the account of a modern victim of racial bigotry as depicted by another skillful writer, Budd Schulberg. A student in the writers' workshop founded by Schulberg in the Watts section of Los Angeles immediately after the prolonged riots there, the young man known as "T" objected to a policeman's manhandling of a citizen in a simple traffic violation. As in the cases collected by Stowe the initial offense is minor but events escalate rapidly. T's mild protest led to his immediate arrest. In the car one officer reviled and struck him repeatedly: " 'You motherfucker, you think you are smart, don't you? . . . You wait until you get down to the station. We're going to kick your black ass. We're going to see how tough you are.' "[23] T. is thrown in jail for three days and is eventually tried and acquitted. His penalty is not on a scale with the slave-victim's. Yet, by using the materials in a skillful way, Schulberg is able to develop a fifteen-page account of T's dilemma that is nearly as moving. There is even less editorial comment than with Stowe, but the episode is extended well beyond the limits of an ordinary newspaper story both in its length and in the dramatic sense which guided the story's presentation. Here is at work the same hand that produced such effective exposes as *On the Waterfront* and *The Harder They Fall*.

Long before muckraking got its name there was a close affinity between newsprint and protest. Garrison loved his type cases almost as much as he hated slavery. Even after emancipation had allowed the *Liberator* to cease publication, Garrison would return to the shop, run his hands fondly over the type, then set up a few paragraphs out of sheer nostalgia. Horace Greeley, another prominent foe of slavery, was—in spite of his loyalty to a surfeit of causes—a newspaperman first, last, and always. Thus it is no surprise to find Weld and Stowe relying heavily on newspaper accounts. Schulberg's "Trial of T." walks the line between reporting and creating.

On the other side of that line—the side occupied by fiction, drama, autobiography, and verse—lie a number of works that have furthered the cause of social change even beyond the impact of journalism. If a single work had to be selected from the many that have attacked social problems, Harriet Beecher Stowe's *Uncle Tom's Cabin* could easily claim to have lit the greatest conflagration. Abraham Lincoln may or may not have remarked, on making Mrs. Stowe's acquaintance, that he was "glad to meet the lady who caused the Civil War." The remark would have been an oversimplification, to be sure, but it would have contained more than a grain of truth. The effectiveness of the literary imagination in arousing the public has been so often demonstrated that a crusader for any cause might be well advised to start searching out a Stowe, a Whittier, a Schulberg, or a Steinbeck as a matter of first priority. Thus the real question becomes not so much whether Stowe's *Key* might have proved more effective than Weld's compilation but whether it is possible to measure on any scale the difference in degree of impact between a skillfully constructed documentary— with all its careful aura of objectivity—and the emotional response generated by the creative imagination.

Mrs. Stowe's success has been explained in a number of ways, no one of them adequate. Surely timing was a crucial element. Another reason for *Uncle Tom*'s impact became apparent with the publication of the *Key*: namely, the amount of careful research that had preceded the composition of the narrative. A modern reader, who has known the novel only by reputation, will be surprised to discover that the case against slavery is not made in any rigid, single-minded way. The problems of emancipation are neither glossed over nor underestimated. There are stereotypes, but they are varied. There are good slaveowners and bad, good slaves and bad. Uncle Tom himself, now used ignorantly as a stereotype for servility, is in fact a courageous practicing Christian who risks and suffers death rather compromise his moral sense. His martyrdom proved as moving to Americans as any event in the antislavery crusade except for the hanging of that flesh-and-blood martyr, John Brown, from a "sour apple tree." As *Uncle Tom's Cabin* was read, discussed, argued, refuted, and defended, the mood of the controversy seemed to change. The Great Emancipator, having struggled against this rising tide of emotions, could well have made the remark to Mrs. Stowe that is often attributed to him.

No work of fiction has polarized attitudes on civil rights the way Stowe's did on slavery. The closest parallels come from the realm of autobiography, a genre which black Americans have mastered with exceptional effectiveness. From Booker T. Washington's *Up from Slavery* through Eldridge Cleaver's *Soul on Ice*, autobiographies have probably contributed more to public understanding than any other literary form. The devices of fictional narrative have often abetted these efforts, but the power to move comes from leading the reader to see, from the recounting of a single life, the barriers which Afro-Americans have encountered in the United States.[24] There is no rumor that President John F. Kennedy or President Lyndon B. Johnson ever said to Claude Brown or Malcolm X that they were glad to meet the man who had caused the civil rights explosion of the 1960s. Yet one can be sure that the cumulative effect of works like *Manchild in the Promised Land* and the *Autobiography of Malcolm X* had much to do with promoting the kind of emotional perceptions on both sides of the color line that resulted in a rebellion against the status quo.

A closer parallel to Stowe can be found in John Steinbeck, one-time proletarian novelist turned conservative then turned again, in his autobiographical *Travels with Charley in Search of America*, into a narrative expositor of contemporary society. Toward the end of that remarkable travel journal, Steinbeck describes a detour into New Orleans to observe in action the notorious "cheerleaders," those white mothers who lined the sidewalks to abuse the black children as they walked to the newly integrated schools. He describes the innocence of the children and the profanity of the adults with an effectiveness reminiscent of Stowe's depiction of some of slavery's worst abuses. Afterward, like the nonsouthern Stowe, he tries to be objective, interviewing and reporting on all shades of opinion and reaction. He lingers longest with a quiet Southern gentleman (reminiscent of Stowe's character, Augustine St. Clare), whose roots go further into the local past than he can document. He describes the problem with patience, resignation, and sympathy, acknowledging the justice of the civil rights crusade but pointing out the inevitable conflict between rising expectations and ingrained attitudes. Steinbeck closes, "the solution when it arrives will not be easy or simple. I feel with [the Southerner] . . . that the end is not in question. It's the means—the dreadful uncertainty of the means."[25]

Along with imaginative reporting, fiction, and autobiography, songs are peculiarly tied to protest on behalf of race. The labor movement has marched to some rousing melodies, and politicians, especially in presidential years, have stumped to the rhythms of their "campaign songsters." The musical legacy of politico-economic reform, however, includes nothing so powerful as "The Battle Hymn of the Republic" or the equally evocative version featuring the words "John Brown's body. . . . " The agitators of the 1960s produced a near equivalent in what one critic called "the Marseillaise of the civil rights movement."[26] The words to "We Shall Overcome" came from a song copyrighted in 1901, the tune from Chicago gospel singers of the 1940s. Modified and copyrighted by Pete Seeger and others, it became an anthem for passive resistance in the face of brutality, while its royalties went to support the "freedom movement."[27]

A musical curiosity links the two eras. In 1962 Bob Dylan wrote what is surely the second singing hallmark of civil rights gatherings, "Blowin' in the Wind."[28] The melody bears a striking resemblance to a work song first sung,

The symbolic power of Frederick Douglass, whose life was a rebuttal to the slavery apologists, is attested by this 1845 song cover. Boston, E.W. Bouvé.

according to Thomas W. Higginson, by slaves being forced to build rebel fortifications at Hilton Head and Bay Point.[29] Although it is impossible to prove that one song derived from the other, they are remarkably similar in key, mood, and chord sequence. Together "Many Thousand Gone" and "Blowin' in the Wind" furnish a melodic echo of two parallel protests a century apart."[30]

Protest uses all forms of the creative imagination: verse and drama, posters and song covers, paintings and cartoons. There is one theme that runs through these media when the subject is the Afro-American. It may be the Tom-show poster depicting Eliza crossing the ice or a contemporary photograph of crowd dispersal by means of cattle prods, mastiffs, or firehoses. Sometimes it takes the form of comparing chattel slavery with cattle; sometimes it is a cry of despair at feeling lower than any creature. This theme is the comparison of men with animals, and it leaps out from the pages of racial oppression with an unavoidable insistence. It was this image that overwhelmed the usually temperate John Greenleaf Whittier as he attended the 1834 convention of the American Colonization Society and listened with mounting outrage to the arguments for sending Americans to Africa. The resulting vitriol took the form of a parody of a hunting ballad depicting maid and mother, priest and statesman—all merrily perched in their saddles as they fly to "the hunting of men!"[31]

Arguments

Today's observer of social patterns might readily assume that the most celebrated echo of the antebellum era occurred when Martin Luther King, Jr., followed in the footsteps of Henry David Thoreau by provoking arrest, going to jail, and sending thence the message. In fact this parallel is much more vivid historically than in context. Thoreau's contemporaries paid little heed to his incarceration, and his famous essay did not achieve its present exalted place until generations after the fact. It was Mahatma Gandhi who found inspiration in Thoreau's blend of civil disobedience and passive resistance; it was Gandhi who, in turn, inspired King.

The most important parallel is in the appeal made by Thoreau and King to the "higher law." Both agreed that when civil law conflicts with conscience it becomes one's duty, as King put it, to break the law "openly, lovingly, and with a willingness to accept the penalty." The Boston Tea Party, wrote King, set an American precedent for principled defiance of temporal statutes.

It was the crusade against slavery, however, that honed moral arguments to their finest edge. King might have found his most appropriate precedent in a fifty-four page anonymous pamphlet whose author was promptly identified as Ainsworth Spofford, a Cincinnati bookseller who eventually became Librarian of Congress. Spofford's essay was given highest marks by his contemporaries. Emerson admitted to having shamelessly stolen from its powerful prose and thoughtful precedents. In the history of reform this work is monumental not only for its contribution to the arguments of more famous writers and social actors, but for the way it combined the moral argument with the other paramount rationales. The parallels can be seen in the two following extracts, the first by Spofford, written in 1851; and the second by Martin Luther King, written in 1964:

> There are some laws which are ridiculous, and fall to the ground by the Higher Law of common sense;—some laws which are obsolete, and are defeated by the Higher Law of human progress;—some laws which are inconvenient and are overruled by the Higher Law of necessity;—some laws which are unnatural, and are null by the Higher Law of instinct and of nature; and some laws which are *unjust*, and are void by the Higher Law of conscience and of God.

> How does one determine whether a law is just or unjust? A just law is a man-made code that squares with the moral law or the law of God. An unjust law is a code that is out of harmony with the moral law. [32]

Both men argued the inevitability, let alone the correctness and duty, of civil disobedience to immoral laws. Both did it in the context of oppressed Afro-Americans. To be sure, Spofford's treatise had the careful, categorical structure that characterized the generation responsible for his education, just as King's appeal is both learned and evangelical. Both men make the identical moral point—*and*, both men go on to buttress their moral point with appeals to logic and practicality.

The other arguments do not produce echoes as literal as the one King provided for Spofford. They do show some remarkable parallels. Sometimes the appeal to reason and the appeal to the practical may seem to merge; but they really are responses to different questions: Is the proposal defensible in terms of a rational system of social thought? And, will it work?

An excellent and important example of the use of logic is Lewis Tappan's *Address to the Non-Slaveholders of the South on the Social and Political Evils of Slavery.* [33] The younger brother of another famous reformer, Tappan was of New England origins and migrated to New York City, where he became a successful businessman, developing the nation's first credit-rating system. His experience clearly reflected reason and order, patience and thoroughness. When the slavery society split, he chose, of course, the branch that endorsed moderation and gradualism. Logic told him that slavery, primarily a Southern problem, was susceptible only to a Southern solution. Arithmetic told him that the adult, white, nonslaveholding males outnumbered by threefold their slaveholding fellow Southerners. If he could convince this clear, enfranchised majority that the minority interest was against their own, then could they not legislate a peaceful end to bondage? Tappan addressed them as fellow citizens:

> We ask your attention to the injuries inflicted upon you and your children, by an institution which lives by your sufferance, and will die at

your mandate. Slavery is maintained by *you* whom it impoverishes and degrades, not by those upon whom it confers wealth and influence. These assertions will be received by you and others with surprise and incredulity. Before you condemn them, ponder the following considerations and statistics.[34]

Tappan proceeded to argue under a number of headings that slavery was ruining the South. He not only posited problems with Southern "Industry and Enterprise," but concerned himself with population growth, with the level and extent of public education, with the state of constitutional liberties, and even with military weakness. He used precise numerical data wherever he could, attempting to shame the region with its rate of illiteracy and its minimal support of education. Perhaps strangely for a successful businessman, Tappan tried to drive a wedge between rich and poor, reminding the nonslaveholders of how they were sometimes known to the planters as "mean whites," or worse.[35] He closed with an exhortation that demonstrates the interrelationship of the primary reform values. Abolish slavery, he urged, and you will regain Christian (moral) values, reestablish the Bill of Rights (social order), and open the doors of opportunity (practical) to the rising generation.[36]

The abolitionists' principal bibliographer called Tappan's work one of the four most telling arguments against slavery.[37] Another of these four, which also stresses reason and experience, is Joshua Leavitt's "Financial Power of Slavery."[38] Leavitt demonstrated that a free economy could win over a slavery economy under any conceivable fixed conditions. The South's only possible tactic, then, was to create uncertainty and instability. Observing that the South's political acumen had enabled it to do just that, Leavitt concluded that the way to combat this destabilizing force was through the founding of a third party; thus he became one of the principals in forming both the Free-Soil and Republican parties.

The most finely tuned of the legalistic campaigns for the peaceful solution of the slavery question was the one led by Congressman John Quincy Adams. Although the "gag rule" had successfully kept from the House floor the question of bondage in the states, Adams found an Achilles heel in the status of the District of Columbia. The governance of the capital city was directly in congressional hands; slavery existed in Washington; therefore Congress could not refuse to consider this particular situation. Assisted by the AA-SS, Adams relentlessly loaded the desk of the Speaker with list after list of petitioners for a hearing on slavery in the District; it was an ambitious parliamentary gambit whose endgame was to have been the legislated abolition of slavery throughout the nation.[39]

Comparable in the civil rights context to the logical arguments and procedural ingenuity of Tappan, Leavitt, and Adams was the courtroom campaign against segregated higher education. The NAACP, whose lawyers were mainly responsible for planning this twenty-year campaign, made some tactical decisions which remind one very much of Adams and his friends.[40] They reasoned that professional education would be a more manageable topic than all of higher education. They knew their point could be made more strongly in an area where state validation was essential. They assumed that the issues would be decided in the courts, and they realized, without undue cynicism, that judges and lawyers are more interested in law schools and bar examinations than in the medical or pedagogical equivalent.

Thus they began a series of prosecutions which, from a 1935 decision, followed one another as neatly as though the steps had been laid down by Euclid. In the first of these cases, *University of Maryland v. Donald G. Murray*, the state argued against admitting blacks because the university was partly private, the number of applicants was small, and the time was not yet propitious. In refusing to accept these familiar excuses the court made the first real dent in *Plessy v. Ferguson* as a bulwark for segregated education. The next case, involving the state of Missouri, undercut the practice of serving blacks by subsidizing training outside the state of residence. With *Sweatt v. Painter* (1950) came the ineluctable direct confrontation with *Plessy* and the concept of "separate but equal." Texas, in this instance, had established a law school for blacks; but was it equal to the white school? One more step (*McLaurin v. Oklahoma*) was taken when a state university's predominantly white law school was challenged for attempting to segregate, within the school, the black students it had admitted.[41]

This carefully planned and relentlessly argued sequence—every case ending with a Supreme Court decision—represented a strategic assault on segregated higher education as surely as Adams's petition campaign represented a deliberate seige of the parliamentary fortress erected by the South. Although these cases are not nearly so famous as the ones that followed where their logic led, they paved the way for *Brown v. Board of Education* and for the social revolution precipitated by that decision and its enforcement. This social revolution may have been unprecedented. The court decision itself, however, was clearly precedented by that series of cases, carefully and logically planned and executed, which eventually diminished *Plessy v. Ferguson* to an unpleasant memory.

The consummate pragmatic argument for reform emerged, during the slavery controversy, from the guiding spirit of the New England Emigrant Aid Company, Eli Thayer. It is a mistake, asserted Thayer, to think that reform can be built only on sacrifice. It is both natural and effective to promote social change in a way that puts all faculties in harmony: namely, by joining altruism with profit.[42] His brainchild responded to the Kansas-Nebraska Act of 1854, which had determined that this new territory would become slave or free on the basis of a plebescite of settlers. To colonize Kansas with Free-Soilers, Thayer offered a plan that included elements of land acquisition and land-use planning, heavy-equipment leasing, mail-order supply, reduced-cost group travel, and a vertically integrated corporation.[43] Thayer, a two-term congressman from Massachusetts and an early supporter of Lincoln, was not able to persuade all of his contemporaries that they could do well while doing good. In offering a scheme which combined the germs of such now-familiar concepts as Sears Roebuck, Hertz Rent-a-Car, and Levittown, Thayer promoted reform in a way that redefined appeals to the practical.

Appeals to the practical do not come only from profit-minded reformers. They come also from Nobel prize winning novelists. William Faulkner, especially during the troubled times of the 1950s, wrote often to his fellow Southerners about the problems of segregation. In his most famous public letter on this subject he told the readers of *Life* magazine that he was against the use of force either to sustain segregation or to enforce integration. He was against force on principle, he said, and added immediately, "I don't believe it will work."[44] In the front of Faulkner's mind at the time was the question of education, and it was to this subject that his letters turned most often. These letters remind the reader less of his idealistic Nobel acceptance speech and more of the pragmatic tests useful to the Southern farmer he often made himself out to be.

The young of the Deep South, Faulkner pointed out, must leave their native states to get the kind of education they require. This is particularly true of the best of the rising generation, and unfortunately for the South, they do not always return. So what does the South do about this condition? Concentrate on improving the existing schools?

> No. We beat the bushes, rake and scrape to raise additional taxes to establish another system at best only equal to that one which is already not good enough, which therefore won't be good enough for Negroes either; we will have two identical systems neither of which will be good enough for anybody.[45]

There is no limit, Faulkner concludes, to how foolish people can get. On grounds of commonsense practicality, the South must abandon segregation.

To illustrate the appeal to the practical with the words of a man who had spent most of his life successfully dramatizing great moral questions is to call attention to the important fact that the classic reform justifications not only recur over the years, but overlap. William Faulkner spent his creative life exploring race and region with a highly moral—not to say Biblical—point of view. He also appealed to reason, using analogies and experiential logic. The confluence of the three main reform justifications is as true of Faulkner as it is typical of the reformer at large. To put a cap on this point, look at a few words taken from the eulogy delivered by Wendell Phillips at the funeral of William Lloyd Garrison, that man who could easily serve as a prototype for the uncompromising, unrelenting, moral zealot—that man whom many, in fact, regarded as mad. About him said Phillips:

> If anything strikes me more prominently than another in this career—to your astonishment, young men, you may say—it is the plain, sober common-sense, the robust English element which underlay Cromwell,

which explains Hampden, which gives the color that distinguishes 1640 in England from 1790 in France. Plain, robust, well-balanced common-sense. Nothing erratic: no enthusiasm which had lost its hold on firm earth; no mistake of method; no unmeasured confidence; no miscalculation of the enemy's strength. Whoever mistook, Garrison seldom mistook.[46]

The comparison of two separate-but-related movements has made evident a number of reform's constant or recurring elements. Some of them, while not limited to the antislavery-civil rights context, have been sufficiently prominent in this setting to have helped define the movement. These traits include the use of violence and nonresistance, the use of the theme of degradation and beastiality, and the dramatic use of documentation, fiction, song, and autobiography. The more general of these recurring traits are characteristic of reform at large: the centrality of voluntary associations among social actors; the crucial involvement of the press and of creative imagination; the constant and interrelated use of appeals to a higher law, to reason, and to the practical.

CHAPTER 4

The Double Cycle
Civil Rights and Civil Liberties

Politico-economic reform illustrates the classic sequence. Each cause, typically, moves through five stages: random negative, structured negative, random positive, structured positive, and—if the process gets that far—institutionalization. It would appear that the important movements on behalf of special groups follow this same sequence but with a vital difference: they experience it *twice*. The first sequence is aimed at rescuing the group from extreme hardship, neglect, or exploitation. The positive stages aim for the creation of an improved setting outside the mainstream but loosely comparable: in other words, "separate but equal."

The first cycle culminates in the establishment of a vocational school in the inner city, a county home for the aged, or a hospital on the Indian reservation. The use of public money to assist those at the lower end of the economic scale induces a feeling of self-congratulation. So long as these special facilities are adequately maintained, the public feels that its responsibility has been met. Indifference sets in. Further petitions are resented. This attitude sometimes lasts for decades.

Sooner or later comes the appreciation that there is no such thing as "separate but equal" and that the concept of opportunity and fulfillment does not admit segregation. At this point the second cycle begins. The target is not only the inequity suffered by the group (as it was the first time) but also the very fact of segregation. Once the principle of "separate therefore unequal" is accepted, then evidence of separation is itself a legitimate object of protest. The goal, the second time around, is full participation in the political and economic life of the nation; or "mainstreaming" as we are now taught to say.

The double cycle has a relatively uncomplicated history for those groups that have been most obviously—sometimes forcibly—set apart: convicted criminals, the mentally and physically handicapped, some large groups of American Indians. In other cases—notably blacks and women—the cycle describes a general movement whose progress from stage to stage is not always regular. The cycle is neither rigid nor inevitable. Throughout the history two attitudes have existed side by side: melioration through separation; melioration through assimilation. For two hundred years the designers of prisons have argued whether their purpose was to punish or to cure. Many segregated groups, especially those with a separate racial or national history, resist integration on the basis of cultural pride. Although the goals of economic democracy and cultural diversity are not contradictory, they are often seen as such. The return to bilingual education in some parts of the country shows that the cycles can be reversed!

Yet the double cycle does accurately reflect a historical direction. If the attitudes implicit in the first cycle have not disappeared, it is clear that the weight of public opinion has shifted from the defense of segregation to the encouragement of integration. Most institutions for special treatment are now seen as way stations. Some always were. Reformers once asked for mental hospitals so the insane could escape the family attic. Today the public judges mental institutions on their rehabilitative success. Penal, remedial, and medical systems are meant to return their charges to full social participation.

One way to test the validity and usefulness of this pattern is to look at the two large groups contained within this category: blacks and women. Although movements on behalf of these groups are as complex as the culture itself, their prominence virtually disallows the choice of other examples. Fortunately each makes an appropriate case for understanding reform dynamics. It must be understood, however, that the following paragraphs do not pretend to resolve controversy but to arrange the materials in such a way that the controversies may be more clearly pursued. It must also be stressed that the subject is not race and sex, but reform movements on behalf of blacks and women.

The Double Cycle and American Blacks

As with the politico-economic issues treated in Part One, the antislavery-civil rights movement reveals a pattern that varies with the distance from which it is viewed. Seen remotely it shows a predictable sequence beginning with the negative goals of ending first the slave trade and then the institution of slavery itself. To many, emancipation was so great an achievement that it distracted attention from the condition of the freedmen and of Afro-Americans in general. Segregation became the accepted answer to the race question and, well into the twentieth century, many reformers were willing to work simply to improve separate institutions without challenging their validity. In this context discrimination meant only that the black school was not as good as the white school. Seen from afar, there have been three major phases: one against slavery, which succeeded; one on behalf of segregated equality, which was abandoned before it approached a full testing; and one aimed at ending segregation and discrimination and making blacks politically and economically indistinguishable from the majority culture.

The sweeping view, however, ignores a number of movements and events. Seen nearer at hand, the history of social change involving this group strongly supports the concept of the double cycle. The random-negative stage of the first cycle began almost as soon as the slave trade. It represented a range of objections including the moral, the economic, and the political. Cotton Mather authored one famous attack on bondage in 1710; twenty-two years earlier the Mennonites of Germantown, Pennsylvania, had issued the first formal protest against slavery in America. Random action and reaction increased with the number of slaves, but the transition to the structured-negative stage did not occur until the founding, in 1816, of the American Colonization Society. Technically the idea of transporting free blacks to Africa is hardly a reform. Yet it was seen as such by its backers and can be understood as a way of moderating the head-on clash between slavery and abolition.

The colonization proposal proved so violently and broadly unpopular that its real contribution lay in stimulating answers which did not deny blacks citizenship in their native land. A number of answers, both gentle and drastic, came forth. At the gentle end of the spectrum were the Free-Soil movement and a number of schemes for gradual emancipation. At the drastic end were *Walker's Appeal* and Nat Turner's rebellion. These activities comprised a random-positive stage.[1]

With time the movement came to center on the American Anti-Slavery Society, founded in 1833. Although its constitution called for "equality with the whites of civil and religious privileges," the organization did not last long enough to make this an attainable goal. The AA-SS, true to its name, was directed *against* something; it led the way into the structured-negative stage of the first cycle. Its leadership, once outspoken for peaceful solutions, became decreasingly tolerant of the peculiar institution. It was the antislavery apostles, convinced of their unassailable moral rectitude, as much as the increasingly defensive slaveholders, who assured that this problem would not be solved with reason and statecraft. Meanwhile, the more stubborn planters, along with David Walker, Nat Turner, and John Brown, deliberately courted the test of combat. Eventually, the crusade against slavery became one of those several, complex, interrelated issues that led to secession.

In the dozen years following Appomattox the status of American blacks was wrenched so violently in enough different directions to guarantee the disruption of any categorical chronology. Three events were of paramount importance:

1. Slavery was ended and the rights of freedmen were assured by the passage of the Thirteenth, Fourteenth, and Fifteenth amendments. These acts climaxed the campaign *against* slavery (structured negative: therefore cycle one, stage two); they also provided a constitutional basis for the attack on discrimination (cycle two, stages one and two).
2. Under the aegis of occupation armies several Southern states allowed Negroes to vote. Consequentially biracial elective bodies governed and, in some cases, revised constitutions. Superficially the Black Reconstruction has the appearance of integrated political equality (cycle two, stage five).

This rendering of the Hampton Institute reading room typifies the stress on the achievements of the affected group during the "separate-but-equal" phase. Harper's New Monthly, *October, 1873.*

3. The compromise of 1876-77 restored segregated white supremacy in the South and inaugurated an era during which the status of Afro-Americans experienced (depending on the topic and place) retrogression, neglect, segregated advance.[2] The period from the mid-1870s to the mid-1890s can be viewed as either a return to the negative stages of the first cycle with bigotry replacing slavery as the target; a random-positive stage in the first cycle where separate equality is the aim; or a hiatus between the two cycles.

The net result of this buffeting was neutral at best. Although revisionist historians of the last generation have rescued Black Reconstruction from ridicule, this positive experience in self-government was long regarded as proof that the former slaves were not equipped for democracy. The South returned to segregation with a vengeance, tolerating violence and secret societies aimed at keeping blacks "in their place." The Thirteenth Amendment was overruled by fiery crosses and lynching parties. Although the incidence of violence was less frequent, attitudes in many parts of the North were no better. It is little wonder that historians of the black experience call the last quarter of the nineteenth century "the nadir."

Two events of the mid-1890s are often taken to mark the lowest point; they also show that the upward struggle had begun. One was the Supreme Court decision (*Plessy v. Ferguson*) which is often said to have paved the way for segregation. This is hardly true. Segregation, *de facto* and *de jure,* was already in full flower. This decision affirmed that the system would not soon be susceptible to successful challenge in the judiciary. But *Plessy* also records the fact that a test had been made. To the observer of social change the remarkable fact about *Plessy* is that a case involving segregation on a Louisiana railroad got as far as the Supreme Court in 1896.

The year before *Plessy*, Booker T. Washington, as though he had anticipated the Court's ruling, delivered his famous "Atlanta Compromise" address at the Cotton Exposition. Elaborating those same principles that marked the founding of Tuskegee Institute in 1881, Washington inveighed against movements that would take the Negro out of the land or even the region of his birth. "Cast down your bucket where you are," he said. Show what you can do within the constraints of law and custom. Washington predicted that merit and diligence would eventually win recognition and equality (integral); but in their setting his words and deeds perfectly exemplify the positive stage of the first cycle: the push for parity on separate terms.

A more obvious version of the first-cycle approach is the separatist spirit against which Washington argued. From the colonization societies through the Black Muslims there have been a number of such movements, none more notorious than Marcus Garvey's convocation of the Universal Negro Improvement Association in 1920. Some of them are useful as reflectors of social discontents, but within the dynamics of social change their meaning is clear and limited. It matters not what presumptions of racial superiority, black or white,

The vitriolic pen of Thomas Nast—in marked contrast to the scene at Hampton Institute—dramatized the underside of segregation. Harper's Weekly, *October 24, 1874.*

underlie these programs. They are all negative in the sense that they abandon the pursuit of integrated social justice in the United States.

Before Garvey came on the scene, however, there were signs that the goals were shifting from acceptance and escape toward integration. Following a series of events that constituted a rebuttal to Booker Washington, the National Association for the Advancement of Colored People was founded in 1909 with a mandate to seek full citizenship for blacks. The next year three agencies that had been assisting migrants from the rural South as they attempted to find jobs and housing in New York City merged and in 1911 formed the National League on Urban Conditions among Negroes, later simply the National Urban League (NUL). The NAACP set forth the essential point of view that defined the second cycle while working to provide structure for a positive movement. The Urban League was ready with practical assistance for the millions of blacks who were to leave the South in favor of Northern cities. In those industrial centers an attractive labor market was being created by the increase of production and the decrease of immigration from Europe as World War I approached. As was the case with female factory workers in World War II, blacks from the agricultural South found in urban life a level of economic self-sufficiency and social expectation that opened new horizons.

Economics and demography, time and experience, transformed the case for black Americans into a positive phase. When? Professor Vann Woodward thought that he could see the "new reconstruction" in action by the mid-1930s and based his opinion on a series of Supreme Court decisions.[3] This view coincides nicely with a sequence of actions sponsored by the NAACP attacking segregated law schools. The first of these was *University of Maryland v. Donald V. Murray* and was handed down in 1935 (see Chapter 3). Most commentators have placed the modern civil rights movement closer to the present, centering it around the legislation passed by Congress from 1957 through 1968, or perhaps going as far back as President Harry Truman's 1948 Executive Order Number 9981, calling for an end to racial discrimination in the armed forces.

For many reasons the quest for black equality began in the 1930s to show signs of changing attitudes for conditions. The momentum continued through World War II, helped produce substantive accomplishments in the 1950s, and accelerated into the 1960s to become (along with the antiwar movement) one of two major public preoccupations. Civil rights had become a full march, its rhythms reverberating in lunchrooms and buses, factories and polling places. Using a wide repertoire of forms and arguments (see Chapter 3), this positive, well-structured program left impressive marks in all the main social areas: housing, education, employment, and political rights.

The movement continues. Hardly a season passes without some sign of crumbling racial barriers. In 1984 a black presidential candidate for the first time entered the convention of a major party with a substantial number of delegates. In spite of signs of continuing momentum, however, the signal lights are not all green (see Chapter 8), and the position of the movement is most difficult to locate. One reason for the difficulty is that race is so powerful a question that it keeps escaping even the broad boundaries of reform. A second reason is that this movement still occupies several stages in the dynamics of reform: stages that are not even consecutive!

Although programs for black Americans are well structured and to an astonishing degree institutionalized, they still point in more than one direction. In some locations de facto segregation of neighborhoods and schools has trapped the movement within the first cycle: the pursuit of separate parity. Pan Africans and Black Muslims seek segregation by choice and by definition. Typical of the transition from the first to the second cycle are those leaders— still highly visible—who stress self-help and achievement in a traditional setting. Meanwhile, the NAACP, the NUL, the ACLU, the Congress of Racial Equality, the Southern Christian Leadership Conference, and other associations actively and effectively move through the stages of the second cycle toward integrated equality. Each of these postures is well defined and readily recognizable. What is remarkable is to see them simultaneously evident within a single movement.

Compounding the distinctiveness of the pursuit of civil rights is the degree of institutionalization already achieved. In addition to the victory over *Plessy v. Ferguson* in the form of a series of court decisions, there are the particularly meaningful Civil Rights Acts of 1957, 1960, 1964, 1968, the Voting Rights Act of 1965 and the agencies that have been established to support their provisions. For a lesser dilemma, this amount of recognition in the three branches of the federal government would surely have meant a solution.

Wherever one places the cause of equality for blacks today, it is clear that its history illustrates the special chronology of Mode II: an opening chapter aimed at separate parity and a second aimed at integrated equality. The first acquired structure early in the nineteenth century, reached one spectacular climax in 1865, and continued in various forms into the twentieth century. A long hiatus, beginning as Reconstruction ended, marks the interval between a dominant public attitude in favor of segregation and the rising acceptance of integration. The second cycle, rooted in the stated ideals of the American Anti-Slavery Society, became a serious movement early in the twentieth century, achieved notable goals in the 1930s, and has made its mark on American institutions with increasing force.

While no study of reform could afford to ignore the quest for racial justice, no discussion can quite comprehend it. This giant question provides one of the strong examples for the special dynamics of Mode II. It also shows (Chapter 3) why some social crusades are as familiar as they are novel; why civil rights is so full of reverberations of the fight against slavery; why the leaders of the NAACP liked to call themselves the new abolitionists: in short, why abolition and civil rights are not two movements but two cycles of the same movement. The race question also reminds us, in its present complex position, poised between three stages of one cycle with an earlier dynamic not yet dead, that it will never be open to a simple answer. The question remains not just *an* American dilemma, as Gunnar Myrdal called it, but probably *the* American dilemma, as Alexis de Tocqueville prophesied.

The Double Cycle and Woman's Rights

Among reform movements on behalf of special groups, the only quantitative rival to the antislavery–civil rights movement is the only one that represents, potentially, a majority of the population. This—the woman's rights movement—also brings with it an abnormal set of difficulties. The role and status of the female is a cardinal feature of any society and often the most difficult to determine with clarity and accuracy. In the United States the problem is compounded by an extraordinary amount of activity, by a war of attitudes where victory results in only a proportional shift, and by an endless argument over the number of women truly involved in and supportive of the movement.

A fair estimate of the place of woman's rights in reform is also complicated by the very fact that women have been so visibly successful across the whole frontier of social change. From Fanny Wright to Elizabeth Gurley Flynn, women have been active in the labor movement. Carrie Nation and Frances Willard were surely the twin celebrities of the temperance crusade; the Grimké sisters became leaders in the antislavery movement. The development of public and private education overflows with names of female leaders.[4]

To recall this degree of involvement in social change is to give many women their due as effective leaders; it is also to suggest another truth: namely, that the movement toward full rights for woman has often been subordinated to other aspects of social change. In the case of the antislavery campaign, the placement of the woman question second to the slavery question was a deliberate—though not unanimous—decision. In other contexts—education, labor—women took fields that were open to them and accomplished important measures, but they were only occasionally able to use this celebrity and this experience to further the cause of woman per se. In one sense it is natural to expect that a subordinated group should find some way to improve its situation other than by direct assault against some firmly entrenched barriers. For the partisans of woman's rights, however, it may be discouraging to see this movement constantly overtaken by other concerns which even feminist leadership concedes are more pressing: peace, minority rights, labor exploitation. Woman's rights has often been called the unfinished business of American reform.

As a continuing part of the agenda, woman's rights has been given credit for providing a kind of continuity for reform in the United States. The movement often comes into prominence at times when other causes recede and, in so doing, keeps intact the reservoir of individuals interested in social change, the corpus of reform arguments, and the essential lines of communication between social actors. Temperance and woman's rights surely functioned as this kind of reform staple throughout the nineteenth century and until the passage of the Nineteenth Amendment.

Although the woman question far exceeds the boundaries of reform, it is also an integral part of social change. As such it can be viewed in terms of the double cycle which helps define Mode II.[5] The first cycle began before the birth of the Republic. Colonial women had found feminist causes, had acted and spoken in protest, and had even engaged in temporary group actions.[6] After the Revolution there was a continued objection to the Declaration's contention that all *men* were created equal. One of the first organized acts of the feminists was to create a woman's version of the Declaration of Independence.[7] Much of the protest was simply against being overlooked: whether by being placed on a pedestal or confined to the kitchen and nursery.

The most distinctive aspect of the random-negative stage was attuned to an age of millennialism, revivalism, and domestic zionism. It was the religious aspect of the woman question. In a time when evangelism was socially important, it was inevitable that woman's advocates should come to grips with the myth of creation, the role of Eve in the Fall, and the notorious strictures against women in the Gospel according to St. Paul. Sarah Grimké, one of the most eloquent of American women on many subjects, thus began a series of letters on equality by dealing directly with the Bible and by demonstrating that God had granted no human being dominion over another human being, regardless of gender. She ends: "Here then I plant myself. God created us equal:—he created us free agents;—he is our lawgiver, our King and our Judge, and to him alone is woman bound to be in subjection, and to him alone is she accountable for the use of those talents with which her Heavenly Father has entrusted her."[8] The most famous of all antebellum feminist encounters, featuring the giant former slave Sojourner Truth, was a rebuttal to the male jibe that God had chosen a Son to redeem mankind. Just so, responded the legendary black woman; but "Whar did your Christ come from? From God and a woman! Man had nothin' to do wid Him."[9]

Women were not solely occupied with defending themselves against their traditional confinement to subordinate status in the home, in politics, and in religion. Advocates of woman's cause sought some means of turning the momentum from the purely defensive to the constructive. The main answer lay not in the direct promotion of woman's rights but in the use of existing institutions as a showcase for feminine capabilities. The decision to move in this way was neither organized nor explicit; but it was natural and effective. The result was not a direct step toward equality but an indirect and probably essential prelude to outspoken feminism.

All kinds of opportunities were grasped by gifted women. Some, like Emma Willard and the women of Oberlin, used academies, seminaries, and colleges as contexts in which they could demonstrate their abilities to perform successfully by male standards. Some, like Fanny Wright, used workers' organizations and publications as a mechanism for grappling with the public mind. The great wave of antebellum communitarian experiments gave women a variety of opportunities to function outside their traditional roles. The widespread practice of celibacy relieved many women of one form of traditional sexual behavior. In many communities simple, functional dress and hairstyles represented a rejection of materialism and emancipation from worldly fashions. At Oneida, women prepared the commune's food, but they did so at a single daily session and were thus relieved from the repetitive aspect of kitchen chores (see Chapter 5). Brook Farm, Nashoba, New Harmony, and other secular communes witnessed social and intellectual advances for women.

In the context of reform there were two crusades which notably demonstated the capabilities of women to perform in public, to organize social movements, and to bring about political change. One was the temperance effort. Equally important, in the long run, was the female contribution to abolition. At first the colonization and abolition societies seemed to accept the subordination and segregation of women. Female chapters were formed. Women were sometimes denied access to platform seating let alone to the dais. But the presence of able women in large number was a guarantee that traditional roles would be challenged; challenged they were. Questions of sex were prominent enough at times to drown out the slavery issue. Arguments passed back and forth. Even Garrison's single-minded paper opened its pages to the controversy. The victories for women were mainly over segregation; they came gradually to share platforms, publications, and organizational responsibility. The price for these concessions was the relegation of the woman question to the back burner of the reform stove. Both male and female leaders professed their support for woman's rights. They also agreed—most of them—that the woman question must await the resolution of the slavery question.

Whereas most public activity by women was uncoordinated, some sense of order and direction was provided by the series of conferences devoted to woman's rights beginning with the famous Seneca Falls meeting of 1848 where, although no permanent organization was born, a group of leaders was identified and a declaration of sentiments agreed upon. The meeting was chaired by a man; the declaration was representative of the unfocused nature of the woman movement; and the article favoring the suffrage barely won approval. Yet Seneca Falls was a beginning and, considering the spirit of the times, an exhilarating beginning at that.

By demonstrating what they could do in reform organizations, women effectively protested their historic neglect. This tactic provided invaluable experience for woman's rights advocates but, since it was unfocused on positive aims, it represented a negative stage. With Seneca Falls and the meetings that followed, the goals became explicit and positive. Although these goals were random and lacked accepted priorities, they made a case that was increasingly hard to ignore. There is no reason to think that the participants in the California constitutional convention of 1849 (see Encounter 5) had even heard of the Seneca Falls convocation of 1848. Yet the concession made in Monterey to

Yᵉ MAY SESSION OF Yᵉ WOMAN'S RIGHTS CONVENTION—Yᵉ ORATOR OF Yᵉ DAY DENOUNCING Yᵉ LORDS OF CREATION.

In commissioning a well-known satirist to cover the woman's rights convention, Harper's Weekly judged public interest to be abundant and skeptical. J. M'Nevin, June 11, 1859.

married woman's property rights was neither original nor clearly motivated. There is something impressive and startling about the fact that the topic was even broached.

The Civil War allowed women to show a range of skills and characteristics that would have been hard to exhibit in peacetime. There were legions of heroic nurses, including the celebrated Clara Barton, whose abilities went well beyond ministering to the wounded. Dorothea Dix, that most versatile reformer, also served as a nurse while Dr. Mary Walker performed surgery at the front. Women served as spies and scouts, and some, disguised as men, participated in battles. The war brought employmnent in government offices to women for the first time. More important, it allowed them to show how well they could manage farms and businesses while the men were away.

After Appomattox, women became immediately active in binding up the nation's wounds and, particularly, in preparing the freed slaves for independent lives. The end of the war also meant that woman's rights need no longer be subordinated to the slavery question. Thus it is not surprising to see the friends of woman's rights organize nationally in 1869 with the achievement of suffrage as the top priority. The performance of women in numerous causes, in peace and war, had provided an impressive prologue for the assumption of a positive, structured stage.

Suffrage groups were not alone in their effort to provide a positive structure. The Woman's Christian Temperance Union was founded in 1874; women's clubs were federated nationally in 1890. Women were explicitly committed to urging temperance; to improving education; to achieving equity before the law in matters of divorce and property rights; and to expanding access to careers in business, government, and the professions.

As the nineteenth century came to its end, the woman movement received an important, if indirect, boost from technology and the business world. The telegraph, the telephone, and the typewriter had created a new set of commercial conditions where women could be effectively employed in offices. With improved access to education, many women could successfully perform as telegraph key and telephone switchboard operators, typists and stenographers. These jobs were not well paid, but they were not nearly so backbreaking as labor in factories and mills. They brought women to the formerly all-male commercial districts. Here, women did not have to dress for arduous chores but could be neatly and even fashionably attired. The woman office worker saw herself as a whole new breed with only distant kinship to her hardworking sister in the textile mills. She was "smart" both in costume and quip. She could hold her own in a man's world. She could have a measure of independence. A woman need no longer choose between industrial drudgery and an overbearing husband. There was a third choice, even for those without wealth. Although her sphere was limited, the woman office worker was, by circumstances, emancipated.[10]

Along with the office girl came the "new woman," a term as evocative of the 1890s as was "flapper" of the 1920s. The qualities of this abstract female cannot

Women have been notably successful in organizing consumer pressure and in staging demonstrations; here a group pickets a New York meat market in 1948. Prints and Photographs Division, Library of Congress.

be pinned to a methodical definition, but the sense of the term can be grasped from two pieces of occasional verse, one irreverently penned by the man who gave us the *Wizard of Oz:*

> Then shout hurrah for the woman new,
> With her rights and her votes and her bloomers, too!
> Evolved through bikes and chewing-gum,
> She's come! . . .
>
> And shout hurrah for the woman new!
> Who wants a new Bible to suit her view,
> And writes for the papers and eats at the club
> Her grub.[11]

A more sober appraisal read:

> She studies all the questions of the day,
> And gives these problems her earnest thought;
> Wise plans for woman unto her are brought,
> Which shed new light on her advancing way.[12]

For a number of reasons—some not directly related to reform—women were attaining a new plateau as the century approached its end. By 1894 there were 84,000 women attending normal schools and colleges. The "age of association" found women adept at organizing for a plethora of purposes. American magazines had remade themselves from a pattern of sentimentality and traditional views of women to a recognition of women as serious, competent, influential decision makers. Women were already wielding an important force as consumers.[13] As Frank Baum's irreverence shows, women were in for a continuing tradition of deprecating parody. Baum's lines, however, differ from the spirit of his predecessors. They suggest a grudging acceptance and even a kind of admiration for this active, informed woman who had outlived her scriptural stigma and was behaving, in many ways, like a man.

While the female office worker was realizing an economic emancipation, and while the new woman was attracting both resentment and respect, women were continuing to advance in a number of very practical ways. As a separate element in the labor force, women were ceded the right to protective measures in a landmark court decision, *Muller v. Oregon*, in 1907, a departure whose ultimate consequence was the establishment of a Woman's Bureau in the Department of Labor (1920). Healing past differences, the two leading national suffrage associations had joined forces in 1890. By 1900 five states had granted women the ballot in local elections. In 1916 the National Woman's party was formed under the leadership of Alice Paul. This group, having learned from the militant techniques of their English sisters, was to show much less patience and decorum in the face of resistance. The suffragettes gave an unmistakable sense of priority to the structured-positive stage of this first cycle as they spearheaded the final, uncompromising push for the vote.

The ratification of the Nineteenth Amendment constituted a great success story in the anthology of social change. It was a victory for democracy, for activism, for feminism. It institutionalized the woman's rights movement while demonstrating that women had come of age both in their ability to effect change and in their now unchallenged possession of the ballot. Or did it?

About all the close students of the suffrage issue will admit is that the situation would have been worse had the amendment failed.[14] They affirm the contention that the vote was not so much a first step toward a true equality as an insistence that women, being different and in some ways superior to men as citizens, would use their franchise to improve the quality of political life. The suffrage arguments, most of them, adopted this tone rather than insisting simply that women merited the vote on the basis of functional equality. When the expanded electorate failed either to elect substantially more women to office or to improve the quality of elected officials in general, suffrage partisans experienced a considerable letdown.

There is no doubt that the woman movement entered a period of apathy—perhaps even counterrevolution as Betty Friedan insists—shortly following the victory of 1920. The thrill of the action that had preceded the ratification contrasted with the disappointing results to produce a post-partum sense of alienation from the feminists who had brought the vote. As the venerable leaders aged toward caricatures, younger women, according to Friedan, came to regard these heroines as acidulous man-eaters and sought different models.

A more simple reading of this phenomenon of the 1920s is that the leadership had erred in seeing the vote as an end in itself. They had not considered what to do with the franchise once it had been gained. The failure to see this new political power as instrumental left them without a program.[15]

In appraising the reform dynamics of the woman movement it is helpful to understand the Nineteenth Amendment as climactic in contradictory ways. Obviously it granted "equal suffrage."[16] At the same time it seemed to promise "unequal suffrage" in the sense that the woman vote would be distinctive. Thus, in a curious way, it is possible to see this amendment as the culmination of the drive for separate equality for women. The prompt establishment of a League of *Women* Voters tends to support this interpretation. So does the ensuing period of inactivity which typically comes between the end of the first cycle and the beginning of the second.

When tempted by overly stark interpretations, however, it is well to remember that the woman movement has always been balanced between the advocates of female distinctiveness and the advocates of sexual equality. During the interval between the first and second cycle there were strong influences in both directions. As the teachings of Sigmund Freud became compulsive cocktail-party topics, women could respond either by feeling permanently deprived for physiological reasons or by feeling socially liberated for psychological reasons. During this transition period, leaders like Lizzie Boynton Harbert worked not only to get out the vote but to elevate the importance of traditional female roles.[17]

The interval between the two cycles can also be understood economically. In the 1920s women continued to increase their education and their involvement in business and the professions. The next decade, however, dealt women a severe blow in the labor market.[18] With the unprecedented competition for jobs, married women were often fired as a matter of policy; in time of dire need, it was argued, no home deserved more than one breadwinner. That one was assumed to be male. The national disaster was particularly hard on those women who were sent home to cope with problems that the nation's economic collapse had made insoluble. But just as World War II ended the depression, it also created a job climate that was as favorable for women as the depression had been unfavorable. Seven million women, it is estimated, joined the labor force during this period. After the war many of them preferred lives as full-time workers. That moment when women who had enjoyed full-time employment outside the home were turned back to other pursuits constituted, according to one persuasive scholar, the true beginning of the "new feminism."[19]

Although there is very little disagreement that woman's rights was a dead issue from 1920 until sometime after World War II, there is considerable disagreement about what set off the second cycle, the one aimed at full equality. The frustration at losing wartime jobs surely contributed. The reaction against the Freudian put-down may have motivated some. Many housewives may have been as satisfied as Lizzie Boynton Harbert could ever have wished as they manipulated their mechanized homes, reared their healthy children, enjoyed their mammoth station wagons and the pleasures of voluntarism. Still, according to Betty Friedan's interviews and surveys, there were large numbers of housewives who were not content, though they saw themselves as having every reason to be. The putatively happy housewives were rebelling against a mystique that confined them to the children, the kitchen, and the suburbs.

For whatever reason, the new feminism was clearly alive by the middle of the 1960s. One sign was the success of Friedan's book itself. Another was the rising assault by women on the job market. A vital political landmark was the prohibition of discrimination by sex as set forth in Title VII of the Civil Rights Act of 1964. The setting up of the National Organization for Women (NOW) in 1966 promised an eventual structure for the movement. For the 1960s, however, the targets were random and the coordination minimal. As any student of this movement would have predicted, much of the reform energy of American women went toward civil rights for blacks and the campaign to end American presence in Southeast Asia.

Gradually a negative feminist agenda began to appear: eliminate sexist words from the language; do not automatically assume that doctors are male, house-keepers female; and don't be too sure that Our Father in Heaven is not Our Mother. While their boyfriends were burning draftcards to protest the war, the

This rendering of "Women depositing their ballots at the police court polls, Cambridge" suggests that the vote is not an end in itself. Frank Leslie's Illustrated Newspaper, *December 20, 1879.*

young women burned their brassieres to symbolize their refusal to be either sex objects or slaves to fashion.

While NOW was enjoying a period of impressive growth (past 100,000 in the early 1980s), the movement was evolving into a random-positive phase. Important activities included the enforcement of equal employment opportunities and equal pay; the provision, at public expense, of day-care facilities for working mothers; and the completion of jurisprudential reform so that women would be equal before the law in all ways.

At this time two highly controversial issues arose, issues which were to prevent the woman's movement from closing ranks on the positive agenda. One was the proposal to legalize abortion and to provide this operation at public expense for women who could not afford it. This question is not only political but social and moral. Inevitably it created what the feminist orthodoxy considers a defection by those who regard the foetus as a human being and who therefore equate abortion with infanticide. The "right to life" groups, most of them heavily religious, have opposed the feminist leadership in a way that has been disruptive to women's conferences and political campaigns alike.

A similarly complex and volatile issue involved homosexuality. Some women have protested the hiring of homosexual teachers of either gender lest the young be exposed to this minority viewpoint. At first the politically minded feminist leaders regarded the support of the lesbian community as a distinct embarrassment. Although the emergence of the homosexual community from its historic underground status has provided one of the few truly new dimensions to social change in the last decade, the path to full acceptance has not been easy or rapid. Endorsement by the "gay" community may still be more a political liability than an asset. Yet the "woman's liberation" movement, as it called itself through most of the 1970s, was effectively trapped into joining hands with the lesbian cause. If a woman had a right to control her own body when it came to pregnancy and abortion, it would be hard to deny her that same right when it came to other choices. NOW has come to terms with its homosexual element and joins in a commitment to the right of sexual choice. The controversy, however, is by no means ended.

The second cycle of the woman movement entered its structured positive stage when NOW decided that its first priority should be the ratification of the Equal Rights Amendment (ERA). This measure dates from Alice Paul's proposal in 1923 and its consideration in Congress that year. It has been introduced in Congress every year since. It passed the Senate twice in the 1950s but with a rider that would have preserved the statutes intended to afford women special protection. The recent campaign, bolstered by strong new voices in the young adult population, both male and female, opened in 1970 with the presentation to the president of a resolution favoring ERA. Having passed both Houses of Congress, the bill attracted the prompt endorsement of a number of states but fell short of ratification even after the normal time limits had been extended. As soon as the parliamentary rules allow, the amendment will again begin its procedural steeplechase. Most students of social change regard its eventual ratification as inevitable.

One lesson taught by the woman movement reinforces a general pattern pervading all civil rights movements and—to a considerable degree—social change in general. As one approaches the present, governments become increasingly important social actors. In the double cycle, this condition is especially apparent. The first cycle often culminates with the passage of legislation and the establishment of remedial agencies. With the initiation of the second cycle, these agencies, created in order to afford protection for the disadvantaged group, must be converted to a force for integral equality. Thus, although voluntary associations remain important, much of the action takes the form of modifying the role of the government as social actor. In the woman's movement the shift from the protection of female workers to the assurance of equal access and equal pay constitutes the most apparent case in point.

The question of how society views women keeps intruding into the reform agenda.[20] It is tempting to see the first cycle, oversimplified perhaps, as a movement aimed at proving the distinctive aptitudes of women and the second cycle, in contrast, as a push toward undifferentiated equality. In fact these two views have always been concurrent and the shift is better seen as a matter of stress or consensus. The question will never be resolved within the reform context.

Inasmuch as the woman question can be narrowed to a reform movement, it helps exemplify the dynamics of reform on behalf of special groups. Its first cycle evolved through a full set of stages, arriving at national enfranchisement as a realization of distinctive parity. Prior to the move toward integral equality a period of quiet intervened. A second cycle, begun two generations after the first had been completed, pushed toward the end of sex discrimination.

Like the movement on behalf of blacks, the woman movement in the 1980s finds itself with three stages active. The stages are, however, sequential, and their concurrent existence creates no major puzzle. Had the fight for ERA been swiftly won, that achievement might have propelled the whole movement into the watchdog phase. At least until this issue has been settled, other programs will be kept active (random positive); and, as long as full institutionalization remains unfinished business, structured movements will set priorities and maintain political pressures. The institutional phase, which began with the franchise and the monitoring of the workplace, extends itself mainly through the enforcement of equal opportunity in the job market.

Civil Liberties

Movements for blacks and women exemplify (even though they do not typify) the broad patterns in social change as covered in Mode II and as summarized at the end of this chapter. There is another aspect of reform which follows different patterns and which in fact related to social change in very special ways. This is the question of civil liberties, which, for reasons that are historical and functional rather than logical, falls within the boundaries of reform on behalf of special groups.

The concept of civil liberty grows directly out of the concept of human rights: those attributes and prerogatives with which God and/or nature endow the individual.[21] Since governments had constituted the principal threat to these rights, libertarian efforts were devoted to protecting people against their governments. Theoretically, at least, the Bill of Rights was added to the Constitution of the United States in order to forestall encroachments by the federal government, although state constitutions also contained similar guarantees. Those who define civil liberty distinctively do so by equating this term with those freedoms enumerated in the first ten amendments to the Constitution, sometimes adding the Fourteenth Amendment and its assurance of due process which is, in one sense, an extension of the guarantees of justice and equity contained in the Fourth Amendment through the Eighth Amendment.

Civil rights, as opposed to civil liberties, grow directly out of the Thirteenth, Fourteenth, and Fifteenth amendments. These rights have mainly to do with discrimination: with the status, actions, and views of minorities. Whereas civil liberties infer protection from governments, civil rights denote protection not only from governments but also from infringement by other persons or groups.[22]

In the history of reform, civil liberties and civil rights often overlap. It is not useful to insist on too fine a distinction; nonetheless, the two concepts have importantly divergent patterns. The defense of civil liberties takes place along an extremely broad front, yet many of these actions represent the interests of only a very small group. Civil rights tend to involve large groups (blacks, women) whose problem is more than temporary and concerns more than the government's infringement of their rights. Actions in civil liberties typically culminate, for better or worse, in a court decision, whereas civil rights programs seek more extensive remedies, including legislation, executive action, the creation of governmental agencies, and possibly the further amendment of the Constitution. In civil liberties the adversary is, by definition, the government. In civil rights the plaintiff may seek to invoke the action of one government against another (federal against state, in many cases). Whereas the aim of civil liberties is to curtail the power of government, the effect of civil rights activity is often to expand government activity.

The founding of the United States coincided with the climax of a long and painful struggle—in Europe and in the colonies—toward the recognition of individual liberties.[23] It is not surprising, therefore, that a Bill of Rights was so promptly amended to the Constitution, although it is a matter of some curiosity (see Chapter 1) that it was not included in the original document. In any case, this enumeration of civil liberties marked the institutionalization of the first major reform agenda.

Thus civil liberties were not an American crusade but became, with the nation's infancy, a set of constitutional guarantees. This fact placed civil liberties, from the first, outside the normal patterns of reform. Once guaranteed, the inviolability of these rights was assumed; they tended to become passive, or "negative," rights. Except in certain obvious cases dealing with racial and sexual inequality, reformers would make issue of those rights enumerated in the first ten amendments only when they were threatened. The defense of civil liberties soon developed its distinctive, dynamic patterns: one in the narrow politico-legal context and one in the broader social context.

The first of these is the more familiar. The pattern is recurrent. It begins with the threat of war, violence, or subversion. Apprehension produces a curtailment of liberties. Once the threat has passed, there is an inevitable counterreaction in the direction of restoring civil liberties and even augmenting them. The Alien and Sedition Acts of 1798 grew out of a fear of French revolutionary influence. Their enforcement violated the liberties of French immigrants and of Republicans with French sympathies. Public reaction against these measures resulted in sympathy for the party of Thomas Jefferson and contributed to his eventual election as president. Controversy, violence, and war led eventually to Abraham Lincoln's suspension of habeas corpus and to a constitutional amendment proscribing activities of former Confederate leaders. Together with the long-standing denial of civil liberties to slaves, these measures produced, following the Civil War, a reaction in the direction of increased guarantees against suppression and discrimination as reflected in the Thirteenth through the Fifteenth amendments.

The cycle recurred in the years surrounding World War I with sufficient force to generate the founding of the American Civil Liberties Union (ACLU).[24] The level of hysteria preceding America's entry into World War II can be gauged by the "trial" of Elizabeth Gurley Flynn (see Encounter 6). With the war came shocking violations of the civil liberties of Japanese-Americans even while Franklin Roosevelt was enunciating his famous "four freedoms."[25] The postwar witch hunt led by Senator Joseph R. McCarthy produced new outrages and, eventually, a swing of the pendulum toward vigorous restoration and defense of civil liberties.[26]

The second aspect of libertarian reform responds to a number of stimulae. Sometimes libertarian action affected large reform questions as when freedom of speech had to be defended in connection with the discussion of slavery or the organization of labor.[27] Freedom of religion may become an issue when an enlightened state government tries to prevent dangerous rituals (the handling of vipers, for example). Libertarians respond to shifts in public attitude, as when it becomes possible to attack discriminatory acts against homosexuals. The most consistent stimulus to libertarian action comes from technology. With the telephone comes the wiretap and the threatened invasion of privacy. With the computer comes the chance to collect a crushing amount of data on individual citizens without their ever being aware of the compilations and of their use.[28]

Although the American Civil Liberties Union does not speak for all libertarians, its existence has made easier the tracking of libertarian concerns.[29] The trial of Gurley Flynn represents the normal posture of the ACLU much less appropriately than does its notorious defense of the rights of assembly of the American Nazi party in Skokie, Illinois.[30] The activities of the ACLU and of the other guardians of the Bill of Rights are varied and complex.[31] Each one of the enumerated rights has its own history of threat, curtailment, and defense. Assembled, these many threads can be woven into a nearly seamless fabric which reflects many of reform's larger topics. This fabric contains a continuous redefinition of civil liberties in response to shifting currents in religion and politics, changing attitudes toward special groups, and abuses connected with new technology.

Even though the question of civil liberties is difficult to place within the historical and structural reform model, it is, nonetheless, essential to the understanding of reform. The Bill of Rights provides a platform of assumed values on which social change takes place. Inasmuch as the Fourteenth Amendment grew out of the first ten, civil rights, in a curious way, grew out of civil liberties. The modern movements in Mode II, which ask the government to protect against discrimination, owe their origins to those historic libertarian cases which protected the individual against the government. Finally, for reasons that cannot truly be explained either historically or logically, civil liberties has become a part of Mode II because of its constituency. The following list reflects the categories of individuals and groups prominently involved in civil liberties proceedings.[32]

alien residents
arrested persons and suspects
candidates for office
consumers
the handicapped
homosexuals
laborers, labor leaders, and special categories of workers, including the
    military and other government employees
minors
pacifists and conscientious objectors
patients in hospitals and other institutions
political minorities
the poor
the press, including reporters
racial minorities
religious minorities, including atheists
students
teachers
territorial residents, including residents of the District of Columbia

voters

women

To compare this list with the constituency that defines Mode II (see Chapter 3) is to realize that action in defense of civil liberty is indeed a part of reform on behalf of special groups. Such was not always the case. Since civil liberties arose as a defense against governments, and civil rights arose from a governmental determination to protect certain groups, it is curious indeed that opposing philosophies could produce movements that overlap so thoroughly in their concerns. Civil liberties and civil rights are still separated by sharp differences in methods, procedures, and assumptions. When it comes to issues and subjects however, they are inescapably yoked together.

Bearing in mind the movements for blacks and women as cases in point, and the defense of civil liberties as an important exception, it will be helpful to continue the narrative sketch of Mode II as begun at the outset of Chapter 3. As movements for special groups began to take shape early in the nineteenth century, they seemed more a part of the general euphoria than ordered campaigns either to enhance civil liberties or to anticipate civil rights. They smacked of the perfectionism that had inspired the Declaration. They argued from the Enlightenment assumption that, freed of unnatural obstacles and institutional evil, all individuals were potentially benign. Abetted by colonial precedents, humanitarians set forth on a broad spectrum of reforms aimed at improving the general society by attending to its disadvantaged or neglected parts. Where they had good leadership, social reforms made marked headway in spite of the heavy competition for attention among numerous causes. Dorothea Dix, for example, made real progress in the care for the insane; Richard Henry Dana's novel *Two Years before the Mast* highlighted a campaign to humanize the treatment of merchant seamen. There were a number of movements on behalf of temperance, "fallen women," and laborers. Communitarian experiments designed by John Humphrey Noyes and others explored the status of women as well as other social questions. Robert Dale Owen argued a careful education system as a cure for all manner of disabilities produced by ignorance. Horace Mann made large strides toward ending the enslavement to illiteracy.[33]

It is the Jacksonian generation that gets the credit for segregating certain groups and housing them in specially designed facilities. This was done in something like the communitarian spirit. Quotidian society, it was argued, would be improved by having removed from it the orphaned, the poor, the delinquent, the criminal, and the insane. The asylums created for these groups, however, were not meant to be places of incarceration where human beings and their problems were conveniently swept under the rug. These new institutions were themselves thought of as model societies designed to rehabilitate their inmates and prepare them for their eventual return to society. Led by Boston, Philadelphia, and New York, America in the 1830s constructed hundreds of prisons, orphanages, almshouses, and other asylums. Laid along with the cornerstones of these buildings was a foundation of optimism unique to that era. With the blemishes of dependency, deviance, and destitution removed there would be an immediate cosmetic uplift. As soon as these carefully planned institutions had worked their curative magic, society would be that much closer to perfection. The inmates, improved by their segregated treatment, would return to make their own contributions to the health of society at large.[34]

The reformers responsible for the discovery of asylum played a cruel but perhaps inevitable joke on themselves. Most of these institutions were able to work their rehabilitative magic on only a very small portion of the inhabitants. Meanwhile the mainstream had acquired the habit of institutionalizing its dependents and deviants. To judge by the uninterrupted growth of these asylums, the utopian hopefulness had given way to the more resigned expectations of the caretaker. Crowded far beyond their designed capacity, and often neglected by the exchequer, many of these places became dystopias whose inmates suffered inhumane neglect.

Meanwhile, other special groups were being affected by the same general attitude: improvement through segregation. Advocates of woman's rights founded female seminaries and women's organizations. Friends of the native American worked to improve life on the reservation. The well-being of the sons and daughters of African slaves was being sought, in the main, through separate equality. Whatever may have been the intentions of the reformers, nineteenth-century America was prepared to tolerate very little beyond the concept of improved treatment by way of separate treatment.

At the close of Reconstruction two movements emerged from the welter of antebellum reforms to dominate Mode II. One was the woman's rights movement, which has already been summarized. The other was the temperance movement, which is pervasive, multifaceted, and therefore difficult to categorize. It belongs to Mode II insomuch as the victims of alcohol (and other substances) can be considered as a special group. To the Enlightenment mind the drunkard was "enslaved" to rum as surely as the bondsman was chained to his burden. This special group, however, was scattered throughout society and was exposed to a great variety of remedial actions. Much of the early temperance movement was associated with evangelism; the taking of the pledge against strong drink was often done in a religious setting. The Washingtonian movement (a forerunner of Alcoholics Anonymous) relied on conversion, repentance, and mutual help in a secular setting. Habitual drinkers were sometimes segregated in special facilities which played the dual role of caretaking and rehabilitating. Only in this limited context did temperance qualify for the double cycle.

From the early days of the Republic the most visible aspects of the movement were political: the pressure for legislation against the manufacture, transportation, and sale of alcohol. Modest success before the Civil War was brushed aside during the conflict, and the campaign was begun again, leading eventually to nationwide Prohibition. By the end of the nineteenth century, temperance had become closely allied with the woman's movement. Drunkenness was considered a predominantly male transgression. The father squandered his pay at the corner saloon, returning home to abuse his hungry family. The Woman's Christian Temperance Union (WCTU) was a natural outgrowth of this viewpoint and developed a farseeing, gradualistic approach to temperance which invested much of its resources in educating the rising generation. Along with the woman's rights movement, temperance helped keep Mode II alive in the Gilded Age.

The end of the nineteenth century was a time when Americans, along with most of the world's population, thought in terms of groups. Not only were people decisively defined by geography, color, language, and religion, but they were also placed in a hierarchy. The saved were ordained to minister to the heathen. The "white man's burden" was to introduce his "little brown brother" into the modern world. At the time of the Boxer Rebellion the white nations rescued their traders and missionaries from the "yellow peril." Domestically this attitude was reflected in a tendency to identify vast numbers of Americans according to race, religion, and national origin. Some of these minority groups stayed together in an effort to preserve language, religion, and custom. Some groups were forced into segregated communities either by economic pressure or bigotry or both. Each group had its stereotype, its deprecatory sobriquet, and its readily mimicked dialect. From today's more sensitized point of view it is hard to believe how thoroughly this sense of hyphenated identity was built into the language, humor, and public policy of the day.

The point of recalling the spirit of those times is not to suggest that each minority required a reform movement in order to approach the mainstream. The point is, rather, to be reminded of how natural it once was for most Americans to think of groups as distinctive and clearly positioned on a ladder of superiority-inferiority. Against this background the best reasonable hope of the reformer was for improved treatment of the disadvantaged group in its segregated setting: a park on Mulberry Street, a new high school across the tracks, a hospital on the reservation, a college just for women. No wonder the asylums were overcrowded. No wonder the proponents of integration regard the Gilded Age as the worst time ever.

Around the turn of the century, attitudes began to change. Palpable signs were in the emergence of a coordinated campaign for women suffrage, the Niagara movement, and the establishment of the NAACP. The Progressive mind began a reexamination of those swollen institutions built by Jacksonians to rehabilitate dependents and deviants. The process had not worked as intended. It had not worked, reasoned the Progressive reformers, because no single answer could possibly serve a multitude of individuals with varying needs and problems. Each case deserved diagnosis and treatment on merit. The old system had lacked the flexibility requisite for matching treatment to ailment. In some ways the new measures were reminiscent of the preasylum days when the individual was not really removed from society but merely helped or punished or placed in the care of the family. The new tools for dealing with criminals, delinquents, and the mentally disturbed included probation, the indeterminate sentence, juvenile courts, training schools for young offenders, psychopathic hospitals, and therapeutic prison programs. These tools are characterized by their tolerance for flexible, individualized treatment; their variety (as opposed to a single response); their deliberate blurring of the hard line between freedom and incarceration; and their common aim of restoring the individual to society as soon as possible.[35]

There is no doubt that the asylum had become increasingly a solution for dependents and deviants while expectations concerning rehabilitation declined. It is also true, however, that the new century has witnessed a changing attitude toward special groups: not just the poor, the criminal, and the insane but also the deaf, the blind, the victims of all sorts of physical and mental disabilities. "Talking books," captioned news, remedial English, and ramped access to public buildings offer physical evidence of this shift. Along with the stubborn habit of segregating the handicapped comes a fresh determination to integrate all who can accommodate themselves. However felicitous the asylum, it is not the same as the mainstream, where, according to the modern reformer, life was meant to be lived.

Whether the goal has been the asylum or the mainsteam, it is true that the present century has witnessed a steadily increasing effort to improve the lot of special groups. This has happened unevenly at the state and local level for what used to be called "wards of the state." It has happened at the federal level for groups determined by age, race, and sex, as part of the general expansion of the role of government as a primary social actor.

A golden moment in the history of reform arrived at the end of World War I when two long campaigns ended in constitutional amendments guaranteeing woman suffrage and establishing a national prohibition against the manufacture and sale of alcohol. These moments, unfortunately, glittered for but a short while, becoming something considerably less than the millennium their advocates had forseen. Prohibition, repealed after a decade of uneven enforcement, is famous as the reform that failed. There are still towns, counties, and states which practice local prohibition; all communities attempt to keep close control over the manufacture, transportation, and sale of alcoholic beverages. And yet the national experiment did seem to create more problems than it solved. Among them were a disrespect for law among traditionally law-abiding people; a source of dependable income for organized lawbreakers who used bootlegging fortunes as the basis for other illegal enterprises; a set of pressures relating to social drinking that produced—at least in some segments of the population— considerably more consumption of alcohol than had been customary before the "great experiment."

The next decade brought hardships throughout the population in spite of new programs for the jobless and homeless, aged and poor. Hard times are always worst at the bottom of the ladder; unskilled labor, marginal and migrant farmers, women and minorities. Suddenly, with the economic recovery of 1939 and the labor shortage created by conscription, those very groups that had tasted despair were now given unprecedented opportunity. War industry helped dissolve pockets of poverty while offering special opportunities to women and blacks. For more than a decade (1939-1950) a changing pattern of income and wealth distribution suggested that the special groups championed in Mode II were indeed on their way to full participation in the economic life of the nation.

Although the dramatic blows against economic inequality turned out to be more temporary than had been hoped, there has been no turning back toward historic extremes of inequality (see Chapter 8). Some special groups are still outside the mainstream in many ways and still merit the attention of reformers. Some subjects of long-standing crusades have passed important landmarks. The interests of hitherto unrecognized groups (homosexuals, victims of crimes), have been placed on the agenda. The constituency of Mode II continues to expand and, although full immersion in the mainstream has by no means been realized for most special groups, there is also a growing list of injustices that have been to some degree alleviated.

One way of measuring progress in Mode II is simply by recognizing the transition from the first to the second cycle. The first cycle may in fact be the most difficult. Here one comes face to face with the inertia of neglect and a resistance to change backed by centuries of historic rigidity. The argument here is whether society owes *anything* to individuals and groups that do not fully fend for themselves. In the process of social change it is a big step from this argument to the argument inherent in the second cycle: namely, that society owes all individuals the chance for full realization in an unsegregated context. Although this assurance has hardly become universal, the shift in premise from the first to the second cycle, within the pattern peculiar to this mode, is a sign that social attitudes have been far from static and that Mode II has moved toward its ultimate conclusion—disappearance within Mode I.

ENCOUNTER 4

Wabash College Meets Lizzie Boynton

Gazing into the clear blue eyes of Elizabeth Morrison Boynton Harbert, one recognizes a sweet reason that has its limits of forbearance. She was not a large woman, but her comely head, rather wide at the cheekbones, was set on a neck that was far from fragile and a pair of sloping shoulders that would have done credit to an Olympic swimmer. An experienced predator would have known, instinctively, to avoid Lizzie Boynton's nest.

Yet for all her air of strength and self-sufficiency, this woman would never have sought conflict. Though strongly fashioned, she valued most the social, intellectual, and imaginative elements in the human condition. A highly spiritual woman, Mrs. Harbert was at home in churches, worked well within their structure, used scripture with friendly familiarity, and considered prayer a normal form of communication. Next to the word of God was the canon of great literature, divinely inspired, capable of lifting ordinary mortals to an exalted view of the universe and their place in it. Women, she consistently argued, needed the inspired view of life which only religion and great literature could offer. They needed this vision in order to perform their sacred trust: the creation of ennobling homes, the guidance of family destiny, and the moral education of the next generation. This pattern of beliefs, not at all uncommon among women reared in Lizzie Boynton's setting, might have made for her a life of tranquil obscurity highlighted by offices held in local literary and religious societies and for papers carefully prepared and delivered on Goethe, Browning, and the beatitudes. Such a pattern might easily have measured Mrs. Harbert's life had it not been for an almost accidental episode that occurred when she was twenty-five.

Lizzie Boynton, to use the "literary name" she preferred before her marriage, was born in 1843 in Crawfordsville, Indiana. She completed the curriculum of a female seminary in Oxford, Ohio, then the Terre Haute Female College, whence she graduated with honor in 1862. Feeling that her education was incomplete, she joined three other young women in petitioning President Charles White of Wabash College to attend lectures at that young but impressive men's liberal arts college. Permission was granted and the four young women began listening to Edmund O. Hovey on chemistry and to the natural science lectures of John L. Campbell, a local celebrity who was to become secretary of the Centennial Exposition in Philadelphia. To these women President White made a rash promise: should they complete the course he would award them diplomas.

Whether or not this promise could have been kept one will never know; for, while it was still a hypothetical question, President White died. In the interim, the number of local women interested in hearing the Wabash lectures had grown to twenty-three. This augmented group petitioned for formal admission. They were denied. They were denied in terms so unfair, so condescending, and so demeaning that Mrs. Harbert was never able, during her long, full life, rich with accomplishment, to recall this rebuke without experiencing a fresh surge of ire and outrage. All twenty-three of the supplicants were similarly provoked. They decided to take their case to the public, announcing the production of a dramatic sketch titled "The Coming Woman," intended both to arouse sympathy through self-mockery and to raise funds for a town library open to readers of both sexes. The young men of Wabash played into their hands, ridiculing the effort in a manner that only promoted it. The performance succeeded both financially and politically. Introduced in flattering terms by the town's Civil War hero, General Lew Wallace, Lizzie gave a triumphant paper on the plight of women in education. The address was repeated often and successfully. It became an article which brought the estimable sum of ten dollars from a New York newspaper. A public career was launched.

Before this career had ended, in 1925, it had spanned a range and degree of achievement that demand more recognition than it has yet been accorded.[1] In at least four states, where she resided, she made palpable contributions to the organization of social and reform groups. She developed a persuasive argument for suffrage early in her career, presented it at the Iowa state Republican convention and thus gained credit for being the first woman to have a political plank on woman's rights adopted by a major party.

In 1874 the Harberts moved to Evanston, Illinois, where they spent most of their lives and where Mrs. Harbert made her major impact. For seven years she contributed a highly popular feature called "Woman's Kingdom" to the Chicago periodical, *Inter-Ocean.* Resigning from that post she founded a well-known journal of social action: *The New Era: A Monthly Magazine Devoted to Philanthropy and Reform.* From the 1870s on, she was in regular correspondence with the national leaders of the suffrage and temperance movements. In 1875 Susan B. Anthony wrote urging Mrs. Harbert to accept the presidency of the state suffrage association to keep it from falling into the wrong hands. In 1876 Anthony accorded one of her rare compliments, writing that Mrs. Harbert "did splendidly" in addressing the Democratic National Convention at Cincinnati.[2]

Summarizing her own career in 1908, Mrs. Harbert listed the state presidencies of the Iowa and Illinois Equal Suffrage societies and the national presidency of the Household Economics Association. As late as Warren Harding's administration Mrs. Harbert was still memorializing the executive to create a cabinet office responsible for the home and for children. Her efforts in founding the Woman's Club of Evanston were sufficiently special that this group hung an oil portrait of Mrs. Harbert as its first act on opening their own building. In Chicago she was a charter member of the Woman's Press Association. As a peace advocate she enlisted her friends from the other humanitarian movements and served as national associate chairman of the World's Unity League. Her platform lectures were in constant demand. In addition to her considerable newspaper and magazine columns, she wrote and published novels, collections of essays, music, and verse. The most famous of her songs was "Arlington Heights," and of her books a didactic novel entitled *Out of Her Sphere*.[3] Her favorite pastime, she wrote, was nature study and "entertaining progressive people" at 1671 Raymond Street, Pasadena, her final residence. The advanced degree she coveted in Crawfordsville was awarded her in 1884, as an honorary doctorate, by Cincinnati (later, Ohio) Wesleyan College.

The neglect of this woman is to be regretted not only because of the wide range of her achievements but also because of the essential dichotomy in the woman's movement which her career illustrates so compellingly. As Mrs. Harbert she argued that most women could best be served by improving their status and effectiveness in the context of home, church, and school. Housekeeping, as she saw it, was indeed a science and an art. Educated women appropriately performed as home managers and as guides to spiritual and intellectual growth. Her campaign for a cabinet level "department of the home" was an expression of her conviction that woman's traditional role could be psychologically gratifying if it were only accorded the social recognition it deserved.

This attitude is typical of the first phase of the woman's movement which aimed at equal treatment without necessarily calling for a redefinition of sex roles. As a journalist Mrs. Harbert helped to found a woman's press club without seeming to resent female exclusion from the male associations. In pushing for the vote she wrote consistently of "equal" rather than female suffrage, yet she clearly thought women would use the franchise distinctively.

On the other hand, as Lizzie Boynton, she clearly resented segregation at the polls as much as in the classroom. She announced her agreement with Anthony that women must go beyond examples of individual achievement and concern themselves with the status of the entire gender. While Mrs. Harbert never lessened her efforts to bring recognition to woman in her traditional roles, Lizzie Boynton, from the first time she appeared as a member of "the Crawfordsville 23," was simultaneously pushing toward integral equality.

If Mrs. Harbert is an example of a naturally active woman who was almost accidentally turned onto reform interests, then her career would also seem to show that this kind of momentum, once imparted, is almost impossible to check. Mrs. Harbert's life was a series of projects and crusades, some overlapping, few abandoned, one growing out of the other. But she never forgot where it all began. In 1885, already a woman of major accomplishments and about to inaugurate her most influential publication, she wrote to Wabash College—her own honorary doctorate firmly in hand—and asked if Crawfordsville were not at last ready for collegiate coeducation. The answer, for all its maddening circumspection, might have provided the impetus—had one been necessary—for a full second phase of social action.

It would be somewhat premature to anticipate the actions of our Board of Trustees regarding any new departure for Wabash College.

The practical difficulties connected with so radical a change are very great and I would not be willing to make the change unless I could also be assured that it would be successful.[4]

There is no record that Lizzie Boynton Harbert either wrote another article on coeducation or staged another show. She neither tore the letter to bits, nor used it to light a suffrage campfire. She saved it.

Planners and Dreamers

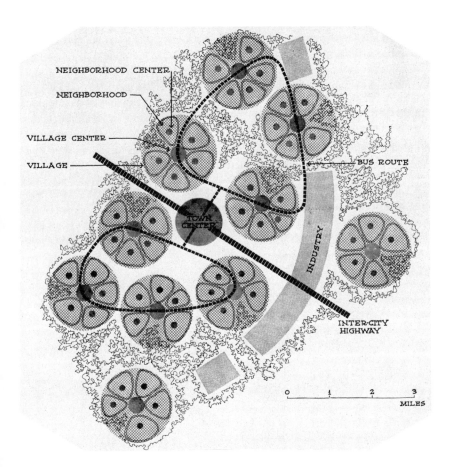

A flower-like design, reminiscent of Frank Lloyd Wright's obsession with the "organic," appears in the promotional literature for the idealistic James Rouse's New Town, Columbia, Maryland, ca. 1963.

The common style of reform—the attack on social imperfections and the protection of rights and liberties—gives way now to the treatment of a much less typical but hardly less important aspect of social change: the establishment or depiction of an alternative order. In this category are the planners who offer a safe harbor when the mainstream becomes roiled and fractious, and the dreamers whose visions provide a direct view of social goals and cultural values.

Chapter 5, except for tracing the communitarians up to the present, is devoted to nineteenth-century alternatives: the intentional settlement and the literary utopia. In Chapter 6 are covered the twentieth-century diffusions of the utopian spirit into science fiction, visionary architecture and planning, and models for world government. As separate movements these dreams and plans are reasonably well understood. It is the burden of Part Three to establish these varied models as a continuous and often interrelated aspect of the reform spirit.

CHAPTER 5

Communes and Literary Utopias

Prone, exhausted from endless hours at a power loom, the worker dreams of a world in which no human becomes the slave of a machine. Triumphant after creating an empire of drygoods, the entrepreneur imagines an entire society based on the organization and efficiency that brought him success. Having witnessed warfare—the blood of battle, the brutality of industrial conflict—the visionary labor leader conjures up a way of life exempt from destructive competition. If I were king . . .

The lure of the ideal is universal. Those diverse delegates who assembled to give California a constitution agreed on a limited utopia where married women could be propertied and where the wealthy would underwrite education for all. Jack London often wrote of a worldwide brotherhood of the common people, whose collective altruism would lift them above the self-interest of kings and corporations. Elizabeth Gurley Flynn savored the same heady atmosphere from a more consistent politico-economic point of view. (See Encounters 1, 5, and 6).

Not all plans and dreams are related to social change. Some are so limited in scope as to have negligible social consequences even if fully realized. Some are so formless or fantastic as to have little probability of application in the world we know. Among the more literate and palpable of these plans and dreams is located reform's most distinctive mode: the impulse to alter society by reference to a substantially different model.

Mode III arises from discontent with the status quo as surely as do its companion modes. In place of the vivid particularized muckraking that generates the movements described in the preceding chapters, these reformers begin with a glimpse of the ideal. Occasionally utopian romancers will tell their readers how to get from the present mess to the remote nirvana; sometimes planners will contrast a real city with one on the drawing board; most of the reformers in this mode, however, are content to offer, with a minimum of comparison, their ideal alternative. In common these planners and dreamers assume that the present system is beyond repair. They propose to replace all or part of it with a dramatically different model.[1]

At the beginning of this story are the millennial prophecies of the Bible, the *Republic* of Plato, the wilderness of Shakespeare's *Tempest*, the imaginings of anyone who ever thought the earthly experience might produce an inspired order conducive to mankind's full realization. The discovery of a Western hemisphere gave a focus to these imaginings: "Here was opportunity for humanitarians dissatisfied with the economic and political absolutism that burdened Europe's peasantry. They would describe the New World not as it was, but as Europe should be. . . . They would create a model . . . of abundance and liberty too tempting to resist."[2] This particular passage from the most recent and thorough synthesis of European views of the New World evokes an unmistakable reform resonance. It was the "humanitarians" dissatisfied with politico-economic inequity who would "create a model," a new Golden Age. As Ray Billington made clear, this was not the only impression of America, but it was one of the very strong and lasting ones. It helps explain how philanthropists like James Oglethorpe could view Georgia as an orderly asylum for debtors; how practical idealists like William Penn could see a green, symmetrical, Quaker town in the woods along the Delaware; how morally preoccupied children of a Calvinist God could imagine in Massachusetts "an HOLY CITY . . . the STREET whereof will be *Pure* GOLD."[3]

Before the colonial era had ended, both facts and expectations had altered. Nature could not have lived up to its opulent advance billing. The "savages" did not prove entirely "noble" in the sense of either the Garden of Eden or the metaphysical paradise of Jean Jacques Rousseau. Colonial governments developed their share of problems both within and across their borders. The Hundred Years War in Europe puffed the flame of colonial friction like a handful of gunpowder tossed into winter's fire.

Yet the euphoria of independence, overriding the force of memory, somehow created a fresh set of hopes that the United States might yet offer Europe a transcendent model. For the religious, these hopes took the shape of a millennium visited on a recent wilderness finally freed from the cumulative evil that was Europe. For those who took the equality of the Declaration in material terms, like Thomas Skidmore, there was to be a giant raffle distributing the nation's wealth in equal parcels to each family. For those who sought their meaning in history, the new Republic meant an opportunity to recreate, and simultaneously surpass, the achievement of antiquity on a Capitol Hill of their own and in towns named Athens, Utica, and Rome.[4]

Among those buoyant young republicans who thought that the whole nation might readily be transformed into a model society, some had particular relevance to the reformers who define Mode III. They were the ones who compounded a utopia out of free land, the single-family dwelling, and the absence of oppressive debt. T. Thomas, a leading merchant of this dream, offered original designs of healthful dwellings on austere classical models, available to the workingmen of towns and cities for less than $300. Thomas thought it important that young adults begin their family lives promptly but without incurring the kind of encumbering debt that would not only shadow their personal lives but also jeopardize their political freedom. Toward this end the members of a community were to lend to one another, at low interest rates, so that all could be freed from the tyranny of landlords and banks. Along with his architectural plans and specifications, he printed articles for incorporating building and loan associations.[5]

Thomas's ideas for the workingman were paralleled by views of the celebrated Andrew Jackson Downing on country houses. Downing favored the cottage style over the neoclassic. He accompanied his floor plans and elevations with instructions for making cheap, becoming furniture. A rude dwelling suits the "lynch law and the use of the bowie knife," Downing wrote, but "when smiling lawns and tasteful cottages begin to embellish a country, we know that order and culture are established." Regardless of what the Old World may value, the New World needs a carefully planned environment of single-family residences in order to stimulate education, truth, refinement, "the highest genius and the finest character."[6]

Thomas and Downing were in a vein that has strong connections outside Mode III: with George Henry Evans and the land question; with Horace Greeley and the Homestead Act; with the rise of suburbia and the continuing stress on homeownership and single-family dwellings. They wrote also against the background of hardship suffered in crowded Europe where possessing a debt-free home on its own land amounted to a visionary goal.

Within Mode III the relevance of Downing and Thomas is even stronger. They belong to a tradition of environmental reform traceable to colonial town planners, evident in antebellum communes, recurring in the works of Frederick Law Olmsted, Frank Lloyd Wright, the federal planners of the New Deal and so on down to Buckminster Fuller.[7] To these planners of ideal communities, whatever their scope, the design of the manmade and natural setting was a crucial factor in elevating society. This tradition will be encountered throughout this chapter and particularly as the discussion of urban and regional planning resumes in Chapter 6.

Antebellum Communes

The times that produced Downing and Evans were perhaps too impatient to await the gradual settling of the continent by a rising artisan-yeoman class. Many wanted to exemplify perfection without delay, as Emerson wrote to Thomas Carlyle:

> We are all a little wild here with numberless projects of social reform. Not a reading man but has a draft of a new Community in his waistcoat pocket. I am gently mad myself, and am resolved to live cleanly. George Ripley is talking up a colony of agriculturists and scholars, with whom he threatens to take the field and the book.[8]

These new communities, enumerated by Emerson for the amusement of Carlyle, became the first large movement within Mode III. At least half a dozen experimental settlements had been in place before the Constitution was ratified. The number of these experiments gently waxed through the Republic's early decades, flowering abruptly in the 1840s when roughly one-third of all the antebellum communes were established.[9]

In the 1850s the number of newly founded settlements decreased by more than half, and by 1870 John Humphrey Noyes was willing to perform an autopsy on the presumably expired corpse. Noyes claimed there had been four distinct communitarian waves. Two were religiously motivated by the revivalists Asahel Nettleton and Charles G. Finney in 1817 and 1831, respectively. Each was followed by a secular tide: one led by Robert Owen in 1824 and one responding to the ideas of Charles Fourier (led by Albert Brisbane and Horace Greeley) after 1842. The religious impulse was native, wrote Noyes, whereas the secular impulse responded to imported ideas.[10] The movement had died, according to Noyes's postmortem, because the native soul had never successfully animated the imported body. Until the secular and religious settlements could learn from each other, the movement would be without real hope.[11]

Social historians have been inclined to accept both Noyes's categories and his judgment that the movement had expired. This opinion was never unanimous. In 1875 Charles Nordhoff published an extensive and positive report on America's "communistic societies." William Hinds found abundant activity in his 1902 and 1908 editions of *American Communities*.[12] Recently, a student of the new communes wrote: "In the twenty years following the depression of the 1870s, until the mid-1890s, a much bigger surge of new communal societies (numbering about one hundred) appeared, based on philosophies combining religion, ethnic identity and economic necessity."[13] Rosabeth Kanter, whose analysis of what makes communes work is justly admired, offers a pattern based on the idea that the three main motives for communal life each dominated overlapping periods in the history of intentional societies: the religious through 1845, the politico-economic from 1820 to 1930, and the psychosocial after 1914.[14] Dolores Hayden, stressing the material aspect, implies objections to any simple periodization of the movement.[15] All seem to agree to only one period of in-activity: 1930–1945, precisely the time when the government took a major role in community planning.

At the moment, the question of periodizing communal history is delightfully unsettled. The direction of the newer interpretations is clear: toward replacing the picture of two distinct movements separated by a century of inactivity with the picture of a nearly continuous movement of gently shifting characteristics. As this attempt to alter the perception of the commune movement is exactly parallel to the efforts of this work to alter perceptions about the periodization of reform in general, there is small doubt as to which picture is favored here.

To be instrumental in social change, however, communes have not only to exist but to attract notice; and between the Civil War and World War II the intentional settlements lived and died, for the most part, outside the public's awareness. Interest did reawaken in the 1950s, increased dramatically in the

1960s as the new environmental consciousness, disapproval of the war in Vietnam, and the congeries of ideas now known as the counterculture came together. Whereas there were fewer than 200 antebellum settlements, the New Wave seems to have produced at least 2,000, genuine and self-proclaimed. In spite of the increasing awareness of significant activity in the interim, the movement is presently accessible mainly through the study of these two waves: one ending with the Civil War and one beginning after World War II.

It is hard to imagine any social form more idiosyncratic than the commune; no one or two could be posed as "representative." Nevertheless, in order to provide a modicum of flesh for this otherwise skeletal discussion, it will be useful to look at two communes, Oneida and Twin Oaks, which offer—each in its own era—clear variations on the accepted social order.

Oneida's creator, John Humphrey Noyes, descended from prosperous, respectable forebears and was reared in a large, happy family.[16] Born in Brattleboro, Vermont, in 1811, he came of age admiring his wise, well-educated father who was adept at business and politics and not much interested in religion. Noyes graduated from Dartmouth in 1830 and began the study of law. But 1830 was also the year in which the great revivalist Charles Finney was converting souls by the thousands. One of his disciples came to Putney, Vermont (at that time the seat of the Noyes family), and presided at the meeting which moved the twenty-year-old to prepare immediately for the service of God. This Noyes did at Andover and Yale, only to be rejected for the ministry when he stubbornly and candidly insisted that his conversion had freed him to pursue perfection.

Released from orthodoxy, young Noyes began—with an assurance that was his chief characteristic—the pursuit of his own way. He read, he corresponded, he visited communes, he hammered at the imperfections of society. There were two major influences upon him: the variety of socialism espoused by Charles Fourier and the peculiar form of inspirational Christianity known as perfectionism. Out of them he developed "Bible communism," growing confident enough to issue sermons and tracts; to convert members of his family; and, by 1846, to issue a statement of principles announcing the existence of a Putney community based on religious communism.

To this point the adult experience of John Humphrey Noyes resembles that of many searchers after the ideal. At the back of his mind, however, was a cluster of uniquely related ideas that would mark Noyes and his communes with their distinctiveness. Perhaps because of his own happy childhood, Noyes thought that the ideal community should resemble the expanded family. Yet he could not admire the jealous possessiveness that grew up between couples and within households. Furthermore, his wife's tortures in suffering four stillbirths from her first five pregnancies, led him to pronounce the virtues of male continence. To this he linked the concept of "complex marriage," and the doctrines that made the Perfectionists notorious were born.

Complex marriage meant that all adult males were married to all adult females. Together they were one large family, blessed and sanctified through their Savior. Within this family everyone was urged to be affectionate, no one possessive. Sexual intercourse was neither prohibited (as with the Shakers) nor patterned into male polygamy (as with the Mormons). Instead Noyes divided the two functions of intercourse. Willing couples were allowed this act of affection so long as the male "reserved" insemination. This male continence Noyes publicized in a number of tracts. For some years the community was limited to this style of intercourse until it was decided that children could be accommodated. Thereupon the community began to sanction selective reproduction, or "stirpiculture."

Sex and marriage were not all that set the Perfectionists apart, but these mores contributed heavily to the harassment of the original commune. In 1848 Noyes and his followers joined with other Pefectionists to found the Oneida settlement, by which they are best known. The community maintained its original framework through 1880, when it became a joint stock company, Oneida Community, Ltd., profitable manufacturers of silverware.

Oneida exhibited most of the characteristics of a successful commune, some of them contradictory. Noyes himself represented the sine qua non of the movement: the charismatic leader. Often described as looking as conventional as his ideas were iconoclastic, Noyes's appearance was not dramatic. A stocky man with square shoulders, a little above average height, his generous features were framed by chin whiskers and dark hair, shading a wide jaw and forehead. From middle years on he wore a full beard, graying with time, as his hairline gradually receded. His eyes were large and direct, his mouth bore a pleasant—if rather perplexed—expression. His general mien suggested an alert, thoughtful steadfastness. John Noyes had enormous self-confidence, treated few men as equals, and remained candid and uncompromising concerning his basic beliefs.

To this portrait of a typical messiah Noyes added some rare traits. He was willing to learn. He was willing to delegate. He was able to overlay his self-trust with an interest in others which women, especially, found irresistible. Oneida had more committees than a faculty senate. But their discussions led to real decisions involving important commitments. The residents, who had eschewed conventional religious services, seemed to make community management their religion. Decisions reached at the regular evening discussions led to the establishment of branches, land investment, architectural design, and a gradual shift from a predominantly agricultural to a predominantly manufacturing enterprise. In nearly all respects the Perfectionist family made its own destiny.

Successful communes have a sense of tight-knit loyalty and dedication. Noyes inspired some of this; experience provided the rest. The Perfectionist family was particularly resentful of the accusation of "free love," since, in their judgment, their sexual practices were more controlled, more thoughtful, and—yes—more holy than those practiced on the outside. Being reviled as promiscuous strengthened their bonds. So did the response to crisis. Their early ranks swollen beyond expectation, they struggled to complete their first "Mansion House" before the bone-chilling reality of an upstate New York winter reached them. Everyone pitched in; prodigious feats were performed. This experience not only instilled group pride but led to one of the more distinctive features of Oneida: the adoption by the women of the "bloomer" costume. Loose trousers under short tunics and short hair were in the interest of saving time and allowing freedom of movement. When the building was up, the women decided to stay with their new appearance and did so for the life of the community in spite of the fact that the men dressed according to outside conventions.

The bloomers and short hair were worn proudly at Oneida as a badge of commitment. The sense of putting the welfare of the group above individual prerequisites was also heightened by the famous ritual of the "critique." Everyone but "father" Noyes was regularly subjected to a personal analysis either by a committee convened for the purpose or by the entire group. The severity of these sessions was tempered by the subject's awareness of a profound concern for his own development and by the fact that one day's inquisitor would be the next day's subject. Such meetings were not rare in communes; the ones at Oneida were the most helpful in resolving the inevitable tension between the individual and the group.

Although bloomers were worn at home, the Oneida women kept a wardrobe of conventional dresses for travel outside. This fact is indicative of a healthy attitude toward outsiders in spite of abuse and prurient curiosity. Oneida welcomed visitors, greeting them with specially prepared literature. The community responded alertly to consumer interest whether for canned fruit (an early, temporary success), for the famous game traps (complete with instructions for skinning), the travelers' lunch bags invented by Noyes himself, or for the silverware that eventually became their lodestar of profit and their spiritual doom. Although the Oneida library was current and wide-ranging, members were urged to leave the community to pursue useful courses of study at neighboring schools and colleges. Noyes himself traveled often, spending considerable time at the Brooklyn branch commune whence many of his publications were issued. Oneida thus avoided the fundamental error of many settlements: the determination to sink or swim in isolation.

The question of who does what work has also sunk a number of experimental groups. At Oneida the basic decisions were made by committees. After the strain of the first seasons had past, the labor was not arduous. Jobs were deliberately rotated so that boredom would be minimized. Labor-saving techniques and inventions were much prized. Some of the unpleasant work was done by paid outsiders. Women were not regarded as equals in the work force, but they achieved considerable recognition. They prepared a large, hot breakfast while fixing food for the rest of the day and placing it in covered dishes on the pantry shelves. When they left the kitchen, still early in the morning, their "slavery" was finished until the next dawn. Women were allowed to work at all tasks for which the community found them suited, and this definition was quite broad considering the times.

THE KITCHEN, ONEIDA COMMUNITY.

This homely sketch attests to communitarian willingness to sacrifice fashion to utility. Wearing bloomers and tunics, the Oneida women prepared the day's food at a single session. Prints and Photographs Division, Library of Congress.

Oneida was special in its ability to allow common sense to triumph over rigid adherence to principle. Its unique traits produced a precarious set of balances: Christianity with socialism, authority with participation, community with privacy.[17] Oneida resembled other settlements in its idealistic foundations, its commitment to shared property, and its dependence on an inspirational leader. Like so many others this community ended with a fight over the succession of leadership. Although the large precepts of Perfectionism had failed to move the outside world, there was at the time of dissolution (January 1, 1881) the happy fact of material prosperity to soften the blow. "We made a raid into an unknown country," declared the ever-optimistic founder, "charted and returned without the loss of a man, woman, or child."[18]

Modern Communes

Several modern communes have shown an awareness of antebellum prototypes, but only one named a major building "Oneida." This is Twin Oaks, a rural commune near Louisa, Virginia, whose founders discovered a kinship between the ideas of Noyes and those of B.F. Skinner. Skinner, in *Walden Two*, had developed a detailed picture of a new social order based, like that of Noyes, on a combination of religious and secular views. A behavioral psychologist, Skinner sketched a kind of social engineering utilizing positive reenforcement. His great "discovery" was in the teachings of Jesus.

It was to discuss the ideas of Skinner that the founders of Twin Oaks first came together. Before long they had developed a strong belief in their own capacity to create, in miniature, a society that would work much better than the mainstream. In 1967 this idea became Twin Oaks, a society without distinctions by race, class, sex, age, seniority, or even by ability. Harmless titles like "Mr." or "Mother" were avoided and only first names used. Work was performed equally by males and females. Property was owned in common. Labor was assigned through a complicated system of points that would give all the best chance to do what they wanted while performing a fair share of the required work.[19]

Using the terminology of *Walden Two*, Twin Oaks began by appointing "planners" to make decisions and "managers" to oversee activities. Conflicts are settled by discussion or by lot. Almost nothing is compulsory at Twin Oaks. Mutual criticism, modeled on the Oneida "critique," was tried and abandoned. Instead there is a "generalized bastard" who receives and passes on complaints, and "feedback sessions" which sometimes entail criticism but which are not compulsory. Complex marriage was discussed but never tried. People live alone, mate in conventional or unconventional ways, change their patterns and attachments. Although sexual behavior is theoretically liberated, jealousy is still a recognized problem, and at least a few members have left the commune because they felt that the sex life was too inhibited.[20]

Oneida did not prosper as an agricultural enterprise mainly because of the climate; at Twin Oaks the problem was a degree of inexperience that made farming a very costly way to produce food and income. Instead, along with several other ventures, the commune makes and sells hammocks and rope chairs. When necessary, a small, unwilling group has commuted to Richmond to bring back earnings. In shifting from agriculture to manufacture, the members of Twin Oaks not only repeated the Oneida experience but automatically alienated themselves from most of the New Wave communes. Organic foods are just too expensive, complains founding member Kat Kinkade. Twin Oaks welcomes technology and seeks efficiency just as surely as the counterculture communes reject both. It does not matter that the settlers at Twin Oaks use their *efficiency* to create time for love, song, or meditation; the word itself creates a cultural barrier.

Like Oneida, Twin Oaks also traded isolation and self-sufficiency for survival. Not only does the budget sometimes depend on the money brought in by the Richmond commuters and the paying guests, but the outside world is recognized as a legitimate retreat *from* the commune. Kat's daughter left for a year; Kat herself, according to recent reports, is off on a prolonged sabbatical but intending to return. (Communards who wish to reserve their places while absent can do so through fixed, regular payments; otherwise they would have to reapply and buy in like any newcomer.) Everyone takes a two-week vacation from the commune; extra labor points earn extra time. The outside world is a source of income, necessities, emotional release, and visitors. Like the Perfectionists, these settlers make a ritual of educating visitors, fellow communards, and the reading public as to what they are doing and trying to do. How else can they reform society at large?

The degree to which Twin Oaks reflects Skinner's views was once an important controversy. One of the founding members, interviewed by Robert Houriet, thought that Twin Oaks was growing closer to *Walden Two* every day. Kat Kinkade, although she welcomed Skinner's introduction to her book, states that Twin Oaks is far from a model of the Skinner prototype. Kinkade watched practical considerations consistently override theoretical models until the weight of heuristic experience threatened to break the last tie with the original inspiration. The current leadership admits that the preoccupation with survival has completely covered the trail leading back to *Walden Two*.[21]

Twin Oaks is that rare example of a sustained, successful commune. Its preoccupation with economic survival can be seen in its prohibition of drugs, in its lack of interest verging on antipathy toward religion and mysticism. It has not attempted to revolutionize sexual mores except by downplaying possessiveness and convention. It has succeeded in developing a unique system of voluntary cooperation built on the elimination of private property, competition, and discrimination. To some visitors it has seemed depressingly impersonal. Kat Kinkade argues that the communal experience succeeds only when it replaces the loneliness of the individual with a "warm group of friends." A committed group can and must encourage "a lot of different dreams" ranging from "the inner reaches of the soul" to "a brighter future for mankind."[22]

To join a commune is not necessarily to make a social statement. Charles Nordhoff described the members of certain antebellum religious settlements as stodgy, healthy, honest, abstemious, with no great interest in art, or labor, or meliorism.[23] For them the communitarian impulse was limited to religious freedom. Gilbert Seldes and Victor Calverton found in the secular communes a group of elite eccentrics whose mission was to challenge conformity wherever they found it.[24]

Yet for many others the act of leaving conventional society was itself a social statement. The language of Emerson's contemporaries—come-outers, millennialists, Fourierists, Perfectionists—shows more impatience with than disapproval of the mainstream. These were the believers who took Joseph Smith's Urim and Thummin on faith and followed him and his disciples to the promised land. These were the Shakers who banished evil through their fingertips, the accolytes of George Rapp the divine Harmonist, the faithful who followed Noyes to Perfection itself! To stay behind was to miss out on exaltation!

With the new communes the statements were more secular. Many of the more eloquent of this group complained that American society did not value the dissenters or that it had wasted a generation by using Ph.D.s to drive taxis. They were against the draft and, Mark Vonnegut added, against cities, capitalism, racism, and industrialization.[25] They saw the ship of state as guided by conformity, consumerism, and the pursuit of an immoral war. Their communes were life rafts, as Paul Goodman called them, deliberately taking other directions. Some of them, it is true, were merely bobbing along with the tides, provisioned with sunflower seeds and beansprouts, shrouded in a fog of marijuana smoke. At the helm of many of these craft, however, were individuals who had tried their best to influence society at large, who had been jailed for protesting the draft or clubbed for promoting civil rights.[26] The course they steered was deliberate.

Once established the commune tended to reflect many of the same reform interests that animated conventional society. The early communes opposed slavery, some serving as underground railway stops and at least one, Nashoba, representing a method of gradual emancipation. Similarly, the new communes are strong on civil rights not only for blacks but for other minorities as well. Except for the Mormons, the antebellum communards tended to avoid the Indians or get along with them. With the new communes the native Americans amount to a fetish as their ways are honored and their costumes aped. The early settlements furnished examples in the use of public lands—to the extent that they were sometimes accused of land hunger. The new communes are self-conscious about ecology, preserving woodlands, avoiding chemical fertilizers and pesticides. Alcohol prohibition was almost universal in the old communes, even when whiskey was manufactured and sold for cash revenue. Although some new communes took the opposite tack in fostering the use of mind-expanding drugs, there is evidence that the more serious, long-lived communes of the 1970s have placed restraints on the use of both drugs and alcohol. Educational reform was also paramount in such early settlements as Round Hill and New Harmony, and in such modern communes as Twin Oaks and Synanon.[27]

One of the more striking reform echoes in the communes involves woman's rights and the new feminism. Yet it is more germane to point out that the challenges to the traditional roles of women were part of an attack on the most fundamental of all social institutions, the nuclear family. The alternatives ranged from celibacy to free love, both of which conditions wre present in both waves. One of the metaphors for a new polity was that of household management wherein the whole settlement was considered an enlarged family unrelated by blood. Oneida was the prime example of the familial model, but all communes tended to equate family with community to some extent. Wrote Vonnegut, "I needed a family now and not just something that was a family five years ago. And I got it."[28]

In several instances women headed these extended families: Mother Ann Lee of the Shakers; Jemima Wilkinson, the Universal Friend; Frances Wright at Nashoba; and Kat Kinkade at Twin Oaks. Partly for this reason women often occupied a notably different place, yet the shift from tradition was not always smooth. Vonnegut admitted that the "traditional male-female division of labor would have made a lot more sense" but that "we stuck as closely as possible to these newfangled urban notions of equality."[29] Burdened less with traditional chores and freed from fashion's dictates, the female communard was able to escape the repugnant notion of being a male possession.[30]

The redefinition of family took place against a background of politico-economic experimentation which invariably attacked at least some aspect of the system based on private property and competition. The primary attack took the form of simplifying life from a materialistic viewpoint and—self-consciously in the New Wave—resisting anything that smacked of consumerism.[31] In most communes the land was jointly owned and property was shared. Labor was assigned by some equitable system. Buying and selling were sometimes done through cooperative arrangements that extended beyond the boundaries of a single settlement. The degree to which socialism replaced free enterprise varied from commune to commune, but the motive for economic rearrangement was consistent. The aim was not to test and reward the abilities of the indiivdual but to create a set of conditions within which all members had a fair share of both the labor and its fruits. The rewards of labor were in freedom from the struggle for survival and time dedicated to social pleasure and to moral and intellectual improvement. These political experiments were indeed a response to the problems of society: the exploitation of labor, the unequal distribution of wealth, the value placed on competition and on material achievement. But they were more than simply protest: they were a proposed solution based on religion, socialism, or social engineering.[32]

The social impact of communitarianism is heightened by the fact that these settlements were more than a series of separate events. The Harmonists learned from their own experience, building three distinct settlements. The Owenites, who bought the site for New Harmony from the Rappites, built literally on the Harmonists' wisdom. A shuttle for visitors carried word from one settlement to another. A league of communes was formed in 1846. Perhaps even more coherence was provided by the fact that, as Nordhoff has pointed out, seventy-two of the principal nineteenth-century communes sprang from but eight fundamental societal plans. Starting with John Humphrey Noyes, the students of the movement have considered it a self-conscious network of experimental societies eager to learn from one another for the sake of survival and to communicate their experience back to the mainstream for the sake of reform.

The new communes were no less interested in keeping in touch and, because of the advantages they had in communications, they may have done a better job. Many individuals visited the new communes and circulated their impressions. Some groups were connected by religious lines as the Shakers had been in the early nineteenth century. To avoid misunderstandings and disappointments the commune leaders have been ready to classify themselves and to assist potential settlers in matching their aims with those of the commune. At one time a computerized service was available. Commune newsletters exchanged practical advice; eventually a single publication, *Communities*, absorbed several others and made itself the recognized connection. The network, as with the antebellum communes, collects experience, shares it, and passes it back to the waiting world.[33]

Most communes did not last very long. Some failed for ludicrous reasons: no one remembered to bring matches. Some were filled with eccentrics or troublemakers. Many were nothing more than hedonistic, anarchic life rafts. Others, in urban settings, remind one of nothing so much as an old-fashioned boarding house without the proprietor.[34] Beyond all these half-way communes and pure retreats there is a core of solid, lasting experimentation. There was and is something both impressive and unsettling in the picture of these communitarians as Nordhoff, Kinkade, and Vonnegut allow one to see them: living their smiling, generous lives; laboring not overly hard and often with joy; feeling close kinship without the aid of blood or statute; freed from many of the anxieties of conventional society while eschewing some of its most fundamental attitudes and institutions. Neither inspiration, nor cooperation, nor social engineering may yet have produced a microcosmic model capable of transforming the national polity; but the movement has laid some worthy evidence on the table. When the crops are in and the sun is shining; when the communal family has shelved its gripes and shared its achievements—at such times the alternative experience may indeed be transcendental whether in the 1850s:

As to the people of the community in general I have a strong respect for them as earnest, unselfish, hard-working livers in the faith of a higher life for man here below as well as hereafter "above." I think they are living devoutly and more in accordance with the principles of Christ *among themselves* than any neighborhood of an equal number that I know of.

or the 1960s:

It was really Eden, there was no other way to describe it. Our crazy gamble had paid off. . . . In a way I almost wished it had been harder. I wouldn't have minded putting in ten or fifteen really bitchy hard years to feel this good. I had fully expected to and it would have been nice to feel that I had really earned it. But it felt so good that earned, begged, or stolen didn't really matter much.[35]

Literary Utopias

The same general urge that produced settlements in the wilderness also produced written versions of the ideal community. Each tradition has its ancient roots. Whereas some of the communes were modeled on a literal reading of the New Testament, utopias have their secular roots in Plato's *Republic*. Over the centuries the two traditions have existed side by side and have affected one another. Some of the utopias are written as though they describe actual settlements, and some of the communes sought to practice ideas described in the literary utopias. In the United States the two movements also have distinct traditions and characteristics. The most obvious difference is that, whereas most communes offered agricultural or village models, the literary utopias tended to accept cities and technology and to redeploy them in ideal terms.

"Utopian" means, in one sense, something so impractical that it will never work. There is another variety of utopia called "cockaigne" where

. . . the little streams of alkyhol
Come trickling down the rocks . . .
There's a lake of stew and whiskey too,
And you can paddle all around in a big canoe . . .

in the Big Rock Candy Mountains.[36] The history of reform avoids the first of these meanings and excludes the second. It centers on a very explicit meaning: a literary work that describes an ideal, fictional society remote in time and/or place. There are isolated examples of this genre in most periods but in only one era did this form become a movement generating a hundred works within twenty-five years.[37]

Like the communes, utopias have a certain negative weight, implying (at the very least) disapproval of the contemporary world. Like the communes, the utopias often share current reform enthusiasms ranging from woman suffrage to fiat currency. The classic utopian romance places a visitor from the contemporary world in the midst of a fictional society which is presented to him in the form of a guided tour. This device allows the guide (author) to project the virtues of the strange new world against the background of the visitor's (reader's) picture of current problems. Sometimes the reader is given directions for getting from "here" to "there." More often the dramatic impact arises from the harsh contrast between the real and the ideal.

The simplest kind of utopia is a tract that disguises itself as fiction in order to achieve narrative impact. A good example is Frederick Upham Adams's *President John Smith, or the Story of a Peaceful Revolution.*[38] The author, a mechanical engineer, inventor of the standard electric street light and designer of a record-breaking railroad train, founded a reform journal, *The New Time*, which he edited together with Benjamin O. Flower. In his magazine he advertised this novel as "the best reform book ever written" and listed in his claque luminaries ranging from John P. Altgeld and Senator Tillman to Frances Willard and Eugene V. Debs. Adams called his work a "masterly exposition of scientific socialism." Although he admired the efficiency of the industrial trusts, he saw no hope for leadership in the self-interested policies of either business or labor. The major parties had produced no true leaders. The economy was being strangled by a metal-based currency, by wasteful and greedy middlemen, and by artificial cycles.

Into this gloomy setting enters Judge Smith, a man who "looks like a banker and writes like a labor agitator."[39] The ensuing scenes recount a familiar tale of popular will thwarted by indirect democracy and corruption. Smith, on a platform halfway between populism and progressivism, wins at the ballot box only to be defeated in the electoral college. The Republican victor, however, declines the tainted triumph; Smith assumes the presidency and ushers in an "age of government" based on the assumption that "*a true government is one which profits by the lessons of the past, governs for the people of to day, and erects no bars for the generation of to-morrow.*"[40]

If this is a utopian novel, it is because of Adams's grand view of the ages of man presaging a glorious future. The past has witnessed great ages of art, philosophy, poetry, music, and navigation. The recent past has been shaped by the machine. Now, at last, it is time for the "applied science of government" to free mankind from historic tyrannies. Like his fellow politico-economic reformers, Adams saw the problems as centrally economic and the solutions as lying essentially in the purification of democracy. Like many model builders, he had no fear of seeing society move closer to socialism. Like Jefferson, whose generation he never tired of praising, Adams saw the triumph of democracy as a process wherein no generation had the right to commit another. His vision was indeed kinetic. President John Smith was to be inaugurated in 1901 on a platform very familiar to Adams's contemporaries. But the utopia predicted in his tale would arrive only when the process revitalized by Smith had been allowed to pursue its evolutionary course.

Adams anchored his utopia on a generalized politico-economic process. Many architects of the ideal society took as their model something more particular and familiar. Thus Bradford Peck, for example, following a successful career as a retail merchant, imagined *The World a Department Store*.[41] Peck united producer and consumer in one great cooperative headquartered in buildings designed to produce both efficiency and unquestioning respect. He turned his back on the past in favor of a kind of administrative perfection that would create health, education, and purchasing power for all.

Startlingly parallel to Peck's utopia, albeit from the opposite end of the spectrum, was the ideal society designed by Thomas J. Hagerty, which Samuel Gompers liked to call "Father Hagerty's Wheel of Fortune." Like Peck, Hagerty assumed that utopia would depend on the ownership by the consumers of the means of production. Like Peck he realized that the administration of this rearranged economy would not be easy. As a friend of labor, Hagerty used the favorite metaphor of the Industrial Workers of the World (IWW): One Big Union. He shaped this union like a wheel, putting administration at the center and radiating responsibilities to departments of building, manufacture, foodstuffs, and so forth, all subdivided by occupation.[42] Father Hagerty's Wheel, while neither so original nor sophisticated as Peck's department store, shows that labor as well as business had its utopian aspects.[43]

Just as the communitarians had their religious wing, so the utopian romance shared its vogue with a near relative, the Christian social novel. Technically (because they were not set in a remote time and/or place) these works do not qualify as utopias, yet they do respond to a parallel impulse.[44] What would the world be like if it were as well run as a good department store? What would the world be like if we were all members of one big union? What would the world be like if we were all true believers in the teachings of Jesus of Nazareth?

Better known than any utopia was the prototype of the Christian social novel, Charles Sheldon's *In His Steps*.[45] Written to enliven the Sunday evening services at the Topeka Central Congregational Church, it told the story of a minister who began to doubt the sincerity of his own commitment and invited his parishoners to join him in pledging to live for one year according to the precepts of Jesus. Spiritual at its core, the work is full of social commentary. The catalyst for the story is a printer turned into a vagrant by the introduction of linotype machines. His wife has died, gasping for breath, in a foul tenement owned by a Christian. When the protagonist, the Reverend Mr. Henry Maxwell, brings his message to the slums, he hears radical political rebuttals to his religious challenge and realizes that the dispossessed have very few choices in their quest for the Savior's path.

Utopia for Sheldon, as much as for Adams, is a process:

Would it not be true, think you, that if every Christian in America did as Jesus would do, society itself, the business world, yes, the very political system under which our commercial and governmental activity is carried on, would be so changed that human suffering would be reduced to a minimum?[46]

Of those who accepted Maxwell's original challenge, most changed their lives dramatically and showed signs of staying in the path. Toward the end of the book Maxwell has a vision fraught with contradictory indications as to whether his small victories will be but temporary and local or whether there will be a national movement emanating from this core. If the great day comes, it will be a millennial experience guided by a Holy Spirit but gradual in its revelation. The utopia of Sheldon is, in fact, consistent with the social Christianity of the day: a middle ground between the idea that religion must be applied to political questions and the more traditional notion that society can be redeemed only through the salvation of the individuals who comprise it. Sheldon knows that only God grants salvation; but he also says that Jesus was a social teacher and that a candidate for salvation should express his commitment through an exercise of social conscience.[47]

Since the end of the utopian outpouring, dystopias—Aldous Huxley's *Brave New World* and George Orwell's *1984*—have enjoyed considerably more prominence than the idealized view of society. Both these English novels built on the fear that large numbers of people could be manipulated by a very small number who understood social and political control. Against this background it is remarkable that the most popular recent utopia, B. F. Skinner's *Walden Two*, has chosen to make a virtue of social engineering.[48] With Skinner, however, there is a difference that links him to Sheldon rather than Huxley. Skinner's spokesman argues that the techniques applied in his ideal community have been available for centuries. He credits not only the transcendental ideal suggested by his title, but also the ideas of Thomas Jefferson, Edward Bellamy, and John Dewey. At bottom, however, were the ideas of the New Testament:

> "If a man can succeed in 'loving his enemies' and 'taking no thought for the morrow,' he will no longer be assailed by hatred of the oppressor or rage at the loss of his freedom or possessions. . . . We are only just beginning to understand the power of love because we are just beginning to understand the weakness of force and aggression."[49]

Unlike the early religious communards who saw the millennium at hand, and unlike the Christian socialists who saw a millennium in the offing, Skinner saw utopia as the introduction of a new set of social processes, available from present knowledge, that would produce a world without the customary fears, frustrations, and limitations. It is interesting that this modern American utopian vision—based as it is on social engineering—contains a strong Christian strain.

To look at Skinner, Sheldon, Hagerty, Peck, and Adams is to appreciate that utopias had a variety of sources, viewpoints, and timetables. It is also true, however, that no genre in the history of American social literature is so completely dominated by a single work. The year 1888 saw the publication of only one utopia, Edward Bellamy's *Looking Backward.* The prior year there had been none. In 1889, however, 9 utopian romances came into print; likewise in 1890. Gradually the vogue fell off; but not until 106 novels had been printed, most directly responsive to Bellamy's work and all enjoying an interest which he had singlehandedly created.

The popularity of this form was fanned, to be sure, by the contributions of popular writers like Edward Everett Hale, political celebrities like Ignatius Donnelly, and major writers like Jack London and William Dean Howells. Still, *Looking Backward* stood alone in its eminence. Solomon Schindler, in *Young West,* did not even bother to create new characters, but simply made Bellamy's hero president and went on with the story. Isaac Roberts wrote *Looking Forward.* J. E. Higgins composed *Looking Backward in Rhyme.*[50] None of these—not even Bellamy's own sequel, *Equality*—ever came close to competing with the original.

The story is still familiar: the device of a long sleep; an awakening to a vision of the year 2000 where technology and cooperation have banished the harsh inequities so oppressive to Bellamy's contemporaries. The telling blows were struck by contrasting the two worlds. The heart of this book, if it can be got into a few words, can be found in these paragraphs from the sermon to which the time traveler Julian West listened on his first Sunday in the future:

> "It is not hard to understand the desperation with which men and women, who under other conditions would have been full of gentleness and truth, fought and tore each other in the scramble for gold, when we realize what it meant to miss it, what poverty was in that day. For the body it was hunger and thirst, torment by heat and frost, in sickness neglect, in health unremitting toil; for the moral nature it meant oppression, contempt, and the patient endurance of indignity, brutish associations from infancy, the loss of all the innocence of childhood, the grace of womanhood, the dignity of manhood; for the mind it meant the death of ignorance, the torpor of all those faculties which distinguish us from brutes, the reduction of life to a round of bodily functions.
>
> "Ah, my friends, if such a fate as this were offered you and your children as the only alternative of success in the accummulation of wealth, how long do you fancy would you be in sinking to the moral level of your ancestors?"[51]

The evil is competition; the solution is cooperation.

Bellamy had the ability to put his finger squarely on the things that concerned Americans most about their society and its apparent direction. He gave advice that was both practical and visionary. His technological foresight was uncanny. He brought more Americans closer to socialism than anyone in his day by avoiding Marxist dogma, stressing moral outrage, and advocating familiar Christian principles.[52]

If Bellamy had something of the evangelist in him, he also had a lot of the planner. It was the explicitness of Bellamy's vision that placed Ebenezer Howard, the inventor of the Garden City, in his debt; that inspired communes in the United States; and that turned Bellamy clubs into the Nationalist party, ready to apply the cures of the year 2000 to the problems of the 1890s. As recently as Lyndon Johnson's vision of the "Great Society," according to Edward Bellamy's daughter, Americans went scurrying back to their utopias for pertinent parallels.[53]

Bellamy created the vogue; he did not necessarily speak for all the members of the literary construction gangs who assembled their own models. The greater number of them tended to follow where Bellamy led, but there was some opposition and there were some questions that almost perfectly divided the group. There was near unanimity as to the condition that concerned them most: the growing inequity in the distribution of wealth linked with the failure of the political system to offer an adequate response. Excessive power and poverty were preserved and exacerbated through political corruption. The result was an unrest which demanded drastic alternatives.

The ideological sources for the new order were the Enlightenment, Christian ethics, the theory of evolution, and socialism. Utopias did not usually come, however, with one of these labels attached; rather, each writer tended to use all four sources. In terms of specific problems, these writers were troubled by the monopolistic aggregation of wealth and power; the exploitation of labor; the profiteering of the middlemen; the scarcity of capital; the corruption of the press and the bench as well as of parties and elected officials; the prevalence of slums and disease; and the lack of adequate education. One-quarter of the utopias made temperance an issue; one-third, woman's rights. Many of the specific remedies were familiar outside the utopian tradition: additional legislation, fiat currency, the organization of labor.

The differences from the mainstream become more apparent when one looks at the system as a whole. The composite utopia made order its first requisite: an order based on equality. The achievement of this order demanded a sacrifice of traditional values. The "rugged individualism" integral to the competitive system was one casualty. Furthermore, to end the "chaos" of contemporary society required some limitation on the historic freedom of choice. About half these writers thought that most traditional values could be maintained while providing the necessary order; the other half saw something much closer to cooperative socialism.

Abundance was the second priority: abundance produced by advancing technology. The payoff was to arrive in terms of leisure and material blessings. Universal good health and superior education would allow each citizen the chance for full expression. This fulfillment was not to be in competitive victories nor in the amassing of private wealth but in altruistic joy in a system that did not exact tribute from the many to garnish the achievements of the few.[54]

The Bellamy model correctly indicates that most utopias were triggered by visions of future marvels; yet it is also true that many ideal societies were inspired by the past: by primitive Christianity or by the agrarian simplicity of preindustrial times. Like the communes, the utopias were also very much a part of their contemporary setting. Arthur E. Morgan argues that William Jennings Bryan's famous "Cross of Gold" speech was but a paraphrase of *Looking Backward*, and that, via Adolph Berle, Bellamy can be identified as an important ancestor of the New Deal.[55] Charles Rooney thinks that much of the utopian platform was absorbed into progressivism, and his analysis of the specific issues supports this point. So does the chronology. Progressive politics climaxed in 1912 when four candidates vied for the most popular version of this political amalgam. Among the candidates was one (Roosevelt) who bore the Progressive label; another (Debs) was the closest thing to a home-grown socialist since Bellamy himself. In this year, as progressivism flowered and socialism almost gained respectability, the utopian romance ended its generation-long vogue. Having inspired an outcropping of backwoods settlements and a literary portrait of the ideal society, the utopian spirit moved on.

CHAPTER 6

Twentieth-Century Models

No single version of the ideal society dominated America in the early days of the present century. The utopian romance, so popular in the 1890s, was fading from view. Although there has never been a time when experimental communities did not exist, these settlements were far from the center of public attention. Yet the utopian spirit was not dead.

Reformers were finding new ways to offer alternative models. At the more practical end of the spectrum were the planners of model cities, suburbs, and regions who were by no means averse to suggesting that social melioration would result from the careful control of architecture, technology, and environment. At the more ambitious end of the spectrum were those visionaries who sought to extend the ideal community to global dimensions. Blending the real and the ideal were those futurists who saw scientific and technological innovation as a means of access to a better world. Each of these forms—at times distinctively, at times overlapping with one another—has helped carry the torch of utopian endeavor.

Science Fiction

Although it is less often directly concerned with social problems, the literary form that most closely resembles the utopian romance is science fiction. The ancestors of this genre include satire (Jonathan Swift); gothic fiction (Edgar Allan Poe); tales of the supernatural (Herman Melville, Mark Twain). Direct descent is from Jules Verne and H. G. Wells. That this kind of writing has flourished in the last two or three generations is usually attributed to the way tchnology has stimulated the storytellers.

Most science fiction is "space opera," a twin of the "horse opera" that used certain frontier conventions as a background for adventure stories offering escape from reality. This term pretty well describes the products of the 1920s, when the sci-fi pulps were established and the sales began to boom. Imaginations were stretched purely for the sake of entertainment with little attention to the direction of innovation or the test of ultimate plausibility.

Two stories published during this decade, however, countered this trend and help to illustrate the relationship between utopian and science fiction. One was by Fred Clough and opened with the awakening of a time traveler, in the year

Norman Bel Geddes' "City of 1960," shown at the 1939 New York World's Fair,
shows the links between the utopian romance, science fiction, and visionary
architecture. Prints and Photographs Division, Library of Congress.

2023, to a "golden age" achieved through advanced technology and social evolution. The greater part of the novel is spent in detailing the political structure of a world freed of man's three great enemies: religion, war, and government. Clough contrasts the inequities of wealth and power in his own day with a world where each family has a home of ultimate convenience on its own plot of ground. Almost apologetically the author inserts those few tricks—a visitor from Mars, space coupés, instant communication—that classify his work as science fiction. At heart it is a piece of political suasion based on three parts Jefferson, one part Henry George, and (unfortunately) one part Rudyard Kipling. In its most important characteristics Clough's *Golden Age* is a direct continuation of the utopian romance.[1]

A novel by Ralph Gernsback, appearing two years later in the same category, illustrates the opposite case. *Ralph 12C 41+* is narrated by an inventor who explains suspended animation, weather control, thought-wave recorders, accelerated growing sites, electric rollerskates, and other wonders.[2] That *Ralph* is sometimes thought of as social fiction is explained by Gernsback's description of his ideal (though far from egalitarian) government. Inequities are accepted (great men carry a "+" after their names, which brings automatic deference); discrimination exists (Martians are not allowed intermarriage with Terrestrials). Gernsback's enthusiasm for delineating the workings of government, however, is on the same level as Clough's aptitude for the workings of the space coupé.

Novels set in a remote time and/or place are sometimes utopias with the trimmings of advanced technology; sometimes vice versa. Sometimes there is a genuine fusion of the two genres. One such appeared during the 1930s when science fiction, perhaps reflecting the mood of that decade, abounded with tales of doom and danger. It was coauthored by Philip Wylie, who enjoyed a subsequent vogue as a harsh critic of American mores. *After Worlds Collide* imagines the destruction of the earth through a predicted planetary collision. Before impact, a number of people escaped on a space ship, landing on "Bronson Beta," a planet newly entered into the solar system, apparently uninhabited but marked by a number of jewellike domes.

On landing, the space travelers discover the remains of a recently departed civilization that had existed in a network of bubble-top cities connected by underground passages. With trepidation they begin their tour, gradually absorbing the cultural implications of this material evidence. The force of the fiction comes to depend on the supernatural impact of these abandoned spaces and objects on the refugees from earth: " 'I can give you no idea of the superlative order in which everything in it was arranged. It would be hopeless for me to try to tell you the skill with which those people combined use with beauty. Beauty and use with imaginative intelligence' "[3] Learning to translate some of the written records of this society, the travelers struggle toward the perception of a remarkable civilization built on a set of delicate balances between beauty and utility, security and mobility, privacy and collective activity. Instead of striving against one another they had learned to strive against nature. Consummate planners, they even foresaw the threat that their planet would become airless (hence the bubble cities). As the travelers from earth repeat their familiar, competitive errors, the cumulative description of the Bronson Betan society emerges as an inspirational alternative in the best utopian tradition.

There is no need to insist that science fiction is a major force for reform. It is both necessary and possible, however, to recognize the fact that, in the midst of a lot of good hearty space operas, there are some important contributions to the literature of social change. Isaac Asimov writes: "The contribution science fiction can make to society is that of accustoming its readers to the thought of the inevitability of continuing change and the necessity of directing and shaping that change rather than opposing it blindly permitting it to overwhelm us."[4] In a society where inventions have so vitally influenced social change, for better and for worse, this is hardly a negligible function. It is quite possible to argue that one way of affecting social goals is to project the accelerating rate of discovery into a future both as wild and as plausible as the imagination can make it. If this projection seems desirable, then we can strive for it; if it seems disastrous, then we can strive to avoid it. Utopia; dystopia. Science fiction offers alternative views of society both in its own special ways and in some other ways that are reminiscent of the utopian romance.

World Government

An invariable characteristic of the ideal community is pacifism. The antebellum communes, whether religious or secular, typically placed nonviolence high on the list of collective values. The modern intentional settlements, because of the negative motivation provided by the war in Southeast Asia, were even more supportive of world peace and more international in their frame of reference. The architects of literary utopias designed a peaceful world, albeit their drawing boards were not always as wide as one might expect. Some of them were bound by strong feelings of patriotism (Josiah Strong, for example), and even the ministerial Charles Sheldon entertained his vision of Christian ethics largely in national terms.[5]

At issue here are two distinct but overlapping movements: peace and world government. The first is an undeniably important aspect of what is usually called humanitarian reform. The American peace movement began, according to Merle Curti, as early as 1636.[6] It includes both religious and secular elements: the Friends, the conscientious objectors. It has a long series of prominent episodes ranging from Henry Ford's Peace Ship to Garry Davis's announcement, in 1953, that he and 750,000 others had become citizens of the world. It has involved eminent Americans, including William Ellery Channing, William Jennings Bryan, Jane Addams, and Norman Thomas. The deliberate use of nonviolent means and pacifism is closely related to what goes on in Mode III but is not contained within it. No single mode or nation circumscribes the peace movement.

Closer to fitting into the present setting is the expansion of the concept of a model community to global scope. The most prominent American example of a world government model is Clarence Streit's Federal Union. In terms of Mode III, its kinship is probably closest to a utopia like that of Frederick Upham Adams.

Frederick Upham Adams began with a single principle: majority rule. Remove the electoral college, let the people vote directly, and a competent leader will be chosen. Yet before he had finished articulating the consequences of his fictional election, Adams found himself compelled to flesh out his ideal community with a revision of corporate practices, of legal processes, and of many institutions far beyond the direct influence of popular sovereignty. At the heart of his novel, however, is the conviction that direct democracy, the essential element in America's original promise, could once more shape the nation in the image of utopia.

Similarly Clarence Streit, while a reporter covering the establishment of the League of Nations, began to argue that a parallel could be established between the sovereignty of the American federal government over the states and the sovereignty of a world government over member nations. He used, and has continued to use, the Constitution of the United States as his model, albeit amended from the experience of Canada and Switzerland. Yet this concept grew well beyond its original, simple, federalism. Today, brochures for Federal Union invite support not only to promote peace and control nuclear power, but also to strengthen individual liberties, contain inflation, stabilize currency, fight pollution, increase jobs, limit population, and provide effective energy sources. Through its several programs and publications, and over its long and interesting history, Federal Union has become one source of a well-articulated international version of the ideal community.[7]

Worldwide models like Streit's can be appreciated as an extension of a certain type of political utopia; but virtually all the forms which define Mode III represent a general momentum away from nationalism and toward a politically unified planet. Edwin Balmer and Philip Wylie projected a continuation of earthly battles on Bronson Beta, but the science-fiction future more typically shows an earth united by threats from space or advances in technology (this is true of Clough and Gernsback). Architects, engineers, and planners also push their models outward from a neighborhood to a region, to a continent. That ultimate engineer-visionary, Buckminster Fuller, reminded us that the world today is one town. The ideal community has neither boundaries nor conflicts. Yet one can no more study the dynamics and progress of peace and world government within the context of a single nation than one can applaud with a single hand.

Visionary Builders and Planners

Alternative models also take the form of plans for structures and communities: sometimes realized, often only visualized. The subject here is not urban and regional planning or urban reform. The subject is a relatively small number of individuals, some of them professionally trained, who hold in common the belief that a carefully constructed environment can substantially alter the quality of individual and collective life. The test for inclusion in Mode III is not the qualifications of the designer, the feasibility of the plan, or the success of the product. Rather, the dream must show a kinship with the experimental commune or the literary utopia. It must offer a model substantially different from the accepted, contemporary norm. It must represent a large step toward perfection.

The roots of this approach to an alternative model are in the Edens and holy cities, in Alexandria and the Acropolis. The impulse came across the Atlantic in the preservation of the village common, in plans for idyllic settlements whether in Georgia or Pennsylvania. T. Thomas and Andrew Jackson Downing represented one of its mutations, the communitarians another (see Chapter 5).

One link between the communes and the planners is in the person of the ubiquitous and seminal Frederick Law Olmsted, sometimes considered the father of planning. Just sixteen years after his enthusiastic report on the socialist commune at Red Bank, quoted in the previous chapter, Olmsted was submitting to the Riverside Improvement Company a prospectus for a new suburb outside Chicago. Over that short span Olmsted might seem to have come a long way from the young man who admired the idealism of the socialists to a businessman talking to investors about property values, drainage, commutation, and return on capital outlay. Not so.

Gently at first, and then steadily, Olmsted infuses his pitch with touches of the ideal. The natural growth and topography will be preserved he writes. Instead of a gridiron ready for extension, the street plan would be curvilinear, suited to the land and to integrity of design. Soon he is describing the broad roadway for getting to work which will have a commuter's train but also paths for strollers, for mounted riders, for carriages. Though all roads were set apart by hedges there would be breaks so that horsemen could pause and converse with the carriage riders. The roadway, in fact, becomes a landscaped promenade. These pleached avenues led to residences of variegated charms in an unfenced suburb suggestive of an informal village rather than an "enclosed and defended" retreat. The planned village was to be more than a green escape from the city, which Olmsted sometimes chose to view as defeating human dignity by its density alone. Riverside would assure, in its very design, "the harmonious association and cooperation of men in a community, and the intimate relationship and constant intercourse, and interdependence between families."[8]

Nor does Olmsted stop with the blending of sociology and design. The people who will inhabit Riverside, he concludes, are not to be "Pagans, fearing one another" but "Christians, loving one another." With these words—with the infusion of moral values into community design—Olmsted turns back the clock those sixteen years and we are visiting, once again, those cheerful, hardworking souls at the Red Bank commune who, he reported, were living "in accordance with the principles of Christ among themselves."[9] The Riverside Improvement Company meant business in dollars and cents. In its way, however, it was a logical extension of the communitarian impulse: an ideal middle-class community for an urban age.

Olmsted's Riverside, for all its communal and moral virtues, would be at best but a lonely blossom. Frank Lloyd Wright, on the other hand, was willing to take what he found best in rural and urban American and combine it into a national utopia called Broadacre City (or, sometimes, Usonia). It was not a city in the usual sense but a way of distributing population over the whole nation with only relatively small variations in density. One effect of this scheme would be to restore to all citizens the right to own their own land and to work on or near it. Wright was very close to Thomas Jefferson in preferring to envisage a nation of small farmers and artisans. He was even closer to Downing and Thomas in finding both political and cultural value in providing each family with tasteful, debt-free housing. The economic coordinate in this utopia came straight from Henry George: taxing the unearned increment in land value to run the state. To attacking capitalism Wright preferred making everyone a landowning capitalist.[10]

Although Wright was a messiah who both expected and attracted disciples, he did not use the religious vocabulary of Noyes, Olmsted, or Fuller. What are the values on which this model is based? "The principles underlying the free pattern called Broadacre City are simply those of an organic architecture."[11] Wright was a designer of the man-made environment whether the setting called for a chair, a walkway, a wall, a chamber, a mile-high building, or a continental landscape. He had the confidence to feel that these designs, if allowed to interrelate in an "organic" (his favorite word) way would provide the setting necessary for individual and social "integrity" (his second favorite word). Life meant relating to a place and being productive. Social life simply expanded this individual definition to the group. Wright's sense of political and social order was so mystical as to be barely present; but he did see society in a way that would have pleased not only Jefferson and Downing but also Walt Whitman, Ralph Waldo Emerson, and Immanuel Kant; for he was a visionary in the transcendental-romantic sense. He followed Bellamy in his easy prophecy of new technology and his willingness to plan a future around capabilities not yet in existence. He was probably—and doubtless deliberately—the most paradoxical of all those who combined plans with dreams; for he saw particulars to the last joint and elevation, land use to the last fraction of an acre, but he was also capable of blowing a cloud of shimmering, enigmatic smoke around those precise ingredients. "Broadacre City is everywhere and nowhere."[12]

Wright is one of the few Americans mentioned in general histories of what Martin Meyerson has called the design utopias.[13] In this tradition utopia is subtly defined as a projection that grows logically out of the cultural past and hovers in the future somewhere between immediate and ultimate feasibility. The true utopian is the genius and the prophet. Ulrich Conrads and Hans G. Sperlich assume that "architects and planners have always been world reformers by virtue of their very calling."[14] Their vision is at least as global as that of Karl Marx. Yet, whereas Marx used "utopian" as a term of derision, Conrads and Sperlich insist that true reform cannot take place without the kind of imagination implied by this very term. They criticize some architects for being too practical or too concerned with simple aesthetics. The planner-reformer must, in order to realize his calling, imagine forms and techniques which respond to contemporary problems by transcending contemporary capabilities.

Mode III is about reformers who are less concerned with applying specific remedies to limited problems than they are with suggesting a whole new way of being or doing. It is not necessary that the recommended model exceed demonstrated limitations; yet, as Conrads and Sperlich help one see, progress sometimes depends on being asked to do something heretofore assumed impossible. The architects of fantasy who interest them, from Leonardo da Vinci to Enrico Castiglioni, illustrate the stimulus provided by those who can break with the past in ways that offer realizable fantasies. Similarly, some of the most important aspects of Mode III—from Oneida through the Tennessee Valley Authority—moved society by their unprecedented propositions.

In the genealogy of visionary design, Paolo Soleri is Frank Lloyd Wright's American son. Although Soleri spent much of his early life in France and Italy, he was a member of Wright's Taliesen group and has been for some years practicing his art in the vicinity of Taliesen West, Wright's Arizona center. Soleri has completed very few projects, although he has designed thousands. He may leave his mark through his endless sketchbooks and through his model megastructures that tour the museums overwhelming the viewer with the eerie visual power of their huge, puzzling lucite ceremonial confections.

Soleri loves wordplay almost as much as juxtaposing forms from nature and geometry. He begins with the neologism "arcology," formed by compressing ecology with architecture. Conscious of the need to conserve natural resources long before the current energy shortage, Soleri responded by creating enormous urban shelters to be built on small parcels of land. For New Jersey, for example, his ecostructure would provide housing and workspace for one million people on only a square mile of land. The interior arrangement saved time and energy by drastically reducing distances between the places where people needed and wanted to be. The other great saving of resources depended on condensing cities and returning land wasted in urban sprawl to agriculture and to natural replenishment.

The megastructure was not simply a horizontal grid turned upward or expanded to three dimensions. Each model contained an original elaboration of cellular interrelations, organic in the double sense of resisting completion while adjusting their alignment functionally. Although Soleri speaks mainly through his shapes, he looks toward a goal which is far beyond mere beauty or efficiency or economy. No less a romantic than his mentor, and more uncompromisingly original, Soleri sees the future as offering a choice between three kinds of value emphases. He collects them under the headings of "sloth man" (regressive and wasteful), "bullion man" (rational and acquisitive), and "aesthetic man" (ultra-rational, destined, compassionate).[15] Utopia is a world dominated by the third of these types. To reach it requires arcology.

Some observers of both planning and culture like to point out an important polarization. One pole is based on the old physiocracy: the fundamental importance of land. It underlay the thinking of Jefferson and Evans, Thomas and Downing, Horace Greeley and Frank Lloyd Wright. Broadacre City might be considered a plan for the utilization of the Homestead Act. It values de-centralization and is reflected in the ideas of Ralph Borsodi and the neo-Jeffersonians. At the other pole is the equally ancient notion that equates cities with ultimate human achievement. Soleri, and sometimes Wright, work in this tradition. Speaking very generally, it has been the imagination of the visionary architects that has, through technology, promised alternative models for the urban dilemma, whereas the government has tended to follow the tradition of Downing and Evans by bringing planning to the land or rural values to the cities.[16]

Such was at least the case when the federal government began its most concentrated effort to serve society by developing new models. During the administration of Franklin D. Roosevelt the federal government sponsored ninety-nine communities, from Arthurdale, West Virginia, to Wolf Creek, Georgia. Nearly eleven thousand units were constructed at a cost of over $100 million. They ranged from industrial housing to agricultural subsistence settle-ments. Although they were by no means all "model" communities, there was not one that did not contain some serious alternative to the way things were being done, whether in terms of landscape design or the extension of homesteading and rural cooperatives.[17]

Paul Conkin calls the New Deal communities "a fascinating adventure in idealism and disillusionment." It is the idealism, clearly, that impresses one most. In a time that called for cynicism and despair, Americans could nonethe-less "dream of a better, more perfect world and could so believe in that dream that they dared set forth to realize it, unashamed of their zeal."[18] Conkin, very properly, goes back to the antebellum communitarian movement as one source for the New Deal ideas and traces the communal spirit through a number of settlements, some of which persisted until the depression itself. Had he not completed his work before the notable upsurge of new communes, Conkin might have seen something about the utopian impulse that would have overrid-den the tone of nostalgia for a lost cause. Although he did not realize it at the time, Conkin has helped us see that the urge to create a model society is unbroken. When extreme economic misfortune shuts off the private expression of this impulse, the government itself, stocked with its own idealists, takes over.

To the planners the most interesting of the New Deal communities were the "green cities": Greenbelt, Maryland; Greenhills, Ohio; and Greendale, Wisconsin. These federal experiments were traceable to the English planner Ebenezer Howard, who oversaw the construction of the first modern, completely designed, low-rise, landscaped settlements in his own country. Howard, some think, was influenced by Edward Bellamy's picture of the city of the year 2000.[19] In any case, that ubiquitous reformer William Dwight Porter Bliss was soon promoting the Garden City movement in America as an answer to a seemingly insoluble problem called the city. Little was accomplished in this direction until 1928 when the Regional Planning Council, which included some of the most imaginative planners in the United States, brought forth Radburn, New Jersey.[20]

Some of these communities are interesting for the way they solved particular problems: as, for example, the Radburn innovation of the "superblock" to separate pedestrian from vehicular traffic. But, as Conkin, David Riesman, Lewis Mumford, and Percival and Paul Goodman keep reminding us, we are also dealing with the attempt to create new social forms. The "garden" or "green" or "satellite" city was designed from the ground up and surrounded by a buffer of protection against the unplanned. Like Riverside, these communities tried to preserve a benign natural setting and to encourage a stimulating balance between familial and communal life. Houses were deliberately faced away from the streets and toward parks and forests. Community centers provided a focus for social life so stimulating in some places that a "stay-at-home week" was prescribed for the sake of equilibrium.[21] Criticized by some as the first Communist cities in America, these experiments did produce neighborhoods more insulated from outside influences, more blessed with natural and recreational amenities, and more self-consciously committed to use these facilities in the full communal sense.

The original garden city concept was an effort to start the urban process again, from the ground up, by building entire, self-sufficient towns on a modest scale. They were to be more than a sociable, well-landscaped retreat from the urban nightmare. In the last twenty years two such communities have been created within commuting range of the national capital. From a model community viewpoint, the more interesting is Columbia, Maryland, a brainchild of an investment banker who, under the corporate name of Community Research and Development, had made a fortune designing and building shopping centers. James W. Rouse found that shopping centers succeeded when they were tied to communal life. He sacrificed rental space to public space and reaped returns in a phenomenally high percentage of occupancy. Rouse observed that he had profited by serving the community's noncommercial needs; he had also positively affected the nature and pattern of local life.

When Rouse acquired 15,000 acres between Baltimore and Washington, he set out to plan a city for 110,000 people without preconceptions beyond his commitment to environmental reform. If the imaginative design of a shopping center can make a better community, then what could one not do for the nation's rising population by putting it into an environment totally designed for the communal good? Before a backhoe or bulldozer had started its engine, Rouse had assembled not only the normal grumble of architects and engineers, but also a choir of consultants expert in family life, class structure, ecology, religion, libraries, and golf. Their eventual product was a low-density, flowerlike design whose petals opened against a spacious backdrop. Columbia's planning seminars concluded that the school was the natural center of each neighborhood; parks, stores, and residences radiated from the schools. In order to interest families with wide-ranging incomes, Columbia kept the cost of housing foremost and suppressed any impulse toward startling appearance. Determined to be less a suburb and more self-sufficient in the New Town manner, Columbia has diligently recruited commercial and industrial employers.

Rouse takes his role as reformer with utmost gravity. In 1963 he delivered a paper stressing the overwhelming responsibility for planning dictated by the sheer growth in population that would take place between that year and 1980. This new population, argued Rouse, gave the chance either to duplicate the errors of the past or to start asking what a community was really for. Challenged by growth, he became as much interested in demography, sociology, and applied science as anyone who builds. But Rouse is also a moral reformer who sincerely believes it possible to improve the quality of human life by lifting the horizons of design. What should be the guide for seeking this new equation? Rouse has several answers but, in the end, finds "no test so embracing and so satisfactory as the Biblical injunction, 'thou shalt love the Lord thy God with all thy heart and with all thy soul and with all thy mind. Thou shalt love thy neighbor as thyself.' " The plan of Columbia, with its petals and pedicels, looks as organic as anything Wright or Soleri might have wished. But in his allegiance to religious precepts as a first criterion, Rouse has also aligned himself with Olmsted and Fuller and with a host of reformers in and out of the present mode.[22]

Eventually Columbia, Maryland, will either prove or disprove the notion that a community thoroughly structured in advance can bring people closer to the Golden Rule. The social ideas of the late Buckminster Fuller will be harder to test. They are so varied in range and scale that they can scarcely be contained, even within a set of concepts as unbounded as those described in this chapter. As a utopian in the vein of Frederick Upham Adams, he imagined a return to direct democracy based on the telephoned, computer-tabulated votes of all citizens on all issues. As an environmental reformer he articulated a faith that the provision of a secure, tranquil, pollution-free environment would produce a capacity in human beings that has not truly been imagined.

Fuller's central discovery, the geodesic dome, is a product of the close study of nature coupled with the logical examination of ideal structures. The plans growing out of this discovery have appealed both to visionary architects and practical contractors. His domes have been used for auditoria, exhibitions,

In contrast to the densely built visions of Norman Bel Geddes and Paolo Soleri, the New Towns hark back to the "green towns" of the New Deal. Undated promotional photo of Reston, Virginia.

military structures, and prefabricated garages. The citizen who needed housing in a Fuller world would simply telephone his order. In a few minutes a single truck bearing the nested parts arrives. In a few hours, with the aid of a helicopter, they are assembled into a "dymaxion" house—metal, completely prefabricated—ready for habitation.

This is only, however, a less-than-ideal microcosmic solution to man's compromise with his environment. Just as direct democracy is meant to do more than reform the United States, so the geodesic principle is macrocosmic as well. Fuller's imagination extends to a geodesic sphere, concentric with the planet, forming an epidermis at the altitude of the earth's highest peaks. Although he will never know whether this concept was the ultimate in the ideal, the practical, or neither, Bucky, as he was fondly called, spent his days serenely strolling along that precipice where utopia threatens to fall by its own weight. The complete reformer, Bucky never tired of promoting his macrocosmic domes, proposing world governments, and praying to that God who urges man to transcend his historic limitations.[23]

Persistence of the Utopian Spirit

The various forms comprising Mode III have roots that go deep into history and were manifested during the American colonial era. Planning was begun with the hope that the whole nation could be one model community; it continued as a function of the custody and dispersal of public land and enjoyed a rebirth with the rise of the modern city. Communitarianism, we are now forced to observe, has not been confined to one or two notable eras but has persisted throughout American history, threatening to disappear only during the years from 1930 to 1945. This was, of course, exactly the period when the federal government set up a hundred experimental communities, including one (the Tennessee Valley Authority) that affected seven contiguous states. The literary utopia is the only form within this mode that had a limited vogue (twenty-five years). Still, when one realizes that the utopian romance is very nearly duplicated in some of the religious social novels, in some kinds of science fiction, and in some models for world government, then even this short-lived form achieves a more impressive span.

It has been possible to meet the central challenge of this section by aligning the histories of those forms that respond most directly to the call for social alternatives. Each form is important on its own terms. Seen together, communes, literary utopias, science fiction, visionary plans, and charters for world government combine to provide an unbroken chronology for Mode III. There has never been a time when at least one of these expressions was not readily visible.

The utopian spirit is not only continuous but, as studies are progressively showing, its various manifestations are interrelated. Some of the new communes have deliberately drawn on the experience of the first wave. Designs and techniques used by intentional settlers have influenced architects and planners in other settings.[24] There is a genealogy of urban planning that begins with Bellamy, descends through the Garden Cities and the New Deal communities to the contemporary New Towns. It is only a matter of time before someone connects (if they have not already connected) the illustrators of science fiction with the visionary architects.

Commentators who start from perspectives as different as those of Harry Laidler and Joyce Hertzler agree that there is little ideological point in distinguishing between communes and utopias. John Humphrey Noyes, although he was well aware of the differences between individual settlements, was able to make a single pattern of them. Paul Conkin composed a number of diverse dreamers and planners into an intellectual prelude for the New Deal. Lewis Mumford, even after dividing the utopian strain into two variants and rejecting one of them, was able to establish an impressive ancestry for contemporary visionary planners. Probably Donald D. Egbert and Stow Persons and their collaborators have found a common denominator for much of Mode III in socialism, broadly defined. With the help of a score of useful studies one begins to see that there are connections, both tangible and ideological, between most important manifestations of Mode III.[25]

The connections between Mode III and the reform agenda are many. They vary from specific issues like abolition, temperance, conservation, and the single tax to broader concerns like socialism, pacifism, and the labor movement. Many have been most interesting for their original concepts of education, the role of woman, and the structure of the family. Although their relevance to reform may vary these alternative models share the assumption that a measurably better social arrangement can be achieved. The first step is usually the removal of the many kinds of waste seen as characteristic of existing societies. A better way depends on curtailed wants, a simplified style of life, shared labor, and the benign use of technology. The harvest will mature in terms of time and energy freed for further education, worship, personal, or cultural growth.

To provide these conditions, institutions must be restructured. Social classes are eliminated; women and minorities cease to be disadvantaged. The polity is arranged either for full participatory democracy or for the absolute rule of a benign governor (the two alternatives, as Rooney's study suggests, are almost evenly balanced). The new political attitudes reject nationalism and war. The new economy unites producer with consumer, restricting private property and competitive enterprise.

At a deeper level is a restructuring of values. Freedom, choice, acquisitiveness, and competitiveness are eliminated or reduced in esteem. In their place come altruism, nonviolence, cooperation, and a respect for the dignity of even the most common forms of labor. At bedrock is an idealistic goal: the harmonious relation of human beings with God and/or nature, and with one another. This goal is sometimes expressed in a formal, religious setting;

times in the mystique of returning to the land and nature; sometimes in the commitment to a secular social order, most often a variety of socialism. Whatever the goal, its shape and intensity will mark a clear departure from the mainstream.

More than by its internal consistency, Mode III is unified by its striking contrast with the other modes. Here the individual social actor can still have an obvious impact. A charismatic leader can still inspire a commune. A powerful literary imagination can produce influential utopian fiction. Sooner or later, to be sure, groups come into play: the tightly knit organization that makes up an effective settlement or the loosely connected admirers of a work of fiction. Such groups bear little resemblance to the voluntary associations which are the principal actors in social, political, and economic reform.[26] Nor does this mode, like the others, feature the steady rise of governments as social actors. Although the federal government has been involved in Mode III all along—through its control of public land, for instance—it has rarely taken an active role in creating alternative models (the 1930s furnish the exception).

The forms used prominently within the mode are small in number. There have been utopian poems and songs; communitarians have sponsored demonstrations and have used boycotts; public meetings and symbols have at times been important. But the principal instruments, as they have been described in Part Three, are the prospectus or plan, fiction, the social use and description of technology, and the model community itself. The dynamics operating in Mode III, when measured by the stages indicated in the taxonomy, are atypically simple. Although presentations of alternative models are protests by inference, they seldom offer the specific and often lurid complaints characteristic of the negative stages of Modes I and II. There is little that is explicitly negative; there is nothing random at all. When the alternative model appears (Broadacre City, *Looking Backward*) it is already in the fourth (structured positive) stage. Sometimes (Green Hills, Oneida) the model is institutionalized (stage five) before the public gets the chance to accept or reject it. Thus Mode III typically utilizes only two of the five stages common in the other modes.

This is not to say that the plans and dreams that define Mode III are necessarily rigid. In fact, long before H. G. Wells called on the new utopias to include kinetic capabilities, many of the American models had continuing change as part of their design. Oneida, for example, was the brainchild of a self-confident but not inflexible leader. Noyes's insistence on the continuous activity of committees and critiques assured a process of self-criticism, revision, and innovation. Evolutionary change also characterized Adams's utopia and Kat Kinkade's Twin Oaks.

Because movements in Mode III either rise or fall without passing through more than one or two stages, the interesting dynamic question reverts to the matter of form. Why do the visionaries present their alternatives in one form at one time and in another form at another time?

There are a few common sense answers. The availability of free or inexpensive land encourages intentional settlement. This helps explain their antebellum popularity and their putative decline later in the century. The New Wave of the 1960s was often forced to choose between remote wilderness and marginal urban neighborhoods. It also seems obvious that the essentially rural character of early America made bucolic models appropriate, whereas the rise of the industrial city led to the fictitious creation of urban utopias based on technology. Finally, it can be observed that wars, revolutions, and conscription sometimes furnish settlers for the communes. This was true, at least, of many Europeans who came to the United States in the 1840s and of many Americans who evaded the draft by joining remote settlements in the 1960s. There is no explanation as to why this kind of exodus did not occur on a similar scale during other seasons of violence.

The best correlation in Mode III is between economic conditions and communitarianism. Although prosperity does not always encourage the outpouring of new settlements, it does seem that hard times are almost universally discouraging. The data collected by Arthur Bestor support this point for the early period. Hugh Gardner was so convinced of the importance of this fact that he titled his study of modern communes *Children of Prosperity*. Although there is still much dispute about the chronology of communitarianism, everyone seems to agree that its low point coincided with the Great Depression.[27]

Lewis Mumford thought that technology was the driving force behind the utopian spirit. Unless one is willing to consider variations in the rate of scientific and technological innovation, however, this observation does not account for the movement of the utopian spirit from one form of expression to another.[28] All speculations are made doubly difficult by the fact that some of the responses are immediate (to prosperity, to the draft), whereas others are sluggish indeed. Much of antebellum communitarianism, for example, seemed to protest not so much against anything happening in the New World as against Old World abuses dating back to the Middle Ages. Beyond a few commonsense explanations and one economic correlation, the shifting forms of Mode III, like reform in general, leave no clear pattern of causation.

The assumptions underlying Mode III contrast sharply with those of other modes. In Mode III it is assumed that the status quo cannot be granted even the provisional acceptance that would tolerate remedial adjustments and gradual change. Instead, drastic change is called for: hence the alternative suggestion. By and large the dreams and plans of Mode III envisage starting over rather than getting from "here" to "there."

The explicit arguments, however, are quite familiar. There is a consistent invocation of the higher law, often exemplified by Christian ethics. The appeal to reason emerges from the logical constructions of ideal societies as they contrast with the irrational world of experience. The architects of the fantastic—whether in science fiction or in three-dimensional models—take considerable pains to connect their inspired imaginings with the laws of possibility.

When David Riesman wrote, in 1947, "A revival of the tradition of utopian thinking seems to me one of the important intellectual tasks of today," he assumed that the tradition was dead.[29] Indeed, if one looks today for a single dominant form, one finds no situation to compare with the 1840s, the 1890s, or even the 1960s. The new commune movement, unborn when Riesman wrote, begins now to fade. There is no successor to Bellamy, either in the classic utopian form or in a related genre. The only popular utopia of recent years, *Walden Two*, was considered a dystopia by an important segment of its readership. Science fiction continues to suggest both a frightening and dazzling future, including robots, clones, and cybernetics; but no powerful ideal has emerged from that canon. Movements for world government continue modestly, paralleled by a United Nations more effective than its predecessors.

Although Buckminster Fuller has enjoyed some grand successes, his efficient domes would not entrance the space traveler approaching this planet as did those glittering urban bubbles on Bronson Beta. Paolo Soleri, whose sketches and models blast the imagination, skippers a ghost ship foundering in the gentle desert breezes north of Phoenix. Wind chimes (made by the students to raise funds) strike an appropriately wistful coda for the ambitious Arcosanti, whose proposed dimensions travesty its present modest size. On many days the curious outnumber the workers as they skirt the occasional wheelbarrow drifting like an unused life raft in the lee of the stranded ark.

If we judge this mode by the health of any single form, Riesman seems to have made a correct assumption.[30] More heartening to those who regard Mode III as a vital part of the process of social change is the fact that all of the extant forms of model building seem now more closely related than they have been in the past. The new communes not only reflect earlier experiments but are less nationalistic than their antecedents. Among the successors to the nationalistic literary utopias are the world government proposals and global domes. When a Bucky Fuller evokes "the world as one town," we are entitled to see an alternative society which draws simultaneously on visionary planning, science fiction, transnational communes, and charters for world government.

The world as one town. . . . If I were mayor . . .

ENCOUNTER 5

California Meets Its Makers

To think of California in 1849 is to think of gold: hillsides pocked with diggings and speckled with hopeful prospectors, picks and rockers in hand. In the valleys erupted the boomtowns, their unpaved roads a muddy avenue to brothels, saloons, and gambling houses. Down by the bay lay that greatest of all the boomtowns, San Francisco, where building sites could be had one day for $15 and the next day brought $8,000, where wheat fluctuated between $20 and $800 a barrel, and where almost everything seemed either too scarce or too plentiful. This setting, chaotic in many respects, seems unlikely as the source of one of the more interesting, orderly, and productive American exercises in self-government.

The particular locale for this event was somewhat removed from the clamor and urgency of the gold rush. It was one of the modest little ports that dotted the Pacific coast turned sleepy by the advent of summer and the exodus of the goldseekers. Monterey is on a small bay that stands almost as a lesson in the congeniality with which water can meet the land. Sun-whitened sand gives way to pebbles and mossy rocks. Scaley, wind-twisted pines edge precipitously near the shore, catching the breakers' spray. In 1849 a few short piers accommodated the regular passage of sailing ships and the new steamers, but there was no feeling of pressing business. The lack of commercial ambition was reflected in the absence of any hotels or restaurants.

There was a military encampment presided over by the governor-general of the territory (Bennett Riley had just replaced Richard B. Mason); but the soldiers had deserted in droves following the end of the Mexican-American War and the gold strikes. Civilians, too, followed the lure, leaving fields half plowed, houses half built, and a village populated by the young and the old.

Yet, as the summer of 1849 wore on, the long warm days had their stillness interrupted by some unaccustomed bustle. Carpenters were attacking the second floor of the town's largest building, Colton Hall, converting what had been a nest of schoolrooms into an auditorium with rostrum and seats. A makeshift hotel was being arranged and places for public dining set up. A sizable party of visitors was clearly expected. Would they come?

The suspense was considerable and arose for a number of reasons. Since California had ceased to be a part of Mexico by the Treaty of Guadalupe Hidalgo, it had what can only be called an interregnum. The settlers in the Mexican parts continued to answer to the alcalde system. The immigrants from the United States were anxious to form a new polity of their own creation. The federal government offered the opinion that a de facto combination of Mexican and military government should continue until something took its place. Exactly what

156

that something should be Congress, caught in the rising agonies of the slavery controversy, was unwilling to say. A mandate to form a state or territory might create an imbalance fatal to the delicate structure of compromise that had kept the uneasy peace between the sections.

Hearing that Congress had adjourned without resolving this dilemma, General Riley issued a "Proclamation of the Governor," making provisions for interim government and calling for an election of delegates to attend a constitutional convention at Monterey on September 1. Riley's proclamation was in some ways reassuring, but it also raised a new series of questions. Would the independent residents, grown resentful of military authority, accept any proclamation issued by an army general? Would the busy farmers and the frantic prospectors halt their work long enough to vote? Would the elected delegates be willing to travel the great distances of this incipient Western giant of a state to attend a meeting where there was no true capital, no library, no printing press, and no real feeling of community on so large a geographic scale? By noon on the first of September the issue was still very much in doubt. Eleven delegates had arrived, including the three who already lived in Monterey. The eleven convened, noted the absence of a quorum and the fact that the next day was Sunday. With some news of other delegates en route, they adjourned until Monday, September 3, hoping for the best.

By noon, Monday, the suspense was ended. The uneasy Californians had realized that a call to organize from the military was far superior to no call at all. Although inconvenienced in varying degrees by the polling process, they had stopped their work, voted, and elected delegates who were willing to make the trek to Monterey, even though it was arduous for many of them. By Monday a quorum was present. Eventually a full roster of forty delegates convened. At least thirty-two of them were under forty years of age; twenty-two had been born in free states, fourteen in slave states; eight were Spanish-speaking natives of a California that was Mexican at the time of their birth.[1] Fourteen described themselves as lawyers, eleven as farmers, eight as merchants. One delegate listed his occupation as "elegant leisure." They were indeed, as the convention chaplain Samuel Willey pointed out, an extremely mixed group, most of them meeting for the first time in Monterey without established cliques or coteries. They did not register political party affiliations and, in truth, very few of them showed an attitude that could be consistently identified as Whig or Democrat according to Eastern criteria. They met assiduously, day and night, and were determined to finish their business as quickly as possible without sacrificing the best interests of the future state. "A few of the members talked a great deal . . . but it was surprising how little they influenced the votes!"[2]

Considering the difficulties and the uncertainties, the simple act of convening an elected constitutional assembly was a remarkable achievement in political democracy. But these men did more than assemble. Given the choice between organizing a territory or a state, they moved toward the more ambitious goal in spite of a clear preference of the Southern delegates for territorial status. Although one delegate proposed creating two Californias by drawing a line eastward from San Luis Obispo, most commentators have rejected Josiah Royce's theory that the attempt to create two territories was part of a conspiracy directed by the slave empire.

Having decided to make a state constitution they went to work in a thoughtfully organized manner, avoiding pitfalls experienced by prior assemblies. They accepted night sessions when necessary. They borrowed wisdom from existing documents. Before they adjourned on Saturday, October 13, 1849, they had made a constitution which achieved easy ratification and lasted for thirty years. It contained a heartening thrust toward public education, a thoughtful provision for an equitable tax structure, a remarkable section on behalf of woman's rights, and, by *unanimous* vote, a prohibition against slavery in California that was to have consequences as profound as they are familiar. In all, these delegates seemed richly to merit the words addressed to them by General Riley following their adjournment. The people were right, he said, to elect this assembly. "They have chosen a body of men upon whom our country may look with pride; you have formed a constitution worthy of California. And I have no fear for California while her people choose their representatives so wisely."[3]

Like all extended events, this convention was a mixture of harmony and friction, enlightenment and ignorance, altruism and self-interest. The friction began on the issue of state versus territorial constitution when some members of that large group who considered themselves already "citizens" by virtue of birth or residence in the United States confronted the Mexican-born Californians. In spite of the latter's assurance that they felt themselves at home in California, the migrants from the East insisted on putting the native Californians in a minority category. This segregated thinking, fortified by the language barrier, continued in force. The right of suffrage was defined, in the end, as belonging to "every white male citizen of the United States" and "every white male citizen of Mexico" who had declared for U.S. citizenship and resided in the state for six months. The curious designation of a "white Mexican" reflected not only a separation of old from new Californians but also a confused effort to legislate a prejudice against another kind of native American—the Indian.[4]

As can be inferred from the suffrage provisions, strong feelings against slavery were not to be confused with a sympathy for Afro-Americans. This situation became manifest when a large group of delegates—mostly from the mining communities—tried to prohibit freed slaves from entering the state. This measure foreshadowed the subsequent resistance to Oriental immigrants. Americans of European ancestry, it was argued, would not, could not, and should not have to labor alongside darker-complexioned workers willing to work immoderately for little gain. Slaveholders, reasoned the miners, might bring their slaves to the borders, free them under contract to dig for gold, and reap the profits. In their fear of this possibility the concerned delegates spoke out against blacks as ignorant, depraved, idle, and ungovernable.[5] Just when it seemed as though bigotry and self-interest might gain the upper hand, a delegate from San Francisco named Edward Gilbert, native of Dutchess County, New York, claimed the floor for a remarkable speech:

> The people will consider our acts in this Convention, and if they ratify them, those acts will go before the Congress of the United States; and not only there, but before the great public of the United States, and before all the nations of the world. Does any gentleman here believe, sir, that there is a man who has ever contended upon the floor of Congress for free soil and free speech, and for the universal liberty of mankind, who will sanction a Constitution that bears upon its face this darkest stigma?[6]

Gilbert knew his audience. He swayed them; the measure to prohibit blacks was defeated. Because he knew his audience, his arguments are interesting. First he argued against hypocrisy, pointing out that the rights granted in principle in this very constitution would be abrogated by this measure. His second argument was more directly logical, pointing out that a freedman, simply by his color and prior servitude, had committed no crime nor disqualified himself for residence in any way. This argument could not have been pursued too far, lest it run against the suffrage question which found nobody—Gilbert not excepted—prepared to argue for enfranchising dark-skinned people regardless of origin. Gilbert then argued that the delegates should put aside self-interest and give the well-being of the entire state their first priority. Finally, as the citation shows, he reminded his audience that the world was watching. This skillful appeal to the better nature of his fellows and to the overriding interests of the state exemplified the qualities praised by Josiah Royce. Balancing the admitted bigotry of the pioneer were certain virutes:

> When on the contrary one turns to his political skill, as it showed itself in this constitutional crisis, one has, as we are well aware, nothing but praise. In fact, the instinctive political skill shown throughout the early history is the one thing in early California affairs of which we can certainly feel quite justly proud.[7]

There is nothing surprising about these delegates from a gold-mining state opposing paper money, as they did. There is nothing surprising about antibank attitudes in any elected body at this time. It may be surprising to see a supposedly rough-and-tumble boom state prohibit lotteries and dueling, which it did. It may be even more surprising to see such a "civilized" directive as Article IX, Section 2: "The Legislature shall encourage, by all suitable means, promotion of intellectual, scientific, moral, and agricultural improvement." This section earmarked for educational use not only the public lands given the state by the federal government but also an additional 500,000 acres of state lands as well as all estates left by intestate Californians.

According to contemporary accounts, the meetings of the delegates were, if not solemn, at least sober and relentless. After more than three weeks of familiarity, however industrious, the delegates may not have been equally sober and diligent at every moment. One session that prompts this speculation took place on the night of September 27, 1849. Most of the discussion related to a proposal that eventually became Article XI, Section 14, of the constitution:

> All property, both real and personal, of the wife, owned or claimed by marriage, and that acquired afterwards by gift, devise, or descent, shall be her separate property; and laws shall be passed more clearly defining the rights of the wife, in relation as well to her separate property, as to that held in common with her husband. Laws shall also be passed providing for the registration of the wife's separate property.[8]

The discussion provoked by this proposal was at times vehement, patronizing, learned, whimsical, and misogynistic. The usually steady H. W. Halleck rose to point out that he was wed neither to the common law, the statutory law, nor to any woman. He urged the bachelors to unite in passing this measure as an inducement to the migration of wealthy single women.[9] It was not Halleck's little joke, however, that settled the argument. Underneath was the recurring concern that the constitution would reveal California as a chaotic community of irresponsible males. Here was a measure that would offer protection for a wife against a reckless husband—drunk with alcohol, gambling, or gold fever—who might easily lose his wife's as well as his own assets on some reckless venture.

The assembly in Monterey was, in its very existence, a remarkable exhibition of direct, effective democracy under trying conditions. The democracy became even more direct when the delegates agreed to move toward statehood instead of territorial status, thus inspiring the Minerva on the California state seal, sprung fully grown from the brow of Jupiter. The delegates were clearly moved to bring to California the blessings of prosperity, world approval, and a settled future. They therefore drafted a constitution which deliberately contradicted the image of the chaotic, brutal frontier settlement. They outlawed dueling and lotteries; they protected the married woman's property; they supported education magnificently. They made California a free state, regardless of the sectional consequences, and voted down a motion to exclude free blacks. They laid the groundwork for an equitable system of taxation. They turned the converted classrooms of a sleepy coastal hamlet into a workshop in progressive democracy, conducted at a decidedly unlikely time and place.

Conclusion

Traditional values, as embodied in the rural Fourth of July, were linked with protest and populism. Charles G. Bush, *Harper's Weekly*, July 6, 1867.

Inasmuch as this work aims at establishing a pattern for comprehending reform, the logical conclusion is in the continued testing of this pattern. Within these pages the structure has been exemplified by a number of extensive cases in point: the politics of money as illustrating politico-economic reform; movements on behalf of blacks, women, and civil liberties as representing reform for special groups; and a series of experimental models pulled together to establish a continuous tradition offering communal alternatives while expressing social goals.

This final section provides three ways of summarizing what has gone before. As promised in the Introduction, reform has been dissected. Chapter 7 fulfills the further promise of putting the principal parts back together, historically and analytically. Chapter 8 entertains two seemingly unrelated questions: Can the effect of social change be measured? Can reform be understood within the American value system? The answers are closely related. Only a revised appreciation of social goals and cultural values can accurately measure the quantitative and qualitative record of reform.

CHAPTER 7

Putting It Together

The new nation enjoyed, at birth, a healthy heritage of protest and reform. For this it owed some debts to the colonists who had cultivated the habit of protest against Crown, parliament, and local authority. Along with their Whig counterparts in England they had developed the telling broadside, the incendiary pamphlet, and the well-argued political essay. There was a militant press. There was a large cast of exceptionally strong individual social actors whom we now call the Founding Fathers.

This social momentum, accelerated by the act of revolution, created a climate which demanded certain political advances. The state and federal constitutions provided them: assurances of equal justice; a degree of representation unknown in Europe; and a Bill of Rights guaranteeing free expression, petition, and assembly. In both negative and positive ways the process of social change was shaped and ensured by the manner in which the first governments were institutionalized.

Those fundamental arguments which were to form the permanent basis for advocating social change had already found expression. The moral argument came over with the settlers of Massachusetts Bay and was echoed by leaders in all debates whether they personally favored the God of Calvin or of nature and humanity. The rational arguments based on the precepts of the European Enlightenment were particularly strong in the days of revolt and nation building. The test of feasibility may have come naturally to a people fresh from solving the material problems of settling a strange land. For whatever reasons, the pragmatic argument soon achieved equal prominence with appeals to the moral and rational.

Composite Narrative

The three main modes of reform were also present from the outset, although to some degree the lines between them were often blurred by the prevailing sense of millennial optimism and Enlightenment promise that tended to fuse all social questions. Even such specific issues as public credit, free land, and suffrage were often colored with the roseate hues of panacea. Although few early reformers would have seen slaves and Indians as an inevitable extension of the concept of the "commonwealthman," few limits were placed on the full expression of nationalism and perfectionism.

The distinctive agenda of Mode I took shape against the background of constitutional debate as the patrician side encountered resistance from those who wished to broaden the suffrage and make the government more directly responsive to the popular will. The more democratically inclined gradually formed themselves into the party of Jefferson and Jackson, attacking privilege and oppression as seen in monopoly (including banks), lien laws, imprisonment for debt, unreasonable hours of labor, and restricted access to public lands.

Mode II was signally fortified by a worldview that saw human beings as innately benign, imperfect only by reason of certain handicaps. If this assumption were true then the brave new world could be realized by removing those handicaps, which included ignorance, slavery, alcoholism, and brutalizing confinement. Thus a sweeping agenda of humanitarian reform soon appeared. Horace Mann led the assault on ignorance while Robert Dale Owen stressed education as the universal solvent. Dorothea Dix made real progress in the care of the insane. Temperance advocates secured state prohibition laws in several of the original states. The advocacy of woman's rights, while often subordinated to other causes, passed some important milestones. Slavery, the most pressing business of reformers who worked in the second mode, steadily became the all-consuming priority of the nation.

The dreams of those who saw America as a chance for immanent perfection often transcended any single mode. Some saw the ultimate solution in a combination of free land, cheap but effective housing, and easy credit. To own one's home on its own land in fee simple was to be assured political freedom in perpetuity. As the full-scale dream was particularized by communitarian experiments, the underlying philosophy shifted from simple economic democracy to various forms of religious and secular socialism and communism. Also tested were such particular issues as educational reform, emancipation, and woman's rights.

Yet what truly distinguished the early expressions of the utopian spirit was the sense of imminent realization. Some saw the settling of the New World as the beginning of the millennium with the day of judgment on the near horizon. Some saw in spiritualism a method of direct contact with another world that could lead promptly to earthly fulfillment. Some saw America as Zion; some found Zion in America. Many thought that isolation and freedom from persecution would soon enable them to develop a social model for the nation at large.

American society moved toward the irrepressible conflict with its reform gears engaged. Communes dotted the landscape. Although the politics of money was relatively quiet after 1846 there was a growing labor movement and a general debate over tariff, public lands, and monopoly. Economic arguments were also prominent in the slavery controversy. As emancipation came to dominate social debate, it was also teaching the nation a lesson in fomenting social change through the press, through lobbying, and through organized voluntarism. The fundamental character of the polity was at stake. Was it to be a stratified Greek democracy built on the backs of a disenfranchised class, or was it to be a fully participatory democracy of free individuals?

The impact of the Civil War on reform was as profound as it was on the general course of national history. It placed women in positions of unprecedented responsibility. It gave factory workers their first real bargaining platform. It used paper currency backed with bonds and thereby created a financial focus for farm and labor protest. It climaxed the first concentrated effort to improve the lot of a large minority of the population and showed the enormous difficulty of opposing the expansion of political democracy.

The Civil War confirmed basic assumptions made by reformers. The mainstream was to be steadily broadened. No large group was to be permanently disenfranchised. Political power would be used to improve economic equity: in this case the right of individuals to work for themselves and not for a master. The agency that confirmed the reform assumptions was the federal government in Washington, D.C., the government that raised an army to defeat secession, monitored a twelve-year reconstruction, and saw to the passage of the Fourteenth Amendment.

The Fourteenth Amendment could easily be taken as the most important single item in the history of social change. Like many such landmarks, however, it did not so much cause a change as make statutory a change that was already in the process of realization. The federal government had transformed itself from the potential tyrant against which the Bill of Rights guaranteed protection into the agent which would itself be responsible for protecting the rights of individuals and groups. The Fourteenth Amendment recognized the emergence of the federal government as the ultimate social actor. The Fourteenth Amendment institutionalized the central evolution from civil liberties to civil rights.

The inevitable wartime manpower shortage produced an improved bargaining position for labor and led to the founding of the first truly national organizations immediately after Appomattox. Although labor reform was hardly unopposed, it was an increasingly active issue. The Great Strike of 1877, the Haymarket Square riot in 1886, and the Pullman workers strike in 1894, kept the conflict in the headlines while the first modern union was enlisting its first million members. Similarly, the Greenbackers and advocates of free silver caught the limelight while farm and labor interests developed a serious economic program based on tax, tariff, the subtreasury plan, railroad regulation, and the war on monopolies. Add civil service, the favorite issue of the patrician reformer, and the sum is a Gilded Age politico-economic program whose full extent and substance has seldom been appreciated.

Women, profiting from augmented wartime opportunities and responsibilities, returned quickly to the campaign launched at Seneca Falls. With some help from the temperance movement and from the office jobs created by new communications technology, the partisans of woman's rights moved steadily and effectively throughout the waning decades of the nineteenth century until, fortified by a handful of powerful national organizations, they stood ready for the final push to suffrage and Prohibition.

For the ill and the handicapped, the criminal and the dependent, the antebellum reformers had built institutions for separating them from society and offering care and treatment. Strained by the wartime swell in their enrollment, these asylums nonetheless survived with augmented custodial responsibilities. Reformers exerted steady pressure to increase the quantity and the quality of these facilities. Although the new century brought new ideas on treatment, the maintenance and improvement of asylums remained a constant concern.

One large group subjected to a roller coaster of changing attitudes and conditions was the Afro-American. The Northern emancipators welcomed the end of slavery with tears and embraces. It was as though a lost child had returned home. With Freedmen's Bureaus and the new democracy of the Reconstruction, hopes and expectations naturally rose. In parts of the North, however, Jim Crow was showing himself to be as much Yank as Reb. And with the end of the military occupation the move toward social equality for blacks abruptly ended. *Plessy v. Ferguson* marked an era when the best hope of the black population was segregated equality.

The condition of black Americans during this period needs to be seen in context. Blacks were predominantly rural, small-town, and Southern. They were not only the victims of discrimination but part of that segment of America—the rural South and West—that was experiencing widespread depression. In spite of the heroic efforts of agrarian reformers, the attention of the nation was focused elsewhere. The great fairs in Philadelphia and Chicago showed clearly that the national fancy had been captured by the march of technology and the rise of the industrial city. So did the utopian romance wherein the simple idyllic life of the bucolic settlement was replaced by efficient cities of ultimate convenience in which machines made competition obsolete while they brought culture to every parlor. These ideal worlds were attuned to a society that prided itself on time-spanning inventions, high-rising cities, and factories smoking with productivity. While utopian authors lectured on peace and universal prosperity, they also sparked the imaginations of those who were to plan actual communities in the rapidly urbanizing world.

What unified reform activity at the end of the century was the recognized need to adjust to this new urban, industrial setting. Reformers, during the Gilded Age, struggled to work out the terms for the federal government's growing role as a social actor. The search was complicated by the fact that the issues were coming more and more to be dominated by the urban environment, the force of technological innovation, and the scope of the new commercial-industrial corporations. Thus the farmer fought the railway owners, the laborer fought the factory owners, and everyone worried about the social impact of unplanned and overcrowded cities. Whether the issue was socialism, utopianism, or temperance, the individual and associational social actor was, each in his own way, writing a part for that new federal star who must eventually steal the show.

To say that the Gilded Age has a bad name in the history of reform is to commit an understatement. Famous scandals competed for the front page: kitchen cabinets, purchased senators, greedy city bosses. The professional politician (elected or not) had replaced the patrician leader. Labor violence punctuated understandable frustrations. Progress in racial tolerance was negative. Inequality of wealth grew toward one of its peaks. In many ways the bad name was deserved.

It would be a mistake, however, to regard these years as apathetic toward social problems. As the more recent social histories have come to recognize, the age of the muckrake may have been named by Teddy Roosevelt but had begun at least a generation before. Mark Twain and Charles Dudley Warner had not only given the era its sobriquet but had contributed their own style of exposure in *The Gilded Age* in 1873. Social critics as diverse as Jacob Riis, Henry George, and John Hay had made their marks well before the turn of the century. To admit that politico-economic reform in this era was characterized more by exposure than by remedial action is not to diminish its importance.

The last years of the nineteenth century, moreover, were not without their positive contributions. Essential steps had been passed on the way to a national banking system capable of responding to public needs. The interests of farm and labor had been marshaled. Railroads had been successfully prosecuted for rate discrimination. A civil service and an antitrust bill had been passed. Henry George and Edward Bellamy had publicly argued their panaceas. The lines of battle in the politico-economic war had never been so clearly defined as they were in the national election of 1896.

If those issues seemed more clearly two-sided then than now it was partially due to the presence of a bi-polar ideological context. On one side was the familiar stress on opportunity, competition, self-help, and individual success. These values were supported by the inspirational biographies of those industrial entrepreneurs who were valid and impressive examples of the self-made man, notably Andrew Carnegie. A new work ethic, with roots in Calvinism and echoes in the Benjamin Franklin school of applied platitudes, supported this viewpoint as did the popular perception of Charles Darwin's theories of evolution and adaptation. The capstone of this philosophy was the idea of stewardship, making each individual responsible to his Maker for the use of his wealth and stressing private philanthropy as a better answer to social problems than any public program, which might blunt incentive.

The opposition to this powerful combination of new ideas and traditional values arose slowly and almost unwillingly. It arose in response to the apparent helplessness of certain classes of Americans, to the widening inequality of wealth, and to the incapacity of the nation's government to temper the consequences of unrestrained industrial and commercial competition. For precedent this side went back to the religious and Enlightenment sense of community responsibility. A new movement, the social gospel, was declaring that the church must engage itself in contemporary problems on the side of the dispossessed. The hereditary patricians called for civil service reform. Socialism, whether imported or homegrown, showed the government a new range of responsibilities toward the means of production. Darwinism was used to justify the evolution of society as a whole instead of the competiton of individuals for survival.

The clash of these two clusters of ideas—one centering on individualism and laissez-faire, the other on collective welfare and social controls—has never again been so stark as it was in the 1890s. Although the general momentum of change has favored the second of these clusters, the debate is by no means concluded. The modern terms of this debate differ notably between the three modes.

The transit from one century to another is less sharply defined in politico-economic reform than in the other modes. Although the progressive era was once depicted as springing fully grown from the brow of Liberty with the tolling of the old century's midnight bell, it is now clear that achievements in the early decades of the new century were but the climax of a movement which had begun no later than the 1860s and 1870s and in some cases well before. As the federal government began to institutionalize its concern for social and economic equity it was in fact realizing aims that had been articulated in general terms in the 1830s and 1840s and in specific terms in the 1880s and 1890s.

The Hepburn Act (1906) must be seen, in part, as a response to the farmers' war on railroad rate discrimination that began in the 1870s. The Clayton Act (1914) was one response to a battle against monopolies evident in the days of Andrew Jackson, and the Federal Reserve Act was a logical consequence of—among other things—Jackson's famous veto of the bank's recharter. Progressivism which had begun in the states returned to the state and local levels in the 1920s; in the 1930s the New Deal again placed the federal government in the direct line of legislating against special privilege while assisting the poor, the homeless, the jobless. In the history of reform the days of FDR are exceptional mainly in the seriousness of the problems confronted. Otherwise they merely institutionalized long-standing efforts to control and to regulate sources of potential inequity. In extending political democracy for the sake of economic equity the New Deal is part of a sequence that has been virtually unbroken from Anti-Federalism through food stamps.

In 1900 Mode II and Mode I were miles apart; but, as the century has progressed, the cause of special groups and the course of the mainstream have come closer together. At the turn of the century, reformers were still seeking improved separate treatment for the disadvantaged. In the first decade of the twentieth century, however, the new leadership of reform for blacks shifted the target to integral equality. The second decade saw the realization of female suffrage. For groups identifiable by place, race, religion, and national origin the timetable has varied, but the momentum has been similar. Many had been physically separated from the mainstream on reservations or in ghettos. All faced social and economic barriers. Almost every group attracted some effort to improve its segregated lot, whether it took the form of vocational training in Appalachia, settlement houses in the slums, or better roads on the Indian reservations. In all instances these reforms were gradually redirected toward efforts to facilitate complete participation in the life of the nation.

It is possible to be even more explicit when dealing with the treatment of orphans, delinquents, paupers, criminals, and the insane. Although the segregated treatment of these groups is still much in evidence, the turn of the century did reflect a shift in the direction of reform away from asylum and toward a number of devices aimed at keeping individuals closer to the mainstream or returning them to it. Although the asylum itself, as envisaged by the antebellum reformers, may have been intended as a rehabilitative device, it had too often become a place of permanent segregation characterized by scandalous conditions. Thus the new century brought a rejection of segregation as a blanket remedy and the introduction of juvenile courts, probation, halfway houses, and other devices aimed at the eventual integration of the individual into the social mainstream. Although the twentieth century has seen no absolute shrinkage in the population of orphanages and sanatoriums, it has seen the relative growth of programs aimed at "mainstreaming."

As these various groups—whether set apart by color or gender or physical handicaps—have entered the second phase of their reform cycle they have approached the agenda of the mainstream. Agencies that oversee the struggle for equal pay for women, equal housing opportunities for blacks, and access to public facilities for people in wheelchairs are all simultaneously engaged in extending the functions of a democratic society as defined by Mode I while assisting the constituency of Mode II toward full participation. Although Mode II is far from disappearing within the currents of the mainstream, it is—when compared with its constrained condition of a century ago—closer to being a part of the same social flow.

It is in the third mode—the presentation of alternative models—that the twentieth century marks the most drastic change. As the nineteenth century matured, this mode, begun as a dazzling assortment of perfectionistic plans, had stabilized into two predominant models: the commune and the utopian romance. The former was essentially an isolated experiment in a rural setting, and the latter, on the Bellamy model, was a fictitious city of the future based on technology and cooperation. Not suddenly but steadily, as the present century grew older, the impulse activating this mode fragmented and proliferated. Visionary architecture and planning, already emerging in the late nineteenth century and to some extent derived from communitarianism and utopianism, moved into the forefront of public attention. Community planning as a means of social reform received a major stimulus from public sponsorship in the 1920s, 1930s, and early 1940s. The fad of utopian fiction faded in the first decade of the century to be gradually replaced by a type of science fiction that was sometimes hard to distinguish from the utopian romance. The disillusion following the nationalistic excesses of World War I helped to expand the concept of the ideal community toward world government and pacifism. Advocates of this approach were disappointed by America's failure to join the League of Nations and, proportionately, heartened by the appearance of a United Nations in New York City following the Second World War. An older form of Mode III, the commune, was revived in the 1960s as a response to new-but-familiar stimulae.

Thus, by the third quarter of the twentieth century, Mode III had lost the linear simplicity which had led from the backwoods utopias of antebellum days to the fictional futurism of the 1880s and 1890s. Instead, the mode could be appreciated only by surveying a number of forms, most of them simultaneously in evidence: movements for peace and world government; intentional settlements; fictional demonstrations of ideal communities; visionary architecture and planning. Technology, once identified by the futurists as the universal solvent for social problems, began to draw suspicion. The reaction to wars, nuclear fission, and various forms of industrial pollution have shaped modern communes as surely as technological imagination marks the architectural fantasies. In one regard, however, current expressions of the alternative ideal are unified. The bell that tolls for thee now tolls for me. No meaningful alternative today can be limited by either geography or national boundaries. The world is one town.

To review the sequence of reform activity is to be struck by the importance of continuity. In spite of the dramatic moments, the colorful figures, and the highly accented eras, there is still more to be learned from what is evolutionary and incremental than from what is peculiar to only a single time or place. Within this continuum only two eras have achieved a level and intensity sufficient to make a lasting imprint across the entire spectrum of reform. One was the constitutional era when the institutions of representative government were created and when civil liberties were enumerated and guaranteed. These events set the ground rules for social change. The other era was that of sectional conflict which, for the student of reform, was of cardinal import for its establishment of the federal government as a prime social actor and for its decisive push in the direction of civil rights.

Comparative Traits

The foregoing paragraphs may be viewed as the consolidation of those narrative summaries that have helped define the three modes. In a parallel manner the rest of this chapter makes use of the taxonomy furnished in the Introduction to provide the structure for a comparative analysis and summary.

ACTORS

To recall the great diversity among the individual social actors who have appeared in these pages is to despair of generalization and to beware of stereotypes. This is, perhaps, the best rule. Prominent reformers have emerged from all imaginable backgrounds. They represent the varieties of racial, religious, and ethnic stock. They come in both sexes and all ages. We can list their goals, analyze their arguments, and deduce their assumptions. Yet any general theory about what motivates them, psychologically or economically, could be effortlessly refuted.

A quick look at just three actors—Eli Thayer, John Jay Chapman, and Buckminster Fuller—will serve as a reminder both of reform's extreme variety and of its American flavor. Eli Thayer, whose colonization proposal was described in Chapter 3, blended altruism with materialism in what must be a singular American manner: "Sir, it is a great mistake to suppose that a good cause can only be sustained by the lifeblood of its friends. But when a man can do a magnanimous act, when he can do a decidedly good thing, and at the same time make money by it, all his faculties are in harmony." John Jay Chapman started life with a religiosity so intense that it caused self-immolation and expulsion from college. Yet this same man rose through a series of political encounters from which he learned the system so thoroughly as to become one of the nation's most sage and cynical political analysts. Buckminster Fuller, a collateral descendant of the noted feminist and transcendentalist Margaret Fuller, attracted public notice through a series of engineering proposals considered wildly unorthodox. Fuller never lost his original evangelical character but became a recognized builder, planner, and designer, devoted to purifying democracy, encouraging world government, and transforming the utopian into the practical.[1]

More colorful than they were typical, Thayer and Fuller show what may be an American tendency to rely on planning and technology to solve social problems. All three men mixed exalted aims with clever tactics to produce what Chapman called "practical idealism." This is surely the same spirit that prompted a Peace Corps advertisement promising to bring "idealists down to earth."[2]

It is tempting to search out a handful of colorful social actors, develop a composite portrait, and offer it as a representation of the American reformer. This technique tempts disaster. Notable figures may help identify notable issues or, in the case of Thayer, Chapman, and Fuller, they may reveal something of the national character. The *last* thing they are, however, is representative.

The most extensive effort to characterize the individual social actor is Henry J. Silverman's "American Social Reformers in the Late Nineteenth and Early Twentieth Century." It is based on the Americans listed in the 1908 edition of W.D.P. Bliss's *Encyclopedia of Social Reform,* a compendium whose subjects include "political economy, political science, sociology, and statistics covering anarchism, charities, civil service, currency, land and legislation reform, penology, socialism, social purity, trade unions, woman suffrage, etc."[3]

Silverman's analysis offers a useful picture of the reformer, a picture that diverges at many points from the stereotype. In 1908 these social actors were, on the average, fifty-four years old. Silverman deduces that they began their activities rather early in life and had achieved recognition while still in their middle years. Most of this group were from the Northeastern United States both by birth and by residence. They were born of middle-class parents, as far as is known, and although they received better-than-average educations they tended to remain middle class themselves. Very few were wealthy. Their professions involved them heavily in writing and editing, teaching and lecturing, organizing and government work. Clergymen stood in a median occupational position and showed an interest in a wide range of activity from Christian socialism to temperance; educators tended to express themselves through economic issues; businessmen worked, unsurprisingly, on economic issues but also for temperance and socialism; politicans, a fairly large group, showed the narrowest range of interests, centering on labor, populism, and temperance. The careers of these actors show clearly that economic issues were by far the most prominent.[4]

This portrait will not astonish those truly familiar with reform, but it does puncture some persistent assertions. Two stereotypes of Gilded Age social fiction, for example, were the wealthy "lady bountiful" and the poor, foreign-born radical. Although social actors born in Europe were much in evidence before the Civil War, reform in Bliss's day had become the business of the natives; and there were few patricians of any stripe. As for radical views, Silverman destroys the notion that the business community was solidly behind the status quo by linking a number of entrepreneurs with socialist crusades. The clergy, alleged by many to be the paramount friends of reform, are revealed by Silverman as squarely in the middle. There is no doubt that reform labels have been used cynically and for profit, yet it is truly hard to imagine how these individuals could have used their reform interests for self-interest. Finally, this study delivers a damaging blow to those who talk about reformers as though they represented a profession. However effective, they were reformers by avocation, not for money, not for power.

The most consistently important social actor has been the association, so much so that organized voluntarism has been identified as a distinctive national trait. The more important of these collective social actors have been characterized by an extended life, a controlled set of objectives, and a competence in the techniques of achieving change. The major examples of these associations are the bread and butter of reform. They include the early workingmen's organizations in New York and Philadelphia; the antislavery and temperance societies that began mostly in New York and New England; the assemblies devoted to the solution of monetary problems, resistance to railroad inequities, and other issues that were of particular concern to the western and southern farmers; leagues devoted to consumer and urban issues, which were prominent in Chicago at the turn of the century; urban organizations that served as power brokers for the poor and the migrants; and on down to the famous twentieth-century associations that have a truly national constituency—the National Association for the Advancement of Colored People, the League of Women Voters, the American Civil Liberties Union, and many others.[5]

Of course not all voluntary associations are social actors in the reform sense. Many are narrowly professional. Some are purely recreational. Some, like labor unions and political parties, mix self-interest with meliorism. Major political parties always have mixed motives, although minor parties sometimes qualify as social actors. One test for a reform organization is that it seek to serve a group either outside or significantly larger than the organization. Like the individual, this type of social actor also stands in need of generalized study.[6]

The voluntary association is as important today as it ever was, but its nature may be changing. Some argue that the single-issue organization has lost its power through the increasingly complicated nature of the public agenda. Many issues have a tortuous history involving subtle court decisions and voluminous legislation. Others are placed beyond common ken by intricate technology. Responding to this problem are a number of multipurpose national associations. "Concerned citizens," rather than spend their efforts on a single cause—which they may or may not understand—can simply send off their checks (tax deductible) to one of these organizations and delegate their social activism to a John Gardner or a Ralph Nader. They could, if they trusted political parties, achieve a similar goal by supporting the party of their choice; however, the type of citizen attracted to these associations is exactly the type who has been dissatisfied with the major parties since at least 1856.

Part of the appeal of these flexible-agenda associations, then, is their position outside structured politics. They are, however, like the parties, centralized and are becoming institutionalized. Headquartered in New York or Washington they are in a good position to deal with the politico-economic leadership. They run the danger—as have political parties and government agencies in the past—of becoming overly identified with just those entities they are trying to reform.

A healthy climate for voluntarism produces a variety of associations arising from the grass roots and applying altruistic activism to specific issues. Instead, goes the complaint, we see a small group of centralized organizations, staffed and perhaps manipulated by a class of professional managers, accepting a blank check from the citizen and applying it where the wisdom of this new kind of institution sees fit. Finally, if one follows the evolution of an organization like Ralph Nader's, it appears as though the very impulse to organize has atrophied and that groups of students and old people must be taught voluntarism as though it were a forgotten craft.

There is, however, another way of looking at the state of voluntarism. This is a point of view which is not totally or conveniently available in print and which depends to a considerable extent on interviews and exchanges with individuals active in this field.[7] What might be called the insider's view of voluntarism proceeds as follows.

Most important reform associations were, sooner or later, run from a national office. There is an important historic dividing line in the way this centralization came about. Associations founded prior to 1920 tended to grow from local and regional chapters and to be run as federations. (The importance of local chapters

Voluntarism, as here portrayed in "The Slum Work of the Salvation Army," by G.A. Davis, remains vital in identifying and solving social problems. Frank Leslie's Illustrated Newspaper, *December 20, 1894.*

to the American Anti-Slavery Society and to the NAACP is discussed in Chapter 3). Newer groups, dating from the Vietnam era, tended to grow from a single item of nationwide concern and originated in a central office. The central office is a necessity, now more than formerly, because of dependence on funds raised through mass mailings generated by computerized information. These techniques are efficient only if they address large numbers. The fact that these associations are centrally administered does not mean that they are insensitive to the voices of their constituency in all of their regional variety. The central office aims for consensus, but only after conscientiously putting its ear to the ground. Nader's efforts to stimulate the formation of local cells on campuses and at centers for senior citizens can be taken as a positive wish to avoid excessive centralization.

Instigators of social action have discovered a responsive group of some 4 million citizens who answer their mailings with checks. This group is passive in that it would rather support with money than by marching or picketing. But these contributors are hardly passive intellectually. They are extraordinarily well read. They believe in the power of ideas. They will respond better to a ten-page letter than to a one-page letter. They will not support institutions, only issues; and they pick their issues with care.[8] In the early 1980s these issues are civil liberties for minorities; civil rights for blacks; abortion; population control; women in the labor force; nuclear nonproliferation; conservation; government accountability and effectiveness.

Voluntarism, according to this view, is not only alive but distinctly healthy. It has never been better organized. Centralization, abetted by technology, has produced efficiency. The headquarters are in effective touch with the constituency, a fact that is to some degree attested by the fiscal loyalty of a membership which has grown even more rapidly than the nation's population. Contributions have also increased. In 1980, Americans recorded $43 billion in gifts.[9] The social impact of this generosity is hard to calculate, since so much of it was given to religious organizations whose social philosophies run the gamut. Even so, there is reason to believe that voluntarism continues to serve its traditional role as a force for melioration in American society. The impact of this force is impossible to measure in a definitive way; but it shows itself in budgets, in membership roles, and in the selection of issues that relate to the fundamental choices of the society.

Many religious organizations function importantly as social actors. Not only do individual congregations continue to exemplify the force of group action as applied to specific problems, but church organizations show explicit commitments.[10] According to at least one analysis, groups with "old-fashioned" methods continue to supply the most effective examples of sustained pressure.[11]

John Gardner argues for the special need of voluntarism to deal with pluralism run rampant. Since the parts of society are complexly interrelated, he says, we cannot afford to have special interest groups—now masterful at manipulating legislatures and media—pulling public interest away from its common center.[12] A new organization plans to apply techniques resembling those of Common Cause to issues that cannot be contained within the national boundary.[13] There may or may not be a pattern in all this concern for voluntarism, but there is assuredly abundant concern.

The main purpose in designating a final category of social actor—the institution—is to force attention to the increasing parts played by governments in social change. Churches, political parties, labor, and business associations could be classified either as associations or institutions, depending on what features are stressed. Governments, however, are functionally discrete. Although governments often initiate social change, they are, at a given moment, the establishment.

It is worth emphasizing that, as a social actor, government is not limited to a single branch or level. Although legislatures have responded more directly to social debate than the other branches of government, they have not acted alone. The executive, through its agencies, has often been responsible for actions ranging from the assurance of credit, the protection of savings, and the provision of financial relief, to the control of impure food and harmful drugs. The courts were traditionally thought to be the last fortress against change; New Deal battles dramatized this relationship. But the famous "Warren Court" startled the nation by taking the initiative in civil rights for minorities in education, voting, housing, and other areas. Students of the courts argue as to whether this aggressive attitude toward change was typical; surely it was not unique.

Some distinction in social actions can be made in terms of modes. In politico-economic reform, actors tend to be defined, eventually, by their organizational settings, whereas in Mode II the powerful leaders (Carrie Nation, Malcolm X) more often seem to transcend the associational context. Mode III may be the natural home for the idiosyncratic leader; yet individuals, in this case, are firmly tied to their communes, their parables, or their visionary plans. Reform for special groups is famous for its classic voluntary altruism; politico-economic reform, on the other hand, depends on the activities of enormous organizations (national political parties, labor unions) where self-interest is an inextricable part of the pressure for social change. Shades of difference among social actors according to time, place, and issue are hard to describe, but they are real enough. These distinctions qualify all broad generalizations about social actors save possibly two: voluntary organizations have exerted a continuous and vital force; governments have steadily increased their engagement at all levels and in all branches.

FORMS

Most of the many forms employed in the process of social change are so closely associated with given issues that they are almost part of their definition. A few forms require special comment because they are controversial, because they have been abnormally prominent, or because they appear to be peculiarly related to social change in America. They are violence, muckraking, literature and the arts, and technology.

It had often been asserted that, with the notable exception of the Civil War, the process of social change in America has been essentially peaceful. The assassinations and riots of the 1960s, however, changed this perception to the point where the opposite assertion is now frequently invoked. Some recent scholarship has added to the notion that physical confrontations are not unusual in either the real or imagined America.[14]

The reform record indicates that the response to violence is not predictable. Violence in the labor movement—whether instigated by labor, ownership, or government troops—has often cost the instigator the support of the public. There are also cases where the authorities feel they cannot respond directly to a show of force but recognize, nonetheless, that demonstrations unquestionably point to problems. The militant protests against the Vietnam War offer an example. In such cases, the violence begets a delayed or indirect result. There are cases, however much the peace-loving would like to deny it, where physical action has directly and immediately affected public attitudes and governmental decisions. The riots following the assassination of Martin Luther King, Jr., are the most recent, widely accepted case in point.

James Bryce was but one of many observers who saw the militant press as a peculiarly important agent for social change in America. The history of journalism, from Peter Zenger through the Pentagon Papers, has only supported Bryce's contention. Social actors have been quick to use the press, from George Henry Evans on land reform to Jacob Riis on slum clearance and William Randolph Hearst on trust-busting. Although the press, with its sensational prose and biting cartoons, is more suited to exposing problems than to solving them, there are also examples of newspapers and periodicals supporting a given social remedy, as with the "greenback press" of the late nineteenth century. Whether or not it is uniquely American in its social role, the press has provided a prominent salient.

Even more characteristic of American culture may be the role of the creative imagination in fomenting and directing social change. A journey through the slums as conducted by Jack London is hardly the same as the report of a commission. Theodore Dwight Weld compiled a best-selling compendium of abuses taking place under slavery, yet it never sparked the fire ignited by *Uncle Tom's Cabin*. The Pure Food and Drug Act owes its life to a novel by Upton Sinclair; the civil rights movement of the 1950s and 1960s owes its momentum to a series of remarkable autobiographies by black Americans. The Federal Theater of the Works Progress Administration highlighted a tradition of using the stage as a public forum while poets from Philip Freneau to Allen Ginsberg have applied their art to social debate. Social crusaders from the antislavery movement to the Wobblies have relied heavily on verses set to music.

Many controversies have been both sharpened and deepened through their

These two views of the same subject show not only the problem of child labor but also the thin line between inspired protest and maudlin melodrama. Photograph by Jacob Riis, ca. 1890, Prints and Photographs Division, Library of Congress. Anonymous drawing, Frank Leslie's Illustrated Newspaper, *January 28, 1888.*

contact with cartoons and serious art. There is, indeed, a whole iconography of reform which includes two-and three-dimensional symbols. Photography has gone far beyond simple muckraking. Documentary and narrative films have made major social statements. Although fiction has lent itself most notably to protest, there is no form of creative art that has not been marked by profound social engagement.[15]

The least controversial assertion about forms of protest is that they have been affected by technology. We may need to be reminded that communitarians like George Rapp succeeded by pioneering community planning and prefabricated building, but we do not need to be told how the bullhorn and the portable television camera revolutionized public demonstrations. We may need to be reminded of how futuristic conveniences furnished the utopias imagined by Edward Bellamy and his followers, but we can hardly have ignored the way Franklin D. Roosevelt and John F. Kennedy built their special effectiveness through a skillful use of radio and television, respectively. Like almost everything else in America, reform is shot through with technological causes, problems, and solutions.

The reliance on technology has, since the beginning of the Republic, been an American constant. In some ways it has also functioned as a variable. As the rate of innovation increased, the American social vision leaped along with it. The camera of Mathew Brady, more than the sketches of Winslow Homer, foreshadowed the way the six o'clock TV news films would make it impossible for Americans at home to ignore the carnage of the battlefield, however distant. The Centennial featured boasts of smoking factories, endless telegraph wires, railroads hurdling rivers and tunneling mountains. Harnessing the power of nature, an inescapable theme at Philadelphia in 1876, identified a preoccupation that would lead not only to nuclear fission but to a network of dams in the valley of the Tennessee River, aimed at bringing a threatened community safely into the modern world. As recently as 1948, whistlestopping was the accepted way to inject the force of personality into a presidential campaign.[16] The televised Nixon-Kennedy debates changed all that. Technology has finally reached the point where the late Bucky Fuller could realistically suggest bringing back the town-meeting style of participatory democracy through the use of high-capacity telephone lines and high-speed computers.

For reformers, advanced technology has often provided an integral part of the ideal community. Routinely technology has been asked to solve social problems, even problems created by technology. Beginning in the 1960s, however, a large number of Americans—not just the "counterculture" but at times the U.S. Congress—began to behave as though technology *was* the problem and that the remedy lay in protecting the environment from toxic wastes as well as heedless exploitation, turning down the rate of innovation, and tuning in to the organic balances of nature.

DYNAMICS

The identification of stages in the reform process, which might seem to be one of the more obvious and therefore unproductive acts of analysis, turns out to uncover some of the more basic and important aspects of the whole subject.[17] To designate some stages as negative, for example, forces attention on movements that have escaped notice because they failed to mature. Such movements are not necesarily less important than the ones that moved closer to institutionalization. In fact, the history of American society has been skewed because of a general failure to recognize social change in any but its final stages.

Concentrating on the difference between negative and positive stages has produced even more insights. It seems never to have occurred to at least some of the prominent antislavery crusaders (Garrison being the best example) that emancipation was not the ultimate solution to the race problem. Leaders like Wendell Phillips, the Grimkés, and Theodore Weld knew, of course, that the organizational charter of the AA-SS was not mere rhetoric and that the attainment of full citizenship for former slaves would require considerably more than that joyful peal of the bells of jubilee. The focus on *anti*slavery, however, may have been at least partially responsible for that awful gap between manumission and the Niagara movement. Similarly, the diversity of positive goals among *Anti*-Federalists may be seen as delaying the emergence of an effective two-party system. Prohibition, another movement that is negative by definition, failed to seize its opportunity partly because the negative aims had no true positive counterparts.

One great general value of identifying dynamic stages is to broaden the social history of reform. This kind of graded description of change ought to discourage flat characterizations of American eras as being totally engaged or completely apathetic. The dynamic scheme helps one to appreciate the fact that all eras are reform eras and that the historian's task becomes one of identifying the issues, the forms, the actors, and the stages.

One particular value of naming dynamic stages is to distinguish between the three modes. Although there are enough exceptions within any of the proposed patterns to comfort those who believe that history will never follow any neat prototype, there are distinctive patterns which help more than any other single trait in establishing and identifying the three major areas of reform activity. The mainstream of politico-economic reform affirms the basic five-stage sequence from random to structured protest, from random to structured affirmative programs, and thence to defeat or to institutionalization.

The concept of the double cycle, with an intervening hiatus, serves to describe what is special about reform on behalf of special groups. The hypothesis, to be sure, is not all that tidy. The various groups are all on different timetables. The inevitable pause between the highest point in the first cycle and the beginning of the second cycle is unpredictably variable. There is also considerable overlapping to the extent that, in the woman movement for example, one finds both cycles in progress from the beginning with a notable shift only in their relative weight. For all these qualifications, the essential point remains. It is of considerable help in understanding Mode II to realize that almost every movement on behalf of a special group began as an effort to improve segregated conditions and ended in the pursuit of integrated equality.

Plans and dreams may go through the early stages of the cycle; if so it is a private process. The social history of Mode III begins with the positive-structured presentation of a New Town, a city of the future, or a charter for world government. It may even, if it is sponsored by an affluent source, appear with budget and building plans in hand. In any case Mode III—unique in all respects—distinguishes itself dynamically by reflecting a minimum progression. The alternative is proposed and/or constructed. It is accepted and prevails or it is rejected and abandoned. Its importance to reform, however, does not depend solely on its physical realization or longevity but on its articulation of social goals.

As a culture matures, its social dynamics become more complex. New movements build on old movements. Variations occur in ways that complicate the cycle. The second mode, save for rare instances of regression, has moved steadily toward the first mode. Time brings to all aspects of reform a growing list of causes that have attained some kind of institutionalization. Thus the student of reform must increasingly become a pathfinder through the bureaus, a registrar of watchdogs, in short, an institutional historian.

ARGUMENTS AND ASSUMPTIONS

As dynamics separate reform modes, so arguments unite them. There are some inevitable differences as one moves from issue to issue and from century to century. What is astounding, however, is the degree to which the three arguments have maintained their interrelated dominance in underwriting the debate over social change.

One might well imagine that, with the strong religious motivations for the seventeenth-century colonization of much of North America, the moral argument would dominate the early crusades. One might as readily surmise that the Enlightenment stress on science and reason would underlie the debates of the revolutionary generation. With a sense of the history of ideas, one might then look for the force of philosophical romanticism—as reflected so beautifully in American transcendentalism—to show itself in appeals that stressed the relativism inherent in an organic view of the universe.

But this just did not happen. One exercise aimed at identifying the colonial origins of reform arguments began with the plausible hypothesis that Cotton Mather might represent the moral argument; Jefferson, the rational; and Franklin, the pragmatic. In their comments on reform issues, however, all three of these alleged archetypes mixed their motivations completely: the religious

George Y. Coffin dramatized the dynamics of social change by depicting a Rip Van Winkle awakening to find his familiar tavern of spoils replaced by a faith in "public trust." Prints and Photographs Division, Library of Congress.

skeptics appeal to morality, the Calvinist urges practical good works, and the adherents to social laws use reason on behalf of an open society.[18]

All reformers, regardless of the time, place, or issue, tend to use—as had Mather, Franklin, and Jefferson—all three of the cardinal arguments. George Henry Evans, editor, friend of labor, and champion of land reform, furnishes an example from the first post-revolutionary generation as he addresses the "Cellar Diggers" in the pages of *The People's Rights*. The "cellar diggers" stand for unskilled urban labor. They have struck. Although a labor strike is logical, Evans argues that experience shows it not to be practical. The entrepreneurial class outlasts the stoppage and recovers any temporary loss by raising prices. Thus labor, Evans argues, is really striking against the poor. Reason shows, moreover, that were the laborer to claim free land to the west he would reduce the supply of workers in the urban market and thus, according to the law of supply and demand, help the unemployed digger by increasing his likelihood of employment at a better wage.

Evans's argument might well have stopped with the appeal to reason and experience. But no. The land is "God's gift to ALL." " 'THE LAND SHALL NOT BE SOLD FOR EVER,' says Moses. . . ." Peppering his appeals to economic necessity with biblical sanctions, Evans ends by pointing out that the settling of available land would remove the hard edge of competition for survival, induce altruism in place of fear, and lead the citizen to "praise his creator for the bounties that surround him."[19] Evans's use of moral strictures to buttress appeals to logic and experience makes him typical rather than exceptional among reformers.

It is not surprising to find moral suasion in the antislavery arguments, but it may be important to observe how thoroughly the great documents of this crusade combine rational and pragmatic appeal in support of the imperatives of the higher law (see Chapter 3). It may be a bit more surprising to find an economic theorist like Edward Kellogg—a man called America's Karl Marx—presenting the idea of paper currency in the rhetorical context of the Bible and advocating convertible bonds as the last stage before the millennium (see Chapter 1).

Appearing in several reform settings are social actors interested in both religious and social philosophy. Many of them also appeal to a strong sense of the practical. An early example is John Humphrey Noyes, who not only invented a distinctive brand of religious communism (the varieties of these combinations of religious principles with social beliefs were legion in the antebellum communitarian movement) but had enough sense of the practical to develop marketable products and manage a profitable corporation. A modern example is furnished by the Reverend James A. Gusweller, who set about to elevate his deteriorating Manhattan parish not by threats of damnation but by battles with landlords, housing authorities, and mortgage bankers.

The integral unity of these three cardinal reform values can be seen nowhere more clearly than in two similar book titles. One is by Adin Ballou, the architect

Comparison of Modes

	Mode I: Politico-Economic	Mode II: Special Groups	Mode III: Alternate Models
Principal actors	Large associations Government: all levels and branches	Individuals Voluntary associations Federal gov't.: all branches	Individuals Communal groups Government agencies at all levels
Characteristic forms	Speeches, tracts Campaigns, conventions Strikes, boycotts Cartoons, symbols, fiction	Speeches, autobiography Demonstrations Cartoons, symbols, music	Plans, designs Futuristic fiction Model communities Social-impact technology
Dynamics	Five-stage cycle culminating in legislative act, court decision, creation of government agency Action tends to be continuous	Same five-stage cycle as in Mode I except it is typically experienced twice: toward segregated equality then toward integrated equality Action tends to be interrupted	Two-stage sequence moving from structured positive to institutionalization or rejection
Arguments and assumptions	Arguments explicitly based on appeals to reason, morality, and practicality Implicit assumptions: the unacceptability of the status quo, the primacy of the collective good, the importance of the United States as a social experiment, and the protection of the Bill of Rights		
	Acceptance of efficacy of gradual change.	Same as Mode I	Drastic change assumed to be necessary

of the Hopedale community, and is called *Practical Christian Socialism*. The other is by Wilbur F. Crafts, prominent in the rise of the social gospel, who called his work *Practical Christian Sociology*.[20]

There are other individuals whose words and actions demonstrate the ubiquity of these three arguments in concert. Perhaps they are descendants of the pragmatic Franklin, who found religion a useful social ingredient. John Jay Chapman, cited previously for his combination of idealism and pragmatism, was not too remote from his progressive contemporaries who prided themselves on social-science objectivity but saw no inconsistency in calling for *good* men and *good* laws. And there is James Rouse, the successful mortgage banker, who plans communities by the Golden Rule, and Bucky Fuller, a physicist and engineer, who wrote

> Yes, God is a verb,
> the most active,
> connoting the vast harmonic
> reordering of the universe
> from unleashed chaos of energy.[21]

The conclusion is as unavoidable as it is antihistorical. Each of the three explicit reform arguments can be derived from a worldview that was prominent during the first two hundred years of European settlement in North America. That these appeals can be seen against strong philosophical settings helps account for their vitality. Yet their popularity with reformers did not rise and fall with the currency of their related philosophies. The most important truth is that three positive, explicit values have appeared so consistently as to put all others in the shade. Almost invariably they appear in combination, supporting one another without regard to time, place, or issue.

These explicit arguments are based on a set of assumptions that are unually implicit. Without always saying so, all reformers find the status quo unacceptable, rely on the presence of the civil liberties guaranteed in the Bill of Rights, and place the general good above the advancement of special interests. Most reformers (without regard to subject) believe in the unique importance of the United States as a social experiment and sometimes use this idea explicitly.

There is only one assumption which varies according to mode. Virtually all programs put forth in the first two modes are based on presumption of gradual, orderly change. Virtually all programs in Mode III envisage a drastic, precipitous shift from one social model to another. In spite of this sharp and notable difference, however, reformers in America share the view of social change as a continuous process. The communes and utopias may start from a fresh plan, but they do not necessarily offer a static solution. As with their fellow reformers in the economic, political, and social modes, the planners and dreamers most often visualize an ideal society built on participatory evolution.

The comparisons and contrasts between the three modes are summarized in the table on page 184. To summarize reform according to its structure is to demonstrate that the three main elements—politico-economic reform, reform on behalf of special groups, and reform through the delineation of alternative models—have enough important distinctions to set them apart and enough in common to identify them as parts of the same whole. To summarize reform chronologically is to make clear that, aside from a few tumultuous moments, the various movements have their separate histories but combine to comprise a generally continuous process of social change. To contemplate the full scope of the subject, whether chronologically or analytically, is to observe that reform has its constants, its variables, and its consistent patterns of change. To assemble the various parts of the reform picture in any manner is to make a case for an extensive and underappreciated national commitment to meliorative altruism: a better society for all citizens. By overemphasizing the distinctiveness of separate movements and eras, we have failed to appreciate the extent and cohesion of directed social change and have, consequently, undervalued this aspect of the national history and character.

CHAPTER 8

Performance and Values
The Meaning of Reform

Can reform be measured? Does the understanding of social change alter the attribution of cultural values? This chapter accumulates evidence in answer to these questions. Although the inquiries begin from totally different perspectives, they lead to strikingly similar conclusions.

Measures of Social Change

The first half of the promise of politico-economic reform is to broaden the access to democratic government and to make participation more effective. In many obvious ways this promise has been repeatedly fulfilled. Offices that once were appointive or indirectly elected are now directly subject to the popular vote. Some state and local governments have tried initiative and referendum, proportional representation and recall. The franchise has been broadened to eliminate the barriers of property, race, and sex. Primary elections have replaced party caucuses in some states. The ballot has been simplified and made secret. Voting rights are better protected at the polls. Although the purification of political democracy is uneven and incomplete, it has registered a number of achievements in statute and in practice.[1]

But has the extension and protection of the right to vote enhanced participatory democracy? Not necessarily. In fact, if one takes election records as a direct answer to this question, the answer is a clear no. As for presidential elections, the percentage of voters who exercised their franchise was distinctly higher in the days when suffrage was more limited. From 1840 through 1900 about 75 percent of the electorate cast ballots each quadrennium. With the broadening of the franchise the proportion has steadily dwindled; since 1904 the average turnout for presidential elections has been much closer to 60 percent.[2]

Nor is that all the bad news. State and local elections typically attract considerably less voter interest (nearer to 40 percent). Those who fail to vote at any level, furthermore, tend to be those who are more in need of political attention: the youngest and oldest eligible voters, females, blacks, voters of Spanish ancestry, the less well educated, the unemployed, the unskilled workers, and the propertyless. If an important reason for participating in the political process is to enhance economic equity, then it seems painfully clear that those who tend to be the economic victims are exactly the ones who fail to take advantage of political remedy.[3]

The discouraging word, however, is not necessarily the last word. Some take comfort in the raw numbers (over 92 million people voted in the presidential election of 1984). Others take comfort in the enforcement of the Voting Rights Act and the assumption that there is now sufficient access to the polls to deal with any real threat to the system. The most interesting affirmations come from those whose study of participation is not limited to voting but includes campaigning, community action, and the pursuit of special interests. Although these studies are tentative and sometimes contradictory,[4] they tend to describe an open system:

> Participation, looked at generally, does not necessarily help one social group rather than another. The general model of the sources and consequences of participation that we have presented could work in a number of ways. It could work so that lower-status citizens were more effective politically and used that political effectiveness to improve their social and economic circumstances.[5]

The system is not rigged to preserve the status quo. Although history does not necessarily reflect a process sufficiently responsive to the needs of the disadvantaged, recent changes show an increase in general participation and a particular upsurge of activity on the part of those that need help.[6] Also, comparisons with other nations show that the American citizen feels a greater obligation to vote and a greater confidence that his political participation will prove consequential.[7]

The indicators quiver with enough uncertainty so that a final judgment may rest on attitude. Is the cup of democracy half full or half empty? Voting percentages are dicouraging both for the broad citizenry and for those who need attention. On the other hand, the raw numbers go up, the comparative studies show relative success, and participation other than voting shows signs of involvement exactly where needed. It is also important to note that the situation is considered wide open. The scholars are not all sure about cause and effect. The research centers are full of political scientists industriously continuing their experiments in the laboratory of citizen behavior. In equal number the reformers press measures ranging from party rules and campaign contributions to self-government for the District of Columbia.[8]

Granted that political participation may have some self-contained satisfactions, it is also true that any political system must eventually be tested by the kind of society it governs. To reformers, especially in Mode I, the second half of the political promise is in terms of economic delivery. Has economic democracy improved?

It is only fair to begin this answer by recalling a number of long-standing and hard-fought battles that have resulted in the institutionalization of safeguards against extremes of inequity. Banks and investment houses have been regulated and minimal savings insured. Monopolies have been restrained; consumers have been protected. The government now guarantees the bargaining rights of organized labor instead of guarding only the owner's property. Wealthy corporations have paid special taxes. After some especially bitter battles, individuals have had to accept graduated income and inheritance taxes. The public coffers have been used, increasingly, to give economic aid to the seriously ill and handicapped, the old, the students, the unemployed, the homeless, and the hungry. Looking back at the days when laissez-faire was a more popular watchword and when government participation often meant subsidies to railroad builders or protective tariffs, the present composite of statutes, enforcement agencies, public interest groups, tax collectors, and court decisions makes a picture colored by the effort to avoid economic extremes.

But has this effort succeeded? By the most basic and simple of measurements, the answer is no. The distribution of wealth in the United States, measured in quintiles, is virtually the same in 1980 as it was on the eve of the Revolution.[9] Nor are these proportions very democratic. The top quintile owns about three-fourths of the wealth in private hands; the three middle quintiles own, in descending order, 16 percent, 6 percent, and 2 percent of this wealth, leaving less than 1 percent for the lowest fifth. These are, among the many measurements of economic democracy, the most harsh. The distribution of annual income, for example, has more democratic trends and proportions, as do other relevant indices. The distribution of wealth, however, is the final measurement of social performance. Therefore these grim statistics need a closer look.

To the historian the most interesting aspect of wealth distribution is that, in spite of the fact that the picture today resembles the picture at the time of the nation's founding, the pattern has been by no means constant. The colonial era appears to have been fairly stable and, especially when compared with Europe, relatively egalitarian. The increase in inequality began shortly after the Revolution, became severe during the second quarter of the nineteenth century, and climaxed in 1860. The 1860s, which included emancipation, were leveling years. Thereafter, inequality began another rise, peaking in 1914. Although World War I witnessed another short move toward equality, the 1920s saw the resumption of maldistributive tendencies culminating in 1929.

While the nation was fighting the Great Depression and World War II, it was also enjoying its most sustained move toward economic democracy, the only such movement that has not been subsequently reversed. The trend began with the crash of 1929 and continued through 1949, causing some observers to think that the key to economic democracy had somehow been discovered. If the social direction imparted by the New Deal were just maintained, they predicted, America could achieve bloodlessly what no number of proletarian uprisings had produced. Unfortunately for the partisans of equality, this trend halted by 1950. Since then the redistributive movements have been either small or contradictory.

These fluctuations fascinate all students of this subject, yet no one seems to be able to account for them. Simon Kuznets announced a very general theory to the effect that, in industrial societies, inequality would tend to rise at first and then level. In a very broad sense he has been justified, while some of his more particular points have been refuted.[10] The correlation between equality variations and what social historians have taken to be reform eras is poor indeed. Of the three apexes of inequality, two occur near the climax of alleged reform eras and one at the end of the supposedly antireform decade of the 1920s. The revised periodization argued in these pages offers no positive correlation, but at least the disjunctions are not so embarrassing.[11] To superimpose the graph of inequality of wealth on the graph of traditional reform periods is to see two wavy lines crossing in opposite directions. As presented here, the line of reform is more nearly level: a gently sloping horizon against the peaks and valleys of inequality. It may also be that extreme inequality—especially when it is flaunted, as in the days of Jacob Riis's "other half" and Thorstein Veblen's "conspicuous consumption"—becomes a stimulus to further reform.

Putting aside the unexplained fluctuations in wealth-distribution one may still ask whether or not the maintenance of a relatively stable pattern is a failure. A degree of inequality (econiomists argue about how much) was imported from Europe. Apparently, it was tempered by the frontier: cheap land and developmental opportunity. The system was then asked to absorb millions of immigrants, most of whom arrived at the lower end of the economic scale. This it did. It also absorbed a number of impoverished former slaves. Responsibility was also assumed, eventually, for an indigenous population whose material wealth was not abundant. If a system can absorb so many new citizens, mostly from the bottom of the economic ladder, and recapture a posture no worse than it exhibited at the outset, is this a defeat?

Then there is the matter of comparisions, a question marred by the apparent difficulty in obtaining reliable data from other nations. The results of existing comparisons are anything but decisive. One may, however, observe with caution that wealth distribution in the United States resembles that of other industrial states only during its seasons of extreme inequality.[12]

Wealth distribution, moreover, is not the only measure of democratic performance:

Inequality of wealth is not necessarily a major social problem per se. Poverty is. The late French philosopher Charles Peguy remarks, in his classic essay on poverty, "The duty of tearing the destitute from their destitution and the duty of distributing goods equitably are not of the same order. The first is an urgent duty, the second a duty of convenience. . . . When all men are provided with the necessities . . . what do we care about the distribution of luxury?" What indeed? Envy and emulation are the motives—and not very good ones—for the equalization of wealth. The problem of poverty goes much deeper.[13]

Very few Americans ever thought that this nation should aim for absolute equality of wealth or income. Many Americans, however, have expressed themselves on the subject of poverty. At various times poverty has been held to be dangerous, deserved, inevitable, and natural. The Bible predicted that poverty was eternal; the Christian was urged to view the poor with charity. Political philosophers thought the poor to be a potentially explosive source of revolution. Social Darwinists thought the poor were an essential by-product of natural selection and must be left to wither. Only recently has a significant portion of the population come to think that a "war to end poverty" could be anything but nonsense. Furthermore, the poor and their spokesmen have come more and more to argue that poverty is not an absolute but a relative condition. It is not enough to be minimally fed, clothed, and housed. If most people expect to have a television set, spend Saturday night at the corner tavern, and have their hair done fortnightly, then one is poor without these amenities. Attitudes have changed.[14]

Yet, however one defines poverty, it still exists. Social critics like Michael Harrington are prepared to make it a primary issue.[15] Since the poor often leave little or no record of their lives, the study of poverty raises unusual difficulties. There are, nonetheless, studies that have penetrated the subject with conclusions that are at least mildly encouraging.

Herman P. Miller shows that poverty (defined here as families earning less than $3,000 per year in 1962 dollars) has diminished from 51 percent of American families in 1929 to 30 percent in 1947 to 21 percent in 1962.[16] Although there are some well-defined pockets of poverty, the condition is not so hopeless and hereditary as was once thought. A sizable number of individuals and families move in and out of this condition each year; the chances of escaping destitution appear more palpable as longer time periods are studied.[17] In spite of what political scientists have discovered about political participation, the poor have even been organized into an effective lobby on the subject of welfare.[18]

Statements in dollars of wealth or income fail to tell the whole story when billions of public dollars furnish help in kind: housing subsidies, health care, day care, and food stamps. The concept of "transfer payments" or "transfer income" helps explain why traditional dollar measurements do not provide all the answers. It seems that, in spite of the rigidity of wealth inequality, absolute poverty has been diminished through services in kind, income leveling, and transfer payments. There is some feeling that we now know how to reduce poverty to a "tolerable" level and we know what it costs.[19] John E. Schwarz, arguing against much skepticism, documents the reduction of poverty by more than half since the Eisenhower years and the comparable relief from malnutrition and disease among the poor. Since he credits most of this to federal programs, Schwarz makes a case for the success of the government as a social actor in this crucial area.[20]

At the other end of the spectrum is wealth, a subject which has also attracted mixed feelings. In a culture that prizes self-help and material success, the rise to fortune is often applauded. The rich man is despised only if he has exploited the poor, profited from unmerited privilege, or followed such parasitical practices as speculation or usury. Extremes of wealth have been reform targets in America on the grounds that riches create all manner of undemocratic advantages from medical care and education to business and politics.

The rich do leave records; and, on the basis of these records, it appears that wealth enjoys a high degree of continuity. One of the best ways to attain wealth is to be born to it. In terms of percentages it appears to be more difficult to fall from riches than to rise from poverty. One may argue that political democracy has done its job in preventing the very rich from attaining undue political power. One may argue that poverty, not wealth, is the social problem. If, however, one finds a test of political democracy in the successful attack on accumulated and inherited fortunes, then that test may well have been failed.[21]

Perhaps the last word on economic democracy should come from Williamson and Lindert, whose timely essay "Long-Term Trends in American Wealth Inequality" has furnished a generous platform for these remarks. "American wealth inequality," they concluded, "paints a fascinating picture, one awaiting explanation."[22] With a better control over data, with categories separating inheritance and public benefits, and with other refinements and distinctions, these authors still hope that what "drives" inequality may one day be understood. As with political participation, the subject is wide open. Scholars prepare new methods for discovering the crucial connections; reformers prepare new plans for mitigating the extremes of wealth and poverty.

The success or failure of reform on behalf of special groups is at least as difficult to measure as is the politico-economic performance of the society at large. Furthermore, since most measurements must be taken group by group, it is not surprising that there are but a few sweeping generalizations that cover this mode and its complex, two-cycle progression.[23]

As with politico-economic reform, Mode II has left its substantive mark on public institutions. The Constitution was amended to correct injustices to slaves and women. The federal executive created bureaus to improve the status of freedmen, women, and Indians. Court decisions have restored property to native Americans and Japanese-Americans. As the aims shifted from improving segregated treatment to facilitating access to the mainstream, legislative acts and executive agencies came to demonstrate commitment to equality in housing, employment, education, and voting. If the standard of success were the institutionalization of social change, then Mode II would get high marks.

Have attitudinal changes matched the march of acts and amendments? To some degree of course they have (see Part 2). Attitudes toward woman's rights, while still polarized, allow many more unobstructed avenues of development than was the case a generation ago when the culture had confined females to a narrow set of roles. Similarly, as J. Milton Yinger attempts to demonstrate, being a black American today is a different experience from what it was before

1955.[24] Bigotry has not disappeared, but attitudes have moved beyond the old stereotypes. The public recognizes the appropriateness of a vast enlargement of black horizons. As one moves from group to group one finds a similar pattern with variations. Perhaps the most conclusive instance of attitudinal shift is in the public recognition of homosexuality and the accompanying move to end discrimination against this group.

In spite of institutional progress and attitudinal changes, there is still plenty of evidence that social justice has not arrived. Blacks and Hispanic Americans are still overrepresented among the poor, the conscripted, and holders of low-status jobs. Enfranchisement and voting rights legislation have been disappointing in the sense that women and minorities do not appear anywhere near their proportional strength in any phase of the political process from voting to officeholding.

For advocates of female equality the most frustrating measurement is that 59 percent which represents the proportion of a male salary that a woman can expect for comparable work. The alleviation of this inequity moves at a snail's pace. During the 1970s, for example, the number of employed female managers more than doubled, reaching 2.9 million. During this approximate period, however, the salaries rose only from 52 percent to 54 percent of those of male managers.[25] In spite of the unequal pay, women are making progress in the job market. One sign is the steady abandonment of the lowest paid traditional occupations. Between 1972 and 1978, 19 percent left household labor. The greatest gain during these years was in transport equipment operatives, where 93 percent more women became drivers of trucks, taxis, busses, and airplanes. Fifteen percent fewer women were farm laborers, but 31 percent more women were farm managers. Observable is a shift away from unskilled drudgery, from jobs for which education is almost irrelevant, to positions where skill and education are essential (professional and technical work increased 35 percent).[26]

The job market has also steadily yielded higher-status jobs to blacks, although these gains are most evident in the young and the female. This improvement is closely connected to advances in education, which have begun to show palpable results for both women and blacks. In 1950, for example, over 70 percent of the black population had completed less than one year of high school. By 1972, 46 percent had graduated from high school and 7 percent had gone on to complete college. The raw numbers are, somehow, even more impressive. In 1950 there were only 1 million black high school graduates and 176,000 college graduates; by 1972 there were 4.5 million of the former and 797,000 of the latter. Measured by the length of stay in school, the black population has made incredible gains in absolute terms and notable gains in relative terms as well, narrowing the gap between black and white performance in most categories.[27]

The bad news concerning blacks comes not so much from the marketplace, where black women have attained parity with white women in some areas, but in housing and the family. Physically, blacks are now better housed; they are more likely than ever before to have a dry place to live with indoor plumbing. But the cost has been an increase of segregation and concomitant problems in education, job integration, and the financial integrity of the inner cities. This is a heavy price. Likewise, the dissolution of the nuclear family continues. Marriages are postponed, ignored, or broken. The home that stands most in need of a two-parent family (the poor with several children) is least likely to have one. The broken homes are worse in almost every way; even more frightening than present hardship is the prospect that these self-destructive tendencies will become institutionalized. At best there has been regression; at worst is the prospect of a permanent underclass.[28]

No aspect of Mode II is as discouraging as the foregoing particulars. In fact, the general picture is not at all discouraging. Available data show general improvement in the job market: more employment, better employment, more equitable pay. As a result, group income is up in absolute terms and, in some instances, in relative terms as well. Women, blacks, and many other groups are now organized, enjoy agency protection, and are better prepared for the economic test.

The more assiduously one labors to grasp the greased marble of tangible results in Mode II, the more apparent becomes the problem. The results are mixed. In many respects, however, the situation is familiar. There is a long history of institutional change accompanied by shifts in attitude. Many of the raw numbers are favorable—employment in higher-status jobs, rising educational level, improved income. It is the relative data that raise the large negative questions: female percentage of male income; black overpresence on the rolls of poverty. There is also room to doubt that gains made in good times can be sustained in bad times, or that the quantitative rise in minority education is not compromised by the dubious quality of this education as test scores suggest. There are many questions like these. But there is also an open situation wherein scholars strive after new answers with new techniques,[29] and where reformers actively pursue an endless agenda from Head Start to affirmative action.

Even if there were a census of model communities or sales figures for utopian novels, there would not be a ready measure for Mode III. The measure of this kind of reform rests not with the number of escapes it has facilitated but in the ways it has helped society at large by identifying problems, introducing meliorative devices, and stating social goals. The contributions have been inventoried in Part 3 with considerably more detail than can be repeated here. Yet, when it comes time to measure reform, it is worth recalling how many public problems—from education and family life to waste and the exploitation of labor—were identified in the communes and utopias and how many alternatives proposed. From the austere Shaker furniture whose functional simplicity wordlessly indicted ostentation, to the nested symmetry of Fuller's dymaxion house, reformers in Mode III have offered physical emblems of a different order. One utopian novel, by itself, contained enough ideas to affect the Garden City Movement, populism, progressivism, and the New Deal.

Beyond particular problems and proposed solutions the planners and dreamers have served by creating emblems of cultural ideals. Toward this end Mode III shows a continuous history of insisting that there must be a better way to relate human beings to one another in a benign natural setting abetted by supportive technology. Beyond competition and material possessions, the planners and dreamers have reminded us, there is an unselfish world where peace reigns and where individuals can become more intellectually, creatively, and spiritually complete. However difficult to measure, this is no small contribution. Today the melioristic alternatives are present in all their forms. The visionaries are vindicated by the seriousness with which contemporary society now accepts the necessity for planning and for studying the future. Meanwhile, cooperative dwellings, arks in the desert, and New Towns founded on the Golden Rule continue to remind a mundane world that there are great horizons.

Can the effectiveness of reform be measured? There are a number of new institutions—from day-care centers to federal enforcement agencies—that were created in response to the demands of reformers. No doubt the social actors were not totally responsible; yet it is clear that reformers have had some part in changing the Constitution, zoning laws, and a number of things in between.

Raw numbers tend to show that the society is moving toward reform goals: more people vote, fewer families suffer poverty and malnutrition. descendants of former slaves achieve each year a higher level of education. Annually, more and more women enter occupations that were formerly reserved for men. When the raw numbers are translated into percentages, however, the picture becomes confused and the efficacy of reform becomes dubious. The percentage of qualified voters who acutally go to the polls is shrinking. The distribution of wealth is the same (in quintiles) as it was two hundred years ago. Too many members of minority groups are poor and ill. Although poverty has lessened, wealth and inheritance seem to pose a rigid barrier to economic democracy.

Sometimes the more subtle percentages dilute the pessimism of the crude figures. The seemingly discouraging indifference of the electorate takes on a more positive hue when compared with that of other nations or when activity other than voting is studied. Apparent pockets of unremitting poverty reveal, under study, that they are instead but transient homes for individuals who seem able to escape indigence as easily as they sometimes succumb to it. Detailed studies of certain groups of formerly disadvantaged citizens show that they have sometimes risen even more in self-esteem and in the esteem of the public than the hard figures might suggest.

In the end, even the quantitative assessment of reform must be subjective. There is no doubt that the nation has moved toward the stated goals of the reformers. Has it moved enough? No one can tell his neighbor how to answer this question. It is germane, however, to point out that all the main social indicators used to measure reform have been subject to fluctuations. Philosophers like Malthus, Ricardo, and Pareto who posited "iron laws" of social behavior appear to be wrong. In most cases no one knows what governs the fluctuations. This ignorance, however, is not taken as defeat but as challenge for continued study and social action. One of the most important things about social change is that it is continuous. Fixed goals have only temporary meaning.

Each section of this summary has ended with a reminder that continuity in all modes is a characteristic not only of the past but also of the present. Social change is alive and well. The time to worry about its health is when it pauses or relaxes either in apparent victory or defeat. One of the great errors is to think that reform can be measured against fixed goals:

> The quest for the Holy Grail is one of the most charming of medieval stories. Its essence is that the Grail could never be found, but that in the course of looking for it, all sorts of interesting things happened. Social justice is perhaps the modern equivalent. It is something we must continue looking for, even though we all know it can never be found.[30]

Kenneth Boulding's refreshing metaphor appears as an oasis to the traveler through the American past who has become parched and tired climbing over the barricades that have been laboriously erected in order to convince us that social change is a series of separate, self-contained episodes. If reform is so good, asks one scholar, why can't it fix society once and for all instead of having to be resurrected in each generation?[31] Yet to move one step outside the limitations of reform is to realize that "process" is a familiar concept for understanding aspects of society that relate to social change.

Talcott Parsons, in 1960, not only put "process" in the title of his book but insisted that it was an essential concept for understanding all modern societies.[32] Political scientists have found many ways to tell their readers that American government is more a series of continuous actions than a fixed structure. Gabriel Almond and Sidney Verba use the concept of cleavage, variety, and balance to make this point.[33] Kenneth A. Arrow argues that voting behavior may show a preference for a less desirable end so long as the preferred process is used to achieve it.[34] Alexander M. Bickel, although he prefers the term "continuity," writes about political change in terms of process.[35] Eugene Rostow prefers the term "consent" and assumes the life of any society is determined by its ability to align institutional with social process; Carl Auerbach, another student of the law, makes a similar and equally forceful statement.[36] Charles E. Lindblom and Bruce A. Ackerman, each in his own way, makes process a prime consideration in shaping political acts and in making creative decisions.[37]

Ralph H. Gabriel, the versatile historian, speaks of his preference for the metaphor of the *body* politic. It is the task of the system to attack disease and to improve healthful living. The resignation-impeachment of Richard Nixon shows that the process works in its negative sense. The design of alternative models has more to do with the positive sense. Many political bodies die; utopia may be a strategy for survival. Jeffrey G. Williamson and Peter H. Lindert would surely accept the first half of this metaphor. As they speculated on the strange riddle of fluctuations in wealth distribution, they thought they might be observing a system that moved to avoid extremes.[38] Alexis de Tocqueville, too, saw a process which would grow into an increasingly powerful force. Even the cataclysmic problem of slavery, he argued, would be solved peacefully if the system were allowed to mature.[39] Very few observers have, like Boulding, Gabriel, and Tocqueville, applied the idea of process explicitly to reform. Charles Sanford does:

> Reform may be defined broadly as the effort to improve existing conditions. In this sense, American reforming zeal is not confined to spasmodic social protest movements or eccentric experiments, but is characteristic of the American people generally, whatever their class or sectional interests. For some three centuries they have been enlisted in a "permanent revolution" dedicated to progress, to social and individual betterment, variously interpreted.[40]

The ultimate measurement of reform is in the continuation of this "permanent revolution."

Reform and American Values

Having taken so many Americans to the frontiers of social change and forced them to argue from the depths of their convictions, reform has created a rich and underutilized opportunity for appraising the national character. The record of reform is indeed extensive and varied as this work has implicitly demonstrated. Examples have been taken from the length and breadth of the nation; from California to Massachusetts, from Wisconsin to Georgia. All periods have been touched upon, from the constitutional era to the latest arguments over the money supply. Special care has been taken to indicate the presence of social movement at times when social historians have found none. A variety of social actors have been described: lonely individuals and large, fully structured associations. Forms of protest ranging from cartoons to novels, from public demonstrations to Supreme Court decisions, have been used to illustrate various causes. Although it is surely true that many of these issues and actors have been important beyond the confines of reform, it should also be apparent that the grand total of energy and commitment represented by these activities is staggering.

There is no way to compare the amount of energy expended on advancing social frontiers with that invested in the frontiers of technology, abundance, or unsettled land. They are all major quantities. They should all be given full consideration by anyone interpreting the national experience. The commitment to social meliorism, however, has been accorded marginal recognition at best. The composite portrait of the American begins with independence and self-reliance. Americans are taken as active, busy, hard-working people; their goals are equated with material success. Pragmatism and inventiveness are illustrated more often by a clever stove than by a workable set of social institutions. The goals and values put at the head of the list are frequently the direct antithesis of those associated with the selfless promotion of the general welfare.

The relative neglect of reform may have something to do with the unfortunate connotations of the term. People who call themselves reformers are often thought of as busybodies, killjoys, or worse:

> But you really have got an awful squad
> Of villains who richly deserve the rod.
> And among the worst, in every case,
> Are the 'special friends of the toiling race'—
> Self-dubbed reformers, selfish and lazy,
> With morals loose and intellects hazy . . ."[41]

It is easy to be cynical about reform; it is just as easy to show how efforts to improve society have fallen short of perfection. To insist on the importance of reform is to risk being regarded as hypocritical, naive, or blindly optimistic. Added to these problems of attitude is the tendency of the scholarly community to regard reform as a series of separate episodes and to neglect those large themes and connections which give this subject its aggregate importance. For whatever reasons, native and foreign observers of the American character have done little to draw attention to social meliorism and the values closely associated with it. The central works of Frederick Jackson Turner, Walter P. Webb, Karen Horney, Margaret Mead, David Riesman, and David Potter have placed little or no importance on reform. The foreign observer James Bryce, in his *American Commonwealth,* came closest to the mark by devoting large sections to public opinion and the press, then describing the way the political process responded to the popular will. Modern visitors, on the whole, have not shown Bryce's awareness, although they have been sensitive to problems of race and status.[42] Had Vernon L. Parrington lived to complete his *Main Currents of American Thought,* he might have contributed even more heavily to the understanding of continuity in service of meliorism. Merle Curti's *Growth of American Thought,* which gives primacy to the dissemination of knowledge and the pursuit of Enlightenment aims, comes closest to measuring the long sweep of social change at its full worth.

When the discussion of values is reduced to a single list, the compilation of Robin Williams is most often cited:

1. Activity/Work
2. Achievement/Success
3. Science and secular rationality
4. Efficiency

5. Practicality
6. Material comfort
7. Progress/Change
8. Moral orientation
9. Humanitarianism
10. Equality
11. Freedom
12. Democracy
13. Individualism
14. Nationalism/Patriotism
15. Racism/Group superiority
16. Conformity[43]

Although Williams's summary gives more weight than most to such qualities as "moral orientation" and "humanitarianism," it still shows the relatively low esteem accorded the process of social change and its related goals. As this list helps make clear, the revision of value-ascription in the light of the reform experience raises more than one problem. There is the case for placing nearer the top of the list—in recognition of reform's importance—some value called "altruism" or "meliorism" or "humanitarianism" or just "concern for the commonweal." There is also the case for taking more seriously the arguments used by reformers to persuade their fellow citizens. These are not, it must be stressed, arguments used only among reformers but are, in fact, designed to appeal to the broadest possible constituency and thus become, in effect, the reformers' perception of the national character. The arguments used by reformers are remarkably few in number and have been employed with a consistency that cannot be explained by the history either of the society or of its dominant ideas. This inexplicable durability itself merits a high ranking for these interdependent values: morality, reason, and practicality.

The reformer's short list of dominant American values does not correlate well, however, with the existing stress on individualism, self-reliance, equality, freedom, efficiency, materialism, progress, conformity, and the sense of special mission. Some of this lack of congruence can be explained by recognizing that there are, in any culture, different kinds of values. Values may be explicit or implicit. Some values are negative or passive as opposed to positive. Some values are static, others dynamic. Some values relate to goals, some to the way these goals are reached.

The concept of implicit and negative values helps explain the brevity of the reformer's list of stated values. Some values are implicit to a culture. It appears that virtually all citizens of the United States believe that America has a special mission among nations. Reformers make this assumption no less strongly than their compatriots; yet, perhaps because they must focus on problems rather than achievements, reformers rarely make this assumption explicit. The concept of negative values was broached in Chapter 4 in connection with civil liberties. The process of social change, as much as other aspects of public life, relies on the freedoms guaranteed in the first ten amendments. Yet, except in special circumstances, the rhetoric of reform contains few appeals to "freedom" or "equality." Only when attacked do these rights rise to the surface of the reform agenda. Important as they are, the libertarian values do not often appear in a positive, explicit way.

Process, as a value, has been identified as one of the most important aspects of reform. If this value is so important, why has it been so well hidden? One possible explanation is in the distinction between static and dynamic values. Compared with the attention devoted to stable and recurring values, there is but a small amount of literature identifying and explaining values related to change and growth. Too, there has been a questionable tendency to equate values with fixed objectives—questionable because it is unrealistic. One sociologist protests: "Values include not only objects and goals thought to be desirable but also the ways in which these objects and goals are obtained. They involve means as well as ends."[44] What appears most likely, however, is that process is typically unexpressed because it is implicit to both the subject and to the culture. Americans accept continuous change as part of their inalienable rights; reformers assume that social change is an unending process.

Values can identify both means and ends; some pertain more to one than the other. Thus, in the rather long list compiled by Williams, many items are really irrelevant to a debate between individual freedom and group welfare. Activity/ Work, Achievement/Success, Efficiency, Practicality, Progress/Change—all of these qualities can be applied to the creation of an ideal department store or an ideal union. True, "work" is sometimes considered an end in itself; so is practicality. As American values are usually construed, however, these instruments are placed in the service of technological efficiency, individual achievement, and material success. Eli Thayer and Buckminster Fuller seem unusual among reformers because they applied some of these instrumental values to the service of social meliorism. In fact these values are the property of neither side of the equation.

The subject of values is complex, and properly so. At the risk of oversimplification, however, it is useful to summarize the impact of the reform experience on this subject in a table. This is not the last word on values; it does not emerge from a study of values. It is only meant to show how the current perception of this subject might usefully be altered by the evidence emerging from the study of social change.

The table helps dramatize a number of things, not the least of which is the presence of opposing values which have provided both conflict and equilibrium.[45] Three paired values have been importantly conditioned by reform. They are: individualism versus democracy, pluralism versus social justice, and morality versus process.

The first of these conflicts was identified by Tocqueville and given lyric expression by Walt Whitman. It is the major theme of *Leaves of Grass* as well as

Reform and American Values

	Reform	Consensus

Explicit long-term positive values	The common good
	Altruism
	Higher moral law
	Reason and experi-
	  ence as applied
	  to social behavior
		Individualism
		Self-reliance
		Competition
		Material abundance

Instrumental values	Activity/Work Achievement/Success Efficiency Practicality Progress/Change Education Science/Technology	
Passive/negative values	Civil liberties	
Implicit values	Special mission of the United States Process as a means and an end	

NOTE: Among explicit long-term positive values, those on the right are most commonly given prominence; those on the left come from reform literature. Both sides believe in religion and morality, but reformers are much more inclined to use a higher moral law as justification for opposing temporal laws. The consensus side sees morality as personal: an aspect of individualism. Both sides believe in feasibility, but reformers believe in the existence of social laws. They assume that reason and experience will dictate adjustments of social institutions in accordance with these laws. Toward this end (compared with the consensus) they accept a greater measure of social control. The lists of instrumental, passive/negative, and implicit values are not meant to be complete. They are arranged so as to dramatize the argument in favor of applying these values equally to both sides of the reform-consensus duality.

of *Democratic Vistas,* and it is just as important and persistent as Whitman and Tocqueville said it was. It is safe to say that, after two hundred years of providing tension and balance, this basic duality will not disappear. In some ways, however, it has modulated. Laissez-faire for individuals has become laissez-faire for groups (Carl Auerbach's phrase). Civil liberties have evolved from protecting individuals against the federal government to protecting groups in class actions. Yet, as the first two parts of this work have illustrated, there has been no significant lightening of the reformer's burden of proving, repeatedly, that individual options can be preserved only at the cost of thinking first about the general welfare.

The second paradox, pluralism versus social justice, is not a logical paradox. It owes its existence to that most unfortunate metaphor "the melting pot" and to the confusion between conformity and equality. This paradox, like the first, ultimately meets outside the limits of reform; some of the confusions engendered by it are discussed in Chapter 4. The nation's population is often divided into groups based on race, sex, religion, region, physical well-being, and criteria which distinguish the advantaged from the disadvantaged. The reformer has worked to end the negative distinctiveness of these groups. All are to have full access to the political process, possess a fair share of worldly goods, and enjoy freedom from invidious discrimination. The movement to remove inequities has sometimes been confused with pressure for total assimilation.

Assimilation is by no means confined to the question of immigrants. Most of the special groups—some with North American ancestry antedating independence or even European settlement—are seen as possessing a distinctive culture. In some quarters it has been assumed that social democracy depends on the abandonment of distinctive subcultures and the merger of all Americans into the mainstream. Thus the success of reform movements in producing better treatment for disadvantaged groups has sometimes been measured by the degree to which these groups have lost their distinctiveness and been "mainstreamed" into the great American current.

Political participation and economic equity need not logically depend on conformity to social mores. But lack of logic has not prevented this apparent paradox from muddying the waters of social change. Reformers have been accused of wishing to limit the nation's rich constituent variety when they wre merely seeking better schools or jobs. The subject has been further confused by the fact that many distinctive groups have been willing to forgo some forms of material betterment in order to retain their own communities, languages, and rituals. The reformer has not been able to make a convincing statement in favor, simultaneously, of cultural pluralism and politico-economic equity. His effectiveness (see Part Two) has been both impeded and misjudged. This fate reflects a deep cultural contradiction, apparently, between the fascination with diversity, the rewards for conformity, and the demands of politico-economic equity.

The third major confrontation is but a particularization of a dilemma that has characterized Western thought with increasing obstinacy during the last century. The general problem is absolutism versus relativism. The confidence in unchanging moral precepts (which was not uniform even among the ancients) received some hard knocks as the nineteenth century progressed. The evolutionary hypotheses of Lyell, Darwin, and others gave new force to the concept of social relativism. If adaptation was the law of nature, why should not the human species be applauded for responding to evolving conditions? The behavioral sciences (especially psychology) cast doubt on the power of reason and (especially anthropology) insisted that supposed moral absolutes varied widely from culture to culture. Popular understanding of Albert Einstein's principle of relativity and of Alfred North Whitehead's theories of process further undermined the old absolutes in a way that was quite reminiscent of the impact of Darwin, Marx, and Freud. From a number of sources came strong suggestions that eternal truths were only mythical and that questions of right and wrong had only very limited meaning.

The conflicts engendered by these views are evident in many discussions of reform issues. The most important contradiction, however, is between reformers' overt insistence on judging social questions according to some higher law and their covert participation in what they recognize as a social process where relative gains constitute their best hope and where there are no definitive goals. There is no denying that these two attitudes are logically incompatible. There is no denying that they have existed side by side throughout the history of American reform.

The idea of social process, as shown above, generously preexisted the speculations of the modern relativists. It is implicit in the reliance on parliamentarianism and in the willingness to accept gradualism as an alternative to violence on even the most highly moral questions. Yet the same reformers who appealed to representation, rational debate, and temperate social remedies were often the very ones who justified their positions on the basis of a higher law emanating from a source above man and society and unyielding in its fundamental definition of good and evil. Among the many examples of this dualism that populate this study, two of the more spectacular are furnshed by Ainsworth R. Spofford and Martin Luther King (see Chapter 3).

Whitman thought that the adversarial struggles between the individual and the group would eventually be reconciled into a third, moral force. John B. Cobb, Jr., feels that the same is true of morality and process. Morality for most people, Cobb admits, lies in allegiance to truths that were revealed once and for all. Cobb, a Christian minister, identifies the true faith as "appropriate participation in the historical movement that owed its decisive impetus to Jesus but lives now in responsiveness to the living Christ within it. This movement is not bound to preserve any specifiable doctrine, even of Jesus."[46] A follower of Whitehead, Cobb has attracted attention to his "process theology," an attempt to locate religious position along the line that shifts with each new examination of the universe.

There are surely reformers who, like Cobb, see no essential contradiction between using enduring moral arguments to defend positions in a relativistic context. Some might point out, like one of Cobb's critics, that when Cobb writes of creative transformations in historic Christianity he is really using some absolute moral principles to distinguish between acceptable and unacceptable processes.[47] Most reformers, to judge from their words and deeds, prefer to rely on moral pronouncements while suppressing the realization that they work in a relativistic setting. Contradictory or not, the acceptance of process and the reliance on moral principles have enjoyed a long history of concomitant effectiveness.

This particular dichotomy leads conveniently to the ineluctable climax of any discussion of reform and values. It is exactly the same place where the discussion of reform's efficacy ended. It is a topic that has furnished a recurring theme for the entire study. It is process. The appreciation of its importance to the understanding of American culture is one of the chief dividends arising from the careful observation of reform.

Process is neither an American invention nor an American monopoly. It can be found in the writings of the ancients: subtly in Plato, less subtly in Aristotle, obviously in Heraclitus. The ideas of Thomas Hobbes were crucial in reminding his contemporaries that political philosophy is based on process.[48] Immanuel Kant made process a vital part of his original worldview. Hegel developed one world-famous application of process to politics. John B. Cobb insists that modern followers of Whitehead are only catching up with Chinese philosophers who, since before Western history, have realized the "primacy of process."[49]

If process is not uniquely American it is still fundamental to understanding this culture. Perhaps because of their own struggles against an unyielding establishment, early Americans were loathe to cast the institutions of the new nation in a manner that would resist change. Each generation of the governed, they iterated, Jefferson most notably, must make a new social contract with its governors. The principle of representation is important for institutionalizing this process of continuous adjustment. If, however, the establishment should turn its back on the flow of revisionary persuasion, then—Jefferson again—the citizen's duty becomes revolutionary. The process must not be obstructed. Among the founding Fathers were an unusual number of political thinkers who, although nurtured on the idea of reasoned social laws, were led by experience to place more stress on continuous change than was usual within Enlightenment orthodoxy.

Two nineteenth-century collections of ideas in which we recognize distinctive American philosophies—transcendentalism and pragmatism—both insist on process as an essential value. Emerson used organic models for his prose and his lessons from nature. Each dawn, he lectured, finds us in a unique position in the processes which define the universe—a place importantly different from any in the past. Emerson leaned on the dynamic precepts of Kant. His transcendental colleagues, though less explicit, shared his assumption that change and growth were the laws of life. William James followed the same general path when he assembled the ideas that became known as pragmatism, but no one put the dynamic equation more explicitly than James's intellectual heir, John Dewey, who flatly stated that the proper moral aim of society was not to reach fixed goals nor to obtain specific results but engage in a continuing process of growth and improvement. The process itself is the only legitimate moral "end." Dewey, whom some consider the most American of all formal philosophers, recognized ceaseless social melioration as an end in itself. In so doing he not only identified process as a moral value but also erased arbitrary distinctions between "means" and "ends."[50] And George Santayana, who was never completely American nor pragmatic, nonetheless recognized process as distinctively American: "Not only was America the biggest thing on earth, but it was soon going to wipe out everything else: and in the delirious, dazzling joy of that consummation, he forgot to ask what would happen afterwards. He glorified in the momentum of sheer process."[51]

Dewey, idealistically, and Santayana, with his characteristic amused detachment, were equally aware that Americans center history and philosophy on process. Evidence of this preoccupation runs the entire gamut of cultural activity. On the level of popular culture John A. Kouwenhoven points to comic strips and soap operas that go on forever, continued in succeeding installments, where ageless characters experience crises and pratfalls which never truly climax or terminate. Prototypical American novelists write tales that are more like flowing rivers than like limited constructions. Of the items that are truly American, writes Kouwenhoven, "the central quality . . . I would define as a concern with process rather than product—or, to re-use Mark Twain's words, a concern with the manner of handling experience or materials rather than with the experience and materials themselves."[52]

Process is not only important in understanding reform, it is also important in providing a method for describing it. Like other aspects of human activity reform is characterized by conflicts, by cycles, and by particular settings that do not recur. Yet more telling, in coming to appreciate this phenomenon, are the tendencies which can be traced without major disruption. Reform is a subject that develops and evolves through time. Its most crucial traits are continous. To study reform is to realize that we may have placed too much stress on what is distinctive to only a limited aspect of the total experience. To study reform is to discover the undervalued importance of treating history as a cumulative process toward aggregate experience.[53] It is no accident that both the measurement of reform's achievement and the evaluation of reform's impact on national values end with the subject of process.

A Final Word

Many remarks along the way have been aimed mainly at historians: the debate over periodization, the arguments for cumulative as opposed to cyclical interpretations of the past. There has been very little added to what specialists already know about the many nooks and knolls of reform, but there has been a continuing invitation for the specialists not only to pursue the elusive detail but also to join in an enterprise aimed at doing full justice to a vast American frontier.

The last words in a book about reform should seek a more universal ear. We should all be a little ashamed when we associate reform only with eccentrics like Horace Greeley, impractical fussbudgets like Stephen Pearl Andrews, ideological chameleons like Orestes Brownson, and naysayers like Anthony Comstock and Carrie Nation. We need to see reform as a major historical force: a force that influenced the settlement of the West, turned tenements into parks, split churches, amalgamated unions, badgered the privileged, and attended to the dispossessed. The understanding of this force provides a strong antithesis to the power of competitive, acquisitive individualism which we may have been asked to see too much in isolation. The opposite of individualism is neither mindless conformity nor philosophical collectivism but a sustained series of altruistic acts and movements designed to preserve a balance between individual liberty and the good of the commonwealth.

Reform is omnipresent; it fails as often as it succeeds. Reform is a process. It is the way an open society has achieved a balance between pluralism and social justice, between relativism and morality, between individualism and democracy. Reform is a cumulative experience based on the most fundamental of American values whose major contributions are in its continuities.

Gurley Flynn Meets the Midnight ACLU

At eight P.M., May 7, 1940, in the City Club of New York, the Board of the American Civil Liberties Union assembled for what was to be the most unusual meeting in its brief history. The air was filled with the same intense political emotions as when, only some twenty years earlier, Roger Baldwin and a few like-minded individuals had founded an organization to protect the rights of those who wished to speak out for unpopular views. In the short time since its founding, the ACLU had come to stand, more resoundingly than any comparable group, for the defense of those freedoms guaranteed in the Bill of Rights. Unpopular minorities of all sorts—religious, ethnic, political—had no better friend than the ACLU. In a number of court actions they had demonstrated that if eternal vigilance were to be the price of liberty, the ACLU would pay this price.

On the night of May 7, however, the board did not meet on behalf of a beleaguered atheist, a muzzled anarchist, or a black activist fighting a trumped-up charge of vagrancy. They met to try one of their own charter members: Elizabeth Gurley Flynn. The primary charge was membership in the Communist Party of the United States (CPUSA); the threatened sentence was expulsion from the board.

In taking on Gurley Flynn (as she was called throughout her life) the board could not be accused of picking on a meek or unknown victim.[1] From her earliest days she had shown as much assurance and love of the limelight as anyone in her generation. Born in New Hampshire of Irish parents, both socialists, she grew up with signs of industrial poverty about her. When she was ten her parents moved the family to the South Bronx, where socialist meetings continued as a normal part of family life. As a high school debater she won medals for arguing in favor of government ownership of industry. Edward Bellamy's domestic socialism further impressed her and by the age of sixteen she was photographed haranguing crowds on the streets of New York. Eventually she became one of the nation's finest speakers, adept at sharp exchange while equipped with the lilting, lyrical quality of address often associated with her Irish forebears.

Nor did her political philosophy ever waver from its initial allegiance to the cause of labor and to the discovery of an alternative to industrial capitalism. In 1906 she joined the Industrial Workers of the World.[2] During World War I she participated in the Mesabi Range strike in Minnesota. After the war she fought for the release of political prisoners and worked tirelessly in defense of Sacco and Vanzetti. Eventually she persuaded herself that communism was a logical extension of the socialism she had accepted as a birthright. Accordingly she applied for admission to the Communist party in 1926, was accepted in 1927, and rose through the ranks to occupy the chair of the national committee in 1961.

When the ACLU tackled Miss Flynn in 1940 they were facing one of the nation's major orators, a labor organizer of proven success, a courageous individual many times arrested and characteristically in the van of strikes and protests, as well as one of the most successful defenders of minority rights that the nation had ever known.

Although it is hard to tell it from her public career, the Gurley Flynn who appeared at the City Club in May 1940 must have been considerably diminished in spirit from those younger days when she faced a public trial with relish. Her stocky frame was on the way to becoming matronly. Her raven hair, once pulled back severely into a bun, was now showing gray and a soft wave. Her habitually alert and quizzical manner, reflected in the piquant angle of her head, was fading into a soft, vertical assurance. No doubt her blue eyes still sparkled and glinted with the lights of controversy, but the curtain of proper, rimless spectacles was frequently placed in front of them. As a young woman she looked bright and unpredictable; as an older woman she looked a composite of one's favorite elementary school teachers. The early months of 1940 had seen her slide rapidly toward age as she sat at the deathbed of her son, Fred, her only child and the individual focus of her life.

Her fellow board members had repeatedly stated, while asking for her resignation, that the request was not personal. In her articles in the press, Flynn made fun of these protestations, yet they were probably true. Most of her colleagues described her with warmth and affection. Her trial had been postponed out of consideration for her son's illness. She thanked them for this. She addressed many of them by their first names, without rancor. The board would doubtless—most of them—have preferred to avoid the confrontation altogether. But the die was cast. The fear and suspicion of radical political philosophies and organizations was growing stronger every day. In spite of the falling out between the leading Facist and Communist nations, America seemed increasingly anxious about alien ideologies. Congressman Martin Dies was then leading the pursuit of un-American activities. The ACLU was not immune.

At first the leadership tried to resist this public hysteria. As late as April 1939 the board of the ACLU issued a statement called "Why We Defend Free Speech for Nazis, Fascists, and Communists."[3] Here was summarized the classic libertarian stand. The ACLU was nonpolitical, began this recapitulation. It made no judgment on politico-economic controversy. It defended all comers on the assumption that no one knew absolutely what was right and wrong and that to deny freedom to any group was to endanger liberty for all. But by February 5, 1940, this same board was tying itself in knots trying to say something different while pretending that nothing had changed. Behind the scenes, apparently, a deal had been made with Dies: if the ACLU would purge itself of Communists in leadership positions, the House Committee would spare them an investigation. A new message stated that the ACLU had never appointed Communists *per se* in the past and would make this unwritten rule a matter of announced policy from that time onward. This change of face divided the membership, but it pacified the Communist hunters and evidently pleased those members whose checkbooks contained the largest balances.

Harry F. Ward, who had chaired the ACLU board since its founding, declared the new departure completely unacceptable. He promptly resigned, giving among his reasons the following:

> In thus penalizing opinions, the Union is doing in its own sphere what it has always opposed the government for doing in law or administration. The essence of civil liberties is opposition to all attempts to enforce political orthodoxy. Yet by this resolution the Civil Liberties Union is attempting to create an orthodoxy in civil liberties, and stranger still, an orthodoxy in political judgment upon events outside the United States. . . .
>
> Furthermore, when the Union disqualifies for membership in its governing bodies [on the basis of party membership] it is using the principle of guilt by association which it has always opposed.[4]

The statement of February 5 had explained away the board's two famous Communists. William Z. Foster was elected when he was an organizer for the American Federation of Labor and had since resigned. Miss Flynn, it was correctly pointed out, had helped found the ACLU before she joined the CPUSA. It was *not* pointed out that Miss Flynn had, quite publicly, become a Communist long before her election to her current term of office as a board member. Flynn had to go. The board chairman, the Reverend John H. Holmes, requested her resignation. She not only refused but she discussed the proceedings in her signed columns in the radical press, remarking that the board, while once a diverse and democratic group, had grown fat with lawyers intent on defending capitalism and employers' rights.

Thus the board, as it assembled that night, was made up of one group outraged by what they saw as the leadership's betrayal of the ACLU's sacred values, and another group which saw at least a temporary necessity to denounce communism in order to stay free of government persecution and to keep the money coming in. The group of compromisers (with Roger Baldwin absent, not voting, but very much pulling the strings) was in no way amused by columnist Flynn's characterization of the board. To the first charge of membership in the CPUSA they added two others, seeking to disqualify her from board membership for her public disparagement of her colleagues.

The meeting was called to order with the Reverend Mr. Holmes in the chair. When Flynn got the floor she first attacked the "star chamber" procedure. How could those who had complained against her serve also as her judges? The presiding officer himself had requested her resignation. Three other voting members were responsible for the three charges. And were not the three separate charges worth separate hearings? Why was the venue so restricted and secret? Why could not proceedings take place before the membership at large?

Where was her right to appeal? Much in the manner of Harry Ward's letter of resignation, Gurley Flynn accused the ACLU board of acting like its historic adversaries. She was, Flynn continued, being banished for her politics, made guilty by association, and tried without anything resembling due process. The chair, though appearing to strive for a formal correctness, showed little openminded-ness. When he could, Holmes overruled any motion that would have made for a more careful or more open hearing.

There were a number of ironies in this procedure beyond the obvious ones. One board member, growing weary toward midnight and feeling that the matter was too serious for a marathon session, proposed adjournment. That motion denied, he walked out taking with him a crucial vote. Another member, though obviously sympathetic to Flynn's side of the issue, refused to vote at all, insisting that there had been nothing to constitute a question. Even so, the vote of the members, at 2:00 A.M., May 8, was deadlocked. The chair unhesitatingly exercised his privilege and broke that tie in a predictable manner. The finding of blame was promptly transferred into a motion of expulsion from the board, and, in a final violation of both due process and courtesy, the members adjourned without informing Flynn of the outcome.

Protests followed, to no avail. Miss Flynn continued her active life, in and out of jail. In 1952 she was tried and convicted under the Smith Act for conspiring to teach the overthrow of the government by force. She served over two years in a federal prison, having completed her autobiography on the eve of her incarcera-tion. After her term she returned to party activities, eventually assuming the chief national office. She continued her work against "oppressive measures" until her death in 1964.

The ACLU, too, lived to fight another day. Perhaps, in voting "only" ten to nine to expel its only overtly Communist board member, the union resisted the pressures of the times with more poise than other groups. The ACLU does not satisfy everyone, but it remains to this day a major weapon in defense of the basic articles of individual freedom. In the darkness between May 7 and May 8, 1940, however, one might have asked some uneasy questions about eternal vigilance. If groups like the ACLU are supposed to be guardians of procedural justice and individual rights, then who was guarding the guardians?

NOTES

Encounter 1

1. For the purpose of this and the other "Encounters" see the Introduction. These episodes are used as cases in point throughout the text.

2. This account is taken largely from Ruth Franchere, *Jack London: The Pursuit of a Dream* (New York: Crowell, 1962), chapter 16. See also, Robert Barltrop, *Jack London: The Man, the Writer, the Rebel* (London: Pluto, 1976), chapter 6; Anna Strunsky Walling, "Memoirs of Jack London," in *Echoes of Revolt: The Masses 1911-1917*, ed. William L. O'Neill (Chicago: Quadrangle, 1966), pp. 117-22.

3. From the Jack London Collection, Henry E. Huntington Library, by permission of Milo Shepard for the Irving Shepard Estate. This is the first one and one-half pages of a long, interrupted letter dealing also with English socialists and with problems with publishers.

Introduction

1. *Complete Works of Ralph Waldo Emerson*, ed. Edward W. Emerson (Boston: Houghton, Mifflin, 1903), vol. 1, p. 255.

2. The difficulty of dealing with reform terminology is also discussed in Robert H. Walker, *Reform Spirit in America* (New York: Putnam, 1976); reprint Melbourne, FL: R. E. Krieger, 1985), p. xviii (hereafter *RSIA*).

3. Throughout the text "reform" and "social change" are used almost interchangeably in order to emphasize the concern with reform movements which parallel the general directions of social change. The organization of *RSIA* reflects the division of reform into these three large areas.

4. For a description of this approach that matches my intentions see Kenneth Boulding, *Primer on Social Dynamics* (New York: Free Press, 1970). The idea of a cycle is used to describe reform dynamics, especially in Mode II; but, as will be noted, this cycle is incomplete and developmental rather than recurring.

5. For a more extensive elaboration of the proposed vocabulary, see my "Anatomy of American Reform", in *Business and Its Environment: Essays for Thomas C. Cochran*, ed. Harold I. Sharlin (Westport, Conn.: Greenwood, 1983).

Encounter 2

1. The best brief biography is that of Franklin B. Dexter, "Abraham Bishop, of Connecticut, and his Writings," *Proceedings of the Massachusetts Historical Society* 19 (2d series), pp. 190-99. The entry for Bishop in the *Dictionary of American Biography* lists further references.

2. Dexter, who also edited the *Literary Diary of Ezra Stiles*, cites this passage in "Abraham Bishop," p. 191.

3. Chilton Williamson, *American Suffrage from Property to Democracy* (Princeton: Princeton Univ. Press, 1960), pp. 165-67. In 1800, Connecticut cast presidential votes through electors chosen by the state legislature. Adams and the Federalists won without difficulty. See also Richard J. Purcell, *Connecticut in Transition, 1775-1818* (1918; reprint ed. Middletown, Conn.: Wesleyan, 1963).

4. The best available version of Bishop's speech is titled *Connecticut Republicanism: An Oration*

on the Extent and Power of Political Delusion; it was printed in Philadelphia for Mathew Carey and dated November 13, 1800 (hereafter *Connecticut Republicanism*). See *RSIA*, pp. 37-45, for an abridged version.

5. *Connecticut Republicanism*, pp. 3-4.

6. Dexter, p. 195.

Chapter I

1. Among the works most helpful in seeing the colonial era in its politico-economic reform dimensions are: Zera S. Fink, *The Classical Republicans* (Evanston, Ill.: Northwestern Univ. Press, 1945); Caroline Robbins, *The Eighteenth-Century Commonwealthman* (Cambridge: Harvard Univ. Press, 1959); Bernard Bailyn, *The Ideological Origins of the American Revolution* (Cambridge: Belknap, 1967); Paul K. Conkin, *Self-Evident Truths* (Bloomington: Indiana Univ. Press, 1974).

2. Rush is quoted in Bailyn, p. 230, and Wilson in Wilson O. Clough, *Our Long Heritage* (Minneapolis: Univ. of Minnesota Press, 1955). J. G. A. Pocock's *Machiavellian Moment* (Princeton: Princeton Univ. Press, 1975) explains, from the viewpoint of the Machiavellian-Harringtonian tradition, why representation was so ideologically complex. Pocock also points out the tension between the fear of a monied class and the interest in success and expansion via available currency and credit, which helps explain why the politics of money quickly became so crucial.

3. *Reports of the Proceedings and Debates of the Convention of 1821* . . . (Albany, N.Y.: Hosford, 1821), pp. 243-44. Buel's remarks are abridged in *RSIA*, pp. 54-61. A most helpful compendium on the state constitutional conventions of the 1820s is the one compiled by Merrill D. Peterson, *Democracy, Liberty, and Property* (Indianapolis: Bobbs-Merrill, 1966).

4. A strong argument for the need to understand the social consequences of financial questions, whether or not one is technically qualified, could well begin with Bray Hammond's *Banks and Politics in America* (Princeton; Princeton Univ. Press, 1957). Irwin Unger pursues this line with vigor in his own work *(Greenback Era* [Princeton: Princeton Univ. Press, 1964]) and points out that Joseph Dorfman's *Economic Mind in American Civilization* is a five-volume elaboration of this position (p. 3). Lacking any special competence in the arcane questions of money and banking, I am nonetheless convinced that an understanding of the important aspects of social change is dependent on appreciating the impact of financial conditions and politics.

5. The congressman is quoted in John C. Miller, *Federalist Era* (New York: Harper, 1960), p. 56. For a more constructive view of banking in early America, see E. James Ferguson, "Currency Finance: An Interpretation of Colonial Monetary Practices," *William and Mary Quarterly* 10 (April 1953): 153-80.

6. *Connecticut Republicanism*, p. 3. See Encounter 2.

7. For useful precedents one need look no further than *Cato's Letters* or the oratory of Jeffersonians like Abraham Bishop.

8. *Compilation of the Messages and Papers of the Presidents, 1789-1897*, ed. James D. Richardson (Washington, D.C.: Government Printing Office, 1897), p. 590.

9. Hammond, *Banks and Politics*, chapter 18.

10. Gouge is not mentioned at all in Louis Filler's *Dictionary of American Social Reform* (New York: Philosophical Library, 1963) or in a leading text by Paul Studenski and Herman E. Krooss, *Financial History of the United States*, rev. ed., (New York: McGraw-Hill, 1963). However, Arthur M. Schlesinger, Jr.'s *Age of Jackson* (Boston: Little, Brown, 1948, p. 300) does explain why Gouge was useful to the workers' partisans both as a theoretician and rhetorician; and Paul K. Conkin's *Prophets of Prosperity* (Bloomington: Indiana Univ. Press, 1980) provides an excellent theoretical setting for antebellum politico-economic issues, including those espoused by Gouge.

11. William M. Gouge, *A Short History of Paper-Money and Banking in the United States*. . . . (2d ed.) New York: Collins, 1835), pp. 41, 42.

12. The two terms came into general use in the mid-1830s. Frances Wright, as will be shown, considered it quite important to use one term rather than the other. Most contemporaries used the terms interchangeably. "Independent" stresses the idea of freeing the government's money from the

influence of private bankers. "Sub" stresses the idea of spreading the funds (and their availability) throughout the country rather than concentrating them in one or two eastern financial centers. The term "subtreasury" came into use again in connection with the agrarian movement and the ideas of C. W. Macune as they were promoted in the late 1880s and 1890s.

13. *Working Man's Advocate* (New York) 1 (October 31, 1829):1.

14. Perhaps because of an episode involving a couple living together outside statutory wedlock, the commune established by Frances Wright at Nashoba, Tennessee, sometimes carries an unfairly radical connotation. As an antislavery measure it was, in fact, quite conservative. Wright purchased the slaves, allowed them to work off their purchase price with five years of plantation labor, then colonized them in Haiti. No wonder Jefferson and Madison approved!

15. Frances Wright, *Whut Is the Matter? A Political Address* (New York: Privately printed, 1838), p. 15.

16. Donald B. Johnson, ed., *National Party Platforms* (Urbana: Illinois Univ. Press, 1978), p. 1.

17. The authoritative work on this subject is David Kinley, *Independent Treasury of the United States* (Washington, D.C.: Government Printing Office, 1910).

18. Esther Taus makes the most thorough argument for this interpretation in *Central Banking Functions of the United States Treasury, 1789–1941* (New York: Russell and Russell, 1943).

19. Local movements do not always follow national patterns. A good way to appreciate this fact as it pertains to this issue and this period is to compare the foregoing generalizations with those provided by Louis Hartz in *Economic Policy and Democratic Thought: Pennsylvania, 1776-1860* (Cambridge; Mass.: Harvard Univ. Press, 1948). In at least one state it appears that the independent treasury was seen as an alternative not to a national bank but to a free banking system.

20. Most of the biographical information on Kellogg comes from a sketch prepared by his daughter, Mary Esther Kellogg Putnam, for an 1883 edition of his work *Labor and Other Capital* (New York: Lovell) slightly retitled *Labor and Capital*. Her account is, of course, subjective. She was not only his self-declared disciple but also his editor and the one who gave final organization to his work. Her esteem for her father is no less than that of John R. Commons, who prepared the useful entry about him in the *Dictionary of American Biography*. Additional information is available in what seems to be a very careful family history: Timothy Hopkins, *Kelloggs of the Old World and New*, 3 vols. (San Francisco: Sunset Press, 1903).

21. Whitehook [pseud.], *Remarks upon Usury and Its Effects* (New York: Harper, 1841).

22. Edward Kellogg, *Labor and Other Capital* (New York: Privately printed, 1849), p. xi. In spite of this direct appeal to labor, Kellogg failed to attract wide support. Robert P. Sharkey tells me that, to many people, Kellogg was on the "wrong side" of a standing argument about whether money should be issued by government or by banks. If the independent treasury was the popular side, then surely this helps account for Kellogg's neglect. It also helps explain why the popularity of these ideas waxed with Alexander Campbell's antibank addenda. See, in particular, Robert P. Sharkey, *Money, Class, and Party: An Economic Study of the Civil War and Reconstruction* (Baltimore: Johns Hopkins Univ. Press, 1959). Most students of the Greenback movement, including Sharkey, credit Kellogg with putting together the ideas—not all of them original—which eventually identified the Greenback philosophy.

23. Kellogg's daughter testifies that her father's ideas were influential at the time the original issue was authorized. The record of the congressional debates does not support her contention. Furthermore, leading supporters of wartime greenbacks (Senator Timothy Otis Howe, Congressmen Samuel Hooper, John B. Alley, and Elbridge Gerry Spaulding) disavowed them in peacetime.

24. John R. Commons et al., *Documentary History of American Industrial Society* (Cleveland: Clark, 1910), vol. 9, p. 33.

25. Alexander Campbell, *True American System of Finance* . . . (Chicago: *Evening Journal*, 1864). The Chronology notes but does not stress the fact that the Civil War banking acts, by eliminating the currency-issue function of state banks, moved toward centralized banking and thus anticipated the Federal Reserve Act. Guy E. Noyes, in his critique of this chapter, makes this point. The fundamental monetary reform of the nineteenth century, he points out, was the establishment of federal control over bank-note issue. He also comments that, although nineteenth-century reformers

equated low interest with increased money supply, modern theory no longer makes this connection. Also relevant is Bray Hammond's *Sovereignty and an Empty Purse* (Princeton: Princeton Univ. Press, 1970). Hammond makes the greenbacks a crucial stage in the emergence of the modern, powerful central government. He finds in William Kellogg (a distant relative of Edward and a coangressman from Illinois who led the pro-greenback fight in 1862) a link between Civil War finance and Western agrarian soft-money politics (p. 191).

26. See *Biographical Directory of the American Congress, 1774-1971* (Washington, D.C.: Government Printing Office, 1971); also, *Chicago Workingman's Advocate* for August 8 and 15, 1874.

27. Campbell is so described in the *Biographical Directory of the American Congress.* Unger's is the only important voice that finds Campbell more important than Kellogg, whom he terms an eclectic borrower. Campbell differs from Kellogg not much on theoretical grounds but because of a different context coupled with a greater sense of political feasibility. As to how Kellogg gets the credit for being "father of the greenbacks," Commons cites Kellogg's daughter's ability to keep *Labor and Other Capital* in print as the century wore on; Sharkey says it was Campbell who added Kellogg to the greenbacks and got a political movement. See Sharkey, pp. 191ff., Unger, pp. 99ff., *RSIA*, pp. 87-94.

28. Edward A. McPherson, *Hand-Book of Politics for 1872* (Washington, D.C.: Philip and Solomons, 1872), p. 211. In other compilations this resolution is numbered as paragraph no. 2, but in all cases it is reported as the first resolution following the preamble.

29. Terrence V. Powderly, *Thirty Years of Labor: 1859 to 1889* (Columbus, Ohio: Excelsior, 1889), p. 398.

30. For discussions of Macune's career, organizational contributions and ideas, see Thomas H. Greer, *American Social Reform Movements* (New York: Prentice-Hall, 1949), pp. 75-77; Charles M. Destler, *American Radicalism 1865-1901* (New London, Conn.: Connecticut College, 1946), pp. 70-72; Lawrence Goodwyn, *Populist Movement* (New York: Oxford Univ. Press, 1978), pp. 51-53, 90-93, passim.

31. For a concise description and defense of this idea see the report of the committee on finance chaired by Macune for the National Convention of the Farmers' Alliance in St. Louis in 1889. See J.E. Bryan, *Farmers' Alliance.* (Fayetteville, Ark.: Privately printed, 1981), pp. 103-104. See note 12 above.

32. Macune referred to a report on a French Revolutionary policy of making crops loans. An article in the *Mississippi Valley Historical Review* (September 1944) by James C. Malin pushes the case of Macune's debts to French and Russian experiments. For a discussion in context, see Destler, p. 71. Although I have not seen the connection made, there is precedent for both successful fiat currency and land credit in the colonial land banks. See the article by Ferguson (note 5, above). Some of Macune's purposes were realized in the Federal Reserve System, but others were addressed only between 1916 (Farm Loan Act) and 1929 (Agricultural Marketing Act).

33. Allen Weinstein *(Prelude to Populism* [New Haven: Yale Univ. Press, 1970]) helps explain why silver, although eventually backed by Populists and reform Democrats, was not an appropriate agrarian issue, having been promoted in the 1870s by urban, hard-money advocates.

34. Although this is true of the candidates, it is not true of their platforms. See Chapter 2.

35. *Congressional Record,* vol. 51, p. 435. For a thorough discussion of the system written by a man uniquely involved in its construction, see H. Parker Willis, *Federal Reserve System* (New York: Ronald Press, 1923).

36. The latest study of the Federal Reserve that both recogizes and attacks its power in ways that Jackson and Gouge would have recognized is Maxwell Newton, *The Fed: Inside the Federal Reserve, the Secret Power Center that Controls the American Economy* (New York: Times Books, 1983).

Chapter 2

1. Taus's *Central Banking Functions of the United States Treasury* is a superb account of the technical performance of treasurers in response to financial conditions but rarely includes the political reasons behind the actions. On the other hand, I have found no political account that appreciates the struggle to win workers from hard to soft money or that adequately explains the technical reasons for the ambivalence of the business community toward the soft-money, low-interest movements.

2. Unger, p. 3.

3. Greer, p. 3.

4. The term "pre-muckraking" testifies to the rigid periodization of reform. "Muckraking," a shorthand for journalistic protest, was so firmly tied to the turn of the century that prior examples of social criticism had to be labeled in a way that suggested prematurity.

5. The standard synthesis is described in *RSIA*, pp. xvi-xvii.

6. In *Prelude to Populism,* Weinstein explains why this was so, historically as well as logically, and throws special light on the way silver complicated the party battles of the 1870s, thus adding to the perceptions of Sharkey, Unger, and Walter T. K. Nugent, "Money, Politics, and Society," in *Gilded Age: A Reappraisal,* ed. H. Wayne Morgan (Syracuse: Syracuse Univ. Press, 1970).

7. For a more extensive explanation of party viewpoints on the money question see Nugent.

8. See Taus.

9. See *RSIA,* pp. 77-79, 214-25, for examples of the oratory of Wright and Roosevelt.

10. *RSIA,* p. 63, reproduces and discusses an early "workie" (labor sympathizer) cartoon.

11. See Robert G. Gunderson, *Log-Cabin Campaign* (Lexington: Univ. Press of Kentucky, 1957); Paul Kleppner, *Cross of Culture,* 2d ed. (New York: Free Press, 1970); Stephen Hess and Milton Kaplan, *Ungentlemanly Art* (New York: Macmillan, 1968); Richard Fitzgerald, *Art and Politics* (Westport, Conn.: Greenwood, 1973). Examples and discussion of both positive and negative symbols occur in *RSIA,* pp. 34-35, 80-82, 145-49, 210-15, 231-34. For American cartooning in its global setting, see Ralph E. Shikes, *The Indignant Eye* (Boston: Beacon, 1969).

12. Verse by Franklin P. Jepson as quoted in Robert H. Walker, *Poet and the Gilded Age* (Philadelphia: Univ. of Pennsylvania Press, 1963), p. 135; see chapters 4 and 5 for considerable additional comment in verse on financial and economic topics. For a sample and discussion of Freneau see *RSIA,* pp. 32-34.

13. From a biographical sketch by Mary Kellogg Putnam, p. xx, in the 1883 edition of *Labor and Capital.*

14. See Walter T. K. Nugent, *Money and American Society, 1865-1880* (New York: Free Press, 1968). One of the main purposes of Nugent's work is to establish the money question as a moral question, not just within the chronological limits of his book but until its alleged disappearance from the headlines in the early twentieth century.

15. A classic example of the technique of linking the Federalists with the English ruling class occurs in the speech of Abrahan Bishop; see Encounter 2.

16. George Henry Evans's *Working Man's Advocate* provides good access to the Mode I agenda of this period. The most helpful interpretive works are those of Edward Pessen.

17. *RSIA,* pp. 153-71.

18. See Arthur S. Link "What Happened to the Progressive Movement in the 1920's?" *American Historical Review* 64 (July 1959): 833-51; Warren I. Susman; "The Persistence of American Reform," in *American Reform: The Ambiguous Legacy,* ed. Daniel Walden (Yellow Springs, Ohio: Ampersand, 1967), p. 95. Some of the most germane interpretive works dealing with the continuity of politico-economic reform from the late nineteenth century through the New Deal are Greer; Eric F. Goldman, *Rendezvous with Destiny* (New York: Knopf, 1952); and Richard M. Hofstadter, *Age of Reform* (New York: Knopf, 1955). All of these works underplay the importance of the 1920s, although the most egregious example is Frederick L. Allen's popular *Big Change* (New York: Harper, 1952). The emphasis on Hoover's progressive side is by no means confined to Joan Hoff Wilson, *Herbert Hoover: Forgotten Progressive* (Boston: Little, Brown, 1975); in fact, her title

might be regarded as misleading in the sense that the serious sudents of Hoover have never forgotten. See the excellent consensus view provided by David Burner in *Herbert Hoover: A Public Life* (New York: Knopf, 1979).

19. *RSIA,* pp. 541-50.

20. *Los Angeles Times,* January 23, 1980, part 2, p. 5.

21. *Miami Herald,* June 22, 1980, pp. 1E, 4E. For an example of Arthur S. Miller's pessimism see his *Democratic Dictatorship* (Westport, Conn.: Greenwood, 1981).

22. *Washington Post,* August 13, 1980, pp. A14, A15. An excellent recounting of the vital interrelationship of political and economic issues in recent decades is by Leonard Silk (columnist for the *New York Times*), *Economics in the Real World* (New York, 1984).

Encounter 3

1. *Walker's Appeal, in Four Articles, Together with a Preamble to the Colored Citizens of the World, but in Particular, and Very Expressly to Those in the United States of America* (1829; reprinted in 1848, New York: Tobitt), pp. 33-36. The 1848 edition used the second, corrected text and contains a helpful sketch of Walker's life by Henry H. Garnet.

2. Ibid., pp. 82-87.

3. *Liberator* 1 (January 8, 1831):6.

Chapter 3

1. *RSIA,* pp. 267-68. The third section of *RSIA* reproduces documents pertinent to Mode II; on the preeminence of the Afro-American question in the reform setting see particularly pp. 269-72.

2. The two quotations are from the second and third articles of the constitution of the American Anti-Slavery Society.

3. W.E.B. DuBois, *NAACP Annual Report, 1929,* p. 69.

4. *Correspondence between the Hon. F. H. Elmore and James G. Birney* (New York: American Anti-Slavery Society, 1838), p. 14 (hereafter *Birney Correspondence*). *RSIA,* pp. 425-55, contains a discussion of the importance of organization as well as a long extract from the above work followed by parallel selections from *Crisis.*

5. The box is described and its principal ornament reproduced in *Emancipator,* October 1, 1840, p. 92.

6. Robert L. Jack, *History of the National Association for the Advancement of Colored People* (Boston: Meador, 1953), chapter 2. Eventually the idea of life memberships to the NAACP bore fruit. In the "jubilee year" alone over a quarter of a million dollors was raised in this manner; the net operating loss for that same year, however, was over $200,000 (*NAACP Annual Report, 1959,* pp. 59, 117).

7. See *Birney Correspondence,* pp. 10-14, for a state-by-state summary of the progress of abolitionism as of 1838.

8. See the *NAACP Annual Report, 1958,* chapter 2; the 1959 report, chapter 2; and excerpts from *Crisis* in *RSIA,* pp. 444-51. For a general discussion of the role of the branches see Jack, pp. 18-21. The evidence compiled by William A. Gamson *(Strategy of Social Protest* [Homewood, Ill.: Dorsey, 1975], chapter 7) indicates that associations are more effective *with* a centralized bureaucracy but *without central authority.* As to the characteristics that made the NAACP politically effective see James Q. Wilson, *Political Organizations* (New York: Basic Books, 1973), especially chapter 9. For an account of how church-related associations functioned, see Clifford S. Griffin, *Their Brothers' Keepers: Moral Stewardship in the United States, 1800-1865* (New Brunswick, N.J.: Rutgers Univ. Press, 1960). As will be discussed below, the matter of local versus national leadership remains crucial to the maintenance of social pressure.

9. In spite of the recognition Weld has received, his role in the antislavery movement may still be

underestimated. In giving the AA-SS a truly national program he seems to have, at the same time, made himself the first systematic and effective Washington lobbyist for a voluntary association. A recent and corrective appraisal of Weld is Robert H. Abzug, *Passionate Liberator: Theodore Dwight Weld and the Dilemma of Reform* (New York: Oxford Univ. Press, 1980). For relevant material on the petition campaign, see *RSIA*, pp. 375-76, 380-404.

10. See *RSIA*, pp. 377-79, 404-25; the use of the courts is also discussed later in this chapter.

11. *Birney Correspondence*, pp. 17-20.

12. For a summary of NAACP ideas on publicity, see Jack, pp. 23-25; for an account of the Huntley episode see the *NAACP Annual Report, 1959*, pp. 68-69.

13. Most of the space in this section is given to those aspects of reform that promote a process of gradual, peaceful change: the exposé, fiction, autobiography, and associations that stress suasion. A valid pattern must include all important aspects of the subject. Thus the stress on *Walker's Appeal* and on the present materials recognizes that violence is a recurrent form for provoking social action and an unavoidable part of the process of social change.

14. *Walker's Appeal*, p. 36. See Encounter 3.

15. *Muhammad Speaks*, May 13, 1963, p. 13. For the context of this passage see *RSIA*, pp. 322-24, 334-36.

16. Wendell Phillips, quoted in *Remarks at the Funeral of William Lloyd Garrison* (Boston: Lee and Shepard, 1884), pp. 5-6; John Jay Chapman, *William Lloyd Garrison* (New York: Moffat, Yard, 1913), p. 7.

17. For a sample of Garrison in action see Chapman's description of Garrison's confrontation with the Rynders mob, in his *William Lloyd Garrison*, pp. 199-218. It should be understood that the leading models for this technique were vigorous, passionate people who did not find severe restraint the easy path. This fact comes revealingly through the discussion of Garrison by Chapman, himself a man of violent, passionate mold who became a firm convert to nonviolence and an important reform link between those antebellum crusaders and turn-of-the-century reform. For a direct comparison of the styles of agitation in the two eras see Howard Zinn, "Abolitionists and Freedom Riders," *Columbia University Forum* 7 (Summer 1964):5-13.

18. Anon., *American Slavery As It Is: Testimony of a Thousand Witnesses* (New York: American Anti-Slavery Society, 1839).

19. Ibid., p. 65.

20. Gilbert Barnes and Dwight Dumond, eds., *Letters of Theodore Dwight Weld, Angelina Grimké Weld, and Sarah Grimké.* (New York: Appleton-Century, 1934), vol. 1, p. xii.

21. The full title is *A Key to Uncle Tom's Cabin; Presenting the Original Facts and Documents upon Which the Story is Founded. Together with Corroborative Statements Verifying the Truth of the Work* (Boston: Jewett, 1853). Stowe's technique was more dramatic than Weld's, featuring fewer instances, each more fully developed. See, for example, the case against James Castleman (pp. 100-104) as discussed in *RSIA*, pp. 278-86.

22. The "Moynihan Report," technically an anonymous Department of Labor paper entitled "The Negro Family: The Case for National Action," had a complicated public history before it was ever officially published. The circumstances and impact are usefully assessed in Lee Rainwater and William L. Yancy, eds., *The Moynihan Report and the Politics of Controversy*, (Cambridge, Mass.: MIT Press, 1967).

23. Budd Schulberg, "The Trial of T.," in Watts Writers' Workshop, *From the Ashes: Voices of Watts* (New York: New American Library, 1967), p. 262.

24. For one good treatment of the black autobiography as a *genre*, see Sidonie Smith, *Where I'm Bound* (Westport, Conn.: Greenwood, 1974). See also Harry Dolan's "I Remember Papa," as reproduced in *RSIA*, pp. 311-18. At the climactic moment in this autobiographical sketch, Dolan's sister screams "you're killing Topsy." Although Topsy is in this case a housecat, the emotional meaning of the occasion harks pointedly back to Stowe. The most recent, important addition to this genre is James Farmer, *Lay Bare the Heart* (New York: Arbor House, 1985).

25. John Steinbeck, *Travels with Charlie in Search of America* (New York: Viking, 1962), p. 242; see also, pp. 220-42.

26. Irving Lowens in the *Washington Star,* July 11, 1965, p. E8.

27. See Robert Shelton in the *New York Times,* July 23, 1963, p. 21.

28. Published by M. Witmark, New York, 1962.

29. John Lovel, *Black Song: The Forge and the Flame* (New York: Macmillan, 1972, pp. 333-34.

30. The two songs are printed, side by side, and discussed in *RSIA,* pp. 319-22.

31. *Anti-Slavery Poems: Songs of Labor and Reform,* Whittier's Poetical Works, vol. 3 (Boston: Houghton, Mifflin, 1888), pp. 33-34. For a documentation of this theme see *RSIA,* pp. 272-76.

32. Ainsworth Spofford's treatise, *Higher Law Tried by Reason and Authority* (New York: Benedict, 1851), had great influence among the antislavery group. The quoted passage is from p. 11. The King quotation is from his famous "Letter from Birmingham Jail" as published in *Why We Can't Wait* (New York: Harper and Row, 1964), p. 185. How the moral argument was used to motivate certain groups in the antislavery movement is recounted by Griffin (see note 9, above).

33. Lewis Tappan, *Address to the Non-Slaveholders of the South . . .* (New York: American and Foreign Anti-Slavery Society, [1843]).

34. Ibid, p. 1.

35. Ibid., pp. 14-15. Tappan was consistent in his attitude toward social classes, arguing elsewhere that wealth was not a natural right.

36. Ibid., p. 58.

37. Dwight L. Dumond, in his introduction to the *Letters of James Gillespie Birney, 1831-1857* (2 vols.; New York: Appleton-Century, 1938), lists the four documents as Birney's published correspondence with Elmore (see note 4, above), Tappan's *Address* (which for some reason he attributes to William Jay), Jay's *View of the Action of the Federal Government, in behalf of Slavery* (New York: J. S. Taylor, 1839) and Leavitt's articles (see note 39, below).

38. There were, in fact, two extended essays by Leavitt, which summed up a number of speeches and editorials. "Financial Power of Slavery," cited by Dumond, appeared in the *Emancipator,* October 22, 1840, p. 102. "Political Power of Slavery," which appeared in the same journal, October 15, 1840, was really the other half of an extended argument. It was the more important half in that it led most directly to his party activity.

39. Adams's ultimate objectives were fully stated in the *Daily National Intelligencer,* April 23, 1839, pp. 2, 3. This is one of the most learned and logical responses to the proslavery arguments on record and, for some reason, it has been relatively neglected. It is reproduced in *RSIA,* pp. 382-404. The gag rule was eventually broken, thus allowing for some of the famous compromises that delayed the eventual armed conflict.

40. The NAACP was joined in this effort by the American Civil Liberties Union (ACLU) as *amici curiae,* which fact illustrates the confluence of civil liberties and civil rights in the modern setting (see Chapter 4).

41. All of these cases (including *Brown v. Board of Education*) are discussed and extracts reproduced in *RSIA,* pp. 375-79, 404-25.

42. *Six Speeches with a Sketch of the Life of Hon. Eli Thayer* (Boston: Brown and Taggard, 1860), p. 12.

43. Eli Thayer, *New England Emigrant Aid Company* (Worcester, Mass.: Rice, 1887).

44. William Faulkner, *Essays, Speeches, and Public Letters,* ed. James B. Meriwether (New York: Random House, 1966), p. 86. The letter appeared March 5, 1956. A more literal parallel to Thayer's carefully planned use of advanced technology to settle the prairies might be found in an idea for rehabilitating slum housing without displacing the population. Using giant cranes, prefabricated units, and large storage lockers, the rebuilders can completely alter a dwelling while removing the occupants for only forty-eight hours. The concept originated with Edward K. Rice and was developed by the T. Y. Lin engineering firm of California for use in New York City (see the Washington *Post,* April 3, 1966, p. G7).

45. Faulkner, p. 216. This letter appeared in the *Memphis Commercial Appeal* on March 20, 1955.

46. Phillips, quoted in *Remarks,* p. 10.

Chapter 4

1. Abolition continues as the subject of lively historical attention: partly because of increased perception of similarities between antislavery and civil rights (see Chapter 3), partly because of a broadening scope, and partly because of a growing appreciation (most congenial to my point of view) of the way in which this leading reform movement helped establish lasting patterns affecting social and institutional change. See, in addition to works cited elsewhere, Ronald G. Walters, *The Antislavery Appeal: American Abolitionism after 1830* (Baltimore: Johns Hopkins Univ. Press, 1976); Lewis Perry and Michael Fellman, eds., *Antislavery Reconsidered: New Perspectives on the Abolitionists* (Baton Rouge: Louisiana State Univ. Press, 1979); Lawrence J. Friedman, *Gregarious Saints: Self and Society in American Abolitionism, 1830-1870* (Cambridge: Cambridge Univ. Press, 1982). Two recent works add importantly to the appreciation of dynamics and institutionalization: Aldon D. Morris, *The Origins of the Civil Rights Movement* (New York: Free Press/Macmillan, 1985) and Charles and Barbara Whalen, *The Longest Debate: A Legislative History of the Civil Rights Act* (Cabin John, Md., Seven Locks Press, 1985).

2. The general terms of the deal that put Rutherford Hayes in the White House had been known virtually since the deal was made; C. Vann Woodward described them in detail in *Reunion and Reaction*, 2d rev. ed. (New York: Doubleday, 1956). For comments on key tendencies and periodization see also Woodward's *Strange Career of Jim Crow*, rev. ed. (New York: Oxford Univ. Press, 1957).

3. Woodward, *Jim Crow*, p. 9. Raymond Wolters *(New Negro on Campus* [Princeton: Princeton Univ. Press, 1975]) summarizes the revolts at black colleges and the consequent responses in a way that makes it possible to see these changes as a half-way point between the organized pursuit of integration in the early years of this century and the court decisions of the 1930s. A recent evaluation of social science theories concerning civil rights is Doug McAdam's *Political Process and the Development of Black Insurgency* (Chicago: Univ. of Chicago Press, 1982). This study helps explain why it is so difficult to pick a precise moment for the transition from negative to constructive phases and why it was necessary to create considerable segregated self-sufficiency before integral equality could be attempted.

4. For a discussion of the special aspects of the woman question in a reform context see *RSIA*, pp. 455-60. Singularly useful in relating the woman's movement to other reform issues is Aileen S. Kraditor's *Ideas of the Woman Suffrage Movement, 1890-1900* (New York: Columbia Univ. Press, 1965).

5. Some students of the woman's movement (including my colleague Professor Phyllis Palmer, for whose help I am grateful) maintain that its fundamental dichotomy is between those who seek to improve the distinctive status of women and those who wish to integrate women more fully. Admittedly, these two attitudes have been present all along and are still much in evidence; however, the first is characteristic of the first cycle, and the rise in prominence of the integral view underlies the second cycle. The aim of this presentation is not to take sides in any special reading of the woman's movement but to provide a more useful perspective on all valid interpretations.

6. See Elizabeth Cady Stanton Susan B. Anthony, and Matilda J. Gage, *History of Woman Suffrage*, vol. 1 (New York: Fowler and Wells, 1881); Eleanor Flexner, *Century of Struggle*, 2d ed. (New York: Atheneum, 1973). The explosion of literature on the woman question includes many works whose special arguments only distract from the task of generalizing; helpful exceptions are listed here and in the following notes. Two useful guides to recent interpretive literature are: Barbara Haber, ed., *Women in America: A Guide to Books, 1963-1975* (Boston: G. K. Hall, 1978); and Virginia R. Terris, *Woman in America: A Guide to Information Sources* (Detroit: Gale, 1980).

7. See Stanton et al., vol. 1, pp. 70-71; see also *RSIA*, pp. 468-71.

8. Sarah Grimké, *Letters on the Equality of the Sexes* (Boston: Knapp, 1838), p. 8. See also *RSIA*, pp. 459-67.

9. Stanton et al., vol. 1, p. 117.

10. See Pastora San Juan, "Woman in the Office" (M.A. thesis, George Washington Univ.,

1966). Supporting the middle-class orientation of a similar group is Cindy S. Aron, " 'To Barter Their Souls for Gold': Female Clerks in Federal Government Offices, 1862-1890," *Journal of American History* 67 (March 1981): 835-53. To understand the circumstances that produced the female office worker, see Margery W. Davies, *Woman's Place Is at the Typewriter: Office Work and Office Workers* (Philadelphia: Temple Univ. Press, 1982).

11. L. Frank Baum, *By the Candelabra's Glare* (Chicago: Privately printed, 1898), p. 39.

12. Anna O. Commelin, *Of Such Is the Kingdom* (New York: Fowler and Wells, 1894), p. 84. For a discussion of the attitudinal setting for these verse comments see Walker, *Poet and the Gilded Age*, pp. 151-59.

13. For a revealing view of both consumerism and the problems of saleswomen at the turn of the century, see Annie Marion LacLean, "Two Weeks in Department Stores," *American Journal of Sociology* 4 (May 1899):721-41.

14. William L. O'Neill *(Everyone Was Brave* [Chicago: Quadrangle, 1969]) deals most directly and thoroughly with the suffrage anticlimax. For a pictorial representation of the split motives in the suffrage campaign, see *RSIA,* pp. 487-90.

15. Betty Friedan, in her famous *Feminine Mystique* (New York: Norton, 1963), makes the disappointment with suffrage the starting gun in the counterrevolution. Jo Freeman, in *Politics of Women's Liberation* (New York: McKay 1975), makes the point that the suffragists failed to see beyond the vote. Freeman, who treats the woman question as a social movement from a political science viewpoint, offers ways of understanding social change that are extremely helpful and very close to the direction of this study. Her conclusions, based on the case study of woman's rights, I see as contructively related to my own efforts to regularize reform vocabulary.

16. Although I have not found direct treatment of this question, I assume that specialists in the woman's movement have noted the important philosophic difference between the concept of "woman suffrage" as opposed to "equal suffrage." The latter would seem to be more suited to the second cycle.

17. Mrs. Harbert, whom I have depicted as a transition figure, used "equal suffrage" consistently. She also regularly petitioned the president to create a cabinet-level "department of the home." See Encounter 4.

18. A summary and interpretation of a number of works on women in the depression is Susan Ware's *Holding Their Own: American Women in the 1930s* (Boston: Twayne, 1982). Ware insists that women did not suffer as much as is usually alleged, but her arguments also show the difficulty in finding any consistent standard by which to measure female status. As to why the Women's Bureau was not more effective in this and other crises, see Judith Sealander, *As Minority Becomes Majority: Federal Reaction to the Phenomenon of Women in the Work Force, 1920-1963* (Westport, Conn.: Greenwood, 1983).

19. William H. Chafe, *American Woman* (New York: Oxford, 1972). Compared with turn-of-the-century labor, workers of the 1940s were sexually integrated, earned higher wages, worked about twenty fewer hours per week, and were made to feel that their contribution to the war effort was both important and glamorous. These facts only partially explain the irony in reporting female emancipation via office work in 1900 versus emancipation by factory work in 1940.

20. For questions that transcend reform see *RSIA,* pp. 490-502, as well as Alice Rossi's "Equality between the Sexes: An Immodest Proposal," in *Women in America,* ed. Robert J. Lifton (Boston: Houghton Mifflin, 1965), pp. 98-143.

21. The concept of human rights was prominent in antiquity as well as in the European Renaissance. Some aspects of this subject as they affect the reform tradition are discussed in the opening pages of Chapter 1. An interesting, self-conscious attempt to project this subject against a background of national concerns seventy years after the Revolution is by Elisha P. Hurlbut, *Essays on Human Rights and Their Political Guarantees* (New York: Fowler and Wells, 1853).

22. *Webster's Third New International Dictionary* agrees with the general distinction pursued here. A good brief explanation is in Edwin S. Newman, *Civil Liberty and Civil Rights,* 5th ed. (Dobbs Ferry, N.Y.: Oceana, 1970), p. x. The most useful finding aid on this subject is Alexander D. Brooks, *Bibliography of Civil Rights and Civil Liberties* (New York: Civil Liberties Educational

Foundation, 1962). As Brooks says, however, the whole subject comes close to being circumscribed in Norman Dorsen, Paul Bender, and Burt Neuborne, *Emerson, Haber, and Dorsen's Political and Civil Rights in the United States,* 4th ed., 2 vols. (Boston: Little, Brown, 1976 and vol. 2 with Sylvia Law, 1979). This work began as a compilation of materials for Professor Thomas Emerson's law class and has been regularly updated and reissued.

23. To appreciate American liberties against their European background see Chapter 1, note 1; Leon Whipple, *Our Ancient Liberties* (New York: Wilson, 1927); and Bernard Schwartz, ed., *Bill of Rights: A Documentary History,* 2 vols. (New York: Chelsea House, 1971). The latter work is confined to England and the colonies. Within those limits it is complete in the sense of political science if not political philosophy.

24. Paul L. Murphy, *World War I and the Origin of Civil Liberties in the United States* (New York: Norton, 1979). It may be true, as Murphy and Henry Steele Commager both allege, that the phrase "civil liberties" was not used prior to World War I, yet the point seems highly technical. Social action on behalf of civil liberties is older than the Christian era and, in North America, predates the forming of the United States. The point can be abundantly documented without going beyond Schwartz or Dorsen et al., cited above, note 22.

25. The trial of Gurley Flynn was used as one of the "encounters" not because it is typical (of the ACLU or anything else) but because, like the other encounters, it helps show the extreme range of reform. In the specific context of reform dynamics, furthermore, this episode illustrates a process of social change well into the "watchdog" stage. My reading in the history of civil liberties failed to show the important influence of such notable efforts to restate libertarian terms as Woodrow Wilson's fourteen points and FDR's four freedoms.

26. The McCarthy era, because of the loyalty oath controversy and the many other academic issues, produced a disproportionate outpouring of publications on civil liberties. A sample of the angry academic response, which also contains ten pages of helpful bibliography, is John W. Caughey's *In Clear and Present Danger* (Chicago: Univ. of Chicago Press, 1958).

27. Theodore Schroeder, *Free Speech Bibliography . . .* (Cos Cob, Conn.: Free Speech League, 1922; reprint, New York: Burt Franklin, 1969).

28. *Challenges of Protecting Personal Information in an Expanding Federal Computer Network Environment,* a report to Congress prepared by the Comptroller General (Washington, D.C.: General Accounting Office, 1978), p. 7. See also Suzan Deighton, *Privacy and Computers: A Bibliography* (London: Library, Institution of Electrical Engineers, 1978). The contemporary issue of privacy contrasts interestingly with one of the good studies of civil liberties in the American colonies: David H. Flaherty, *Privacy in Colonial New England* (Charlottesville: Univ. of Virginia Press, 1972).

29. The ACLU has been central in defining issues as well as acting upon them. A recent journalistic history is Barbara Habenstreit, *Eternal Vigilance* (New York: Messner, 1971). Two more serious works are Donald Johnson, *Challenge to American Freedoms* (Lexington: Univ of Kentucky Press, 1963); and Charles L. Markmann, *Noblest Cry: A History of the ACLU* (New York: St. Martin's, 1965). The ACLU is not without its critics. Daniel J. Popeo, the self-styled "Ralph Nader of the right," claims that ACLU-sponsored court actions have made the public schools into a haven for sexual deviates and pornographers while eliminating the rights of the majority to engage in prayer, celebrate religious holidays, and express patriotic sentiments. This is a summary of material distributed during 1980 by the Washington Legal Foundation, Dulles Access Road, Box 17725, Washington, D.C. 20041.

30. A controversy that still refuses to die was created by the ACLU in Illinois when it defended a local Nazi parade. For contemporary accounts see *Newsweek,* January 30, 1978; *U.S. News and World Report,* April 3, 1978; *New Leader,* August 14, 1978; and *Nation,* August 19-26, 1978.

31. The presidential candidate for the Libertarian party in 1980 got 880,000 votes as compared with 173,000 in 1976. A more serious appreciation of the state of civil liberties today can be synthesized from three recent works, one having to do with political philosophy, one with historical perspective, and one with public policy: Robert Nozick, *Anarchy, State, and Utopia* (New York: Basic Books, 1974); Norman A. Graebner, ed., *Freedom in America: A 200-year Perspective*

(University Park: Pennsylvania State Univ. Press, 1977); and Stephen L. Wasby, ed., *Civil Liberties* (Lexington, Mass.: D.C. Heath, 1976).

32. The list is not exhaustive but reflects the major concerns as reported in histories, source collections, bibliographies, and directories. One convenient inventory is the biennial *Human Rights Organizations and Periodical Directory* (Berkeley, Calif.: Meiklejohn Civil Liberties Institute). In 1977, David Christiano, editor of the directory compiled a 150-page list, ranging from abortion to Women's Soul Publishing to Youth Liberation.

33. In spite of its being outmoded in some respects, Alice Felt Tyler's monumental *Freedom's Ferment* (Minneapolis: Univ. of Minnesota Press, 1944) remains by far the best synthesis of Mode II antebellum reforms. Another good summary (especially in connecting philosophy with social concerns) is Henry Steele Commager's introductory essay in *The Era of Reform, 1830-1860* (Princeton: Van Nostrand, 1960). C. S. Griffin's *The Ferment of Reform, 1830-1860* (New York: Crowell, 1967) also makes sense of the era consistent with valid reform patterns: something more recent works have, unfortunately, failed to do.

34. I am leaning directly here on David J. Rothman, *The Discovery of the Asylum* (Boston: Little, Brown, 1971). Rothman begins by recounting the virtual absence of institutional solutions to social problems in the colonies. Thus the asylum was indeed a discovery. I am somewhat surprised at Rothman's assertion that the inventors of asylum saw rehabilitation as the essential function, whereas my own reading has seen the impetus as almost equally mixed between the curative and custodial.

35. The second part of the asylum story is told by David J. Rothman in *Conscience and Convenience* (Boston: Little, Brown, 1980). While developing my definition of Mode II and my ideas about its dynamics, I was unaware of Rothman's work, this second book having not as yet been published. I am very much in admiration of Rothman's determined ability to generalize about groups that have most often been treated separately. In this characteristic, Rothman's is closer than any other work to the kind of general treatment I have proposed for this broad category. I am also delighted that, in general terms, it supports my concept of a two-phase movement. In fact, the reforms covered by Rothman follow the double cycle more neatly than those used in this chapter, perhaps because of the complexities involved in sex and race as compared with social attitudes toward other special groups.

Encounter 4

1. Mrs. Harbert's granddaughter sold the Harbert papers to the Huntington Library in 1969. They have been beautifully ordered by Harriet McLoone who has my thanks for calling them to my attention. Although Mrs. Harbert's career is given summary treatment in several state and women's compendia, she was not included in *Notable American Women*. She richly merits a full biography.

2. Letters of March 15, 1875, and November 12, 1876, from Susan B. Anthony to Elizabeth Boynton Harbert, Harbert papers, Huntington Library.

3. Elizabeth Boynton Harbert, *Out of Her Sphere* (Des Moines: Mills, 1871).

4. The letter from Mrs. Harbert which produced this response is not preserved, although the subject is not hard to guess. The reply is dated February 16, 1885, and appears to have been signed by the professor whose physics lectures she attended twenty-five years earlier. Mrs. Harbert would have done no better to write the president or the board; for, when the subject of coeducation did come up for serious consideration in 1899, the answer was decisive and apparently permanent. The college had suggested "coordinate education" and invited the town's support for the establishment of a women's school within the college. The townspeople, after some vigorous discussion, astonished the college administration by proposing instead complete coeducation without further delay. This response the college's board tacitly rejected, thus ending the debate. Thanks to the kind help of Gladys Otto and Robert S. Harvey of the Wabash College archives, and of President Lewis S. Salter, I have been able to add to the information contained in the Harbert Papers in a manner which both clarifies and confuses the issue. No record of any discussion of coeducation exists in the

minutes of faculty, trustee, presidential, or other committees. Wabash College, at that time, clearly wished to consign both coeducation and its consideration to oblivion. Newspapers and campus magazines, however, preserve more than a ghost of the event. From these sources it is clear that the protest of "the 23," as they were then known, occurred in the fall of 1868; that it received attention in campus publications beyond the Indiana borders; that a young woman named Mary Hannah Krout may have been at least as prominent in the protest as Lizzie Boynton; and that there was a thread of continuity between the protest of 1868 and the movements for coeducation in Crawfordsville of the 1880s and 1890s.

Chapter 5

1. There is, as usual when abstractions and categories mix, a confusion as to terminology. Some writers make no distinction between literary and actual utopias. One school consistently refers to the communitarians as "utopian socialists." To achieve some clarity without inventing a new set of terms, I will designate only actual settlements as "communes" and their inhabitants and advocates as "communards" or "communitarians." "New," before these terms, indicates the movement of the 1960s and 1970s as opposed to the antebellum, or "old," phenomenon. "Intentional settlement," a more recent term, is used synonymousy with "commune." Thus "utopia" can be reserved for designating a concept that is described rather than performed.

2. Ray A. Billington, *Land of Savagery, Land of Promise* (New York: Norton, 1981), p. 3. There are many works on the idea, the promise, the image of America. Closest in spirit to the present chapter is Charles L. Sanford, *Quest for Paradise* (Urbana: Univ. of Illinois Press, 1961), especially chapter 10.

3. Cotton Mather, *Theopolis Americana* . . . (Boston: Gerrish, 1710), p. 42.

4. On the influence of the classical heritage, see Chapter 1, especially note 1.

5. T. Thomas, *Working-Man's Cottage Architecture* (New York: R. Martin, 1848). For reproduction of a section of this work and a discussion of its setting, see *RSIA*, pp. 505-12. All of *RSIA*, part 4, pertains to this chapter and the next.

6. Andrew Jackson Downing, *Architecture of Country Houses* (New York: Appleton, 1852), pp. v-vi.

7. The term "environmental reform" can be used to cover a multitude of activities that might be considered part of Mode III. The conservation and ecology movements surely aim at improving man's relation with nature and thus qualify at least for the margins of this mode. In the center, however, are reformers who use the term to indicate the creation of a carefully planned environment (natural and/or technological) which aims to improve the individual and collective human condition. Two works that use this term helpfully while expanding its meaning are Albert Z. Guttenberg, *Environmental Reform in the United States*, Council of Planning Librarians, Exchange Bibliography no. 85 (Monticello, Ill., 1969); and Cecelia Tichi, *New World, New Earth: Environmental Reform in American Literature from the Puritans through Whitman* (New Haven: Yale Univ. Press, 1979).

8. Ralph Waldo Emerson to Thomas Carlyle, 30 October 1840, in Charles E. Norton, ed., *Correspondence of Thomas Carlyle and Ralph Waldo Emerson, 1834-1872* (Boston: Osgood, 1883), vol. 1, pp. 308-309. Ripley's colony became Brook Farm.

9. The most efficient way to get a good contemporary view of this movement is to read John Humphrey Noyes, *History of American Socialisms* (Philidelphia: Lippincott, 1870); Charles Nordhoff, *Communistic Societies of the United States* (New York: Harper, 1875); Adin Ballou, *Practical Christian Socialism* (New York: Privately printed, 1854). The indispensable modern treatment is Arthur E. Bestor's *Backwoods Utopias* (Philadelphia: Univ. of Pennsylvania Press, 1950), which leaves off its coverage in 1829, having provided some reliable checklists and compilations through 1860. Robert S. Fogarty, *Dictionary of American Communal and Utopian History* (Westport, Conn.: Greenwood, 1980), includes an updated checklist compiled by Otohiko Okugawa, a bibliographical essay, and a dictionary of individuals and communes.

10. Bestor, p. 5, finds the roots of religious communism in the radical sects of the European Reformation. It is surely true that many of the better-known religious communes were imported directly from Europe, particularly from Germany, to the American backwoods.

11. While contrasting the secular and religious viewpoints, Noyes made little distinction between the varieties of socialism and the varieties of revivalism. Although in his own life he first encountered the religious view, Noyes saw Oneida as, in part, an extension of Brook Farm's final, Fourierist phase. The key to Oneida's success was in refusing either view, in toto, while developing a workable blend of the secular and the religious. See Noyes's *History of American Socialisms*, pp. xv, 22-24.

12. Nordhoff. (see note 9); William Hinds, *American Communities* (Chicago: Kerr, 1902, 1908).

13. Hugh Gardner, *Children of Prosperity: Thirteen Modern American Communes* (New York: St. Martin's, 1978), p. 2. Apparently Gardner bases this conclusion on the unpublished data compiled by Foster G. Stockwell (Gardner, chapter 1, note 2). The "bigger" in the quotation compares post-Civil War with antebellum numbers.

14. Rosabeth M. Kanter, *Commitment and Community: Communes and Utopias in Sociological Perspective* (Cambridge, Mass.: Harvard Univ. Press, 1972), p. 8. Kanter and Gardner provide the most useful works on the new communes.

15. See Dolores Hayden, *Seven American Utopias* (Cambridge, Mass.: MIT Press, 1976) and *Grand Domestic Revolution* (Cambridge, Mass.: MIT Press, 1981).

16. Access to the Oneida experience is unusually rich. John Humphrey Noyes himself issued many publications and wrote an autobiography. There are also accounts by family, visitors, and participating Perfectionists. The basic bibliography is included in Maren Lockwood Carden, *Oneida: Utopian Community to Modern Corporation* (Baltimore: Johns Hopkins Univ. Press, 1969). Since then, Noyes's granddaughter, Constance Noyes Robertson, has collected and edited two volumes of materials relating to Oneida, both published by the Syracuse Univ. Press: *Oneida Community: An Autobiography, 1851-1876* (1970) and *Oneida Community: The Breakup, 1876-1881* (1972).

17. See Hayden, *Seven American Utopias* pp. 199-219, for an analysis of the way the Perfectionists worked out this balance architecturally.

18. Pierrepont Noyes, *My Father's House: An Oneida Boyhood* (New York: Farrar and Rinehart, 1937), p. 176.

19. B. F. Skinner, *Walden Two* (New York: Macmillan, 1948).

20. The best access to the early days of the Twin Oaks commune is Kathleen Kinkade, *Walden Two Experiment* (New York: Morrow, 1973). The most helpful accounts by outside visitors are those of Kanter, pp. 18-31, and Robert Houriet, *Getting Back Together* (New York: Coward, McCann and Geoghegan, 1971), chapter 7. Updating the story is a two-part interview with Kat Kinkade's daughter in the *Washington Post:* May 3, 1981, pp. A1, A14; and May 4, 1981, pp. A1, A2.

21. As of 1982 Gerri Frantz had apparently inherited the role of Kat Kinkade. She is quoted in the *Washington Post* article (see note 20, above) and has also been interviewed by my colleague, Professor Robert Kenny, who teaches a course in the theory and practice of communes. I am obliged to him for having read part 3 critically and having improved the currency of my information. Gerri Frantz sees no link with Skinner. Richard Todd went further by asserting that Skinner would have been disappointed had he visited Twin Oaks. See " 'Walden Two': Three? Many More?" *New York Times Magazine,* March 15, 1979, pp. 24-25, 114-25.

22. Kinkade, p. 2.

23. Nordhoff, pp. 399-409. A view discounting the buoyant perfectionism usually attributed to this period and much more supportive of the group portrait submitted by Nordhoff, is that of Lewis O. Saum, *Popular Mood of Pre-Civil War America* (Westport, Conn.: Greenwood, 1980).

24. Gilbert Seldes, *Stammering Century* (New York: Day, 1928), especially the preface and chapter 26; Victor F. Calverton, *Where Angels Dared to Tread* (Indianapolis: Bobbs-Merrill, 1941), especially chapter 20.

25. Mark Vonnegut, *Eden Express* (New York: Praeger, 1975), p. 31. This remarkable autobiographical fragment is correctly catalogued with works about schizophrenia; it is also in some ways a

singular penetration of what the new commune movement meant to many of its participants; see pp. 41, 48. See also Gardner, p. 239.

26. Gardner, p. 242.

27. Twin Oaks had in mind a separate children's house, on the Oneida model, where the young would be reared as the wards of the entire settlement. Kat Kinkade's daughter, who was thirteen when Twin Oaks was founded, was somehow never considered a child. On educational pioneering at Synanon, see Kanter, chapter 8.

28. Vonnegut, p. 59.

29. Ibid., p. 40.

30. The Perfectionists of Oneida were quite explicit about the parallel between material possessions and the "possession" of wife, husband, and children (see Noyes, p. 625). A comparative look at the roles of women in the Shaker, Perfectionist, and Mormon communities is available in Lawrence Foster, *Religion and Sexuality* (New York: Oxford, 1981).

31. One chink in the armor of asceticism stems from the love of music and the importance of dancing and singing. Thus many communes had elegant musical instruments—only some of them homemade—and, at the new ones, elaborate sound systems.

32. Kanter, pp. 201ff. Kanter observes that many psychosocial techniques had been anticipated at Oneida. For other examples see Gardner, chapter 12.

33. For a sample of such publications, see *RSIA,* pp. 595-606. Some scholars of the new communes (Kanter, Hayden) have been helpfully sensitive to the precedents offered by earlier experiences; it is hard to tell, however, how many of the actual settlers were aware of a prior tradition. At Twin Oaks three buildings were named for earlier communes, but there are few instances of this kind of self-consciousness of continuing an earlier tradition.

34. For two constructive views of urban communes see Carl Bernstein, "Communes, a New Way of Life in the District," *Washington Post,* July 6, 1969, p. C1; Rick Margolies, "Building Communities," in *Good Life,* ed. Jerry Richard (New York: New American Library, 1973), pp. 264-76.

35. The first passage resulted from Frederick Law Olmsted's visit to the phalanx at Red Bank, New Jersey. It appeared in the *New York Daily Tribune,* July 29, 1852, p. 6. For a reprinting of the entire letter see *RSIA,* pp. 519-24. The second passage is from Vonnegut, p. 71.

36. John A. Lomax and Alan Lomax, *Folk Song USA* (New York: Duell, Sloan and Pearce, 1947), p. 281.

37. Unless otherwise noted, my statements about this form rely on Charles J. Rooney, "Utopian Literature as a Reflection of Social Forces in America, 1865-1917" (Ph.D. diss., George Washington Univ., 1968). Rooney's study is based on 106 romances, all but a handful of which appeared from 1889 to 1912. Lewis Mumford *(Story of Utopias* [New York: Boni and Liveright, 1922]) felt that modern utopias were inseparable from the rise of technology, H. G. Wells distinguished the modern utopia by its kinetic, as opposed to static, structure (as discussed in Harry W. Laidler, *Social-Economic Movements* [New York: Crowell, 1944], p. 114); Ellene Ransom, in her "Utopus Discovers America" (Ph.D. diss., Vanderbilt Univ., 1946), argues for an important connection between this genre and the rise of literary realism. Kenneth M. Roemer, ed., *America as Utopia* (New York: Franklin, 1981), pp. 254-304, describes the small number of American utopias that preceded Bellamy's.

38. Frederick Upham Adams, *President John Smith, or the Story of a Peaceful Revolution* (Chicago: Kerr, 1896). Allegedly written in 1893 this work does anticipate some of the Populist recommendations of 1896. Many utopias were penned for political purposes even more specific than those of Adams: for example, Ignatius Donnelly's two works: *Caesar's Collumn,* (Chicago: Shulte, 1890), a direct endorsement of populism, and *The Golden Bottle* (Chicago: Merrill, 1892), an attack on the gold standard.

39. Adams, p. 143.

40. Ibid., p. 165.

41. Bradford Peck, *The World a Department Store* (Lewiston, Me.: Peck, 1900).

42. Joyce L. Kornbluh, ed., *Rebel Voices* (Ann Arbor: Univ. of Michigan Press, 1964), pp. 10-11.

43. For an argument as to the utopian aspects of the IWW see *RSIA*, pp. 574-76. There is no intention, there or here, to suggest that the IWW was simply a utopian movement. It was surely one of the more unusual adventures in American reform partly because of the coloration provided by the dreams of that "one big union" in the sky, and partly because (like most utopias and unlike most unions) it was truly radical. See Aileen S. Kraditor, *The Radical Persuasion, 1890-1917* (Baton Rouge: Louisiana State Univ. Press, 1981).

44. For a thorough discussion of this literary type see Robert G. Wright, "Social Christian Novel in the Gilded Age, 1865-1900" (Ph.D. diss., George Washington Univ., 1968). Most Christian social novels depict the redemption of society through individual acts of sacrifice and charity as opposed to the adoption of a new social order.

45. Charles Sheldon's *In His Steps* was first published in serial form in the religious journal *Advance* in 1896-97, after which it had a publication history as complex as it is extensive. It has been translated into all major and many minor languages, including Esperanto. It may have sold more than 20 million copies. Subsequent references are to the edition published by Universal Book, Philadelphia, 1937.

46. Sheldon, p. 256.

47. For a further discussion of religion and society at this time, with Josiah Strong's *Twentieth Century City* as a case in point, see *RSIA*, pp. 568-74. Throughout *Socialism and American Life* (2 vols., ed. Donald D. Egbert and Stow Persons [Princeton: Princeton Univ. Press, 1952] runs a thread connecting the religious impulse behind various forms of socialism, including communes and utopias.

48. It should be noted that some of Skinner's readers regard his work more as a dystopia. See *RSIA*, p. 597.

49. Skinner, p. 106 of the softbound edition.

50. J. E. Higgins, *Looking Backward in Rhyme* (San Francisco: Carrier Dove, 1892). All the novels mentioned here are fully cited and summarized in Rooney, pp. 264-81.

51. Edward Bellamy, *Looking Backward* (Boston: Houghton, Mifflin, 1888), pp. 278-79.

52. Egbert and Persons, vol. 1, p. 269.

53. Letter from Marion Bellamy Earnshaw to W. H. Ferry, Center for the Study of Democratic Institutions, Santa Barbara, California, April 14, 1965. For more on Howard and the Garden City see Chapter 6, note 19.

54. Because the utopian movement as a whole is less well known than Bellamy's work, I have given some space to it, drawing heavily on Rooney. The composite novel shows that Bellamy was more influential than all other sources combined. What strikes one most is the narrow margin between those who were and were not willing to move toward a controlled, cooperative system at the expense of traditional values.

55. Arthur E. Morgan, *Nowhere Was Somewhere* (Chapel Hill: Univ. of North Carolina Press, 1946), p. 9.

Chapter 6

1. Fred Clough, *Golden Age, or, the Depth of Time* (Boston: Roxburgh, 1923). For discussion of this work, including an excerpt, see *RSIA*, pp. 591-95.

2. Ralph Gernback, *Ralph 12C 41 +* (Boston: Stratford, 1925).

3. Philip Wylie and Edwin Balmer, *After Worlds Collide* (New York: Stokes, 1934), p. 148. This book and its predecessor, *When Worlds Collide*, accurately reflect the catastrophic tone of the science fiction of the 1930s. There is much stress given the question of choosing the limited number of possible survivors, a question not unrelated to the Great Depression. *After Worlds Collide* invokes the religious and patriotic past at every turn. The ships used to escape the doom are christened arks; the leader is called a true Moses; the enemy are the Midianites. Once the "Ark" has touched down, "Moses" sees to the raising of Old Glory and declares a Day of Thanksgiving.

4. Isaac Asimov, "Social Science Fiction," in *Modern Science Fiction: Its Meaning and Its Future*, Reginald Bretnor ed. (New York: Coward-McCann. 1953), p. 196. Asimov's essay offers a knowledgeable taxonomy of the various compartments of science fiction with an eye toward social impact. Lyman T. Sargent catalogs the utopian elements in American science fiction, 1950-75, in Roemer, pp. 347-66.

5. Sheldon's minister, in the final pages of *In His Steps*, has a waking dream of his mission spreading to "Endeavor Societies all over the world"; but the high point of this hopeful prophecy is "the church of Jesus in America" (p. 263).

6. Merle Curti, *Peace or War: The American Struggle* (New York: Norton, 1936).

7. This program is discussed and some publications excerpted with the help of Clarence Streit in *RSIA*, pp. 579-91. Garry Davis's idea is an interesting variation on the world government model. Instead of asking nations to relinquish autonomy, he invites citizens to resign their nationality and join a nonnational World Service Authority. Although Davis might not admit it, he is engaging in a protest movement as opposed to creating a world government model.

8. "Preliminary Report upon the Proposed Suburban Village at Riverside, near Chicago," Olmsted, Vaux & Co., Landscape Architects, September 1, 1868. The report is in the Olmsted papers, Manuscripts Division, Library of Congress. The report and plan were reproduced by Theodora Kimball in *Landscape Architecture* 21 (July 1931): 257-91; the quotation is from p. 289. Sections having most to do with the present approach were reproduced and discussed in *RSIA*, pp. 524-34. Enough of Riverside remains today to repay a visit.

9. See Chapter 5, note 35. Olmsted played a part in the reform drama beyond observing and planning. He was a member of that elite group loosely associated with the Liberal Republican movement. See Geoffrey Blodgett, "Frederick Law Olmsted: Landscape Architecture as Conservative Reform," *Journal of American History* 62 (March 1976):869-89.

10. For a discussion of the idea see Baker Brownell and Frank Lloyd Wright, *Architecture and Modern Life* (New York: Harper, 1937), pp. 308-28. For renderings of Broadacre City see Arthur Drexler, ed., *Drawings of Frank Lloyd Wright* (New York: Museum of Modern Art, 1962).

11. *RSIA*, p. 539.

12. Ibid., p. 536. Wright meant this paradox to enforce the notion that his principles could be applied on any scale from a single county to the surface of the globe. It suggests another paradox pointed out by Helen Rosenau: namely, that Wright was an "anarchist planner." See *Ideal City* (New York: Harper and Row, 1972), p. 151. There is a helpful discussion of Broadacre City in Percival Goodman and Paul Goodman, *Communitas* (New York: Random House, 1960), pp. 88-93.

13. Martin Meyerson proposes a simpler bifurcation between the literary utopias on one hand, which tell how to change social institutions, and design utopias on the other hand. The second stream dates from the Italian architects Leone Battista Alberti and Antonio Averlino and dictates a new physical environment. I am accepting this distinction but arguing that in most important models the two streams come together. Furthermore, within each stream, there are gradations running from the mundane to the fantastic. Meyerson's article, "Utopian Traditions and the Planning of Cities," appeared in *Daedalus* 90 (Winter 1961):180-93.

14. Ulrich Conrads and Hans G. Sperlich, *Architecture of Fantasy*, trans., ed., and expanded by Christiane C. Collins and George R. Collins (New York: Praeger, 1962), pp. 20-21. The other important chronicle of this genre is that of Rosenau, cited in note 12, above.

15. Paolo Soleri, *Sketchbooks* (Cambridge, Mass.: MIT Press, 1971), pp. 4-6.

16. A collection of sources that helps point up this distinction is David R. Weimer, ed., *City and Country in America* (New York: Appleton-Century-Crofts, 1962).

17. Paul K. Conkin, *Tomorrow a New World: The New Deal Community Program* (Ithaca, N.Y.: American Historical Association, 1959). This excellent study is perfectly appropriate for understanding Mode III. In his first chapter Conkin traces the history of communes through a set of sources determined by his interest in economic ideas and by his search for precedents to a particular set of events. He adds fuel to Gardner's assertion (see chapter 5, note 13.) that communes continued importantly beyond the Civil War; for a quantitative summary see pp. 332-37.

18. Ibid., pp. 6, 7. One of Conkin's major points concerns the erosion of individualism, as a

social value, and its replacement with collective experimentation. Thus in this limited context he asserts something that is true of the reform experience in general and which is helpfully corrective of one's sense of national values.

19. David Riesman, *Individualism Reconsidered and Other Essays* (Glencoe, Ill.: Free Press, 1954), p. 81. Hayden particularizes Howard's debt to Bellamy *(Seven American Utopias,* p. 300), while Robert Fishman *(Urban Utopias in the Twentieth Century* [New York: Basic, 1977]) argues that Howard, Wright, and Le Corbusier (while not agreeing with one another) all responded to Bellamy's call for a complete reconstruction of cities to avoid hardening the physical manifestations of social injustice.

20. Conkin, in *Tomorrow a New World,* chapter 3, chronicles the ways different individuals came together in different projects. Clarence S. Stein and Henry Wright were important links between Radburn and the New Deal Communities. See Stein's *Toward New Towns for America* (1957; reprint ed., Cambridge, Mass.: MIT Press, 1971). There is also some overlap between the green cities and the Tennessee Valley Authority, the most ambitious regional plan of ths era. *RSIA* (pp. 541-50) reproduces part of the TVA legislation and raises the question of the extent to which this project can be considered a model in utopian terms as the Goodmans argue (pp. 111-16). Models do not always achieve their lofty aims. For a careful recent evaluatin see Michael J. McDonald and John Muldowny, *TVA and the Dispossessed: The Resettlement of Population in the Norris Dam Area* (Knoxville: Univ. of Tennessee Press, 1982).

21. Conkin, *Tomorrow a New World,* p. 316. The hyperactive communal life at Radburn may not have been reflected in most New Deal communities; Conkin characterizes the planners as visionaries but the residents as interested primarily in economic stability.

22. *RSIA,* p. 554. For a discussion of Rouse and an extract from his address, see pp. 550-58. Included is a photograph of a model for Columbia which is more reminiscent of Broadacre City than of any other precedent. A summary of Rouse's inner-city efforts is in the *Washington Post,* January 17, 1982, p. D2 and May 11, 1985, pp. F21-23; see also February 27, 1982, pp. F1, F18, for an update on Columbia. A booklength attempt to place Columbia in a planning context is Vivian Gurney Breckenfeld, *Columbia and the New Cities* (New York: Ives Washburn, 1971).

23. For a student of reform it is hard to avoid exaggerating the impact of a man who combines as many parts of the total reform picture as did Fuller. A case for Fuller as dreamer-planner is made in *RSIA,* pp. 606-609, where are reproduced pictures of the dymaxion house and a dome over Manhattan as specimens of Fuller's microcosmic and macrocosmic solutions. The larger aspects of his ideas are taken up on pp. 653-64.

24. Hayden, *Seven American Utopias* and *Grand Domestic Revolution;* also Paul Douglas, "Town Planning for the City of God," in *Utopias: The American Experience* Gairdner B. Moment and Otto F. Krausher ed. (Metuchen, N.J.: Scarecrow, 1980), pp. 103-25.

25. Joyce O. Hertzler, *History of Utopian Thought* (London: Allen, 1923). The other works mentioned in this paragraph are cited in chapters 5 and 6.

26. Occasionally an event in Mode III will have repercussions in other modes. The works of Edward Bellamy and Henry George (both of which have been considered utopian) have spawned political and associational activity; this is atypical.

27. Hayden sometimes falls into the trap of oversimplifying the commune movement by calling it a response to the industrial revolution. From this position she is tempted to overplay economic causation. She writes that the panics of 1837, 1854, 1857, 1873 and 1893 increased commune membership *(Seven American Utopias,* p. 14). Even the data from Bestor, which she reproduces, refutes this to some extent. The late 1830s saw only four communes formed (hard times) as opposed to the early 1840s (good times), which saw thirty-six. I am unaware of a panic in 1854; were there one, it would have coincided with a slack time for new communes (eight) as opposed to fourteen in the immediately preceding comparable period (good times). Gardner, on the other hand (p. 242), takes the opposite position with considerably more credibility. He shows that the affluent postwar climate made the New Wave possible and that the stringencies of the 1970s helped undermine the movement.

28. There is a very loose correlation between the two commune waves and the times when the

mainstream was struggling to adjust to a sharp upturn in the rate of scientific and technological innovation accompanied by a related challenge to traditional values. In contrast, periods when value structures are relatively stable and the rate of innovation is constant produce milder forms of expression: futuristic novels and visionary plans. This speculation is more a question than a conclusion and assumes that leaving the mainstream for a planned settlement is a qualitatively different act than sitting down to the typewriter or drawing board.

29. Riesman, p. 70, a revised version of a essay first published in 1947.

30. It occurred to me to ask David Riesman if, twenty-five years later, he still put a high priority on the revitalization of utopian thought. He replied that he was no longer so sure and expressed disappointment that so many authors of social solutions were uninformed as to economics, technology, and demography. At the same time, the letter carried its own distinct, visionary tone (Riesman to author, Cambridge, Mass., July 15, 1981).

Encounter 5

1. These numbers are reported with some variation. The principal source is the official *Report of the Debates in the Convention of California on the Formation of the State Constitution*, compiled by the designated reporter, the writer J. Ross Browne (Washington, D.C.: John T. Tower, 1850), pp. 478-79. See also Samuel H. Willey, *The Transition Period of California* (San Francisco: Whitaker and Ray, 1901), pp. 93-94. Willey was one of two chaplains, residents of Monterey, who opened each day's session with a prayer. See also Josiah Royce, *California* (Boston: Houghton, Mifflin, 1897), p. 260.

2. Willey, p. 94.

3. Browne, p. 477.

4. As a concession to the Hispano-Americans, many of whom had Indian ancestry, a provision was added allowing the future legislation of voting rights for Indians (Browne, p. 341).

5. See Browne, pp. 138-50. See also Rockwell D. Hunt, *Genesis of California's First Constitution*, Hopkins Studies in Historical and Political Science, 13th series, (Baltimore: Johns Hopkins Univ. Press, 1895), p. 43.

6. Browne, pp. 149-50.

7. Royce, p. 255. Royce goes on to point out how this political skill was admirable only as "cleverness" and failed to solve the moral problem it temporized with. There is some contradiction in Royce's admiration of an "instinctive" political skill as opposed to his conspiracy theories.

8. Most commentators have pointed to the convention's action as offering one of the first steps toward codifying married women's property rights. This is, like many legal and constitutional questions, not subject to quick generalizations. In 1897, Jessie J. Cassidy compiled a set of comparative data on this topic in *The Legal Status of Women* (New York: National-American Woman Suffrage Association); as of that date, seven of forty-one states still failed to recognize the married woman's right to her own property. Maine, Pennyslvania, and North Carolina, at least, would appear to have preceded California in passing this kind of statute (see pp. 20-21).

9. Browne, p. 259.

Chapter 7

1. In Part 5 of *RSIA* is a set of documents intended to suggest what may be distinctive about American reform. Thayer, Chapman, and Fuller are all discussed and portions of their works reproduced. The quotation is from Thayer, *Six Speeches*, p. 12. See Chapter 3, note 43.

2. *RSIA*, p. 643.

3. Henry J. Silverman, "American Social Reformers in the Late Nineteenth and Early Twentieth Century" (Ph.D. diss., Univ. of Pennsylvania, 1963). In his *Encyclopedia of Social Reform*, Bliss listed 230 American reformers; Silverman's study is based on those 166 who left substantial records.

A much larger number from the same era (more than 20,000) were identified by Lisle A. Rose, whose bibliography is in the process of being stored on computer at George Washington University. The world of Bliss and Silverman may prove to be a microcosm but, at this date, it is the most comprehensive list. Perhaps because "political actor" is a more controllable concept than "social actor," it has begun to attract some careful study based on structured sampling as opposed to cumulative biographies. The pioneer study in this field, stressing the consequences rather than the causes of political behavior, is Angus Campbell et al., *American Voter* (New York: Wiley, 1960). Sidney Verba and Norma Nie have not only updated the work of Campbell and his colleagues at the University of Michigan Survey Research Center, but they have begun to measure participation other than voting. Their basic work is *Participation in America: Political Democracy and Social Equality,* (New York: Harper and Row, 1972). Some of these findings will be used in Chapter 8.

4. This portrait should be compared with characteristics of the contemporary members of voluntary societies (see especially note 8, below). One group is made up of leaders and the other of givers; yet the similarities are striking.

5. Part Two discusses the American Anti-Slavery Society, the National Association for the Advancement of Colored People, and the American Civil Liberties Union.

6. Although there is no study aimed directly at the reform association, there is a literature of voluntarism most broadly defined by Susan J. Ellis and Katherine H. Noyes, *By the People: A History of Americans as Volunteers* (Philadelphia: Energize, 1978) and most usefully organized by Constance Smith and Anne Freedman, *Voluntary Associations: Perspective on the Literature* (Cambridge, Mass.: Harvard Univ. Press, 1972). Studies by political scientists bear on reform questions as with J.Q. Wilson, *Political Organizations.* Sociological studies often pertain to reform as, for example, Kenneth E. Reid, *From Character Building to Social Treatment: The History of the Use of Groups in Social Work* (Westport, Conn.: Greenwood, 1981). Although Ralph M. Kramer's pretentiously titled comparative study, *Voluntary Agencies in the Welfare State* (Berkeley: Univ. of California Press, 1981), deals only with agencies serving the handicapped, it does correlate strongly with what David Rothman (in particular) and I (in general) have proposed concerning goals and attitudes. Although he designates only seventeen of the fifty-three groups he studied as "reform," W. A. Gamson in his *Strategy of Social Protest* has come close to answering questions germane to the history of reform. Anne F. Scott argues the harmful neglect of voluntarism and the particular consequences for misunderstanding the woman movement: "On Seeing and Not Seeing," *Journal of American History,* 71 (June, 1984), pp. 7-21. The careers of Gurley Flynn (Encounter 6) and Elizabeth Boynton Harbert (Encounter 4) make rich comments on women and voluntarism. So does Anne M. Boylan, "Women in Groups," *Journal of American History* 71 (December 1984): 497-523.

7. I have studied the literature issued by contemporary organizations. I have also enjoyed extensive conversations with Claire Nader and brief talks with John W. Gardner, and I have helped direct a doctoral dissertation on the Ralph Nader organizations. My best insights, however, have come from a series of interviews with fund-raiser Roger Craver, founder of Craver, Mathews, Smith and Co. (CMS), whose clients include the American Civil Liberties Union, Common Cause, the League of Women Voters, National Organization for Women, Planned Parenthood, and the Sierra Club. After the 1980 presidential campaign of John Anderson, CMS gave up serving individual candidates for the sake of the National Democratic Committee. CMS, to be sure, represents the classic liberal bias in fund-raising, but then, so does most of social change.

8. Craver discovered this group through its reading habits: magazine subscription lists. He calls them "the extreme middle" and compares them with European liberals in that they are fiscally conservative and socially liberal; he thinks of them as the gyroscope for the middle class. They seek to avoid turmoil by anticipating issues and preventing extreme positions from developing. They are process-oriented. The causes they back win in the long run. The mean age of this group is fifty, typical of "givers." By occupation they are professional and managerial; thus they are definitely *not* antibusiness. Rather, they *are* business management. Although they will not attack their own institutions, they show no evidence of financial self-interest in the causes they support. Compared with the general population they are better educated, more urban and coastal, slightly more female

and notably more Jewish. Given seventy years of geographic and demographic change, the modern giver sounds remarkably similar to the reform leader of 1908 (see the Silverman study, note 3, above). A link between Silverman and Craver, based on a geographically limited sample, is Kathleen D. McCarthy's *Noblesse Oblige: Charity and Cultural Philanthropy in Chicago, 1849-1929* (Chicago: Univ. of Chicago Press, 1982); much of this book is tied to local circumstances, but it offers some interesting examples of the shift from personal participation to financial support.

9. The amount of money raised by CMS increased from $25 million to $85 million between 1977 and 1981. Some of this reflects increased public participation; some reflects the growing number of CMS clients.

10. The spectacular impact of the Reverend James A. Gusweller on the housing conditions in the neighborhood of his Church of St. Matthew and St. Timothy was chronicled in a *New Yorker* magazine profile, August 1 and 8, 1964. A symposium directly addressed to the church and social action was sponsored by the Board for Homeland Missionaries of the United Church of Christ. See *Journal of Current Social Issues* 9 (Autumn 1971):3-30; an annotated bibliography is included.

11. J. Q. Wilson uses the example of the NAACP to make this point in *Political Organizations.*

12. John Gardner, "The War of the Parts against the Whole," in *Seventeenth Cosmos Club Award* (Washington, D.C.: Cosmos Club, 1980).

13. Undated mailing from New Directions, 2021 L St., N.W., Washington, D.C., 20036, from Russell Peterson, President (1979).

14. There has been new attention to slave revolts and the Woman's party as sources of violence. Gamson estimates that 25 percent of his sample "challenge groups" engaged in some form of violence (see chapter 3, note 8). In contrast Rhodi Jeffreys-Jones argues in *Violence and Reform in American History* (New York: New Viewpoints, 1978) that both the amount and effectiveness of violence—actual and threatened—has been overestimated.

15. In Part 2 of this work and in *RSIA* (pp. 272-321), the literature of emancipation and civil rights has been used to illustrate the use of creative forms in the service of social change. Monographs on literature and society are plentiful, and include works by Daniel Aaron, Alfred Kazin, Edmund Wilson, and many other discerning critics. These works tend to stress fiction. I have myself tried to make a case for the social relevance of verse in *The Poet and the Gilded Age*. A work that connects both cartooning and serious painting is Richard Fitzgerald's *Art and Politics*.

16. In 1984 both major candidates campaigned from trains. The effect was nostalgic, with Walter Mondale deliberately attempting a parallel with Harry Truman's whistlestop triumph of 1948. The impact of this direct appeal to voters proved insignificant when compared with that of the televised debates.

17. There are other models for the stages of social change but most of them are offered in a severely limited setting. The nearest thing to a usable general model was proposed by Albion W. Small eighty-five years ago. He identified four stages: namely, discovery (of the problem/solution), persuasion, individual adjustment, and social adaptation. Small is willing to consider both the individual actor and the social institution as integrally involved in the same process, but he does not see the importance in distinguishing protest from remedial action. See "Sanity in Social Agitation," *American Journal of Sociology* 4 (November 1898):335-51.

18. *RSIA*, p. 11.

19. George Henry Evans, *The People's Rights*, n.s. 1 (May 25, 1844):1. See *RSIA*, pp. 83-87. This collection of documents, *RSIA*, was arranged to show among other things the universality of all three main reform arguments. This pattern is also given prominence in the foregoing chapters of the present work, especially in Chapter 3, where the antislavery and civil rights movements are compared.

20. Adin Ballou, *Practical Christian Socialism* (Hopedale: Privately printed, 1854); Wilbur F. Crafts, *Practical Christian Sociology* (New York: Funk and Wagnalls, 1895).

21. For a discussion of Rouse and Fuller in context see Chapter 6, above; the lines are from Buckminister Fuller, *No More Secondhand God* (Carbondale: Southern Illinois Univ. Press, 1963), p. 18. For additional comment on Fuller, as well as socially pertinent extracts from his verse, see *RSIA*, pp. 653-64.

Chapter 8

1. See Part 1 and Chapter 7.
2. William J. Crotty, *Political Reform and the American Experiment* (New York: Crowell, 1977), chapter 2.
3. Angus Campbell et al., especially chapter 20.
4. Richard G. Niemi and Herbert F. Weisberg, *Controversies in American Voting Behavior* (San Francisco: Freeman, 1976); Norman H. Nie, Sidney Verba, and John R. Petrocik, *Changing American Voter* (Cambridge, Mass.: Harvard Univ. Press, 1979); Paul Kleppner, *Who Voted? The Dynamics of Electoral Turnout, 1870-1980* (New York: Praeger, 1982).
5. Sidney Verba and Norman H. Nie, p. 342; see also chapters 3 and 4.
6. Gabriel Almond and Sidney Verba, *Civic Culture* (Princeton: Princeton Univ. Press, 1963), especially chapters 9 and 11. Melvin B. Mogulof *(Citizen Participation* [Washington, D.C.: Urban Institute, 1970]) considers citizen involvement the responsibility of federal agencies and finds some evidence that pariciption waxes.
7. It must be stressed that these studies are based on the very recent past and make no comment on issues prior to World War II. Sidney Verba, Norman H. Nie, and Jae-On Kim, *Modes of Democratic Participation: A Cross-National Comparison* (Beverly Hills, Calif.: Sage, 1971); and, by the same authors, *Participation and Political Equality: a Seven-Nation Comparison* (Cambridge: Cambridge Univ. Press, 1979).
8. For a reasonable inventory of contemporary concerns, see William J. Crotty, ed., *Paths to Political Reform* (Lexington, Mass.: Heath, 1980), especially as summarized in the Introduction. This work also contains a helpful treatment of specific solutions to the problem of nonvoting (pp. 97-107). Robert A. Dahl has developed his own way of assessing democracy; it is not particularly optimistic, yet it, too, is interesting for the number of constructive recommendations it contains. See his *Democracy in the United States: Promise and Performance* 3d ed. (Chicago: Rand McNally, 1976), chapters 6 and 29, especially. Crotty, *Political Reform and the American Experiment* reviews a number of problems but also ends with a positive view of the progress toward effective democracy.
9. Unless otherwise noted, the historical reading of wealth distribution in the United States is taken from Jeffrey G. Williamson and Peter H. Lindert, "Long-Term Trends in American Wealth Inequality," in *Modeling the Distribution and Integrational Transmission of Wealth*, ed. James D. Smith (Chicago: Univ. of Chicago Press, 1980), pp. 9-93. This essay is not only timely but incorporates and synthesizes a very broad range of studies and includes an excellent bibliography. Much useful information still comes from the landmark study by Robert J. Lampman, *Share of Top Wealth-Holders in National Wealth, 1922-1956* (Princeton: Princeton Univ. Press, 1962). I am grateful for the personal help provided on this subject by Joseph A. Pechman of the Brookings Institution and James D. Smith, senior project director, Institute for Social Research, University of Michigan.
10. Kuznets is discussed by Williamson and Lindert, p. 10; he is refuted by Gabriel Kolko in *Wealth and Power in America* (New York: Praeger, 1962), pp. 24-29. It could be that the last word on politico-economic cause and effect belongs to Robert Kuttner whose *Economic Illusion: False Choices between Prosperity and Social Justice* (Boston: Houghton-Mifflin, 1984), argues that those nations that have moved most effectively toward social justice also hold the current lead in economic growth and innovation.
11. The best correlation I can see is between the inequality peaks and crises in the politics of money. The first coincides with greenback issue; the second with the establishment of the Federal Reserve; and the third with the crash and its attendant financial problems.
12. A guide to a number of comparative studies is Ethel L. Chamberlain, *Bibliography on the Distribution of Income and Wealth, 1945-1970* (Rand, 1971); the entries are selective and the coverage is piecemeal. One comes with anticipation to a book like Martin Schnitzer, *Income Distribution: A Comparative Study of the United States, Sweden, West Germany, East Germany, the*

United Kingdom, and Japan (New York: Praeger, 1974), but ardor is considerably dampened by the absence of direct comparisons.

13. Dwight Macdonald, "Our Invisible Poor," *New Yorker,* January 19, 1963, p. 86.

14. A historical development of attitudes is presented by Robert H. Bremner, *From the Depths: The Discovery of Poverty in the United States* (New York: New York Univ. Press, 1956); also by Oscar Handlin, "Poverty from the Civil War to World War II," in *Poverty and Affluence,* ed. Leo Fishman (New Haven: Yale Univ. Press, 1966).

15. Michael Harrington, *The Other America: Poverty in the United States* (New York: Macmillan, 1962). Harrington today thinks that the problem has not disappeared, only redefined itself. *New American Poverty* (New York: Holt, Rinehart and Winston, 1984).

16. Herman P. Miller, *Rich Man, Poor Man* (New York: Crowell, 1964), p. 29.

17. Robert J. Lampman, *Ends and Means of Reducing Poverty* (Chicago: Markham, 1971), chapter 3; Sar A. Levitan, *Programs in Aid of the Poor for the 1980's* (Baltimore: Johns Hopkins Univ. Press, 1980), chapter 1. I owe a lot to my colleague, Sar Levitan, not only for the extensive publications on subjects that more than span my own interests, but also for his kind patience in helping me to understand some of the things he knows.

18. An interesting view of the National Welfare Rights Organization is provided in Nick Kotz and Mary Lyn Kotz, *A Passion for Equality* (New York: Norton, 1977).

19. See Levitan, especially chapter 6, and Robert A. Levine, *The Poor Ye Need Not Have with You* (Cambridge: MIT Press, 1970).

20. John E. Schwarz, *America's Hidden Success: A Reassessment of Twenty Years of Public Policy* (New York: Norton, 1984). See also Spencer Rich, "The Skeptics are Wrong—Anti-Poverty Programs Do Work," *Washington Post,* May 6, 1984, pp. F1, F4. In addition to the works already cited I have drawn on James N. Morgan, ed., *Income and Welfare in the United States* (New York: McGraw-Hill, 1962); James D. Smith, ed., *Personal Distribution of Income and Wealth* (New York: National Bureau of Economic Research, 1975); Kenneth E. Boulding and Martin Pfaff, eds., *Redistribution to the Rich and the Poor* (Belmont, Calif.: Wadsworth, 1972); Robert J. Lampman, *Transfer Approaches to Distribution Policy* (Madison: Univ. of Wisconsin Press, 1973); Sar A. Levitan and Robert Taggart, *Promise of Greatness* (Cambridge, Mass.: Harvard Univ. Press, 1976). The most pertinent and recent bibliography is the one compiled by Williamson and Lindert. More extensive is *Distribution of Income and Wealth: A Bibliography of Recent Materials,* comp. Library of Congress, Congressional Research Service (Washington, D.C., 1978).

21. In addition to works already cited, see Jonathan H. Turner and Charles E. Starnes, *Inequality: Privilege and Poverty in America* (Pacific Palisades, Calif.: Goodyear, 1976); John A. Brittain, *Inheritance of Economic Status* (Washington, D.C.: Brookings Institution, 1977), and *Inheritance and the Inequality of Material Wealth* (Washington, D.C.: Brookings Institution, 1978); Joseph A. Pechman, *Who Paid the Taxes, 1966-1985* (Washington, D.C.: Brookings Institution, 1985).

22. Williamson and Lindert, p. 74.

23. The pattern followed in these generalizations is suggested by Sar A. Levitan, William B. Johnston, and Robert Taggart, *Minorities in the United States* (Washington, D.C.: Public Affairs, 1975). This knowledgeable summary concentrates on only five minority groups, yet the patterns seem as broadly applicable as any I have found.

24. "Characterological Change among Black Americans: A Contextual Interpretation," in *We, the People,* ed. Gordon J. DiRenzo (Westport, Conn.: Greenwood, 1977), p. 219. See also a nationwide survey based on a balanced sample of 1,872 individuals of whom 446 were black published in the *Washington Post,* March 24-26, 1981, on pp. A1, A2 for all three days. The dramatic difference in responses to similar situations can be illustrated by two recent reports on experiences by blacks in the South. Twenty years ago Samual Adams, traveling with his wife, found the situation measurably improved *(Washington Post,* December 6, 1964, p. E5). In 1981, however, Chet Fuller was so disheartened by threats and outrages that he ended by asking "What New South!" *(I Hear Them Calling My Name* [Boston: Houghton, Mifflin])

25. A summary of various reports by Joann S. Lublin, *Wall Street Journal*, August 4, 1981, p. 1. The most useful summary of the job market is Ralph E. Smith, ed., *Subtle Revolution: Women at Work* (Washington, D.C.: Urban Institute, 1979). On the particular topic a symposium of views with an excellent annotated bibliography is *Women in Management* ed. Bette Ann Stead (Englewood Cliffs, N.J.: Prentice-Hall. 1978). In a report just published by the Rand Corporation, James P. Smith and Michael P. Ward contend that pay differentials in the 1920s were much greater than we have thought and have narrowed much more than reported. Women's pay is now 64% of men's, they say, and will rise to 74% by the end of the century if the present trends continue. The changes are attributed by the authors to women's rising education and experience rather than to politics and legislative programs. See discussion in the *Washington Post*, October 31, 1984, pp. A1, A10.

26. R. E. Smith. See also *Statistical Report of Women in the United States: 1978* (Washington, D.C.: Bureau of the Census, 1980).

27. Sar A. Levitan, William B. Johnston, and Robert Taggart, *Still a Dream: The Changing Status of Blacks since 1960* (Cambridge, Mass.: Harvard Univ. Press, 1975), chapter 4. The figures cited are for the population over twenty-five years of age. Black progress is even more impressive if one includes the under-twenty-five age group.

28. Unless otherwise indicated, the data and generalizations abut the current state of black Americans are taken from the remarkably useful synthesis by Levitan, Johnston, and Taggart, *Still a Dream*, and the comprehensive work by the Bureau of the Census, *Social and Economic Status of the Black Population in the United States: An Historical View, 1790-1978*, series P-23, no. 80 (Washington, D.C. Government Printing Office, 1980). On this topic see Levitan, Johnson, and Taggart, chapters 5 and 7.

29. Some of this scholarship is directly connected with public policy: e.g., Stanley H. Masters, *Boack-White Income Differentials* (New York: Academic Press, 1975). Of even more consequence to the designers of social programs is Stanley Lieberson's *A Piece of the Pie: Black and White Immigrants since 1880* (Berkeley: Univ. of California Press, 1980), which constitutes a direct attack on the work of Daniel P. Moynihan and Nathan Glazer by demonstrating with elaborate quantification, that black economic problems in the twentieth century have nothing to do with the legacy of slavery.

30. Kenneth Boulding, "Social Justice as a Holy Grail: The Endless Quest," in *Quest for Justice: Myth, Reality, Ideal*, ed. Melvin J. Lerner and Michael Ross (Toronto: Holt, Rinehart and Winston of Canada, 1974), p. 9.

31. Susman (see Chapter 2, note 18, above) has no trouble recognizing that "each generation of Americans seems to have had its rendez-vous with reform . . ." (p. 95). Far from finding this circumstance either creditable or inevitable, Susman sees the need for repeated attention to the same general problems as "a basic 'failure' " (p. 96).

32. Talcott Parsons, *Structure and Process in Modern Societies* (Glencoe, Ill.: Free Press, 1960).

33. Almond and Verba, chapter 15.

34. Kenneth Arrow, *Social Change and Individual Values*, 2d ed. (New york: Wiley, 1963), p. 90.

35. Alexander M. Bickel, *Reform and Continuity* (New York: Harper, 1971).

36. Eugene V. Rostow, ed., *Is Law Dead?* (New York: Simon and Schuster, 1971); see particularly chapter 2 by Rostow, "The Rightful Limits of Freedom in a Liberal Democratic State"; and p. 133 for the heart of Auerbach's thesis.

37. Charles E. Lindblom, *Policy-making Process*, (Englewoqd Cliffs, N.J.: Prentice Hall, 1968); Bruce A. Ackerman, *Social Justice in the Liberal State* (New Haven: Yale Univ. Press, 1980).

38. Williamson and Lindert, p. 56.

39. Alexis de Tocqueville, *Democracy in America* (New York: Random House, Vintage Books, 1944), vol. 2, p. 271.

40. Charles Sanford, *Quest for Paradise* (Urbana: Univ. of Illinois Press, 1961), p. 9.

41. Anon. [Frederick Hollick?], *Devil's Visit* (New York: Excelsior, 1891), p. 37.

42. See William Torrence and Paul Meadows, "American Cultural Themes," *Sociology and Social Research* 43 (September-October 1958):3-7.

43. It is unfair to Robin Williams to boil his fine chapters on values down to a single list. His *American Society* (New York: Knopf), which first appeared in 1951, contained one of the most courageous and comprehensive treatments of American values, a treatment that has grown and changed with succeeding editions.

44. J. Kenneth Morland, *Race, Values, and American Unity* (DeLand, Fl.: Stetson Univ., 1969), p. 9.

45. This idea of opposing value-clusters is far from original and was put most strongly by Seymour M. Lipset in *First New Nation* (New York: Basic Books, 1961). I have learned from Lipset and from his work, but I cannot agree with the stress he places on the alternate dominance of the clusters nor on the timetable he projects for this alternation. It is much more important to see both forces as continuously present. See Michael Kammen, *People of Paradox* (New York: Knopf, 1972).

46. John B. Cobb, Jr., quoted in David R. Griffin and Thomas Altizer, eds., *John Cobb's Theology in Process* (Philadelphia: Westminster, 1977), p. 187.

47. This argument is made by Griffin, p. 23, *ibid.*

48. See Leo Strauss, *Political Philosophy of Hobbes*, trans. by Elsa M. Sinclair (Chicago: Univ. of Chicago Press, 1952); Strauss stresses the importance of going beyond *Leviathan* in appraising Hobbes's contributions. Paul F. Kress *(Social Science and the Idea of Process*, Urbana: Univ of Illinois, 1970), offers a derivation of the idea of process in Western thought and ends by focusing on political science and the contribution of Arthur F. Bentley.

49. The quotation is from John B. Cobb, "Post-Conference Reflection on Yin and Yang," manuscript. A good place to see Cobb in the broad setting of the process question is in Griffin and Altizer.

50. John Dewey, *Reconstruction in Philosophy* (1920; reprinted., Boston: Beacon, 1948), p. 177; see above, note 21.

51. George Santayana, *The Last Puritan* (New York: Scribner, 1936), p. 126. The author is describing the lectures of a high school history teacher in such a way as to illustrate the dangers of process orientation. As Dewey made clear, process is a legitimate value but not a legitimate end in itself. A society uses its commitment to process in order to move not aimlessly but from one goal to the next.

52. John A. Kouwenhoven, *Beer Can by the Highway* (New York: Doubleday, 1961), p. 66. Of all the studies of American character and values, this one deals with process most forthrightly, illustrating not only from literature and popular culture but also from architecture, planning, and technology. It is a playful book in some ways, but it is singularly useful in forcing the consideration of process outside its philosophic setting.

53. The most careful demonstration of this assertion is in the Appendix as interpreted in Chapter 2, above.

Encounter 6

1. Miss Flynn married a fellow labor organizer, John A. Jones, in 1908; three years later she had a son. Jones and Flynn separated not long after and were officially divorced in 1920. The son, who was always known as Fred Flynn, died prematurely in 1940; to him Miss Flynn dedicated her autobiography. Gurley Flynnn lived with the flamboyant Italian syndicalist, Carlo Tresca, for about a dozen years beginning in 1913. See her autiobiography, *I Speak My Own Piece* (New York: Masses and Mainstream, 1955). A corrected version, retitled *The Rebel Girl*, was issued in 1973 by International Publishers, New York. See also *Current Biography* (New York: Wilson, 1961), and the *New York Times*, September 7, 1964, p. 15b.

2. All her life Flynn remained attached to the IWW and its associations. She left instructions that her autobiography be reissued as *The Rebel Girl*, the title of a song the IWW composer Joe Hill dedicated to her. She also instructed that the sheet music be included as a frontispiece.

3. Corliss Lamont, ed., *The Trial of Elizabeth Gurley Flynn by the American Civil Liberties Union* (New York: Horizon, 1968), pp. 181-84. This book contains an introduction by the editor, a member of the board present at the trial. It reproduces the stenographic transcript and a number of related documents.

4. Ibid., p. 210.

A Chronology of the Money Question

The purpose of this compilation is to bring together enough events, central in their focus but varied in their nature, to support certain generalizations about social change. Of special interest are the related matters of periodization, dynamics, cause and effect. Only a chronology forces attention to sequence, coincidence, and relative degrees of activity. By supplying more factual detail than could be reasonably contained in any narrative this compilation furnishes an essential kind of support for the interpretations in Part 1. Although the case at hand is the politics of money, the chronology also illustrates politico-economic reform, and, in some respects, social change in general.

The principle of selectivity was shaped by these purposes. No single aspect of the money question is completely recorded. Noted are the most germane speeches, congressional debates and enactments, publications, and programs and platforms of associations and political parties. Although the technical side of the money question is not as important as the impetus toward social change, it was essential to record some of the conditions that prompted response: currency supply, interest rates, loan criteria, reserve requirements, federal surpluses or deficits. The stress is on events of national—as opposed to local or international—importance. The chronology covers the years between Andrew Jackson's veto of the bill to recharter the second Bank of the United States and the passage of the Federal Reserve Act.

Background

The bank question began in 1781 with the establishment by the Continental Congress of the Bank of North America followed by the chartering of the first Bank of the United States in 1791. Although the constitutionality of the bank had been challenged, it was affirmed in 1819 by the Supreme Court (*McCulloch v. Maryland*). Opposition was aroused by the apparent favoritism toward business as opposed to farm loans and, as early as the 1790s, the Anti-Federalists were alleging a conspiracy between Federalist bankers and businessmen.

Although Congress had established a mint and a national system of coinage in 1792 there was little stability. The situation was exacerbated after 1820 by the rapid growth of banks without proper regulation, security for loans, or adequate currency. At the same time opposition to the BUS was increasing as a result of competition with state banks; disputes about the bank's location; and resentment, especially from the West and South, concerning currency and credit restrictions. Some of these objections were unfair, since the second BUS, between 1823 and 1836, actually increased the amount of currency and credit available in the West and South. In 1829 President Jackson began to attack the BUS in favor of a government depository with limited functions.

Year-by-Year Chronology 1832–1913

1832 President Andrew Jackson seizes the recharter of the Second Bank of the United States (BUS) as a political issue. Roger Taney advises that it is unconstitutional. Jackson's famous veto message pits interests of common man against the special privilege of the wealthy banker. Former foe Thomas Hart Benton helps defeat attempt in Congress to override veto.

Reelection of Jackson considered affirmation of his stand on bank.

1833 Nicholas Biddle, president of the BUS, bills government for services, withholding funds when bill is refused. Government sues bank. Jackson gets Congress to pass resolution investigating bank's solvency.

Jackson twice replaces secretary of treasury in order to get government deposits made in state "pet banks" instead of the BUS, which still had three years remaining on its charter. This act precipitates war with Congress; House passes resolution of support; Senate passes resolution of censure.

Treasury circular encourages industrial and commercial loans.

1834 Mathew Carey and others memorialize Jackson to restore deposits to BUS.

Second coinage act approves bimetalism with 16:1 ratio of silver to gold.

Early discussion of independent treasury idea by Senators Gordon (Va.) and Wright (N.Y.).

1835 Twenty-nine "pet banks" now identified as recipients of federal deposits.

Government retires debt, making available more money, specie, credit.

Philadelphia Radical Reformer and Working Man's Advocate publishes verse attacking the way "paper coin" robs the worker of his pay. Radical Democrats identified with workers meet in New York City, call for hard money, and regard Jackson as too inflationary. These were the "locofocos" whose political influence is a matter of controversy.

William M. Gouge publishes *A Short History of Paper-Money and Banking in the United States. . . .*

Riot in Baltimore against Bank of Maryland overseers.

1836 Second BUS completes term and is rechartered as a state bank in Pennsylvania.

Deposit Act attempts to control banks by prohibiting small denomination money issue and by requiring interest to government on deposits held over three months. It also required the treasury to designate at least one bank in each state for federal deposits.

Jackson, following a deflationary, hard-money line, pocket vetoes bill to repeal specie circular.

Treasury circular, in attempt to force specie westward and to curb land speculation, requires (after December 15) payment for land in specie or "Virginia land scrip." In practice this measure worked to discredit western banks.

Another act prohibited transfer of federal funds except for disbursement. This measure hurt the newer banks, inhibited flexibility, currency supply, and credit.

Locofocos publish platform expressing "unqualified hostility to bank notes and paper money." *Philadelphia National Laborer* also blasts workingman's victimization by paper money.

1837   In his farewell address Jackson attacks paper currency and the power of private banks.

Van Buren speaks in special session of Congress against state-chartered banks and alludes to a plan for removing federal deposits from them. Favors specie. Helps obtain House passage of Independent Treasury Bill and keeps this issue before Congress steadily through 1840.

Panic of 1837 caused in part by deflation. Treasury responds by issuing new notes for business loans and distributing $28 million to states as loans. Business failure in this panic caused Edward Kellogg to begin his studies of banking and credit.

Gouge publishes his second influential volume, *An Inquiry into the Expediency of Dispensing with Bank Agency and Bank Paper.* . . .

1837–41: period of federal deficits (except 1839).

1837–43: period of declining federal revenues; issuance of over $47 million in treasury notes.

1837–48: period of wholesale bank failures, including state banks whose failures entail loss of federal funds, discourage foreign investments and hurt credit abroad.

1838   Benton-Jackson specie circular of 1836 repealed.

New York free banking act encourages more competitive banking by no longer requiring special legislation for each charter, by setting a modest specie reserve requirement (12.5 percent), and by backing bank notes with bonds.

Frances Wright publishes *What Is the Matter?* which hails the independent treasury idea as a second Declaration of Independence. Orestes Brownson, a noted conservative, also supports this measure in the *Boston Quarterly Review,* calling it one of the most important measures in the government's history.

1840   Independent Treasury Act passed, which event has a slight deflationary effect on the economy.

1840–43: years of panic; treasury, caught in its own strict rules, cannot move funds to relieve stricken banks.

Democratic platform argues against a national bank as dangerous to the Republic and the people, and as unconstitutional.

Henry C. Carey completes publication of his *Principles of Political Economy.* Here and elsewhere Carey found high interest rates the main financial problem; thus this conservative Whig became a soft money advocate and led this cause, especially after 1865. Upon his death in 1879 his nephew, Henry

Carey Baird, continued the cause. Carey converts included Joseph Wharton and Peter Cooper.

1841 With support from Henry Clay, Independent Treasury Act repealed, but Clay's push for a new national bank twice vetoed by Tyler. Whig majority defeats new subtreasury efforts.

1841–46: return to state banks as federal depositories.

Publication of first in a series of pamphlets by Edward Kellogg leading up to his major work. This one, released under a pseudonym, was titled *Remarks upon Usury and Its Effects*.

Philadelphia Public Ledger prints arguments against banks and high interest.

1842 Gouge, in the *Journal of Banking*, defends his subtreasury against accusation of its being an idea for the "rabble" by citing eminent proponents in church, business, and society.

1843 1843–60: period of general growth of private banking under state regulation except in the West, where bank failures continue to be common and antibank sentiments high. In 1852, for example, there were no incorporated banks in Arkansas, California, Florida, Illinois, Iowa, Michigan, Wisconsin, Oregon, or Minnesota, while in Indiana and Missouri banking was a state monopoly.

1844 Democrats again adopt bitter plank against national bank, calling for the "separation of the money of the government from banking institutions," while the Whig platform calls for a "well-regulated currency."

George Henry Evans's *People's Rights* comes out for the independent treasury idea.

1846 Independent Treasury Act passed and signed into law, a victory for Democrats who favor hard money and oppose a national bank. Subtreasury depositories identified in Washington, D.C., Philadelphia, New Orleans, New York, Boston, Charleston, and St. Louis.

1846–49: Mexican War financed mainly by loans, thus creating a deficit of over $53 million.

1847 Treasury notes issued to help finance Mexican War.

Courts finally decide against Biddle in his 1833 suit against the government.

1847–61: height of Independent Treasury's success.

1847–64: only period when no federal money is deposited in banks.

1848 Democratic platform opposes national bank and distribution of land-sale funds among the states; calls for continued separation of government monies from private banks. Free-Soil party platform calls for increased federal spending in the states.

1849 Edward Kellogg publishes *Labor and Other Capital*, arguing for government control of credit and issuance of paper money. Thought by many to be the most influential nineteenth-century American work in economic theory.

Federal surplus returns; used to buy up bonds, prepay debt, and thereby relieve financial stringency.

Gold strikes in the West create new abundance and eventually help to drive silver from circulation, creating a growing problem later in the century.

1849–60: period during which New York City establishes itself as investment capital center attracting increasing foreign investments outweighed by domestic money market. Stock exchange and brokerage houses affirm the city's financial dominance.

1852 Democratic platform again opposes national bank and supports continuation of Independent Treasury. Free Democrats take same position.

1853 New York clearinghouse established to serve banking community.

Treasury uses income surplus for silver coinage in effort to offset panic. Amount of silver in coins under $1 reduced; $3 gold piece authorized.

1856 Federal surplus again used to buy up bonds and ease money shortage.

Democratic platform again supports Independent Treasury and denounces national bank.

1857 Panic of 1857 caused by seasonal withdrawal of deposits coupled with failure of some lending institutions. Specie payments temporarily suspended. First overinvestment panic.

1858 1858–60: period of increased federal expenses, annual deficits, hence low credit. Government-supported credit becoming increasingly a political issue.

1860 Democrats drop subtreasury and antibank planks, reverse themselves to join opposition by supporting internal improvements.

Beginning of several republications of Kellogg's work (subsequently under the title *A New Monetary System*) as his ideas increase their influence on farm, labor, and other protest movements.

1861 Wartime demands prove too much for Independent Treasury. Its rules are suspended as treasury notes are issued, $250 million in bonds and notes authorized by Congress; two loans of $50 million floated.

1861–65: many new taxes passed to aid war financing, including first income tax (mildly graduated) and a light inheritance tax excluding husband-wife bequests.

Banks suspend specie payment.

1862 In spite of much opposition, especially from bankers, greenbacks are authorized. Lincoln supports them as a necessity of wartime; Secretary Chase first opposes and then reluctantly supports them. Federal treasury suspends specie payment.

Pliny Freeman offers a non-Kellogg version of interconvertible bonds: a soft-money plan at higher rates aimed at keeping credit constant and paying interest on idle funds. Appeals to business more than Kellogg's plan.

1862–64: $431 million issued in greenbacks.

1863 National Banking Act passed. Modeled on the New York free banking system, it suspends the Independent Treasury for the duration of the war; forces cooperation between treasury and private banks for issue of bond-backed currency, notes, and bonds.

Some reformers regard the National Banking Act as a banker's act leading to large profits for the financial community and threatening the government's perquisites.

$900 million loan authorized.

1864 Alexander Campbell publishes *The True American System of Finance,* arguing for expanding use of greenbacks. Some scholars trace to him (rather than Kellogg) the idea of the interconvertible bond as a device to keep currency plentiful and interest rates low. Campbell had immediate political appeal because he combined the ideas of Carey and Kellogg with the antibank, antiaristocratic prejudices utilized by Jefferson and Jackson.

Andrew C. Cameron founds the *Chicago Workingman's Advocate* as the organ of the trades assembly; it soon becomes an important outlet for Campbell and other "people's money" spokesmen.

Republican platform favors payment of the government debt and circulation of the "national currency."

Income tax made slightly more progressive; inheritance tax raised minimally.

National Banking Act amended to encourage participation of more branch banks. State bank circulation taxed (2 percent) as further incentive for national banks.

1865 New treasury secretary, McCulloch, announces his aim to retire war debt, contract greenbacks, and return to specie. Congress suspends rules and overwhelmingly endorses this plan.

High interest rates to government creditors attacked in Ohio gubernatorial campaign. The *Cincinnati Gazette* first voices the "Ohio Idea" of paying the debt in greenbacks. George Pendleton adopts a version of this idea, "the Pendleton plan," which would move away from gold, replace bank notes with greenbacks, and curtail interest to bondholders, but which is only mildly inflationary.

A seven-percent-thirty-year government loan is rapidly subscribed.

1865–75: period during which many prominent antebellum reformers are converted to Kellogg-Campbell greenback ideas. They include Wendell Phillips, Edward M. Davis, Albert Brisbane, Charles Lewis Sears, John Drew, Susan B. Anthony, Elizabeth Cady Stanton, Abby Hopper Gibbons, Victoria Woodhull.

Tax on state bank circulation raised, effective in 1866, from 2 to 10 percent, thus increasing pressure for state banks to become national branch banks. Federal power to tax state banks upheld by Supreme Court (*Bank v. Fenno*) in 1869.

1865–97: period of severe deflation.

1866 National Labor Union founded, center of movement through 1871 and locus of financial debates.

Campbell publishes condensed version of his plan in *Chicago Workingman's Advocate.*

A mixed group of farm and labor leaders, manufacturers, and businessmen (Boutwell, Stevens, Sherman, Kelly, Butler, Sprague, Morton) begin increasing pressure for repeal of greenback contraction act of 1865–66 with eventual success in 1868.

Marcus M. "Brick" Pomeroy strikes his first hard blow against eastern bondholders in his pamphlet *Soliloquies of the Bondholder, the Poor Farmer, the Soldier's Widow. . . .* Indicates renewed sectionalism pitting western farmer against eastern creditor.

Trying to curb gold speculation, treasury sells excess gold to private banks, which further violates Independent Treasury rules and creates reform issue.

1866–69: period of rural prosperity, with midwestern corn prices especially high. This helps explain why farm interest in monetary reform failed to become a political issue till the 1870s.

1866–70: wartime taxes repealed, excesses return, debt converted to long-term bonds, greenbacks contracted to $356 million under act of 1866.

1867   Oliver H. Kelley founds the National Grange of the Patrons of Husbandry, eventually an important prepolitical force for rural discussions of the currency issues.

National Labor Union meets, with some farm representation, and endorses Kellogg-Campbell ideas, marking the first organized labor support for this concept. Andrew C. Cameron and William Sylvis active.

George F. Train pushes greenbacks as a panacea and typifies unreliable fringe of this idea.

Congressional debates on contraction bills indicate shift in majority away from contraction and association of contraction (unfairly) with hard times. Nonetheless, contraction continues.

Ohio politics further demonstrate popular shift. *Cincinnati Enquirer,* a Democratic paper, promotes inflationist Ohio idea and, with Pendleton's help, defeats contractionist Republicans.

1868   Congress repeals contraction act of 1865 in order to relieve stringency in money supply.

Sherman introduces bill to place gold/silver ratios in international setting but is defeated.

Labor leaders meet in New York during Democratic convention and unsuccessfully urge Kellogg-Campbell ideas on platform committee but take credit for inclusion of Pendleton plan. This platform, together with the candidacy of gold-Democrat Horatio Seymour, shows party split. Platform also calls for one, uniform, lawful, money.

Republicans call for gradual debt repayment with lowered interest rates.

Central Committee of National Woman's Suffrage Association advocates 3 percent convertible bond.

Farm and labor spokesmen urge Kellogg-Campbell ideas on President Johnson and, after election, on Grant.

William Sylvis, leading labor spokesman and recent convert to Campbellism, joins Cameron as co-editor of *Chicago Workingman's Advocate.*

1869   Public Credit Act passed in 1868, pocket vetoed by Johnson but signed by Grant. The act calls for payment of government debts in coin and thus scuttles the "Ohio Idea." This act contradicts the 1868 act against further contraction of greenbacks. Thus a middle position is established which opposes any kind of "repudiation" of the war debt but which holds the line against further currency contraction.

Grant himself announces resumption of specie payment.

Hepburn v. Griswold allows the Supreme Court to rule that greenbacks are not legal tender for debts contracted before their issue was authorized (February 25, 1862).

Jay Cooke, along with many other speculators, endorses an expanding currency.

Black Friday (September 24) results when Grant orders government sale of $2 million of gold to frustrate Jay Gould and Jim Fisk, who were trying to influence gold prices upward by involving Grant in rumors of government refusal to sell. This kind of episode, even when collusion was absent, made reformers worry about the consequences of the present system.

In an atypically early rural expression of interest, the *Minnesota Monthly* publishes an article attributed to C. A. Robertson, which calls for an expansion of credit to farmers and a People's National Bank to assure low interest rates. Ideas attributed to Kellogg.

First meeting called, by Uriah Stephens in Philadelphia, of a group that is to become the Knights of Labor, an important voice on the monetary questions.

1869–70: *Chicago Workingman's Advocate* serializes Kellogg's *A New Monetary System.*

1870   Year opens with protracted congressional debate in progress concerning full implications of specie resumption and characterized by much dramatic rhetoric on the "people's money" (greenbacks) versus the moneylenders.

1870–73: period of rural hardship climaxed by panic. Farmers hit by low prices, scarce credit and high interest rates. Thus, pressed farmers begin to organize politically and to adopt the ideas of Kellogg, Campbell, and others. Representing 47 percent of the population but having only 7 percent of Congress (by occupation), farmers begin a long campaign toward full political status.

Congress passes refunding measures in 1870, 1871, designed to take advantage of falling interest rates but, in some cases, paying more than would have been necessary. Nearly $2 billion refunded at nontaxable rates of between 4 and 5 percent.

1871   Supreme Court, with two new appointees, reverses first legal tender case and allows greenbacks as legal tender for all debts.

1871–74: treasury issues $26 million legal tender notes by purchasing bonds.

Claiming membership of 80,000, Knights of Labor adopts that name.

Grange chapters established and growing in Midwest, especially Illinois, Iowa, Minnesota, and Wisconsin.

1870s: a period in the spreading influence of Kellogg's ideas, through Campbell in Congress; through the conversion of Horace Greeley; through the National Labor Union, the *Chicago Workingman's Advocate.* In 1871–72, Horace H. Day and other labor reformers try to get the Liberal Republicans (Carl Schurz) to accept a Kellogg plank. The Greenback party vice presidential candidate in 1876 (Gen. S. F. Cary) is an avid exponent of Kellogg-Campbell ideas.

1872   National Labor Reform party's first resolution stated: "That it is the duty of the Government to establish a just standard of distribution of capital and labor by providing a purely national circulating medium, based on the faith and resources of the nation, issued directly to the people without the intervention of any system of banking corporations, which money shall be legal tender in the payment of all debts, public and private, and interchangeable, at the option of the holder, for Government bonds bearing a rate of interest not to exceed 3.75%, subject to future legislation by Congress." This is a full endorsement of Kellogg-Campbell, as full as these ideas were ever to get in a narrow political setting; in many ways this plank is also a big step toward a federal reserve system.

Democratic platform shuns repudiation and, along with Liberal Republicans, calls for a quick return to specie.

Orthodox Republicans call for resumption; also congratulate themselves on lowering the war debt and the interest rate on the remainder.

Prohibition party (whose planks are sometimes here cited as a kind of disinterested bellwether) calls for a national currency that is sound, adequate, and convertible into gold or silver.

Income tax expires.

Period of heavy growth of Grange commences.

1873   Panic of 1873 further evidence of an overinvestment cycle, of the weakness of the banking system, and of the incapacity of the government to respond. A $26 million greenback issue (1873–1874) insufficient to offset currency shortage. Panic heightened by failure of Jay Cooke's bank along with seventeen national and eighty-seven state banks.

The fourth coinage act, the "Crime of '73," fails to mention silver among coinage activities (although silver coinage was not prohibited).

Act of March 3 tightens National Banking System; limits greenbacks to $354 million. Most important aspect of this act from currency standpoint is the establishment of variable reserve requirements between big city banks (25 percent) and small town and rural banks (15 percent). This measure was meant to relieve the seasonal rural shortages and stop the flow of funds to the large cities.

National Labor Union declaration of principles (1873–74) includes a form of Kellogg's ideas leading to their adoption in the Knights of Labor preamble in 1878.

Founding of *Industrial Age*, prominent Illinois farm journal with announced hard-money views, shifts during its first year of publication to greenbacks and the interconvertible bond: symptomatic of the spread of Kellogg-Campbell ideas in rural areas as witness also *Indiana Farmer* and *Iowa Homestead* (later *Western Farm Journal*), which shifted also in this same year.

1873–75: period of growing political influence of Grange, often through a variety of third parties. Illinois is the first state fully organized by the Grange and in 1873 the Grange wins elections in sixty-three of sixty-six contested counties and eventually defeats the judges who ruled against them in the railroad cases.

1874 Grant vetoes bill to increase greenbacks further; calls for specie resumption.

Congress limits greenbacks to $382 million and calls for resumption by January 1, 1879.

High point of Grange marked by 20,000 clubs.

1873–75: Illinois State Farmers Association joins with labor leaders to support Kellogg plan as shown in 1876 greenback platform.

Alexander Campbell elected to Congress as Independent with Greenback commitments.

1875 Act passed calling for resumption of specie payment in 1879. Although it was vague as to details and considered but a gesture by others, it did signal resistance to greenbacks. The act also encouraged the issuance of national bank notes and, for every $100 of new notes, the retirement of $80 of greenbacks.

1875–93: period of consistent revenue surplus used to retire debt at unprecedented rate.

Peter Cooper (as interviewed in *New York Herald*) supports unfluctuating greenbacks; opposes government borrowing as a friend of the people and foe of creditors and manipulators.

Timely publication of fourth edition of Kellogg's work and also Britton H. Hill's *Absolute Money,* which signals the beginning of a decline in support for the Kellogg-Campbell interconvertible money/bond to be replaced by a demand for pegging currency at a fixed (higher-than-existing) rate per capita; complete repayment of government debt; termination of national banks; and an attack on high interest in general and the New York money market in particular.

1876 Republican platform affirms progress toward specie resumption. Democrats attack GOP for not achieving resumption nor retiring the debt; call for a new financial "system" to restore confidence. Prohibition party calls for an independent treasury to issue paper money redeemable in gold or silver.

Independent (Greenback) party becomes the first national party to carry an important expression of agrarian discontent, picking up farm support as the number and power of the Grange declines. Platform calls for repeal of the specie resumption act of 1875, for the issue of fiat currency convertible to bonds limited to $0.01/day/$100 interest. Cooper and S. F. Cary are nominated. Although the party gets but 80,000 votes nationally, it polls over 6,000 in the states of Illinois, Iowa, Indiana, Michigan, and Kansas.

1877 Pomeroy publishes *Democrat* and later (1878) *Good as Gold,* proposing expanding currency to pay off the debt but opposing the interconvertible bond of the Kellogg-Campbell plan as well as some features of the Pendleton plan.

1878 Bland-Allison Act, allowing silver coinage, passed over Hayes's veto. The vote was a victory for western and southern farmers, yet the act was only a compromise between monometalism and full parity for silver.

Congress makes $347 million of greenbacks still in circulation part of permanent money supply; meanwhile $200 million gold reserve is accumulated in order to bring fiat currency to par with specie.

Greenback Labor party is organized at Toledo, with eight hundred delegates from twenty-eight states. Its national platform contains Kellogg planks, opposes specie resumption, and favors silver coinage. Some state platforms substitute "absolute money" ideas for those of Kellogg. This is the height of Greenback political power, with victories in fifteen congressional races.

Founding of S. F. Norton's *Chicago Sentinel,* acclaimed as the nation's leading Greenback paper. Norton, an avid Kelloggite, also published a more general reform journal, *Chicago Express,* and an influential allegorical pamphlet, *Ten Men of Money Island.* As a publisher he distributes the work of Donnelly and Kellogg. As a politician he is given credit for selling fiat money views to the Populists. In 1896 he is offered to the Peoples' party convention as a presidential candidate by those who opposed merger with the Democrats; he loses by slightly more than 3:1 ratio.

Knights of Labor abandon secrecy and publish a constitution with a preamble endorsing a flexible currency without banks issued directly to the people.

1879 Resumption of specie payment begins January 1. Greenbacks hold their value although lower denominations are replaced by silver certificates because of unpopularity of large silver coins.

To reduce interest burden on debt House authorizes treasury to call in the five percent-twenty-year bonds in exchange for four percent bonds with a three-month premium at the old rate.

Warner Silver bill, calling for unlimited coinage, passes the House but dies in Senate committee.

T. V. Powderly, ardent advocate of flexible currency, replaces Stephens as head of Knights of Labor.

Early organization of Farmers' Alliance both in Texas, where it fought the ranchers, and in Illinois, where it was antimonopoly and was led by Milton George. These groups, with quite different local circumstances, recover the momentum of the Grange and the Greenbackers, become an important voice on monetary questions, and help create populism.

1880 Democratic platform calls for "honest" money: gold, silver, or paper redeemable in metals. Republicans congratulate themselves on reducing the principal and the interest rate on the public debt.

The Greenback Labor platform, more vague and rhetorical than formerly, abhors banks, private manipulation of money and credit, and calls for more active government regulation. With James B. Weaver as candidate, the national vote slips to 300,000 and the congressional representation to ten seats.

First Farmers' Alliance charters issued in the Southwest. National (Northwest) Farmers' Alliance forms in Chicago and elects Matt Anderson president.

The 1880s see the spread of Kellogg-Campbell ideas through the Knights of Labor. Rural voices lend support but also add stress on land loans and the new subtreasury idea. See the *Chicago Express* and *Western Rural.*

1880–83: period when Civil War bonds mature and are refunded for another twenty years. A basis for paper money issue is thus maintained, but some essential questions are postponed until the years immediately preceding discussions of a federal reserve system. Later, surpluses are used to buy up bonds at a premium, thus endangering the base for bank currency issue and highlighting the treasury's inconsistency.

1881 Congress sees battle along party lines concerning interest rates on new bonds. Republicans prevail, with the aid of Hayes's veto, and get rate raised from 3 to 3½ percent, at which level it is so rapidly subscribed as to suggest that a lower rate would have sufficed.

1882 New funding bill passed at 3 percent to buy up previous year's bonds.

The Wheel, one of many farmers' groups later to turn political, founded in Arkansas.

Greenbackers down to one congressman.

1883 Arkansas Wheel goes statewide.

Fifth and cheap edition of *Labor and Other Capital* is issued, showing continuing interest in Kellogg ideas.

1884 Panic causes failure of some large New York banks and raises questions about reserve requirements pyramided in such a way as to exaggerate the power of large eastern urban banks.

Republican platform calls for international meeting to establish the relative values of gold and silver for coinage.

Democrats support "the gold and silver coinage of the Constitution" or redeemable paper. Bimetalism at this time would have meant a virtual "silver standard."

One branch of the split Prohibition party calls for "ample and sound" currency.

Greenback Labor party nominates a presidential candidate for the last time. The platform demands money in "sufficient quantities" for the nation's needs and the substitution of greenbacks for national notes. The candidate, Benjamin Butler, gets only 175,000 votes out of some 10 million.

The Anti-Monopoly party draws up a platform which condemns banks along with other monopolies but contains no plank on currency.

In *Julliard v. Greenman* the Supreme Court reverses the Hepburn case (1869) and upholds the legitimacy of greenbacks for all debts.

1884–89: period of withdrawal of national bank notes at the rate of about $7 million per year, average.

1885 The Wheel unites with other farm groups and spreads to Kentucky and Tennessee.

Knights of Labor, at their Hamilton, Ontario, meeting, endorse Kellogg's land loan plan and petition Congress for its adoption. This is one of the signs of the reemergence of Kellogg's central ideas as the greenback issue, which his ideas also supported, fades from prominence.

1886   Knights of Labor reaffirm their support of Kellogg's ideas in the General Assembly at Cleveland and are endorsed by several rural papers.

Texas organizes its statewide Farmers' Alliance with 2,700 "suballiances." In the border states, the "Grand Wheel" denounces all monopolies and takes the new name of National Agricultural Wheel of the U.S.A.

1886–92: period during which Kellogg-Macune ideas (land loans, interest controls and eventually crop loans) pervade farm and labor organizations eventually to appear in the Populist statements of 1892.

1887   New national banking act, in response to the panic of 1884, sets more strict reserve requirements but allows more banks into the system. Central and branch banks both must have 25 percent of deposits in reserve.

C. W. Macune unites the Texas and Louisiana Farmers' Alliances and is elected president of the newly renamed National Farmers' Alliance and Co-operative Union of America. At this point they decide not to unite with the northern groups, and Macune continues to organize the South through 1890.

Northern Alliance meets in Minneapolis calling for free silver, payment of the debt, and paper money issued directly to the people.

National Agricultural Wheel meets again, this time in Tennessee, counting a membership of 500,000. Delegates appointed to explore merger with Southern Alliance.

1888   GOP and Democratic platforms argue about extravagances and surpluses. GOP endorses international bimetalism and scores Democrats for trying to demonitize silver.

Union Labor platform asks for a fiat currency in the interest of the producer, issued without the intervention of banks, and for low-interest land loans. A. J. Streeter, a former Alliance president, is nominated for president and gets 146,000 votes.

United Labor platform abhors the payment of interest on the government debt and endorses government-issued fiat currency.

The southern branch of the Farmers' Alliance holds first national meeting in Shreveport and requests the repeal of the national banking system and favors government-issue currency. Wheel and Farmers' Alliance delegates meet in Meridian, Mississippi, and discuss merger.

1889   Farmers' Alliance and Wheel merger completed, although southern groups are never fully integrated into national associations because of difference in racial viewpoint. Delegates from the newly formed Farmers' and Laborers' Union of America are sent to the St. Louis meeting, where an important step toward a People's party is taken. Farm, labor, and Greenback interests are well represented (including Powderly, Macune) at this founding meeting of the National Farmers' Alliance and Industrial Union (NFAIU).

A national office and periodical established in Washington, D.C. *The National Economist* becomes an important voice not only for the NFAIU but particularly for the Macune subtreasury plan. L. L. Polk elected president, and Macune, chairman of the board. Statements issued by the convention oppose banks, support free silver, call for treasury notes issued on a per capita basis and regional subtreasuries offering low-interest credit to the farmer so that he need not be a victim of the season, the railroads, the speculators, and the banks.

T. V. Powderly publishes his *Thirty Years of Labor,* revealing his intense preoccupation with the issue of currency and credit. His Knights of Labor decide not to merge with the NFAIU but endorse their statement of purpose.

National Farmers' Alliance meeting in Des Moines memorializes Congress on behalf of the land loan ideas of Kellogg.

A new secretary of the treasury reverses prior policy by withdrawing federal money from national banks: another example of the manner in which treasury actions often reflect personal philosophies rather than responses to economic conditions.

1890   National (Southern) Alliance meets in Ocala, Fla., simultaneously with Colored Farmers' Alliance. This is the last real meeting for the Alliance, which lost money on its co-op ventures. Importance of this meeting is the endorsement of Macune subtreasury plan, calling for a branch of the U.S. Treasury in every county with more than $1 million to $2 million in farm produce annually; storage facilities; available loans on 80 percent of crop value at 1 percent interest redeemable in one year. Thus the farmer would be relieved of the necessity to sell his crops immediately or else face high storage and interest rates. Southern and Western Alliance begin more direct political activity, claiming a part in the victories of three governors, three senators, and thirty-eight U.S. congressmen, and majorities in seven state legislatures.

1890–91: Kellogg's land loan plan is endorsed by National Grange and Farmers' Mutual Benefit Association.

Statewide People's party is formed in Kansas.

Publication of Ignatius Donnelly's best-selling dystopia, *Caesar's Column,* which pushes Populist ideas, including the abolition of fixed metallic standards for currency.

Sherman Silver Purchase Act stipulates fixed monthly purchase of silver by weight at market price. After an initial flurry of price rise and currency increase, this act succeeds neither in raising the price of silver and farm commodities nor in putting more money in circulation. Currency redundancy also leads to a run on gold reserves, exacerbated by the failure of Baring Brothers (London), whose receivers hasten to redeem American notes in gold. This pressure is temporarily relieved by shipping silver, freight-free, to the interior and by a temporary upturn in the balance of trade.

1891   Cleveland speaks forcefully against free silver.

1,400 delegates meet in Cincinnati and resolve to form a new party (Populist).

Tom Watson founds the *People's Party Paper* in Georgia as throughout the South the subtreasury issue separates the friends of agrarian fiscal reform from the traditional hard-money conservatives. Silver, although of no regional importance, is recognized as an issue that could unify agrarian protest.

J. E. Bryan publishes his *Farmer's Alliance,* a volume combining history, exhortation, songs, and arguments for free silver and the subtreasury.

1891–1900: period of increase in number of state-chartered trust companies whose lack of close regulation is to be source of difficulties.

1892 The People's party of the U.S.A. (Populists) has its first official convention in Omaha. The platform attacks banks, supports free silver and a $50 per capita level of currency, and endorses "the subtreasury plan of the Farmers' Alliance, or a better system." Ignatius Donnelly is author of much of the platform; he also publishes *The Golden Bottle,* a utopian sketch invoking the government to issue money for the good of the many instead of the bankers. James B. Weaver, who published his pro-labor, anti-bank *Call to Action,* is nominated as presidential candidate and makes impressive inroads for a new party: over 1 million popular and 22 electoral votes.

Democratic platform calls for bimetalism while Cleveland stays firm for gold. Democrats also attack the Sherman Act and ask for repeal of the 10 percent tax on state bank issues, thus further confusing their financial posture.

Republican platform asks for a fixed per capita rate of government-issued currency: gold, silver, paper, each equally valuable. This platform marks the beginning of monetary reform statements by the GOP.

Socialist Labor platform ignores the silver issue but calls for government control of all currency issue.

Free silver passes the Senate but is ignored by the House.

1893 Panic as a result of decline in tariff revenue, shrinking reserves, and consequent currency stringency and foreign mistrust. 491 banks, including 69 national banks, fail. It is this panic that points out banking system inadequacies and leads to careful study, including the examination of foreign banking systems.

The American Bankers' Association (ABA) recommends a system of mutual bank guarantees modeled on the recently reformed Canadian system but known thereafter as the Baltimore plan after the place of the ABA meeting.

Dockery-Cockrell committee appointed in Congress to review treasury procedures.

Cleveland gets congressional repeal of Sherman Silver Purchase Act; silver certificates gradually withdrawn.

Periodical first called *New Occasions* and then *New Time* is founded in Chicago by F. U. Adams with the assistance of B. O. Flower. It becomes an important voice for "a scientific money system" in the progressive mold. Merged into *Arena* in 1898.

1894 Responding to the 1893 panic, Secretary of the Treasury Carlisle calls for repeal of laws requiring bond deposits to secure currency; recommends that up to 74 percent of a bank's capital be freed for bank-note issue and that a safety fund for emergency use be accumulated through taxation. Convention of private bankers also recommends the issue of notes based on general assets.

Carlisle twice sells $50 million issues to shore up gold reserves, second sale totally subscribed by J. P. Morgan.

Dockery Act tightens treasury's administrative procedures without providing a much-needed system for control of appropriations.

Coxey's Army marches on behalf of more jobs but also advocates increased money in circulation.

William H. Harvey publishes *Coin's Financial School,* the most politically effective bimetalist tract.

1895   Free-silver bill passes both houses of Congress but vetoed by Cleveland. Free-silver conventions held in South and West. Bland and Bryan write the "Appeal of Silver Democrats" and seek the endorsement of House Democrats. Ignatius Donnelly publishes *American People's Money,* an argument for free silver.

Gold reserves dip to $41 million, prompting series of negotiations between Morgan and Cleveland. Without congressional approval Cleveland authorizes Morgan to organize New York bankers to refrain from withdrawing U.S. gold and to purchase gold abroad. Gold drain is prevented for only a six-month period but in a way that is quite profitable for the bankers and which produces rabid criticism of Cleveland for collusion with private interests.

1896 $100 million public bond sale solves gold shortage problem for the time.

Complicated convention year with many splinter parties and "third parties." Bryan and free silver get the support of three parties: Democrats, Populists, and Silver Republicans. In addition to supporting silver, the Democratic platform attacks interest-bearing bonds, national banks, and (as a sop to the hard-money wing) paper money not redeemable in coin.

People's party (Populists) endorse the independent treasury and the increase in the volume of the circulating medium.

"National Democratic" party attacks the Chicago platform of the Democrats and endorses gold, hard money, and fiscal economy.

Republican platform affirms specie resumption and opposes unlimited coinage of silver without an international, established ratio with gold.

Prohibition party splits over the issue of whether they should take a stand on issues other than alcohol. The "broad gaugers" call themselves the National party and support silver, the Independent Treasury, and fiat currency.

Socialist Labor party comments only that the government should issue all money and that workers should be paid in good money.

1897   Indianapolis Board of Trade calls conference which results in the appoint-ment of important monetary commission.

High-water mark for Populists with twenty-seven congressmen; all gone by 1903.

1898   Report of Indianapolis monetary commission lists faults in national banking system, including lack of flexibility and uniformity in currency supply; unequal geographical availability of currency and credit. The report, tied to a premature gold standard bill, represents problems which reformers had stressed and which eventually affect the Federal Reserve Act.

Spanish-American War adds to annual deficit, but not seriously. Private banks used to add prestige to the government bond sales.

1899   Period of late 1890s and early twentieth century is characterized by rise of international issues (war, imperialism, colonialism) which, together with rising farm prices, have the effect of cooling the particular financial issues (greenbacks, silver) while a general consensus grows in favor of broad reform of the monetary, credit, and banking systems.

1900 Treasury functions increasingly like a central bank, making deposits in national banks again, advancing money to rural banks for seasonal needs, and deliberately influencing the New York money market.

Gold Standard Act is passed; bullion reserve is increased to $150 million; silver notes of 1890 are redeemed. World supply of gold increases markedly.

Democrats and "fusion" Populists again support Bryan and give free silver prominence (though not as much as in 1896) and attack the Gold Standard Act. Democratic platform otherwise is hard money, while Populists manage to sound more like Gouge and less like Kellogg-Macune. Silver Republicans also condemn gold standard for its adverse effect on silver and the "patriotic" greenback.

People's (middle of the road) party remains faithful to the idea of flexible currency sufficient to need. Wharton and Donnelly are its candidates.

GOP boasts of sound finance and affirms the gold standard but then steals the reform ball from the Democrats-Populists with: "We recognize that interest rates are a potent factor in production and business activity, and for the purpose of further equalizing and of further lowering the rates of interest, we favor such monetary legislation as will enable the varying needs of the season and of all sections to be promptly met in order that trade may be evenly sustained, labor steadily employed and commerce enlarged. The volume of money in circulation was never so great per capita as it is today."

1901 Charles N. Fowler becomes chairman of the House Banking and Currency Committee and begins introducing measures aimed at providing elastic currency and controlled growth through credit.

1901–15: era of financial and corporate growth and consolidation with regular appeals for government regulation.

1902 Secretary of the Treasury Shaw takes office and, probably illegally, increases number of bank notes to relieve stringency; also purchases bonds at a premium and increases the number of depository banks.

1903 Treasury discounts notes in anticipation of seasonal, rural use.

Shaw redefines treasury so that he can move deposits and thus bypass the strictures of the Independent Treasury Act.

1904 Democratic presidential candidate (Alton B. Parker) demands a platform without a silver plank, gets one, suffers landslide defeat.

Republicans, unpressed on the money issue, reaffirm the gold standard and take credit for sound money.

People's party platform keeps money at the top of the list but mentions neither silver nor greenbacks and begins to sound like antebellum Democrats in their stress on stable, redeemable money issued by the government without bank intervention.

1906 Shaw asserts in his annual report that it is the government's duty to protect the people from panics as from contagious disease. Uses $60 million, by way of example, to provide a variable money supply in rural areas, in spring and fall, to avoid the nearly annual shortage and depression.

1907 Act of Congress affirms Shaw's actions and makes the treasury more flexible. George B. Cortelyou succeeds Shaw and suggests regional zones to prevent accumulation of reserves in the Northeast.

Panic due mainly to poorly regulated trust companies. Bank failures double (to 200 per year) during 1907 and 1908. J. P. Morgan intervenes to stop run on the banks, thus illustrating again the power of the "money trust."

1908 Aldrich-Vreeland Act creates special bank note fund for times of crisis and establishes the National Monetary Commission which eventually made and published a series of exhaustive studies on banking and related issues providing the research background for the Federal Reserve Act.

Populists nominate Thomas E. Watson, who gets only 28,000 votes as the call for banking and currency reform pervades the major parties.

Democratic platform blames the Republicans for causing the panic of 1907 and for being in league with bankers. The idea of emergency currency is accepted only on the basis of adequate security and direct government issue. (This is only a small step into the twentieth century from their 1904 platform.)

Republican platform admits the need for monetary reform, points to the work-in-progress of the National Monetary Commission, and calls for "a more elastic and adaptable system. . . . automatic in operation, minimizing the fluctuations of interest rates" and relying at bottom on the value of gold. Except for the gold plank, this is a decidedly progressive statement, more so than that of any other party.

People's party calls for government issue of money sufficient to meet need. Independence party (a one-time-only creation of the friends of William Randolph Hearst) recommends a central bank to issue and control money.

1909 Postal savings facilities established.

1910 Banker Paul Warburg publicizes plan for a "United Reserve Bank" and Fowler introduces a bill "to Establish a Complete Banking and Financial System" based on European models. These events and others presage the Federal Reserve.

1911 Senator Aldrich pushes the Monetary Commission findings as supportive of a national bank.

Woodrow Wilson, governor of New Jersey, cites the money monopoly as the most dangerous foe to the nation's development.

T. Cushing Daniel publishes *Real Money versus Bank of Issue Promises to Pay*. This work is symptomatic of rising interest in banking problems. Daniel submits a 23-page testimony before the Senate Banking and Currency Committee in favor of expanding currency, freedom from banks, and a more international view of money. He does not exactly support the Aldrich bill but is taken to be sympathetic.

1912 Democratic platform contains a mild call for banking reform, suggests opposition to the money market and competitive bidding by private banks for public business.

Republican platform is practically populistic in its stress on farm loans and the need for seasonal money in the rural West and South.

Progressive platform opposes Aldrich bill as putting too much power in private hands and calls for "soundness and elasticity."

Socialists, having eschewed specific monetary planks heretofore, now call for "collective ownership and democratic management of the banking and currency system."

The Aldrich bill, mentioned in several platforms, is introduced and calls for a National Reserve Association having some of the features of the Federal Reserve System. The Democrats, as well as the Progressives, explicitly oppose it.

Robert La Follette speaks against monopolies which control credit and money while free from outside regulation.

Arsène Pujo becomes chairman of a subcommittee of the House Committee on Banking and Currency, established to investigate money and banking conditions.

1913 Pujo committee reports on sensational abuses in financial and investment circles.

Sixteenth Amendment adopted legalizing the graduated income tax, another indicator of the government's expanded role in economic matters.

The Federal Reserve Bill becomes a partisan matter opposite to the platforms. It is introduced by the Democrats with Wilson's strong backing and opposed by the Republicans, led by Aldrich, on the grounds that currency would be insecure and the act would produce an undesirable kind of national bank. Its passage created a new agency with a mission to:

Assure a reliable currency at home and abroad
Establish adequate reserve requirements
Lessen the influence of private banks and partisan politics in favor of the general good
Create a system sensitive and flexible enough to head off the consequences of excessive inflation or deflation
Encourage discounts, loans, and interest rates which favor large numbers of citizens
Allow regional responses to regional conditions

The act contained many features familiar to reformers who had spoken in favor of farm and labor interests. But it was a compromise at best. It did not fully separate the government's role from that of private banks. It did not allow for crop loans dear to farmers and essential to the Macune viewpoint; but it did authorize the land loans dear to Kellogg and Campbell. During the Federal Reserve's first two years of operation, $46 million in land loans were made.

After 1913

The Federal Reserve banks were actually set up in 1914, although it was not until 1918, following a recommendation by the Bureau of Efficiency, that the last of the subtreasuries were written off. By 1920 the Independent Treasury had been completely merged into the Federal Reserve System.

Within the twenty years following the passage of the Federal Reserve Act there were further responses to the agrarian demands noted in the chronology. In 1916 the Federal Farm Loan Act established twelve regional banks whose function was to provide low-interest loans to farmers at rates determined locally. In 1923 the government established Federal Intermediate Credit Banks for indirect, short-term farm loans; in 1929 the Agricultural Marketing Act made $500 million available to assist farmers in marketing their crops at favorable terms. In 1932 the Emergency Relief and Construction Act made farmers eligible for help under the Reconstruction Finance Corporation. Although none of these measures represented a long-term solution, they all responded to aspects of agrarian protest and, in particular, to the ideas of C. W. Macune.

To chronicle the money question after 1913 would be relatively easy because the Federal Reserve itself maintains an elaborate record of financial events relating money-market operations to discount rates, reserve requirements, and other pertinent conditions. (See, for example, David P. Eastburn, *Federal Reserve on Record*. Philadelphia: Federal Reserve Bank, 1965.) No one supposes that the Fed controls the money situation. Yet the transition of social change to its institutional stage can be marked by the establishment of a national agency which, among other things, takes responsibility for maintaining the record.

Sources

The principal sources for the chronology are listed below. These works represent various levels of seriousness and reliability but have the common trait of including a number of pertinent items and usually in strict chronological order. Conflicts in facts and interpretation have been resolved in favor of the more recent and/or special study.

Bryan, J. E. *Farmers' Alliance*. Fayetteville, Ark., 1891.

Commons, John R., et al. *Documentary History of American Industrial Society*. 10 vols. Cleveland: Clark, 1910.

Destler, Chester M. *American Radicalism 1865–1901: Essays and Documents*. New London, Conn.: Connecticut College, 1946.

Dwinell, Olive C. *Story of Our Money* . . . [a source collection]. Boston: Meador, 1946.

Greer, Thomas H. *American Social Reform Movements: Their Pattern since 1865*. New York: Prentice-Hall, 1949.

Hammond, Bray. *Banks and Politics in America from the Revolution to the Civil War*. Princeton: Princeon Univ. Press, 1957.

Huntington, A. T., and Robert J. Mawhinney. *Laws of the United States concerning Money, Banking, and Loans*. Washington, D.C.: Government Printing Office, 1910.

Johnson, Donald B. *National Party Platforms*. Vol. 1. Urbana: Univ. of Illinois Press, 1978.

Kinley, David. *Independent Treasury of the United States*. Washington, D.C.: Government Printing Office, 1910.

Kull, Irving S., and Nell M. Kull. *Chronological Encyclopedia of American History*. New York: Popular Library, 1969.

Morris, Richard B. *Encyclopedia of American History*. New York: Harper, 1953.

Pessen, Edward. *Most Uncommon Jacksonians*. Albany: State Univ. of New York, 1967.

Sharkey, Robert P. *Money, Class, and Party: An Economic Study of Civil War and Reconstruction*. Baltimore: Johns Hopkins Univ. Press, 1959.
Studenski, Paul, and Herman Krooss. *Financial History of the United States*. New York: McGraw-Hill, 1963.
Taus, Esther R. *Central Banking Functions of the United States Treasury, 1789–1914*. New York: Russell and Russell, 1943.
Unger, Irwin. *Greenback Era: A Social and Political History of American Finance, 1865–1879*. Princeton: Princeton Univ. Press, 1964.

BIBLIOGRAPHICAL NOTE

As this work does not purport to cover reform, a comprehensive bibliography would not be appropriate even if such a compilation were possible. Several volumes would, in fact, be required just to document social change in the areas stressed herein. What follows, then, is an inventory of the main types of sources and materials. Each category is illustrated by works chosen not on some absolute scale of value but on grounds of their utility and consanguinity in the present setting. The order is first by type, second by sequence parallel to the text, and last by date of publication.

The foundation for this study is the record of reform, much of which is contained in public documents: for example, the memorable argument of David Buel for the extension of suffrage in *Reports of the Proceedings and Debates of the Convention of 1821* (Albany, N.Y., 1821); the annals of the petition campaign to open Congressional debate on slavery as detailed in the Daily *National Intelligencer.* Only the *Congressional Globe,* 37th Congress, 2nd Session, 523-681 and Appendix, January 28-29, 1862, shows the range of public reasoning as the controversial greenbacks were introduced as legal tender. Movements often climax in legislative debate as with the Federal Reserve Act (*Congressional Record* 51 Part 1, 426-43, December 8, 1913) or the Adamson Act (53 Part 13, 13579-608, September 1, 1916). The language of the enactment may be crucial to understanding reform as in the voting rights acts of the 1960s (for example, *United States Statutes-at-Large* 79:437-444) or a piece of social legislation like the authorization of the Tennessee Valley Authority (United State Code IV, Title 16, Section 831, 1970 edition). Messages from the White House must also be scrutinized as, for example, President Harry S. Truman's landmark Executive Order No. 9981 calling for the end of racial discrimination in the armed forces. Sometimes court decisions form the crucial nexus of social change, as in the numerous verdicts leading to the desegregation of state university law schools: 169 Maryland 478-89 (1935); 305 US 337, 342-52 (1938); 339 US 632-36 (1950); 332 US 640-42 (1950); and culminating in the famous Brown v. Board of Education of Topeka, 347 US 490-96 (1952, 1953) and 349 US 298-301 (1955) (the pages cited are those of most interest in the reform context).

Political platforms are a lively part of the reform record. They show how major parties wish to be seen and remembered. Sometimes minor party platforms can be used as a litmus for detecting shifting views as were the prohibition/temperance platforms on the money question (see Appendix). This study also rests on charters, constitutions, and statements of purpose of unions and associations of all types. Sometimes there are invaluable aids in interpreting these manifestoes as, in the case of the American Anti-Slavery Society, *The Correspondence between the Hon. F.H. Elmore and James G. Birney* (New York, 1838). Robert L. Jack's *History of the National Association for the Advancement of Colored People* (Boston, 1953) is of parallel utility.

Journalism is a vital element in social change. The antislavery movement cannot be understood without familiarity with the *National Intelligencer,* the *Emancipator,* the *Liberator,* and many others. In the present century the main line on civil rights appeared in *Crisis* while other points of view can be sampled in a range of periodicals from *Alexander's* and *Colored American* to *Muhammad Speaks* and the numerous urban papers known collectively as the "black dispatch." Students of progressive reform have made good use of the *Nation, Munsey's, McClure's,* the *Outlook,* and *Arena.* But the student of the money question must also consult such obscure publications as the

Chicago Express, Western Rural, National Economist, People's Party Paper, New Occasions, and *New Times.*

Special collections have many uses to the student of reform. At the Hoover Institution one can assemble a unique background for appreciating an individualistic president's reluctant move toward federal action. At the Huntington Library I found the materials for studying the California constitutional convention of 1849, as well as the papers of a champion literary muckraker (Jack London) and those of a very interesting if relatively neglected feminist (Elizabeth Boynton Harbert). There is no corner of the Library of Congress that does not possess some grist for the reform student's mill: from the collection of song covers and commercial lithographs, with their uncanny ability to mirror the concerns of the day, to the papers of singular social actors such as Eli Thayer.

One is grateful for published correspondence and interviews ranging from Ralph Waldo Emerson's with Thomas Carlye to Ralph Nader's in *Playboy.* One is especially fortunate when one can talk and correspond with Guy E. Noyes (about the Federal Reserve), with Clarence Streit (about world government), with Sar Levitan (about the social role of the federal government), with Roger Craver (about voluntarism and politics) and with the late Buckminster Fuller about environmental meliorism.

The literary imagination has contributed actively to social change in this country, not only in political orations and journalistic essays but also in all forms of *belle lettres.* Scholars from Moses Coit Tyler and Vernon L. Parrington to Daniel Aaron and Alfred Kazin have illustrated this point abundantly. Collections such as Upton Sinclair's *Cry for Justice* (Philadelphia, 1915), anthologize the argument.

Literature is so intertwined with reform that it is impossible to separate the subjects. The same is true with other forms of expression. Without leaving the Prints and Photographs Division of the Library of Congress one can see the photographic record of urban problems (Lewis Hine, Jacob Riis) and of the Depression (Farm Security Administration, Office of War Information). A singular collection of cartoon originals shows how the issues were dramatized.

The record of reform is more than two-dimensional. The Division of Political History at the Smithsonian Institution's Museum of American History allows one to see not only buttons and banners but also useful objects (jugs and pitchers, tie pins and snuff boxes) transformed into social and political statements. The artifacts used in communes and architectural models—from a Shaker chair to a Soleri megastructure—project their own forms of meliorism. One may see this record not only at the Smithsonian but also at the Winterthur Museum, the Corcoran Gallery, Oneida, the Amana villages, Arcosanti, and other museums and sites.

The record of reform has been collected under many headings, although the act of selection inevitably instills a point of view. Three document collections are eminently attuned to this work: John R. Commons, et al., eds., *Documentary History of American Industrial Society* (New York, 1958, 10 vols.); Alpheus T. Mason, ed., *Free Government in the Making* (New York, 1956), and my own collection, which furnishes a deliberate echo of the present work, *Reform Spirit in America* (New York, 1976).

In attempting to understand the process and pattern of social change and in developing a method for describing it I have drawn on a number of works, many of them representing disciplines other than my own. At the top of the list are Kenneth E. Boulding, *Primer on Social Dynamics* (New York, 1970); Roberta Ash, *Social Movements in America* (Chicago, 1972); and Thomas C. Cochran, *Social Change in Industrial Society* (London, 1972). Also helpful were: Francis B. Allen, et al., *Technology and Social Change* (New York, 1951); Eva Etzioni-Halevy and Amitai Etzioni, eds., *Social Change: Sources, Patterns, and Consequences* (Westport, Conn., 1964); Joseph R. Gusfield, ed., *Protest, Reform, Revolt* (New York, 1970); Rudolph Heberle, *Social Movements* (New York, 1951); Seymour Lipset and Richard Hofstadter, eds., *Sociology and History: Methods* (New York, 1968); Barry McLaughlin, ed., *Studies in Social Movements* (New York,

1969); and Talcott Parsons, *Structure and Process in Modern Societies* (Glencoe, Ill., 1960).

More congenial to my own primarily historical orientation, but no less generally helpful, were a number of major works that have, at or near their center, an integration of reform with broader American experience: Merle Curti, *The Growth of American Thought*, 3rd ed. (New York, 1964); Ralph H. Gabriel, *The Course of American Democratic Thought*, 2nd ed. (New York, 1956); Thomas H. Greer, *American Social Reform Movements* (New York, 1949); John Bach McMaster, *The Acquisitions of Political and Industrial Rights of Man in America* (Cleveland, 1903); Arthur M. Schlesinger, *The American as Reformer* (Cambridge, Mass., 1959). Outside these pages I have commented on my own methods most fully in *Reform Spirit in America* (above) and in an essay appearing in Harold Sharlin, ed., *Business and its Environment* (Westport, Conn., 1983).

The *Encyclopedia of Social Reform* compiled by William D. Bliss (New York, 1897) is a unique inventory of reform. With the aid of Henry J. Silverman's dissertation, "American Social Reformers in the Late Nineteenth and Early Twentieth Century" (University of Pennsylvania, 1963), it becomes the source of a rare collective portrait of the individual social actor. To this may now be added Alden Whitman, ed., *American Reformers* (New York: H.W. Wilson, 1985), which depicts 508 individuals from four centuries. To shift from social to political actor brings into focus a number of studies at the center of which are Angus Campbell, et al., *American Voter* (New York, 1960); Sidney Verba and Norman Nie, *Participation in America: Political Democracy and Social Equality* (New York, 1972).

Among the many studies of collective social actors the most pertinent is William A. Gamson, *Strategy of Social Protest* (Homewood, Ill., 1975). Also germane are Constance Smith and Anne Freedman, *Voluntary Associations: Perspective on the Literature* (Cambridge, Mass., 1972); and, in the broadest sense, Susan J. Ellis and Katherine H. Noyes, *By the People: a History of Americans as Volunteers* (Philadelphia, 1978). *Promise of Greatness* by Sar A. Levitan and Robert Taggert (Cambridge, Mass., 1976) is one of the more recent and incisive studies of the increasing role of the federal government as a social actor.

Because of my insistence on reform's continuity I ought, perhaps, avoid mentioning period studies altogether; nevertheless, some are useful in ways that do not always attract citations. John G. Sproat's *"The Best Men"* (New York, 1968) shows why one prominent group of self-proclaimed reformers constituted a dead end. Conversely, studies like Harold U. Faulkner's *Politics, Reform and Expansion 1890–1900* (New York, 1959) and Arthur Mann, *Yankee Reformers in the Urban Age* (Cambridge, Mass., 1954), while limited in time and place, particularize conditions that characterize the larger canvas. *Freedom's Ferment* by Alice Felt Tyler (Minneapolis, 1944), while outmoded in many respects, offers a more usable synthesis than any of its successors. There are also collections of documents which, while limited to a narrow chronology, shed important light on matters of continuing concern to students of reform: for example, Henry Nash Smith, ed., *Popular Culture and Industrialism, 1865–1890* (New York, 1967) and Daniel Aaron and Robert Bendiner, eds., *Strenuous Decade* (New York, 1970).

Each of the four main parts of this work draws on some works which, by their breadth or by their ability to make connections between some of reform's diverse elements, merit inclusion here as well as in appropriate citations.

Two works from a viewpoint unfamiliar to me helped test and organize thoughts on the politico-economic aspects of social change: Robert A. Dahl, *Pluralist Democracy in the United States* (New Haven, 1961); Dahl and Charles E. Lindblom, *Politics, Economics and Welfare* (Chicago, 1953). A trio of works helped identify one powerful but often overlooked protest tradition: Zera S. Fink, *Classical Republicans* (Evanston, Ill., 1945); Caroline Robbins, *The Eighteenth-Century Commonwealthman* (Cambridge, Mass.,

1959); Bernard Bailyn, *Ideological Origins of the American Revolution* (Cambridge, Mass., 1967).

To connect the money question to larger issues I used Joseph Dorfman, *Economic Mind in American Civilization* (New York, 1946–1959, 5 vols.); Bray Hammond, *Banks and Politics in America* (Princeton, N.J., 1957); Irwin Unger, *Greenback Era* (Princeton, N.J., 1964); and Robert P. Sharkey, *Money, Class and Party* (Baltimore, 1959).

To understand the antebellum politico-economic climate I used several of Edward Pessen's works, especially *Most Uncommon Jacksonians* (Albany, N.Y., 1967) and Paul K. Conkin, *Prophets of Prosperity* (Bloomington, Ind., 1980). Of the many comparable works dealing with the last half of the century, I found much of what I needed in Chester McA. Destler's *American Radicalism 1865–1901* (New London, Conn., 1946).

Although there are serviceable studies of women and of individual minorities it is difficult to find works that establish useful patterns beyond a single group or era. That is why the work of David J. Rothman has been so gratefully noted. In *The Discovery of Asylum* and *Conscience and Convenience* (Boston, 1971 and 1980) he takes a number of subjects outside my particular focus and sees a reassuringly similar dynamic pattern. I am also unusually impressed by Jo Freeman's *Politics of Women's Liberation* (New York, 1975) for its identification of patterns that apply outside the particular subject and by Clifford S. Griffin for his analysis of one of the prime reform ingredients as it cuts across a number of issues in *Their Brothers' Keepers: Moral Stewardship in the United States, 1800–1865* (New Brunswick, N.H., 1960). A comprehensive contemporary treatment is Sar A. Levitan, William B. Johnston, and Robert Taggert, *Minorities in the United States* (Washington, D.C., 1975).

There is no single work that surveys civil liberties/civil rights in the reform context. The most helpful to me were Norman Dorsen, et al., eds., *Emerson, Haber and Dorsen's Political and Civil Rights in the United States*, Boston, 1976, 1979, 2 vols.); Donald Johnson, *Challenge to American Freedoms* (Lexington, Ky., 1963); and Norman A. Graebner, ed., *Freedom in America: a 200-year Perspective* (University Park, Pa., 1977).

Of the many works that treat the idea of America as an ideal society, the most recent and applicable is Ray A. Billington's *Land of Savagery, Land of Promise* (New York, 1981). On the impulse to improve society by controlling its setting Cecelia Tichi's *New World, New Earth* (New Haven, 1979), makes some original connections.

In establishing the categories that distinguished the first communitarian wave no work has yet surpassed John Humphrey Noyes' *History of American Socialisms* (Philadelphia, 1870). Other studies that take the communes out of their narrow setting are: Arthur E. Bestor, *Backwoods Utopias* (Philadelphia, 1950); Lawrence Foster, *Religion and Sexuality* (New York, 1981); and, concerning the later settlements, Rosabeth M. Kanter, *Commitment and Community* (Cambridge, Mass., 1972), and Hugh Gardner, *Children of Prosperity* (New York, 1978).

To understand the literary utopias as a comment on social change one begins with Lewis Mumford, *Story of Utopias* (New York, 1922); continues through Harry W. Laidler, *Social-Economic Movements* (New York, 1944); and ends with Charles J. Rooney's *Dreams and Visions* (Westport, Conn., 1985).

In tying together some of the scattered threads of the utopian impulse in the twentieth century the following works stand out: Reginald Bretnor, ed., *Modern Science Fiction* (New York, 1953); Paul K. Conkin, *Tomorrow a New World* (Ithaca, N.Y., 1959); Percival and Paul Goodman, *Communitas* (New York, 1960); Helen Rosenau, *Ideal City* (New York, 1972); Robert Fishman, *Urban Utopias in the Twentieth Century* (New York, 1977); and Kenneth M. Roemer, *America as Utopia* (New York, 1981).

In addition to several titles mentioned in other settings, the following proved instrumental in evaluating the politico-economic performance of American reform: Robert J. Lampman, *Ends and Means of Reducing Poverty* (Chicago, 1971); Robert A. Dahl, *Democracy in the United States: Promise and Performance* (Chicago, 1976, 3rd ed.);

William J. Crotty, *Political Reform and the American Experiment* (New York, 1977); Norman H. Nie, Sidney Verba, John R. Petrocik, *Changing American Voter* (Cambridge, Mass., 1979); Paul Kleppner, *Who Voted? The Dynamics of Electoral Turnout, 1870–1980* (New York, 1982); and most especially, Jeffrey G. Williamson and Peter H. Lindert, "Long-Term Trends in American Wealth Inequality," in James D. Smith, ed., *Modeling the Distribution and Integrational Transmission of Wealth* (Chicago, 1980).

In evaluating reform as it has affected blacks and women the historical statistics tell the main story. Useful interpretations, in addition to those already mentioned, are: Sar A. Levitan, William B. Johnston, and Robert Taggert, *Still a Dream: the Changing Status of Blacks since 1960* (Cambridge, Mass., 1975); Ralph E. Smith, ed., *Subtle Revolution: Women at Work* (Washington, D.C. 1970); and Stanley Lieberson, *A Piece of the Pie* (Berkeley, Ca., 1980).

Robin Williams deserves credit for being one of the first scholars to publish a weighted list of American values in his *American Society* (New York, 1951). Subsequent variations in the list are as interesting as the original rating. In dealing with the clash between presumed values and those implicit to the reform experience, the following treatments shed the most light: David Riesman, *Individualism Reconsidered* (Glencoe, Ill., 1960); John A. Kouwenhoven, *Beer Can by the Highway* (New York, 1961); Seymour M. Lipset, *First New Nation* (New York, 1961); Charles L. Sanford, *Quest for Paradise* (Urbana, Ill., 1961); Michael Kammen, *People of Paradox* (New York, 1972); Ralph H. Gabriel, *American Values: Continuity and Change* (Westport, Conn., 1974); and Gordon J. DiRenzo, ed., *We, the People: American Character and Social Change* (Westport, Conn., 1977).

Among the notes to the individual chapters may be found bibliographies on the many topics covered in this work from the distribution of wealth to civil liberties. The sources listed at the end of the appendix provide a good starting point for further readings on the money question. Donald D. Egbert and Stow Persons, in the two volumes of *Socialism and American Life* (Princeton, N.J., 1952), have not only compiled a list of pertinent readings but have published a set of essays that touch on many aspects of reform. A guide to articles appearing between 1973 and 1982, *Social Reform and Reaction in America* (Santa Barbara, Ca., 1984), is organized first by period and then by categories. To be broadly helpful to the study of social change general bibliographies must transcend a single approach: as, for example, the Library of Congress *Guide to the Study of the United States of America* (Washington, D.C., 1960, and supplements); Robert H. Walker, ed., *American Studies: Topics and Sources* and (with Jefferson Kellogg) *Sources for American Studies* (Westport, Conn., 1976, 1983).

INDEX